Born Divine

Born Divine

The Births of Jesus & Other Sons of God

Robert J. Miller

Born Divine: The Births of Jesus and Other Sons of God

Published in 2003 by Polebridge Press, P.O. Box 6144, Santa Rosa, California 95406.

ISBN 0-944344-95-X

Library of Congress Cataloging-in-Publication Data

Miller, Robert J. (Robert Joseph), 1954-
  Born divine : the births of Jesus & other sons of God / Robert J. Miller.
    p. cm.
  Includes bibliographical references and indexes.
  ISBN 0-944344-95-X
    1. Jesus Christ--Nativity. 2. Infancy narratives (Gospels) 3. Apocryphal infancy Gospels. 4. Virgin birth. 5. Bible. N.T. Gospels--Criticism, interpretation, etc. I. Title.

BT315.3.M55 2003
232.92--dc21

2003051747

TO CELINE AND BOB

with heartfelt gratitude

CONTENTS

BORN of A VIRGIN?

UNDERSTANDING THE VIRGIN BIRTH

INFANCY GOSPELS

Boxes

Cameo Essays

Preface

This book is designed for the general reader. Since it is neither short nor easy, it demands a high level of interest in the subject matter; yet it does not presuppose any specialized knowledge. While I hope this book will make its contribution to the field of biblical studies, and while I hope that my academic colleagues find this book helpful, I have not written it for them. Rather, my goal has been to share the benefits of scholarly work on the infancy narratives with non-specialists. To keep from getting bogged down in detailed analysis, this book bypasses a great deal of technical information about the stories of Jesus' birth and childhood, information that, though fascinating to scholars, makes little difference to our overall interpretation of the texts. My role has been to survey the available information, decide how much is important and useful to the general reader, and then explain its significance as clearly and concisely as I could. Occasionally I found it helpful to deal with some aspect of the original language of a certain passage, but the reader will need no knowledge of that language in order to follow the discussion. Nearly all the information and interpretations presented in this book fall well within the broad consensus of critical scholars. Occasionally I take a position against the consensus, or against a longstanding traditional interpretation; but in those few cases I trust that I have made my dissent clear.

Consequently, rather little in this book is original. Having elected to write for those who are not specialists in the academic study of the Bible, I have not tagged the scholarly source of every item of information or every inference in every argument. That sort of citation is expected when a scholar writes for his or her peers, but to have followed that practice meticulously throughout this book would have added hundreds of footnotes and dozens of pages, without enhancing anyone's knowledge of the subject matter itself.

Since I have decided against using footnotes for academic citations, I am eager at the outset to acknowledge my major intellectual debts and express my gratitude to my sources. In preparing Chapters 2–5, I benefitted enormously from *The Birth of the Messiah*, by the late Raymond Brown. This monumental commentary from 1977 remains the single most important work on the infancy narratives, unparalleled both in its scope and in its depth. I also mined much information and many insights from the learned commentaries on Luke by Joseph Fitzmyer and by C. F. Evans, and from those on Matthew by Ulrich Luz and by W. D. Davies and Dale Allison.

It is a pleasure for me to acknowledge *Documents for the Study of the Gospels,* that gem by David Cartlidge and David Dungan. Their anthology of hellenistic texts on the birth of Greek and Roman heroes was the inspiration for my Chapter 7, where my selection of texts is heavily indebted to theirs.

I am grateful to Jane Schaberg for *The Illegitimacy of Jesus*, a work of careful scholarship that achieves a rare combination of intellectual passion and balanced judgment, a book whose publication in 1987 was also an act of scholarly courage. Although I am unable to agree with Schaberg's central thesis, I could not have written my Chapter 13 without her book to guide me. It also influenced Chapters 11 and 4.

The Infancy Gospels of James and Thomas, by Ronald Hock, is the basis for my Chapters 17 and 18. Hock's critical edition of the Greek texts of these neglected gospels is a gift to the scholarly world, and his exposition of them exemplifies the state of the art. Many of my comments on those two gospels are taken directly from his.

My deepest debt is to John Dominic Crossan. Although he has not written extensively on the infancy narratives, it is from him that I have learned the most important concept that informs the present book. According to Crossan, the Christian claim that Jesus was the son of God was originally put forth primarily to counter Roman propaganda about the divinity of Caesar. This insight is for me the key that unlocks the basic message of the infancy narratives and the original meaning of the belief in the virgin birth. Crossan's thinking has influenced my own in several places in this book, most profoundly in my arguments in Chapter 16. The cameo essay in Chapter 15, "Emperors as Sons of God," derives directly from his work. In addition, Crossan's work on Moses and Jesus is the basis for my Chapter 6.

In preparing the translations of the primary texts presented in this book, I have benefitted from the work of translators before me. They are acknowledged on p. 325.

Style

I use masculine pronouns for God when discussing the beliefs of ancient Jews and Christians, because that is how they themselves referred to the Deity.

It is the normal custom at present to print the titles of biblical books in Roman type face and to italicize the titles of non-canonical religious writings. This typographic distinction reflects a theological privileging of the canonical writings which is inappropriate in historical-critical study. Besides, the distinction between what is inside and outside the canon is anachronistic for the first few centuries of the Common Era. I therefore use Roman type face for all ancient religious texts.

Capitalization and lower case

gospel / Gospel. A gospel is a kind of writing, and so the word "gospel" is a common noun. The "Gospel of Luke" is the title of a specific gospel, and so the title is capitalized. The "Gospel of Matthew" and "Matthew's gospel" are two ways to refer to the same work, but only the first is a title.

Law. I capitalize "Law" when it refers to the Torah.

gentile. I use the word as a common noun because it means "non-Jew," which to ancient Jews meant "foreigner."

Terminology

A *pagan* is someone who was neither a Jew nor a Christian. I use the word purely descriptively, with no evaluative connotation.

Jew. I sometimes refer to early Jewish followers of Jesus (e.g., Paul and Matthew) simply as Jews because that is how they understood themselves. If, for our convenience, we refer to them as Christians, that is not because they practiced Christianity—which did not yet exist as a distinct religion—but because they believed that Jesus was the Christ, the Anointed.

Hebrew Bible / Old Testament. The Hebrew Bible is the Jewish scriptures in the Hebrew language. The early Christians knew the Jewish scriptures mostly in Greek translation, and so I use (somewhat unhappily) the term "Old Testament" to refer to the Jewish scriptures as adopted by Christians, except in those specific cases where the Hebrew text is meant.

Virgin Birth. I use "virgin birth" to refer to the belief that Jesus had no human biological father. In this book the term is usually synonymous with "virginal conception," which is a more precise term, but less familiar to general readers. See also my comments on p. 195.

Acknowledgements

In 2001 it was my privilege to be Scholar in Residence at Westar Institute in Santa Rosa, California, where most of this book was written. I am grateful to Robert Funk for the invitation to come to Westar and to James Kasper and Lucy Hansen for funding my year there. Their generosity afforded me that most coveted of scholarly privileges: time for unhurried reading, thinking, and writing. During my time in Santa Rosa, Bob Funk and Char Matejovsky graced me with their hospitality, friendship, and encouragement.

Marianne Sawicki, my wife, endured the absurdities of a bicoastal marriage with a generous spirit and shouldered stressful burdens imposed by the absence of her spouse. This book could not have been written without her encouragement and support. The book has also been greatly improved by her editing.

Gail Dawson graciously provided invaluable assistance to this project by acting as my long-distance reference librarian. Tom Hall edited the manuscript with an eagle's eye, for which I am most grateful. Daryl Schmidt generously shared with me his expertise in the Greek language and made several suggestions which have improved this book. Eric Freed supported me with his friendship, hospitality, and enthusiasm for my work. With their quiet competence and cheerful attitude, Lee Masters and Nancy Gaspard make Westar a happy place to work. Their kindness has meant more to me than they know.

Writing a book about the birth of Jesus has made me acutely aware of how utterly dependent all of us were as infants on the selflessness and sacrifice of those who cared for us. In gratitude for the love and kindness that I cannot remember, I dedicate this book to my parents.

Abbreviations

Acts	Acts of the Apostles	Mal	Malachi
BCE	before the Common Era	Mark	Gospel of Mark
CE	of the Common Era	Matt	Gospel of Matthew
1, 2 Chr	1,2 Chronicles	Mic	Micah
1 Cor	1 Corinthians	Neh	Nehemiah
Dan	Daniel	Num	Numbers
Deut	Deuteronomy	1 Pet	1 Peter
Ex	Exodus	Phil	Philippians
Ez	Ezekiel	Ps	Psalm
Gal	Galatians	Ps Sol	Psalms of Solomon
Gen	Genesis	Rev	Revelation
Hab	Habakkuk	Rom	Romans
Hag	Haggai	1, 2 Sam	1, 2 Samuel
Heb	Hebrews	Sir	Sirach (also known as
HistJos	History of Joseph the		Ecclesiasticus)
	Carpenter	Wis	Wisdom (also known as
Hos	Hosea		Wisdom of Solomon)
InJas	Infancy Gospel of James	Zech	Zechariah
InThom	Infancy Gospel of Thomas		
Isa	Isaiah		
Jdt	Judith		
Jer	Jeremiah		
John	Gospel of John		
1 John	First Letter of John		
Josh	Joshua		
Judg	Judges		
1, 2 Kgs	1, 2 Kings		
Lev	Leviticus		
Luke	Gospel of Luke		
LXX	the Septuagint (Greek translation of the Old Testament)		

INTRODUCTION

This book is a comprehensive resource for the study of the stories about the birth and infancy of Jesus, and for thinking through the historical and religious questions they raise. The book approaches those two projects by treating the infancy narratives[1] in *four dimensions* (literary, exegetical, historical, and theological) and within *three contexts* (Jewish, pagan, and Christian).

FOUR DIMENSIONS

This book treats the infancy narratives in four dimensions:

1. *literary*: how were the infancy narratives composed and how do they tell their stories?
2. *exegetical*: what did the stories mean to their original authors and audiences?
3. *historical*: which parts of the stories are historically reliable, and which are not?
4. *theological*: what are the implications of these stories for Christian life and practice, both then and now?

Literary and Exegetical Dimensions

Chapters 2–5 deal primarily with the literary and exegetical dimensions of the infancy narratives. These four chapters make up a modest commentary on the infancy narratives of Luke and Matthew. The introductory remarks to the individual sections of the narratives, along with the comments on specific items in the text, provide the information necessary for a critical, respectful, and, I hope, enjoyable engagement with the ancient texts.

---

1. The term "infancy narratives" usually refers to the stories about the conception, birth, and childhood of Jesus (and John the Baptizer) found in Matthew 1–2 and Luke 1–2. When I use the term to refer to stories about people other than Jesus, that will be clear from the context.

1

The gospel passages can be studied one section at a time and in any order that suits the reader. Topics that are discussed more fully elsewhere are so noted.

Throughout the book, but mostly in the commentary, there are two types of sidebars: boxes and cameos. *Boxes* have two purposes: 1) to provide excerpts from other ancient (mostly biblical) texts that illuminate the gospel passage under discussion; and 2) to present the biblical data in formats that facilitate comparison and contrast. *Cameos* are brief, stand-alone essays on various topics relevant to the main subject under discussion.

The genealogies of Jesus in Luke and Matthew are not stories, and so, strictly speaking, are not part of the infancy narratives. Nevertheless, the genealogies are an essential part of the gospel presentation of Jesus' origins, and their highly contradictory contents are so useful for understanding the relationship of the infancy narratives to the facts of history that no comprehensive consideration of the infancy narratives is complete without them. The genealogies are the subject of Chapter 4.

Historical Dimension

A crucial task for the modern study of the gospels is to discern which parts of them are historical and which are not. Critical scholars widely agree that very little history can be found in Matthew 1–2 or Luke 1–2. Yet few authors have emphasized this finding, perhaps because there is so little scholarly disagreement on the topic. Some scholars hedge their conclusions with so much nuance that the reader may be uncertain as to what position an author takes. Other scholars state their positions clearly enough, but without drawing the reader's attention to them. In a book on the infancy narratives, readers deserve to know whether the author thinks that the events in the stories really happened, but oftentimes readers have had to hunt to find the answer.

Historical questions are confronted directly and forthrightly in this book. I discuss the evidence, present my arguments, and draw my conclusions in plain language and in clearly marked sections of the book. You might not always agree with me, but you will know what I think and why.

The historical value of the infancy narratives as a whole is treated in Chapters 8, 9, and 12, along with questions about the historicity of the central episodes and the key facts they report. Other historical questions less central to the story are treated as they arise in Chapters 2–5.

Theological Dimension

Reflection on the theological dimension of the infancy narratives raises questions that go far beyond stories about the baby Jesus. Some of these questions are:

- What did it mean in the ancient world for someone to be called a son of God?
- What was the meaning of the claim that Jesus was born to a virgin? What might be the meaning of that claim today?
- Did the events of Jesus' birth and infancy fulfill biblical prophecies? How does our answer to this question affect our understanding of the relationship of Christianity to Judaism?

Historical investigation and theological reflection intertwine as we work through these questions, because they require us to reconsider both the past and the present. We examine the past to ask how the early Christians understood the religious meaning of the infancy stories. Only after we have made our best effort to discern that, can we go on to address our own time and seek to understand what implications those ancient stories have for Christian faith today.

Chapter 8, "Did Jesus fulfill prophecy?" analyzes the claim in the Gospel of Matthew that certain events at the beginning of the life of Jesus happened in order to fulfill specific prophecies from the Old Testament. I discuss the original meanings of those prophecies and Matthew's use of them. I then assess whether the events in question actually occurred. The notion that Jesus fulfilled prophecy, I argue, is exegetically untenable, theologically obsolete, and religiously dangerous.

The Virgin Birth

Belief in the virgin birth of Jesus is only a marginal element in the theologies of the New Testament, and it is not a prominent feature even within the canonical infancy narratives. Yet as the system of mainstream Christian belief developed, the virgin birth took on an importance far out of proportion to its place in the Bible. It became a cornerstone Christian doctrine, with powerful implications for what Christians believed about the divinity of Jesus and the role of Mary in the economy of salvation. More generally, it profoundly influenced how Christians would come to view human sexuality. Because of the theological importance of the virgin birth in the history of Christianity, this book takes up this topic at some length and examines both its historical and its theological dimensions.

Chapter 10, "What is a virgin?", looks closely at the precise meanings of the ancient terminology used in the biblical texts. We will see that "virgin" usually meant something different in the ancient world than it does to us.

Chapter 11, "Is there a virgin birth in Matthew?" investigates whether that gospel writer intended to claim that Jesus had no biological father. I argue that Matthew probably had no such intent.

Chapter 12, "Is the virgin birth historical?" asks whether there are any grounds for claiming that the virgin birth is an historical fact. My answer is no.

Chapter 13, "Was Jesus illegitimate?" analyzes the insinuations and accusations in ancient Christian, pagan, and Jewish sources that Jesus had a biological father other than Joseph. After sifting the available evidence, I argue that this is unlikely.

Chapter 14, "Son(s) of God in the Bible," describes the kind of people whom the Bible calls sons of God and explains the range of meanings attached to that title. This knowledge is necessary for an understanding of what was going on when the earliest Christians referred to Jesus that way.

Chapter 15, "The Virgin Birth in Context," compares the early Christian belief about Jesus' conception with two sets of ancient stories about miraculous births: stories from the Hebrew Bible about infertile women who conceive through God's intervention, and stories about Greek and Roman heroes who had divine fathers and human mothers.

Chapter 16, "The Meaning of the Virgin Birth," pulls together the findings of Chapters 10–15 and explores the implications of this belief for ancient and modern Christians. I argue that the virgin birth remains a vital and challenging belief even for those of us who cannot take it literally.

THREE CONTEXTS

This book situates the infancy narratives within three contexts: Jewish, pagan, and Christian.

1. The Jewish context within which the infancy narratives must be understood has two components: the scriptures of Israel, primarily in their Greek translation, and the popular legends about the birth and infancy of Moses, known as the Moses Haggadah. The commentary in Chapters 1–5 analyzes how Luke and Matthew draw extensively on the Old Testament. The relevant selections from the Moses Haggadah are presented and analyzed in Chapter 6.

2. The infancy narratives should also be understood in the context of the stories about the births and childhoods of Greek and Roman heroes who were considered sons of God. Chapter 7 offers selections from hellenistic texts, in fresh translations, with introductions and comments. Ranging from the first century BCE to the third century CE, they present stories about seven heroes.

3. The Christian context for the infancy narratives is made up of two sets of texts. The first is passages from the New Testament and other early Christian writings that shed light on this or that topic in the infancy narratives. These passages are presented and discussed throughout the book. The second set of texts is the long tradition of infancy gospels. These Christian writings elaborate and embellish the birth and childhood of Jesus with imaginative stories that fill in the gaps in the early life of Jesus left by the gospel narratives, and supply detailed background stories about the lives of Mary

and Joseph. (For a fuller introduction to the infancy gospels, see the cameo on pp. 260–61.) Chapters 17–22 present the full text of one infancy gospel and excerpts from six more (from the second century to the Middle Ages), all in fresh translations, with introductions and comments.

THE INFANCY NARRATIVES

OVERVIEW

Starting the Story

If you were telling the story of Jesus' life, where would you begin? The answer seems obvious: you start with the Christmas story. Yet a quick check of the first pages of the four gospels shows that this answer was not at all obvious in the first century. Mark, the earliest gospel, begins with John the Baptizer preaching by the river. When Jesus enters the narrative a few verses later, he is already an adult presenting himself for baptism. The Gospel of John, written perhaps thirty years after Mark, opens with a theological prologue ("In the beginning was the Word") and then tells of John the Baptizer. Outside the gospels, the only texts that come close to being recitals of events in the life of Jesus are two brief summaries of his life in the Acts of the Apostles. The first one is attributed to Peter. It begins,

> You know the word God sent to the Israelites as he proclaimed peace through Jesus Anointed, who is Lord of all, what has happened all over Judea, beginning in Galilee after the baptism that John preached, how God anointed Jesus of Nazareth with the holy spirit and power. (Acts 10:36–38)

The second one is ascribed to Paul and begins,

> God has brought to Israel a savior, Jesus. John heralded his coming by proclaiming a baptism of repentance. (Acts 13:23–24)

In both of those capsuled narratives, as in the Gospels of Mark and John, the story of Jesus commences with John's baptism. For many early Christians, the good news about Jesus did not include anything about his birth. Either they knew nothing about it, or they saw in it nothing of religious significance. Our earliest Christian writings, the letters of Paul, develop elaborate and sophisticated theological assessments of Jesus but devote less than one sentence to his birth: "born of a woman, born under the Law" (Gal 4:4).

There was nothing inevitable about beginning with a birth story as Matthew and Luke did. That those two writers independently decided to begin the story that way reflects ancient expectations about how to write the biography of a famous man, not some inherent tendency in Christian belief about Jesus. Ancient audiences expected extraordinary men to have had extraordinary births and childhoods. A story of Jesus' life designed to appeal to readers from the mainstream hellenistic culture (as Luke's gospel certainly was) needed a proper birth story, ideally one that included a miraculous conception and a scene highlighting the precocious abilities of the child. Matthew's gospel, written for a Jewish audience, portrays Jesus as the new Moses, and so begins by showing how the birth and infancy of Jesus recapitulate the history of God's relationship with Israel in general and popular legends about Moses in particular.

The infancy narratives of Luke and Matthew were innovations in early Christian literature. In writing them, these two authors were entering uncharted territory. Each of them had to devise his own narrative strategy and story outline. That they had no shared template for their projects is immediately apparent from the very different narratives they produced. The differences between the two infancy narratives are both broad and detailed, greater than any other disparities in the gospels.

Differences Between Luke and Matthew

We can analyze these differences in four categories:

1. the general shape of the narratives;
2. the atmosphere of each story;
3. how the stories are told; and
4. the actual contents of the two narratives.

Shape
The two narratives are completely different in shape, with very different beginnings, middles, and endings (see Box 1.1).

Luke's narrative begins and ends in the temple. The first half of the story is concerned mostly with the annunciation, birth, and presentation of John the Baptizer; the annunciation of Jesus' birth occurs after that of John's. The second half opens with a journey from Nazareth to Bethlehem, the place of Jesus' birth, where the event is hailed by angels and the baby is visited by shepherds. The infant Jesus is later presented in the temple in Jerusalem, where he is recognized and acclaimed by a holy man and woman. Luke's narrative concludes with an epilogue, in which Jesus visits the temple at the age of twelve.

1.1   Outlines of the Two Infancy Narratives

Luke	Matthew
(genealogy of Jesus not included in infancy narrative; see 3:23–38)	genealogy of Jesus *(1:1–17)*
John's birth announced to Zechariah (1:5–23)	
John's conception (1:24–25)	
Jesus' birth announced to Mary (1:26–38)	Jesus' birth announced to Joseph (1:18–25)
Mary visits Elizabeth (1:39–56)	
John's birth and presentation (1:57–80)	
Jesus' birth (2:1–7)	*(Jesus' birth not narrated)*
shepherds visit Jesus (2:8–20)	
Jesus' circumcision and his presentation in the temple (2:21–38)	
family returns to Nazareth (2:39–40)	
	magi meet with Herod (2:1–8)
	magi visit Jesus (2:9–12)
	the family flees to Egypt (2.13–15)
	Herod's massacre of babies in Bethlehem (2:16–18)
	the family returns to Israel and relocates to Nazareth (2:19–23)
Jesus' visit to the temple at age twelve (2:41–52)	

By contrast, Matthew's gospel begins with a genealogy, followed by the annunciation to Joseph. Jesus is born between scenes; the birth itself is not narrated. The magi follow a star to Jerusalem, where they visit King Herod. A short while later they find Jesus in Bethlehem, presumably his parents' home. We read of Herod's plot to kill his infant rival, Jesus' escape to Egypt, and the slaughter of the babies in Bethlehem. The narrative closes with the family's move from Egypt to Nazareth.

Atmosphere
There is a marked difference of atmosphere in the two narratives.

Luke's story is pervaded by a sense of happiness: a joyful expectation whose fulfillment evokes more rejoicing. Most of the scenes feature people who praise, thank, or bless God. Every active character in the story contributes to the atmosphere of celebration, including both individuals (Gabriel, Zechariah, Mary, Elizabeth, Simeon, and Anna) and groups (Elizabeth's neighbors and relatives, the chorus of angels, and the shepherds). Greek nouns and verbs for joy, glory, praise, blessing, and thanks occur twenty times in Luke 1–2. The canticles of Zechariah, Mary, and Simeon are suffused with rejoicing, gratitude, and confident hope for the future. The mood darkens only in the brief oracle of Simeon (Luke 2:34–35), which hints at the strife that Jesus will catalyze toward the end of his life.

The atmosphere in Matthew is as different from Luke's as night is from day. Matthew's gospel begins with the emotionless recitation of a formal genealogy; only its mathematical structure merits an interested comment from the narrator. The story itself opens on a somber scene, with Mary in jeopardy and Joseph in an anxious dilemma, which is resolved by the revelation of the angel and Joseph's obedience. The rest of the story—except for a brief scene in which the magi venerate the child (Matt 2:11)—is dominated by the grim atmosphere emanating from Herod's murderous designs: his evil plotting, a close escape, a horrific atrocity, and a haunting scriptural reminiscence of inconsolable grief. The danger ends only with the monster's death. Even then, the family's return to Israel is revised to avoid the threat of another menacing ruler.

How the Stories Are Told

There are five striking differences in how the two stories are told.

1. Luke tells the story of John the Baptizer along with that of Jesus. It is not the case that Luke simply happened to tell about John and then about Jesus. Rather, the pairing is basic to Luke's literary and religious purposes, for he carefully integrates the two stories into a pattern called step parallelism. By contrast, Matthew is silent about John.

2. Matthew's narrative is told primarily from Joseph's perspective. Joseph receives angelic revelations and the plot revolves around his responses to them. Matthew also tells portions of the story from the perspective of the magi or Herod. All the active characters in this narrative are male (Joseph, magi, Jewish religious experts, and Herod). Mary does nothing on her own. Joseph decides her fate, takes her to Egypt, and moves her to Nazareth. Matthew does not even narrate her giving birth to Jesus. Mary's name is used only three times in the story.

In Luke's infancy narrative Mary is the central character. Jesus' birth is announced to her and she declares her willingness to participate in God's plan. Joseph is a mere bystander. He is named only twice and never speaks. Luke's story balances pairs of male and female characters: Zechariah and Mary are the primary parents for John and Jesus respectively, while Elizabeth and Joseph are supporting spouses (though Elizabeth has a much stronger role than Joseph); and Simeon and Anna are the embodiment of expectant Israel greeting the messiah.

3. Both Matthew and Luke use the Old Testament as their primary literary resource, but they use it in markedly different ways. Matthew spotlights

five prophecies, each of which he formally introduces and directly quotes, and around which he composes the five episodes that frame his narrative.

Luke does not quote the Old Testament (except in passing in 2:23–24), but it pervades his narrative as he draws on it in nearly every verse, in three distinctive ways. First, from beginning to end Luke imitates the style of the Septuagint (the Greek Old Testament) and continually alludes to it by recycling bits of its language. Second, he unmistakably models his characters after Old Testament figures. Third, he composes (or adapts) lyrical celebrations of the fulfillment of Israel's hopes in the canticles, which are themselves built out of paraphrases of scriptural poetry.

4. In Matthew, all the major plot movements are directed by dreams. Joseph obeys an angel in a dream (1:20) by completing his marriage to Mary (see pp. 87–88) and adopting Jesus. The magi are advised in a dream not to report back to Herod (2:12). An angel in a dream tells Joseph to flee to Egypt with his wife and child (2:13), and sometime later directs him to go back to Israel (2:19). Finally, Joseph is warned in a dream not to return home to Bethlehem (2:22).

There are no dreams in Luke's story. There are messages from heaven delivered by angels, but these come in visions (to Zechariah in 1:11, to Mary in 1:26, and to the shepherds in 2:9). There are also intimations by the holy spirit, prompting people to inspired speech (Elizabeth in 1:41, Zechariah in 1:67, Simeon in 2:27–28). However, only once does a heavenly communication direct a physical movement when the shepherds go to find the newborn Jesus.

5. Matthew's narration is laconic and stripped down. Only the episode with the magi features human interactions and narrative details. For the rest, the narration is kept to a minimum, with only enough to describe the fulfillment of prophecy. Outside the magi episode there is no human speech; not even Joseph has anything to say. The only spoken words come from the angel in Joseph's dreams or the prophets speaking from the past through the words of scripture.

The contrast with Luke could not be more pronounced. For Luke, human speech is the primary means for expressing the message of the story, with the set-piece canticles at center stage.

Contents

The most obvious difference between the two infancy narratives, and the most striking one, is in their actual contents. The disparities are totally unlike those among Mark and the rest of Matthew and Luke, most of which arise from variations in parallel versions of the same scene or from the diverse sequences in which the three gospels arrange similar scenes. But the two infancy narratives do not have a single scene in common. The only comparable scenes are the two annunciations of the birth of Jesus, one to Mary (Luke 1:26–38) and one to Joseph (Matt 1:18–25). Though these share some common elements—the couple is betrothed, a holy spirit is involved in the conception, and the child's name is chosen by an angel—these are two very different stories. Another structural similarity between the two gospels is that both include a genealogy, though Luke's is not incorporated into his infancy narrative. Nevertheless, the discrepancies between these two family trees are so extensive that no two parallel passages in all the gospels have a higher rate of contradiction.

The genealogies are only one example of how the infancy narratives frustrate those who want to believe that the variations in the gospels are due merely to different perspectives on the same events. Defenders of the historical truth of the infancy narratives point out places where Matthew and Luke can be plausibly harmonized—a task, by the way, not undertaken by critical scholars. For example, it is pointed out that Matthew's silence about the birth of John the Baptizer does not exclude Luke's story about him: Luke gives information that Matthew does not. It is also argued that nothing in the two annunciation stories rules out the other: Joseph and Mary found out separately about God's plan. But that is as far as harmonization can go. Apart from the two annunciations and the stories about John, the two narratives are irreconcilable. The magi and the shepherds stand side-by-side in Christmas nativity displays, but they do not appear together in the actual gospels. The shepherds (only in Luke) visit the newborn in a travelers' shelter and see him in a feeding trough (Luke 2:7); the magi (only in Matthew) visit Jesus at the family home (Matt 2:11). The harmonizer's wishful thinking that both visits happened, but at different times—the shepherds' on Christmas night, the magi's several months later—is a futile contrivance, for these two scenes are woven into mutually exclusive narratives.

In Luke, Mary and Joseph live in Nazareth and travel to Bethlehem to register in a census (Luke 2:4–5). Jesus is born in makeshift surroundings, apparently in some sort of stable (Luke 2:6–7). Forty days later (Luke 2:22) the family goes to Jerusalem to meet its religious obligations in the temple, after which they straightaway return home to Nazareth (Luke 2:39).

In Matthew, Mary and Joseph reside in Bethlehem[1] and presumably Jesus is born at home. Magi arrive in Jerusalem (Matt 2:1) some time (between several months and two years) later. King Herod directs the magi to Bethlehem (Matt 2:8). They pay their respects to Jesus and depart, under angelic instructions not to report back to Herod (Matt 2:12). When the king orders the murder of all the baby boys in the Bethlehem area, a dream warns Joseph of

---

1. See the comment on Matt 2:11, p. 108.

Herod's plan and he takes the mother and child to Egypt (Matt 2:14), where they stay until Herod dies (Matt 2:15). The family returns to Israel, but another dream directs them away from Bethlehem to Nazareth, where they settle (Matt 2:22–23).

The timelines in both narratives are seamless and irreconcilable. Luke's story has no gaps that allow for a visit from Matthew's magi or a stay as refugees in Egypt. The differing accounts of how Jesus was born in Bethlehem and grew up in Nazareth are likewise seamless and equally irreconcilable. In Luke the family resides in Nazareth and Jesus is born during a brief trip to Bethlehem. In Matthew, the family lives in Bethlehem, flees to Egypt, sets out to return to Bethlehem, but ends up relocating to Nazareth.

Points of Agreement

Although Luke and Matthew have no scenes in common and hence no places where the action in their narratives agree, they do agree on several points.

- Mary became pregnant after she and Joseph were betrothed but before they lived together.
- Joseph was not Jesus' biological father.
- Jesus was a descendant of King David.
- Jesus was born during the reign of Herod the Great.
- Jesus was born in Bethlehem and grew up in Nazareth.

These agreements are not trivial. Since they also seem too specific to be coincidental, scholars generally take them to be elements that Luke and Matthew independently inherited from earlier tradition. Whether any of these points is based on accurate historical memories is another question, which we will take up later in the book. The last three items will be discussed in Chapter 9. The first two are aspects of the question of the virgin birth, which will be evaluated in Chapter 12.

LUKE 1–2

1 [5]In the days of Herod, king of Judea, there happened to be this priest named Zechariah, who belonged to the priestly clan of Abijah. His wife, a descendant of Aaron, was named Elizabeth. [6]They were both righteous in the sight of God, obediently following all the commandments and ordinances of the Lord. [7]But they had no children, because Elizabeth was infertile, and both were well along in years. [8]While he was serving as priest before God when his priestly clan was on temple duty, [9]it so happened that he was chosen by lot, according to the custom of the priesthood, to enter the sanctuary of the Lord and offer incense.

[10]At the hour of incense, while the whole congregation of the people was praying outside, [11]there appeared to him a messenger of the Lord stand-

ing to the right of the altar of incense. [12]When he saw him, Zechariah was deeply disturbed and overcome by fear. [13]But the heavenly messenger said to him, "Don't be afraid, Zechariah, for your prayer has been heard, and your wife Elizabeth will bear you a son, and you are to name him John. [14]You will be joyful and elated, and many will rejoice at his birth, [15]because he will be great in the sight of the Lord; he will drink no wine or beer, and he will be filled with holy spirit from the very day of his birth. [16]He will cause many of the children of Israel to turn to the Lord their God. [17]He will precede him in the spirit and power of Elijah: he will turn the hearts of the parents back towards their children, and the disobedient back towards the ways of righteousness, and will make people ready for their Lord."

[18]But Zechariah said to the heavenly messenger, "How can I be sure of this? For I am an old man and my wife is well along in years."

[19]And the messenger answered him, "I am Gabriel, the one who stands in the presence of God. I was sent to speak to you, and to bring you this good news. [20]Listen to me: you will be struck silent and speechless until the day these things happen, because you did not trust my words, which will come true at the appropriate time."

[21]Meanwhile, the people were waiting for Zechariah, wondering why he was taking so long in the sanctuary. [22]And when he did come out and was unable to speak to them, they realized that he had seen a vision inside. And he kept making signs to them, since he could not speak. [23]And it so happened, when his time of official service was completed, that he went back home.

[24]Afterwards, his wife Elizabeth conceived, and went into seclusion for five months, telling herself: [25] "This is how the Lord has seen fit to deal with me in his good time in taking away my disgrace."

[26]In the sixth month the heavenly messenger Gabriel was sent from God to a town in Galilee called Nazareth, [27]to a girl betrothed to a man named Joseph, of the house of David. The girl's name was Mary. [28]He entered and said to her, "Greetings, favored one! The Lord be with you."

[29]But she was deeply disturbed by these words, and wondered what this greeting could mean.

[30]The heavenly messenger said to her, "Don't be afraid, Mary. You see, you have found favor with God. [31]Listen to me: you will conceive in your womb and give birth to a son, and you will name him Jesus. [32]He will be great, and will be called son of the Most High. And the Lord God will give him the throne of David, his father. [33]He will rule over the house of Jacob forever; and his dominion will have no end."

[34]And Mary said to the messenger, "How can this be, since I'm still a virgin?"

[35]The messenger replied, "A holy spirit will hover over you, and the power of the Most High will cast its shadow on you. This is why the child to

be born will be holy, and be called son of God. [36]Further, your relative Elizabeth has also conceived a son in her old age. She who was said to be infertile is already six months along, [37]since nothing is impossible for God."

[38]And Mary said, "Here I am, the Lord's slave. I pray that all you've told me comes true." Then the heavenly messenger left her.

[39]At that time Mary set out in haste for a town in the hill country of Judah, [40]where she entered Zechariah's house and greeted Elizabeth. [41]And it so happened, when Elizabeth heard Mary's greeting, that the baby jumped in her womb. Elizabeth was filled with holy spirit [42]and proclaimed at the top of her voice, "Blessed are you among women, and blessed is the fruit of your womb! [43]Who am I that the mother of my lord should visit me? [44]You see, when the sound of your greeting reached my ears, the baby jumped for joy in my womb. [45]Congratulations to her who trusted that what the Lord promised her would come true."

[46]And Mary said,

> My soul extols the Lord,
> [47]and my spirit rejoices in God my Savior.
> [48]For he has looked on the lowly status of his slave.
>   And, look, from now on every generation will congratulate me.
> [49]The Mighty One has done great things for me,
>   and holy is his name.
> [50]His mercy will come to generation after generation
>   of those who fear him.
> [51]He has shown the strength of his arm,
>   he has routed the arrogant, along with their private schemes.
> [52]He has pulled the mighty down from their thrones,
>   and exalted the lowly.
> [53]He has filled the hungry with good things,
>   and sent the rich away empty.
> [54]He has come to the aid of his servant Israel,
>   remembering his mercy,
> [55]as he spoke to our ancestors,
>   to Abraham and to his descendants forever.

[56]And Mary stayed with her about three months, and then returned home.

[57]The time came for Elizabeth to give birth and she had a son. [58]Her neighbors and relatives heard that the Lord had shown her great mercy, and they rejoiced with her. [59]And so on the eighth day they came to circumcise the child; and they were going to name him Zechariah after his father.

[60]His mother spoke up and said, "No; he is to be called John."

[61]But they said to her, "No one in your family has this name." [62]So they made signs to his father, asking what he would like him to be called.

⁶³He asked for a writing tablet and to everyone's astonishment he wrote, "His name is John." ⁶⁴And immediately his mouth was opened and his tongue loosened, and he began to speak, blessing God.

⁶⁵All their neighbors became fearful, and all these things were talked about throughout the entire hill country of Judea. ⁶⁶And all who heard about these things took them to heart and wondered: "Now what is this child going to be?" You see, the hand of the Lord was with him.

⁶⁷Then his father Zechariah was filled with holy spirit and prophesied:

⁶⁸Blessed be the Lord, the God of Israel,
　　for he has visited and ransomed his people.
⁶⁹He has raised up for us a horn of salvation
　　in the house of David his servant.
⁷⁰This is what he promised in the words of his holy prophets of old:
　　⁷¹deliverance from our enemies,
and from the hands of all who hate us;
　　⁷²mercy to our ancestors,
　　and the remembrance of his holy covenant.
⁷³This is the oath he swore to Abraham our ancestor:
　　⁷⁴to grant that we be rescued from the hands of our enemies,
　　to serve him without fear,
　　⁷⁵in holiness and righteousness before him all our days.
⁷⁶And you, child, will be called a prophet of the Most High;
　　for you will go before the Lord to prepare his way,
⁷⁷to give his people knowledge of salvation
　　through the forgiveness of their sins.
⁷⁸In the heartfelt mercy of our God,
　　the dawn from on high will visit us,
⁷⁹to shine on those sitting in darkness,
　　in the shadow of death,
　　to guide our feet to the way of peace.

⁸⁰And the child grew up and became strong in spirit. He lived in the desert until the day of his public appearance to Israel.

2 In those days it so happened that a decree was issued by Emperor Augustus that a census be taken of the whole civilized world. ²This first census was taken while Quirinius was governor of Syria. ³Everybody had to go to his own town to be counted in the census. ⁴So Joseph too went up from Galilee, from the town of Nazareth, to Judea, to the town of David called Bethlehem, because he was a descendant of David, ⁵to be counted in the census with Mary, to whom he was betrothed; Mary was pregnant. ⁶It so happened while they were there that the time came for her to give birth; ⁷and she gave birth to a son, her firstborn. She wrapped him in strips of cloth and laid him in a feeding trough, because the travelers' shelter was no place for such things.

[8]Now in the same area there were shepherds living outdoors. They were keeping watch over their sheep at night, [9]when a messenger of the Lord stood near them and the glory of the Lord shone around them. They became terrified. [10]But the messenger said to them, "Don't be afraid: I bring you good news of a great joy, which is to benefit the whole nation; [11]today in the city of David, your Savior was born—he is the Anointed, the Lord. [12]And this will be a sign for you: you will find a baby wrapped in strips of cloth and lying in a feeding trough."

[13]And suddenly there appeared with the messenger a whole troop of the heavenly army praising God:

> [14]Glory to God in the highest,
> and on earth peace to people whom he has favored!

[15]It so happened when the messengers left and returned to heaven that the shepherds said to one another, "Come on! Let's go over to Bethlehem and see what has happened, the event the Lord has told us about." [16]And they hurried away, and found Mary and Joseph, and the baby lying in a feeding trough. [17]And when they saw it they reported what they had been told about this child. [18]Everyone who listened was astonished at what the shepherds told them. [19]But Mary took all this in and reflected on it. [20]And the shepherds returned, glorifying and praising God for all they had heard and seen; everything turned out just as they had been told.

[21]Now eight days later, when the time came to circumcise him, they gave him the name Jesus, the name assigned him by the heavenly messenger before he was conceived in the womb.

[22]Now when the time came for their purification according to the Law of Moses, they brought him up to Jerusalem to present him to the Lord [23]as it is written in the Law of the Lord, "Every male that opens the womb is to be considered holy to the Lord," [24]and to offer sacrifice according to what is dictated in the Law of the Lord: "A pair of turtledoves or two young pigeons."

[25]Now there was a man in Jerusalem, named Simeon, a righteous and devout man who was waiting for the consolation of Israel, and the holy spirit was with him. [26]It had been disclosed to him by the holy spirit that he would not see death before he had laid eyes on the Lord's Anointed. [27]And so he was guided by the spirit to the temple area. When the parents brought in the child Jesus, to perform for him what was customary according to the Law, [28]he took him in his arms and blessed God:

> [29]Now, Master, you can dismiss your slave in peace,
> since you have kept your word.
> [30]For my eyes have seen your salvation,
> [31]which you have prepared in the sight of all the peoples:
> [32]a light of revelation to the gentiles,
> and glory for your people Israel.

³³His father and mother were astonished at what was being said about him. ³⁴Then Simeon blessed them and said to Mary his mother,

> This child is linked to the fall and rise of many in Israel,
>   and is destined to be a sign that is rejected—
>   ³⁵you too will have your heart broken—
>   and the schemes of many minds will be exposed.

³⁶A prophetess was also there, Anna, daughter of Phanuel, of the tribe of Asher. She was well along in years, since she had married as a young girl and lived with her husband for seven years, ³⁷and then alone as a widow until she was eighty-four. She never left the temple area, and she worshiped day and night with fasting and prayer. ³⁸Coming on the scene at that very moment, she gave thanks to God, and began to speak about the child to all who were waiting for the liberation of Jerusalem.

³⁹And when they had carried out everything required by the Law of the Lord, they returned to Galilee, to Nazareth, their own town. ⁴⁰And the boy grew up and became strong, and was filled with wisdom; and God regarded him favorably.

⁴¹Now his parents used to go to Jerusalem every year for the Passover festival. ⁴²And when he was twelve years old, they went up for the festival as usual. ⁴³When the festival was over and they were returning home, the young Jesus stayed behind in Jerusalem, without his parents knowing about it. ⁴⁴Assuming that he was in the traveling party, they went a day's journey, and then began to search for him among their relatives and acquaintances. ⁴⁵When they did not find him, they returned to Jerusalem to search for him.

⁴⁶And after three days it so happened that they found him in the temple area, sitting among the teachers, listening to them and asking them questions. ⁴⁷Everyone who listened to him was astounded at his understanding and his responses.

⁴⁸And when his parents saw him they were overwhelmed. "Child," his mother said to him, "why have you done this to us? Don't you see, your father and I have been worried sick looking for you."

⁴⁹"Why were you looking for me?" he said to them. "Didn't you know that it is my destiny to be in my Father's house?"

⁵⁰But they did not understand what he was talking about. ⁵¹Then he returned with them to Nazareth, and was obedient to them. His mother took careful note of all these things. ⁵²And Jesus, precocious as he was, continued to excel in wisdom and gain respect in the eyes of God and the people.

MATTHEW 1–2

This is the record of the origin of Jesus the Anointed, son of David, son of Abraham.

²Abraham was the father of Isaac, Isaac of Jacob, Jacob of Judah and his brothers, ³and Judah and Tamar were the parents of Perez and Zerah. Perez

was the father of Hezron, Hezron of Aram, ⁴Aram of Amminadab, Amminadab of Nahshon, Nahshon of Salmon, ⁵and Salmon and Rahab were the parents of Boaz. Boaz and Ruth were the parents of Obed. Obed was the father of Jesse, ⁶and Jesse of David the king.

David and Uriah's wife were the parents of Solomon. ⁷Solomon was the father of Rehoboam, Rehoboam of Abijah, Abijah of Asaph, ⁸Asaph of Jehoshaphat, Jehoshaphat of Joram, Joram of Uzziah, ⁹Uzziah of Jotham, Jotham of Ahaz, Ahaz of Hezekiah, ¹⁰Hezekiah of Manasseh, Manasseh of Amos, Amos of Josiah, ¹¹and Josiah was the father of Jeconiah and his brothers at the time of the exile to Babylon.

¹²After the Babylonian exile, Jeconiah was the father of Shealtiel, Shealtiel of Zerubbabel, ¹³Zerubbabel of Abiud, Abiud of Eliakim, Eliakim of Azor, ¹⁴Azor of Zadok, Zadok of Achim, Achim of Eliud, ¹⁵Eliud of Eleazar, Eleazar of Matthan, Matthan of Jacob. ¹⁶And Jacob was the father of Joseph, the husband of Mary, who was the mother of Jesus. Jesus is known as the Anointed.

¹⁷In all, the generations from Abraham to David come to fourteen, those from David to the Babylonian exile number fourteen, and those from the Babylonian exile to the Anointed amount to fourteen also.

¹⁸The origin of Jesus the Anointed is as follows: While his mother Mary was betrothed to Joseph, but before she moved into his house, she was found to be pregnant by a holy spirit. ¹⁹Her husband Joseph was a righteous man, but did not want to expose her publicly; so, he planned to break off their betrothal quietly.

²⁰While he was thinking about these things, a messenger of the Lord surprised him in a dream with these words: "Joseph, son of David, don't hesitate to take Mary as your wife, since a holy spirit is responsible for her pregnancy. ²¹She will give birth to a son and you will name him Jesus, because he will save his people from their sins." ²²All this happened in order to fulfill the prediction of the Lord through the prophet:

> ²³Look, a "virgin" will conceive a child
> and she will give birth to a son,
> and they will name him Emmanuel

(which means "God is with us").

²⁴Joseph got up and did what the messenger of the Lord told him: he took Mary as his wife. ²⁵He did not have sex with her until she had given birth to a son. Joseph named him Jesus.

2 Jesus was born at Bethlehem, Judea, when Herod was king. Magi from the East showed up in Jerusalem just then. ²"Tell us," they said, "where to find the one born to be king of the Judeans. We have observed his star at its rising and have come to pay him homage."

³When this news reached King Herod, he was visibly shaken, and all

Jerusalem along with him. ⁴He assembled all the ranking priests and local experts, and pressed them for information: "Where is the Anointed supposed to be born?"

⁵They replied, "At Bethlehem, Judea. This is how it is put by the prophet:

> ⁶And you, Bethlehem, in the land of Judah,
>> in no way are you least among the leaders of Judah.
> Out of you will come a leader
>> who will shepherd my people, Israel.

⁷Then Herod called the magi together secretly and ascertained from them the precise time the star became visible. ⁸Then he sent them to Bethlehem with these instructions: "Go make a careful search for the child. When you find him, report back to me, so I can also go and pay him homage."

⁹They listened to what the king had to say and continued on their way.

And there guiding them on was the star that they had observed in the East: it led them until it came to a standstill above where the child lay. ¹⁰Once they saw the star, they were beside themselves with joy. ¹¹And they arrived at the house and saw the child with his mother Mary. They fell down and paid him homage. Then they opened their treasure chests and presented him with gifts: gold, frankincense, and myrrh. ¹²And because they had been advised in a dream not to return to Herod, they journeyed back to their own country by a different route.

¹³After the magi had departed, a messenger of the Lord appeared in a dream to Joseph, saying, "Get up, take the child and his mother and flee to Egypt. Stay there until I give you instructions. You see, Herod is determined to hunt down the child and destroy him."

¹⁴So Joseph got up and took the child and his mother under cover of night and set out for Egypt. ¹⁵There they remained until Herod's death, in order to fulfill the prediction of the Lord through the prophet:

> I called my son out of Egypt.

¹⁶When Herod realized he had been duped by the magi, he was outraged. He then issued instructions to kill all the children two years old and younger in Bethlehem and the surrounding region. This corresponded to the time of the star that he had learned from the magi. ¹⁷Then the prediction of Jeremiah the prophet was fulfilled:

> ¹⁸In Ramah the sound of mourning
>> and bitter grieving was heard:
> Rachel weeping for her children.
> She refused to be consoled:
>> They were no more.

[19]After Herod's death, a messenger of the Lord appeared in a dream to Joseph in Egypt: [20] "Get up, take the child and his mother, and go to the land of Israel; those who were seeking the child's life are dead."

[21]So he got up, took the child and his mother, and went to the land of Israel. [22]He heard that Archelaus was the king of Judea in the place of his father Herod; as a consequence, he was afraid to go there. He was instructed in a dream to go to Galilee; [23]so he went there and settled in a town called Nazareth, in order to fulfill the prediction of the prophets:

He will be called a Nazorean.

LUKE 1

JESUS AND JOHN

The most distinctive feature of Luke's infancy narrative is that it tells the story of John the Baptizer along with that of Jesus. The stories are structured the same, as if Luke designed them to be set in parallel columns (see Box 2.1). There are two scenes in which the angel Gabriel announces and provides confirmatory signs for the boys' miraculous conceptions, John's to his father Zechariah and Jesus' to his mother Mary (1:5–25 and 1:26–38). Both Mary and Zechariah recite canticles of praise and thanksgiving (the Magnificat, 1:46–55, and the Benedictus, 1:68–79.) Both births are joyfully celebrated by visitors (1:58 and 2:17, 20). At their circumcision ceremonies both babies are given names mandated by an angel (1:59–63 and 2:21). The future greatness and God-given destinies of both boys are publicly foretold in spirit-inspired proclamations (1:68–79 and 2:25–38). Both stories are concluded by nearly identical summary statements about the boys' physical and spiritual development (1:80 and 2:40).

Luke's purpose in this point-for-point parallelism is to show that John is great but Jesus is greater. Scholars call this kind of literary structure a "step parallelism." The clearest example of how this works can be seen in what the angel says about the futures of the two boys. John "will make people ready for their Lord" (1:17), whereas Jesus "will rule the house of Jacob forever" (1:33). Luke weaves this step parallelism into the details about Elizabeth's and Mary's conceptions, pregnancies, and childbirths. John will be filled with holy spirit "from the very day of his birth" (1:15), whereas holy spirit is involved in Jesus' conception (1:35). The scene where the two pregnant women meet reinforces Jesus' superiority to John in two ways. When Mary greets Elizabeth the unborn John "jumps for joy" in her womb (1:41, 44) and Elizabeth declares her unworthiness to be visited by "the mother of my Lord" (1:43). John's birth

2.1	Similarities in the Stories of John and Jesus

Annunciations

John (1:5–25)

5–7 introduction of Zechariah and Elizabeth

11   the angel appears

12   Zechariah is disturbed

13   "Don't be afraid, Zechariah."

13   "Elizabeth will have a son."

13   "You will name him John."

15   "He will be great."

15–17 the child's destiny is described

18   "How can I be sure of this?"

19   the angel responds

20   sign: you will be mute

23   Zechariah departs

Jesus (1:26–38)

introduction of Mary and Joseph 27

the angel appears 26, 28

Mary is disturbed 29

"Don't be afraid, Mary." 30

"You will have as son." 31

"You will name him Jesus." 31

"He will be great." 32

the child's destiny is described 32–33

"How can this be?" 34

the angel responds 35

sign: Elizabeth is pregnant 36

the angel departs 38

Public Presentations of the Infants

John (1:59–80)

67 spirit-inspired prophecy

68–79 Zechariah's canticle

65–66 all were astonished

80 the boy grew up and became strong

Jesus (2:22–40)

spirit-inspired prophecy 27

Simeon's canticle 29–35

parents were astonished 33

the boy grew up and became strong 40

is greeted by neighbors and relatives; Jesus' by angels. John's future greatness is prophesied by Zechariah at home; Jesus' by two prophets in the temple. Finally, while the story about John in Luke 1–2 ends at his circumcision, the story about Jesus continues past his infancy with an episode about him at age twelve.

Despite the inequality between John and Jesus, Luke's portrait of John is wholly respectful. John is a great prophet, inspired by the holy spirit and commissioned by God. Luke's insistence that John is less than Jesus is not meant to demean him. The step parallelism by which Luke coordinates the two infancy stories is his way of responding to the rivalry between followers of John and those of Jesus after both leaders had died. Each side considered its leader superior to the other. The earliest Christians were at a disadvantage in this debate because John had preceded Jesus, and so it could be argued that Jesus had merely carried on the work that John had started. Worse yet, there was the undeniable memory that Jesus had been John's disciple, or at least had acknowledged his authority, because Jesus had submitted to John's baptism (Mark 1:4, 9). Matthew copes with this embarrassment with a heavy-handed rewrite of Mark's baptism scene in which he makes John recognize

Jesus' superior status (Matt 3:13–17; (see Box 2.2). Luke handles the problem very differently, by having Jesus baptized *after* John is imprisoned (Luke 3:19–21). While this makes a bit of a mess in Luke's narrative by raising the question of just who has baptized Jesus, it neatly pre-empts any worry that Jesus' baptism proved that he was subordinate to John.

2.2   The Baptism of Jesus

Mark 1:9–11

Matthew 3:13–17

Luke 3:19–22

[19]But Herod, who had been denounced by John over the matter of Herodias, his brother's wife, [20]topped off all his other crimes by shutting John up in prison.

[9]During that same period Jesus came from Nazareth, Galilee, and was baptized in the Jordan by John.

[13]Then Jesus comes from Galilee to John at the Jordan to get baptized by him.
[14]And John tried to stop him with these words: "I'm the one who needs to get baptized by you, yet you come to me?"
[15]In response, Jesus said to him, "Let it go for now. After all, in this way we are doing what is fitting and right." Then John deferred to him.
[16]After Jesus had been baptized, he got right up out of the water, and— amazingly—the skies opened up, he saw God's spirit coming down on him like a dove, perching on him, [17]and—listen!— there was a voice from the skies, which said, "This is my special son—I fully approve of him!"

[10]And just as he got up out of the water, he saw the skies torn open and the spirit coming down toward him like a dove.

[11]There was also a voice from the skies: "You are my special son—I fully approve of you."

[21]And it so happened, when all the people were baptized, and after Jesus had been baptized and while he was praying, that the sky opened up, [22]and the holy spirit came down on him in bodily form like a dove, and a voice came from the sky, "You are my son; today I have become your father."

Our knowledge of John's self-perception is severely limited by the scant evidence we have about him. What is clear, however, is that John understood himself to be preparing Israel for God's coming judgment. Mark, Matthew, and Luke all associate John the Baptizer with a quotation from Isa 40:3, indicating that John was sent to "prepare the way of the Lord." Taken on its own, "the Lord" here means God. Neither John nor his followers thought the Baptizer was preparing for Jesus—that is a Christian interpretation of John's work. But Luke works this view into his version of John's preaching when he has John declare, "I baptize you with water; but someone more powerful than I is coming. He'll baptize you with holy spirit and fire" (Luke 3:16; see also Acts 1:4–5, 11:16), a prophecy which Luke sees fulfilled at the first Christian Pentecost (Acts 2:1–5). In Acts, Luke has Paul quote John: "I am not the one. No, you are looking for someone who will succeed me, whose sandal straps I am not fit to untie" (Acts 13:25).

This Christian subordination of John to Jesus takes its most blatant form in the Gospel of John. There it is emphasized that John the Baptizer is "not the light; he only came to attest to the light" (John 1:8). The Baptizer is made to say that he is neither the Anointed, nor even Elijah, the Anointed's forerunner, nor "the Prophet" (John 1:20–21). John neither baptizes Jesus nor even meets him. When he sees Jesus at a distance, he tells his own disciples, "There is the Lamb of God" (1:29, 35–36). The Baptizer of the Fourth Gospel declares that he must decrease and Jesus increase (3:30). His entire purpose is to testify to Jesus (1:7, 30–31).

Bear in mind that the Gospel of John was written at the end of the first century. This gospel's overt and thoroughgoing subordination of John to Jesus suggests that the rivalry between their followers was still keen nearly seventy years after their deaths. To be sure, Luke's demotion of John is less strident than that of the Fourth Gospel. Nevertheless, the care Luke lavished on the elegant step parallelism, as well as the clumsy chronology of Jesus' baptism scene, indicate that Luke takes seriously the claims of the Baptizer's disciples. Luke mentions John's followers twice in the Acts of the Apostles (Acts 18:24–28 and 19:1–6, (see Box 2.3), and both times he tells the story in such a way as to put John respectfully but firmly in his "proper" place by insisting that the purpose of John's message was to pave the way for Jesus.

All of this is a showcase example of how strongly the concerns of the later Christian movement have shaped the telling of the Jesus story in the gospels. It reminds us how complex these narratives are, and how vital it is to distinguish between two sorts of information they contain: historical reports based on memories about Jesus, versus interpretations of or free elaborations on the life of Jesus that are driven by the agendas of his followers generations later.

LUKE 1:5–25
The Announcement of the Birth
of John the Baptizer

Old Testament Models

Though we do not know who the author of the Gospel of Luke was, we can learn some things about him (assuming the author was male) from the way he wrote his gospel. One thing we can tell is that he had carefully studied the Greek translation of the Old Testament, known as the Septuagint (abbreviated LXX). This writer had a thorough knowledge of its characters and stories. He was so familiar with its language and so skilled at his craft that he could imitate its style, as he does to great effect in chapters 1 and 2. Although Luke rarely quotes directly from the Old Testament (in Luke 1–2, only at 2:23–24), in his infancy narrative he constantly incorporates phrases from the scriptures into his narration, and structures his scenes and models his characters after ones in the Old Testament. Luke fills his infancy narrative with so many echoes of Old Testament passages and so skillfully adopts its style that Jewish members of his audience might almost have taken the scenes in Luke

---

2.3   Disciples of John the Baptizer

Acts 18:24–28

[24]Now a Jew named Apollos, a native of Alexandria, came to Ephesus. He was an eloquent man, well versed in the scriptures. [25]He had been instructed in the way of the Lord and he spoke with intense enthusiasm and taught accurately about Jesus. However, he knew only about the baptism of John. [26]He began to speak boldly in the synagogue; but when Priscilla and Aquila heard him, they took him aside and explained the Way of God to him in more detail. [27]When he wanted to make the crossing to Achaia, the believers encouraged him, and wrote to the disciples to welcome him. When he arrived, he was of great help to those who through grace had become believers, [28]for he powerfully refuted the Jews in public, demonstrating from the scriptures that Jesus was the Anointed.

Acts 19:1–6

[1]While Apollos was in Corinth, Paul passed through the upper country and came to Ephesus, where he discovered some disciples. [2]He asked them, "Did you receive the holy spirit when you became believers?" They said, "No, we haven't even heard that there is a holy spirit." [3]And Paul said, "So what kind of baptism did you receive?" They said, "John's baptism." [4]Paul explained, "John baptized with the baptism of repentance, telling the people to believe in the one who was to come after him, that is, in Jesus." [5]When they heard this, they were baptized in the name of the Lord Jesus. [6]And when Paul had laid his hands upon them, the holy spirit came over them, and they spoke in tongues and prophesied.

1–2 as passages from their own scriptures. A modern equivalent might be the effect created by a Christian preacher who can tell stories in "King James English."

Two specific ways that Luke drew on the Old Testament are on display in the first part of Luke 1. The first has to do with how he portrays his characters. The second has to do with how he outlined the two scenes in which the angel announces a miraculous birth.

1. Luke models Zechariah and Elizabeth on two Old Testament couples: Abraham and Sarah, and Elkanah and Hannah. Both couples were unable to have children, the first because of Sarah's advanced age, the second because of Hannah's infertility. In both cases God miraculously enabled these women to have sons, Isaac for Sarah and Abraham, and Samuel for Hannah and Elkanah. Both boys grew up to play vital roles in carrying out God's plans for Israel. Isaac continued God's covenant with Abraham when all seemed lost. Samuel was a mighty prophet who struggled for the cause of God in dark times and who anointed Saul and David to be kings.

The particular details of how Luke drew on these Old Testament figures are noted below in the comments on individual verses. He recycles parts of the scriptural stories to create an atmosphere of continuity between the old and the new. This enables Luke to sustain the vivid impression that God is acting in the events surrounding the births of John and Jesus just as he acted in the lives of ancient Israelite heroes of the faith. Luke's use of these scriptural figures is more subtle than setting up one-to-one correspondences between them and the characters in his gospel. For example, he uses descriptions of the young Samuel in his reports about the childhoods of both John and Jesus.

2. Another interesting aspect of Luke's use of the Old Testament is how he structures his two annunciation stories (of John to Zechariah in 1:11–20 and of Jesus to Mary in 1:26–38) in imitation of analogous annunciation scenes in the Jewish scriptures.[1] There are four Old Testament scenes in which an angel of God (or God himself) foretells the birth of a boy with an important destiny.

- Ishmael's birth is announced to his mother Hagar (Gen 16:7–13).
- Isaac's birth is announced in two separate stories to his father Abraham (Gen 17:1–9 and 18:1–13).
- Samson's birth is announced to his parents (Judg 13:2–21).

These scenes all have a similar five-part structure (See Box 2.4):

---

1. Luke seems also to have used a pagan literary model in his composition of the annunciation scenes. See Appendix, pp. 317-21.

1. An angel (or God) appears.
2. The person reacts in fear, reverence, or amazement.
3. The message is delivered.
4. The person objects or asks for a sign.
5. A sign is given to confirm the message.

In addition to these four annunciation scenes, there are two other scenes in which an angel or God appears to a grown man to tell him that his life is about to change because God has chosen him to lead his people.

- God appears in a burning bush to tell Moses that he will lead Israel out of Egypt (Ex 3:1–12).
- An angel appears to Gideon to tell him that God has chosen him to lead the people to victory against the Midianites (Judg 6:11–24).

These two scenes are built on the same five-part outline as the annunciation stories.

Not every story has the identical structure (see Box 2.4). The Ishmael story does not have parts 4 and 5, for example. Some stories have the parts in somewhat different order. Still, the structural similarities are sufficiently strong to show that Israelite storytellers used a standard outline for these six scenes.

LUKE 1:5–25

1:5–7   Introduction of John's parents
1:8–23   Announcement of John's birth
1:24–25 John's conception and Elizabeth's pregnancy

⁵In the days of Herod, king of Judea, there happened to be this priest named Zechariah, who belonged to the priestly clan of Abijah. His wife, a descendant of Aaron, was named Elizabeth. ⁶They were both righteous in the sight of God, obediently following all the commandments and ordinances of the Lord. ⁷But they had no children, because Elizabeth was infertile, and both were well along in years. ⁸While he was serving as priest before God when his priestly clan was on temple duty, ⁹it so happened that he was chosen by lot, according to the custom of the priesthood, to enter the sanctuary of the Lord and offer incense.

¹⁰At the hour of incense, while the whole congregation of the people was praying outside, ¹¹there appeared to him a messenger of the Lord standing to the right of the altar of incense. ¹²When he saw him, Zechariah was deeply disturbed and overcome by fear. ¹³But the heavenly messenger said to him, "Don't be afraid, Zechariah, for your prayer has been heard, and your wife Elizabeth will bear you a son, and you are to name him John. ¹⁴You will be joyful and elated, and many will rejoice at his birth, ¹⁵because he will be great in the sight of the Lord; he will drink no wine or beer, and he will be

Biblical Annunciations

2.4

	Ishmael **Genesis 16**	*Isaac* **Genesis 17**	*Isaac* **Genesis 18**	*Samson* **Judges 3**
1.	The angel of the Lord found Hagar 16:7	The Lord appeared to Abram 17:1	The Lord appeared to Abraham 18:1	The angel of the Lord appeared to the wife of Manoah 3:3
2.	"Have I really seen God and survived?" 16:13	Abram fell on his face 17:3	Abraham prostrated himself 18:2	Manoah said to his wife, "We will surely die because we have seen God" 3:22
3.	"You shall give birth to Ishmael," etc. 16:11–12	"Your wife will give birth to a son," etc. 17:19	"Your wife will have a son." 18:10	"You will give birth to a son," etc. 3:3–5
4.		"How can a child be born to aged parents?" 17:17	Sarah laughed: "At my age am I going to have pleasure?" 18:12	"Lord, I pray, let the man of God come to us again." 3:8
5.		"I will establish my covenant with Isaac." 17:21		The angel of God came again to the woman. 3:9

Moses Exodus 3	Gideon Judges 6	John Luke 1	Jesus Luke 1
1. The angel of the Lord appeared to Moses in a burning bush. 3:2	The angel of the Lord appeared to Gideon. 6:12	An angel of the Lord appeared to Zechariah. 1:11	The angel Gabriel was sent from God to Mary. 1:26, 28
2. Moses hid his face because he was afraid to look at God. 3:6	"Help me, Lord God! For I have seen the angel of the Lord face to face." 6:22	Zechariah was deeply disturbed and overcome with fear. 1:12	Mary was deeply disturbed. 1:29
3. "I will send you to Pharoah to bring my people out of Egypt." 3:10	"I commission you to deliver Israel from the hand of Midian." 6:14	"Your wife Elizabeth will bear you a son," etc. 1:13–17	"You will conceive and give birth to a son," etc. 1:30–33
4. "Who am I that I should go to Pharoah?" 3:11	"How can I deliver Israel? I am the lowest member of the weakest clan . . . Show me a sign." 6:15, 17	"How can I be sure of this? For I am an old man and my wife is well along in years." 1:18	"How can this be, since I'm still a virgin?" 1:34
5. "This will be the sign that it is I who sent you: you shall worship on this mountain." 3:12	The angel sends fire. 6:19–21	"You will be struck silent and speechless until the day these things happen." 1:20	"Your relative Elizabeth is already six months pregnant." 1:36

filled with holy spirit from the very day of his birth. ¹⁶He will cause many of the children of Israel to turn to the Lord their God. ¹⁷He will precede him in the spirit and power of Elijah: he will turn the hearts of the parents back towards their children, and the disobedient back towards the ways of right-eousness, and will make people ready for their Lord."

¹⁸But Zechariah said to the heavenly messenger, "How can I be sure of this? For I am an old man and my wife is well along in years."

¹⁹And the messenger answered him, "I am Gabriel, the one who stands in the presence of God. I was sent to speak to you, and to bring you this good news. ²⁰Listen to me: you will be struck silent and speechless until the day these things happen, because you did not trust my words, which will come true at the appropriate time."

²¹Meanwhile, the people were waiting for Zechariah, wondering why he was taking so long in the sanctuary. ²²And when he did come out and was unable to speak to them, they realized that he had seen a vision inside. And he kept making signs to them, since he could not speak. ²³And it so hap-pened, when his time of official service was completed, that he went back home.

²⁴Afterwards, his wife Elizabeth conceived, and went into seclusion for five months, telling herself: ²⁵ "This is how the Lord has seen fit to deal with me in his good time in taking away my disgrace."

1:5 *his wife, a daughter of Aaron, Elizabeth.* No other canonical source reports the names of John's parents. Perhaps Luke named his mother (*Elisabet* in Greek) after the only woman in the Old Testament with this name: Elisheba (*Elisabeth* in Greek), the wife of Aaron, the first priest (Ex 6:23), and therefore a distant grand-mother of this ancient priestly caste.

the priestly clan of Abijah. According to the roster of priestly clans in the Old Testament, the eighth is the clan of Abijah and the ninth is the clan of Joshua/Jesus (1 Chr 24:10–11). Perhaps this sequence, rather than some biographical informa-tion, is Luke's source for this identification of Zechariah's family line.

1:6 Luke describes John's parents as paragons of Jewish piety and observance.

1:7 *But they had no children.* Childlessness was interpreted as a sign of God's disapproval or even as punishment. Luke's *but* signals that this is not the case for Zechariah and Elizabeth.

well along in years (literally, "advanced in their days") is borrowed from the Old Testament description of Abraham and Sarah, who "were old, advanced in age" (Gen 18:11 LXX).

1:8 Priests were divided into twenty-four *clans*, each one serving in the temple twice a year for one week.

1:9–10 Selection *by lot* was thought to reflect the choice of God. Luke also reports that the apostles used lots to select the replacement for Judas (Acts 1:26).

Incense was offered in the temple every morning and evening, in accord with

Ex 30:7–8. To be chosen for this duty would be a once-in-a-lifetime honor. If selected, a priest was not eligible to be chosen again until all the other hundreds of priests in the clan had each had his turn. Luke sets the scene with high drama: Zechariah receives the news from the angel at the high point of his priestly service, in an especially holy place in the temple, at a solemn liturgical moment, and while *a huge crowd was praying outside.*

1:11 *messenger of the Lord.* Though the Greek word *angelos* simply means "messenger," the word has come into English ("angel") to refer to the supernatural messengers mentioned in the Bible. The angel identifies himself as Gabriel in 1:19. The only place in the Hebrew Bible where this angel appears is in the Book of Daniel. Luke has modeled Gabriel's appearance to Zechariah after his appearances to Daniel (see Box 2.5).

Why does Luke rely on Gabriel's appearance to Daniel for his story of the annunciation of John's birth? Daniel 7–12 contains symbolic visions of the future and Gabriel is the one who reveals their secret meanings. Gabriel tells Daniel that God's plans for humanity will come to fulfillment after "seventy weeks of years" (Dan 9:24). For Luke, the life, death, and resurrection of Jesus begin "the last days," the fulfillment of prophecy (see Acts 2:16–17). Gabriel is thus an appropriate messenger to announce the beginning of this new age. Luke does not understand "the last days" in a chronological sense, as if the end of the world were near, but in a theological sense, that is, the completion of all that God's people were awaiting.

1:13 *your wife Elizabeth will bear you a son and you are to name him John* quotes God's news to Abraham in Gen 17:19: "Sarah your wife will bear you a son and you are to name him Isaac."

Your prayer has been heard implies that Zechariah had been praying for a son. In light of Elizabeth's advanced age, this detail does not fit well into the narrative, for it would mean that Zechariah was hoping for a miracle. Luke's phrase here more likely is influenced by 1 Sam 1:17, in which Eli, the priest at the sanctuary at Shiloh, reveals to Hannah that she will have a son.

1:15–17 describes John's vocation in phrases based on the prophet Malachi's description of the coming of Elijah and anticipating Jesus' later assessment of John's unique importance (see Box 2.6).

1:15 *No wine or beer* echoes the description of the nazirites, men specially consecrated to God's service. Abstention from alcohol was one of the signs of their consecration (Num 6:1–4).

- Samuel's mother promises to raise her boy as a nazirite, not giving him any wine or beer (1 Sam 1:11 LXX).
- Samson's mother is directed by an angel not to drink wine or beer during her pregnancy because her son will be a nazirite from birth (Judg 13:4–5).

1:16 *Turn* is the standard Old Testament term for repentance.

1:18 Zechariah's question echoes Abraham's reaction when told by God that he would possess the land (Gen 15:8). Zechariah's objection is the same as Abraham's in Gen 17:17.

2.5   The Appearances of Gabriel

to Zechariah	Luke		Dan	to Daniel
At the hour of incense, while a huge crowd was praying outside, there appeared to him an angel of the Lord standing to the right of the altar of incense.	1:10–11	*Gabriel appears at a time of liturgical service*	9:20–21	I was still occupied with my prayer . . . on behalf of his holy mountain — I was still occupied with this prayer, when Gabriel came to me in rapid flight at the time of the evening sacrifice.
When he saw the angel, Zechariah was shaken and overcome by fear.	1:12	*Zechariah, Daniel are frightened*	8:17	When he came near where I was standing, I fell prostrate in terror.
"Don't be afraid, Zechariah, for your prayer has been heard."	1:13	*Gabriel tells them not to fear*	10:12	"Fear not, Daniel, from the first day you made up your mind to acquire understanding and humble yourself before God, your prayer was heard.
"I am Gabriel, the one who stands in the presence of God. I was sent to speak to you, and to bring you this good news."	1:19	*Gabriel explains that he was sent to speak to them*	10:11	"Listen to the words I speak to you . . . for I have been sent to you."
"Listen to me: you will be struck silent and speechless until the day these things happen." . . . And when he came out, he was unable to speak.	1:20, 22	*Zechariah, Daniel become speechless*	10:15	While he was speaking to me, I fell to the ground and was speechless.

> "How can I be sure of this?
> I am an old man and my wife is
> well along in years." (Luke 1:18)

> "How can I be sure?" (Gen 15:8)
> "Can a child be born to man who is
> one hundred years old?
> Can Sarah, who is ninety, bear a
> child?" (Gen 17:17)

1:20 Zechariah's sign is a punishment. When Mary makes an objection similar to Zechariah's in 1:34, the sign she is given is not a punitive one. The Christian tradition has alleged a major difference between the two responses, usually arguing that Mary's question is a sincere one, not a stubborn objection like Zechariah's. Yet their questions are not really different.

2.6	John and Elijah	
Malachi on the coming of Elijah	*Gabriel on John's future mission*	*Jesus on John's importance, after his death*
Mal 3:1; 4:5, 6	**Luke 1:15, 17**	**Luke 7:27, 28, 33**
		7:27 This is the one about whom it was written:
3:1 I am sending my messenger to prepare the way before me.	1:15 He will be great before the Lord;	"Here is my messenger whom I send on ahead of you to prepare your way before you."
		7:28 I tell you, among those born of women none is greater than John
		7:33 John the Baptizer appeared on the scene, eating no bread and
	he will drink no wine or beer.	drinking no wine
4:5 I will send you the prophet Elijah before the great and terrible day of the Lord.	1:17 He will precede him in the spirit and power of Elijah.	
4:6 He will turn the hearts of parents to their children and the hearts of children to their parents.	He will turn the hearts of the parents back towards their children, and the disobedient back towards the ways of righteousness, and will make people ready for their Lord.	

That Zechariah's sign is his own muteness probably comes from Luke's modeling of the annunciation to Zechariah after Gabriel's revelation to Daniel, who was rendered mute after hearing the angel's words (Dan 10:15), though in Daniel the muteness is neither a sign nor a punishment.

1:22 It is not clear why his inability to speak should make people deduce that *he had seen a vision.*

1:23–24 *He went home and afterwards his wife Elizabeth conceived* parallels the story of Elkanah and Hannah:

> They went back home to Ramah. Elkanah knew his wife Hannah and Yahweh remembered her. In due time Hannah conceived and gave birth to a son. (1 Sam 1:19–20)

1:24 Elizabeth's *five months in seclusion* does not reflect any actual custom of the time. Nor is it explainable in terms of Elizabeth's motivation. She has no cause to be embarrassed. Quite the opposite: her words in 1:25 explain why she would want to publicize her pregnancy. The reason for her seclusion has nothing to do with her. Luke contrives this detail to prepare for the sign the angel gives to Mary in 1:36. The angel's news of Elizabeth's pregnancy works better as a sign if it is a secret.

1:25 *Taking away my disgrace* echoes the words of Rachel when she gave birth to Joseph: "God has taken away my disgrace" (Gen 30:23).

LUKE 1:26–38
The Announcement of the Birth of Jesus

[26]In the sixth month the heavenly messenger Gabriel was sent from God to a town in Galilee called Nazareth, [27]to a girl betrothed to a man named Joseph, of the house of David. The girl's name was Mary. [28]He entered and said to her, "Greetings, favored one! The Lord be with you."

[29]But she was deeply disturbed by these words, and wondered what this greeting could mean.

[30]The heavenly messenger said to her, "Don't be afraid, Mary. You see, you have found favor with God. [31]Listen to me: you will conceive in your womb and give birth to a son, and you will name him Jesus. [32]He will be great, and will be called son of the Most High. And the Lord God will give him the throne of David, his father. [33]He will rule over the house of Jacob forever; and his dominion will have no end."

[34]And Mary said to the messenger, "How can this be, since I'm still a virgin?"

[35]The messenger replied, "A holy spirit will hover over you, and the power of the Most High will cast its shadow on you. This is why the child to be born will be holy, and be called son of God. [36]Further, your relative Elizabeth has also conceived a son in her old age. She who was said to be infertile is already six months along, [37]since nothing is impossible for God."

[38]And Mary said, "Here I am, the Lord's slave. I pray that all you've told me comes true." Then the heavenly messenger left her.

⌒⌒⌒

1:26 *in the sixth month*: of Elizabeth's pregnancy.

1:27 *girl*: traditionally translated as "virgin." For an explanation of the present translation, see Chapter 10.

betrothed: Ancient betrothal was unlike our modern custom of engagement in that it was a formal and binding step in the process of a legal marriage. See pp. 87–88.

1:28 *Greetings, favored one!* No translation can do justice to the alliteration in the Greek: *chaire kecharitomene*.

1:31 *Jesus* is the Greek form of the name Joshua. See the comment on Matt 1:21, p. 89.

1:32 *his father David*. It is unclear how Luke could understand Jesus to be a descendant of David. Unlike Matthew, Luke does not present Joseph as Jesus' legal father. Nor does Luke think that Jesus is Davidic through his mother. The only information about Mary's lineage offered by Luke is that she is a relative of Elizabeth, who belonged to the Aaronite priestly caste (1:5). At any rate, royal descent was not reckoned through the maternal line.

1:32–33 The angel declares that Jesus will be the permanent king of Israel (*the house of Jacob*). Luke constructed these verses out of phrases from the passages in 2 Samuel 7 where God promises David that his descendants would rule forever.

> [9]I shall make for you a *great* name. . . [13]I shall establish the *throne* of his *kingdom forever*. . . [14]I shall be his father, and he will be *my son*. . . [16]And your *house* and your *kingdom* will be ensured *forever*. (2 Sam 7:9–16)

> [32]He will be *great* and will be called *son* of the Most High. And the Lord God will give him the *throne* of David, his father. [33]He will rule over the *house* of Jacob *forever*; and his *kingdom* will have *no end*. (Luke 1:32–33)

For Luke to say that Jesus is the Davidic king is another way of saying that he is the Anointed. Jesus' everlasting kingdom (*basileia*, elsewhere translated as "imperial rule" or "domain") is eschatological—a matter of the end times. This will be made clear in the only passage in which Jesus claims to be a ruler with his own domain, a claim made in private (Luke 22:28–30). Everywhere else in the gospel, the kingdom that Jesus proclaims is God's, not Jesus'. A crowd of followers will hail Jesus as a king (19:38), but when Pilate asks him whether he is "king of the Judeans," Jesus replies with sarcasm (23:2–3), an insult that Pilate returns by crucifying him under that title (23:38).

1:34 Mary's question is a strange one. If the angel had told her that she was already pregnant, her question would be appropriate. But since the angel tells her that she *will* conceive, her question makes no sense. Mary is betrothed and so is looking forward to starting a family with her husband. A teenage woman preparing for marriage would naturally also be anticipating marital sexuality. Luke phrases Mary's question not in the interests of realistic storytelling, but to signal to the reader that she is a virgin in the strict sense. Since Mary is *betrothed* and since betrothed couples were allowed to have sex, Luke's readers would not automatically assume that she and Joseph were abstaining. Mary's question clarifies the issue.

1:35 Although Luke wants the reader to understand that Mary will conceive while a virgin, he also wishes to head off the impression that would come naturally to hellenistic readers familiar with stories about gods who father children with human women. Luke is careful to imply that Jesus' divine begetting did not involve any kind of physical contact between Mary and God. The two verbs in this verse, *hover over* and *cast a shadow*, reflect Luke's delicacy in this matter. Neither verb connotes conception, much less sexual activity. "Hover over" occurs again in Acts 1:8 when the risen Jesus promises that the holy spirit will visit the disciples. "Cast a shadow" is used in Acts 5:15–16 to report that sick people were healed when Peter's shadow fell on them.

In 1:35 it is the descent by holy spirit and the overshadowing by divine power that makes Jesus a son of God. These two equivalent notions also appear in two later key scenes. The holy spirit descends on Jesus at his baptism (3:22) and the divine presence overshadows him at his transfiguration (9:34). Both scenes culminate in God's announcement that Jesus is his son, confirming what is told to Mary in 1:35.

1:36 *your relative*. Only in Luke's gospel are John and Jesus relatives. By contrast, the Gospel of John emphatically denies that John the Baptizer ever knew Jesus prior to seeing him at the Jordan (John 1:29–33).

1:37 *Nothing is impossible for God*. The angel's words of assurance to Mary are a nearly verbatim quotation of what the divine visitor said to Abraham after Sarah laughed at the news that she would have a son in her old age: "Is anything impossible for God?" (Gen 18:14 LXX).

1:38 *slave*. Mary's declaration that she is the Lord's slave (*doule*) echoes Hannah's response when she hears that she will have a son: "Let your slave find favor in your sight" (1 Sam 1:18).

Mary's response of complete submission to God's will should be appreciated in connection with Luke 8:19–21, where Luke deftly reverses Mark's negative portrait of Jesus' mother and brothers. Luke's source, Mark 3:20–21, 31–35, is a bitter scene in which Jesus disowned his mother and brothers, clearly excluding them with the announcement that his family are those who do God's will. But Luke gently rewrites this scene to make it just as clear that Jesus' words *include* his mother and his siblings.

Mark 3	Luke 8
[20]Then he goes home, and once again a crowd gathers, so they could not even grab a bite to eat. [21]When his relatives heard about it, they came to get him. (You see, they thought he was out of his mind.) . . .	
[31]Then his mother and his brothers arrive. While still outside, they send in and ask for him. [32]A crowd was sitting around him, and they say to	[19]Then his mother and his brothers came to see him, but they could not reach him because of the crowd.

him, "Look, your mother and your brothers and sisters are outside looking for you." [33]In response he says to them: "My mother and brothers—who ever are they?" [34]And looking right at those seated around him in a circle, he says, "Here are my mother and my brothers. [35]Whoever does God's will, that's my brother and sister and mother!"

[20]When he was told, "Your mother and your brothers are outside and want to see you,"

[21]he replied to them, "My mother and my brothers are those who listen to God's message and do it."

"SON OF GOD" IN LUKE 1:35

By itself Luke 1:35 does not foretell a virginal conception. The verse is structured in two parts that are linked by a "therefore." The divine influence in the first half of the verse (*holy spirit* and *power of the Most High*) is what causes Jesus to be *holy* and a *son of God* in the second half. One does not have to be born of a virgin to be holy or a son of God. 1:35 thus states that God's influence will determine *what kind of* person Jesus will be; it does not say that God will influence *how* this person will be conceived. It says that God will somehow be with Mary as Jesus is conceived and born, endowing him with the spiritual qualities that will empower him to fulfill his destiny as a holy son of God. On its own terms, then, 1:35 does not describe a miraculous birth.

However, 1:35 does not exist on its own. Its immediate context is the contrived question in 1:34, which signals that Mary will not conceive Jesus through intercourse with Joseph. The larger context for 1:35 is the step parallelism between John and Jesus. That is the key evidence that Luke is narrating a virginal conception for Jesus. The births of John and Jesus were both miracles, but, according to the logic of Luke's elaborate step parallelism, Jesus' birth has to be a greater miracle than John's. John is born to a woman long past the age of childbearing, a miracle for which there is biblical precedent, but Jesus is born to a virgin, an unprecedented act of divine power.[2] Luke reinforces this understanding of Mary's conception when Elizabeth congratulates her for "trusting that what the Lord promised her would come true" (1:45), praise which would make no sense if Mary had conceived naturally.

The *that is why* (literally, "therefore") in Luke 1:35 makes it clear that Jesus is God's son because of his divine begetting. However, for Luke this does not mean that Jesus has a divine nature. Although that notion comes easily to Christians familiar with the doctrines of the Incarnation and the Trinity, respect for the Bible requires us to understand each author's meaning within its own context. Luke's

---

2. Non-Christians in the ancient world might not agree that it is a greater miracle for a young virgin to conceive than for an aged woman to do so. See pp. 236–37.

context here is the Old Testament, not Christian doctrines defined long after his time.

Within the Old Testament passage from which Luke quarried the building blocks for Luke 1:32–33, God says of David's son Solomon, "I will be his father and he will be my son" (2 Sam 7:14). Similarly, the words of God in Ps 2:7, "You are my son; today I have begotten you," are addressed to the Davidic king on the day of his coronation. God's calling the king "my son" does not mean that the king is divine. It means that God will treat him as a father treats his son, appointing him to a special mission, expecting his obedience, and sharing with him his honor and intimacy.

For Luke, "son of God" means more or less what it means in 2 Sam 7:14 and Ps 2:7. From Luke's perspective, Jesus' status as son of God does not make him divine. It does not even make him unique. Jesus teaches that those who imitate God's indiscriminate generosity are also sons of God (Luke 6:35). In the speech to the people of Athens that Luke writes for Paul in Acts, Luke can even assert that all human beings are "God's offspring" (Acts 17:29). The Christian tradition is inclined to see in Luke 1:35 the idea that Jesus is God's son in a unique sense because of the extraordinary role God played in his conception. Yet Luke's geneal-

---

"a holy spirit"

When Mary asks the angel how she will conceive while still a virgin, the angel attributes her imminent pregnancy to the work of "a holy spirit" (Luke 1:35). Matthew also associates Mary's pregnancy with "a holy spirit" (Matt 1:18, 20). In all three verses the term "holy spirit" appears without the definite article; hence the translation "*a* holy spirit." That may sound strange to Christian readers, but that is good if it disrupts the uncritical habit of assuming that early Christians understood terms like these the way Christians do today. Neither Luke nor Matthew means that this holy spirit is a personal, conscious spiritual entity. Even less do they have in mind the third person of the Trinity, a doctrine defined centuries after the gospels were written. They use this term the way "spirit of God" is used in the Hebrew Bible, where it refers to God's creative power. In Hebrew, the same word means "spirit" and "breath," breath representing the life force itself.

- The Creation Story begins with the spirit/wind of God sweeping/blowing over the waters of Chaos.

> The earth was a formless void and darkness covered the face of the Abyss, while a wind from God swept over the surface of the waters. (Gen 1:2)

- The first human being comes to life when God breathes the breath/spirit of life into it.

> Yahweh God formed the human being from the dust of the ground an breathed into his nostrils the breath of life. And the human became a living being. (Gen 2:7)

- God's spirit is the creative force in all earthly life.

When you send out your spirit/breath, they [all living things] are created; and you renew the face of the ground. (Ps 104:30)
• In a dramatic vision, the prophet Ezekiel proclaims a divine message of resurrection to a valley full of bones.

O dry bones, hear the word of Yahweh. Thus says Yahweh God to these
bones: "I will cause breath/spirit to enter you and you shall live. I will
lay sinews on you, and will cause flesh to come upon you, and cover
you with skin, and send breath/spirit into you, and you shall live." (Ezek
37:4–6)

That the gospel writers are using "holy spirit" in its Old Testament idiom is especially clear in the way Luke uses the term in 1:35. There he sets out the angel's words
to Mary in two parallel phrases:

A holy spirit will hover over you
and *the power of the Most High* will cast its shadow on you.

This kind of arrangement is called synonymous parallelism, a literary device,
common in Old Testament poetry, in which two lines repeat the same thought in
different words. This shows that Luke understands "a holy spirit" to be the same
thing as "the power of the Most High."

In Luke, God's power enables Mary to conceive without male involvement.
Matthew is more vague, saying only that her pregnancy is "of a holy spirit." This
does not imply (nor does it deny) that Mary was a virgin when she conceived. It
means only that God is responsible for Mary and her pregnancy (see pp. 198–200).

ogy of Jesus concludes with "Adam, son of God" (Luke 3:38). For Luke, what Jesus
and Adam share, and what sets them apart from the rest of us, is not a divine
nature, but a miraculous origin for their human life.

THE CANTICLES

A prominent feature of Luke's infancy narrative is his insertion of poetic
prayers of praise and thanksgiving at key points in the story: by Mary when
she meets Elizabeth (1:46–55), by Zechariah at the circumcision of John
(1:67–79), and by Simeon when he encounters the infant Jesus in the temple
(2:27–32). Christian tradition has referred to these psalm-like prayers as "canticles" and named them after their opening words in the Latin translation: the
Magnificat (Mary's canticle), the Benedictus (Zechariah's canticle), and the
Nunc Dimittis (Simeon's canticle).

The canticles of Mary and Zechariah are much longer than Simeon's and
have some unusual qualities in common.

• They are made up mostly of phrases taken from prayers in the Greek Old
Testament. The canticles are, in effect, literary collages, compositions built by
the skillful arrangement of pre-existing pieces (see Boxes 2.9, 2.10, and 3.1).

• These canticles have little to do with their contexts in the narrative. In the Magnificat, only 1:48 refers to Mary's circumstances. In the Benedictus, only 1:76–77 refer to Zechariah and John.

• These canticles allude to certain kinds of events that have no connection with the situations of the speakers. In the Magnificat, 1:51–52 has nothing to do with Mary's pregnancy. In the Benedictus, 1:69, 71, and 74 have nothing to do with the birth of John.

• Both canticles fit awkwardly in their literary settings. If they were removed their absence would not be noticed. In fact, they interrupt the action in the narratives, which would move along more smoothly without them. Each canticle comes at the end of its scene, followed only by a brief report that closes the episode (1:56 and 1:80). Those concluding reports seem abrupt and artificial in their present positions after the canticles, but flow smoothly from the actions of their scenes if we delete the canticles (see Box 2.7). The poor fit of the Benedictus is even more noticeable because the way it is intro-

---

 2.7   The Story without the Canticles

Luke 1:39–45, 56
with Magnificat omitted

³⁹At that time Mary set out in haste for a town in the hill country of Judah, ⁴⁰where she entered Zechariah's house and greeted Elizabeth. ⁴¹And it so happened, when Elizabeth heard Mary's greeting, that the baby jumped in her womb. Elizabeth was filled with holy spirit ⁴²and proclaimed at the top of her voice, "Blessed are you among women, and blessed is the fruit of your womb! ⁴³Who am I that the mother of my lord should visit me? ⁴⁴You see, when the sound of your greeting reached my ears, the baby jumped for joy in my womb. ⁴⁵Congratulations to her who trusted that what the Lord promised her would come true." . . .

⁵⁶And Mary stayed with her about three months, and then returned home.

Luke 1:65–66, 80
with Benedictus omitted

⁶⁵All their neighbors became fearful, and all these things were talked about throughout the entire hill country of Judea. ⁶⁶And all who heard about these things took them to heart and wondered: "Now what is this child going to be?" You see, the hand of the Lord was with him. . . . ⁸⁰And the child grew up and became strong in spirit. He was in the desert until the day of his public appearance to Israel.

In both cases, omitting the canticle leaves a coherent narrative with no noticeable gaps. This reinforces the impression that the canticles were added to stories that were originally written without them in mind.

duced in 1:67 leaves the reader confused about when Zechariah recited the canticle. It would go more logically between 1:64 and 65. In its present location the canticle seems to have been pasted on to the end of the scene.

• Analysis of the Greek in these canticles turns up little that is distinctive of Luke's style. In other words, these prayers don't sound like Luke's writing, except—and this is very important—in just those few verses that specifically refer to the situations of the speakers (1:48 in the Magnificat and 1:76–77 in the Benedictus).

These features of the canticles have led scholars to conclude that Luke did not compose them himself. Because they fit so awkwardly into his story, it also seems likely that Luke did not write his narrative with them in mind. He probably found them afterwards and added them to his story with minimal adaptation.

Christian tradition naturally has assumed that Mary and Zechariah came up with these canticles on the spot. But this is untenable as a critical theory of their origin. Not only do the canticles closely follow the wording of the Septuagint, in a few places they repeat phrases that are found only in that translation, phrases absent from the original Hebrew of those passages. Whoever composed these canticles relied on the Greek Old Testament for source material.

If Mary and Zechariah did not compose these prayers, and neither did Luke, then who did? The only clues are in the form and content of the canticles themselves.

On the one hand, these prayers are clearly Jewish. They resemble the biblical psalms, and every line quotes or echoes some Old Testament prayer. They mention Israel (1:54, 68) and Abraham (1:55, 73).

On the other hand, the canticles reflect a Christian perspective. They celebrate "salvation" coming through "the house of David" (1:69) and the fulfillment of the promises made to Abraham (1:55, 73).

This evidence leads to the conclusion that the canticles originated among Jewish Christians, who used the words of the Jewish Bible to praise and thank God for what he had done in Jesus. These canticles are also prayers of people whose religious outlook is in continuity with the teachings of the historical Jesus, for they identify themselves with the lowly, the hungry, and the downtrodden and they celebrate a God who takes their side against the rich and mighty who oppress them.

LUKE 1:39-56
Mary Visits Elizabeth

After narrating the two annunciation stories, Luke now brings these parallel plot lines together by having Mary and Elizabeth meet. This scene achieves two main purposes. First, it confirms that Mary has conceived, verifying the fulfillment of the miracle promised by the angel in 1:35. In this respect the scene has the same function as the one in 1:24–25, which immediately follows John's annunciation and tells of its fulfillment. The similar designs of these two scenes show that Luke composed them as a matched set of epilogues. Each begins with a formulaic time reference: literally, "after these days" in 1:24 and "in these days" in 1:39. Each praises God for his role in the miraculous conception. Each is dated by noting the months of Elizabeth's pregnancy (five months in 1:24 and three more in 1:56).

The second major purpose of 1:39–56 is to bring the two expectant mothers together in such a way that the superiority of Jesus to John is established even before they are born. The scene leaves no room for the thought that there was ever any competition between them. As soon as Mary walks through the door, a holy spirit reveals to Elizabeth what has happened to her young relative and she bursts out ("proclaimed at the top of her voice," 1:42) with blessings on Mary and her unborn son, proclaiming Jesus' spiritual identity, and congratulating Mary for her trust in God's word. Even John joins in the celebration, "jumping for joy" in his mother's womb (1:44).

Luke's objectives in this scene do not include telling a realistic story. He provides no motive for why Mary makes the trip (though readers can easily fill that in), or why she sets out in a hurry (though readers can guess at this too). The trip itself is unrealistic. From Nazareth to the hill country of Judah is about eighty miles, which means at least a four-day trip, on a route that may have passed through inhospitable Samaritan territory—by a young woman traveling alone. As we saw also in 1:34 when Mary questioned the angel, the words and actions of Luke's characters are controlled by his literary and theological interests, even at the cost of a contrived or unrealistic story.

LUKE 1:39-56

1:39–45   The mothers meet
1:46–55   Mary's Canticle (the Magnificat)
1:56   Mary returns home

[39]At that time Mary set out in haste for a town in the hill country of Judah, [40]where she entered Zechariah's house and greeted Elizabeth. [41]And it so happened, when Elizabeth heard Mary's greeting, that the baby jumped in her womb. Elizabeth was filled with holy spirit [42]and proclaimed at the top of her voice, "Blessed are you among women, and blessed is the fruit of your womb! [43]Who am I that the mother of my lord should visit me? [44]You see, when the sound of your greeting reached my ears, the baby jumped for joy in my womb. [45]Congratulations to her who trusted that what the Lord promised her would come true."

[46]And Mary said,

My soul extols the Lord,
>   [47]and my spirit rejoices in God my Savior.
[48]For he has looked on the lowly status of his slave.
>   And, look, from now on every generation will congratulate me.
[49]The Mighty One has done great things for me,
>   and holy is his name.
[50]His mercy will come to generation after generation
>   of those who fear him.
[51]He has shown the strength of his arm,
>   he has routed the arrogant, along with their private schemes.
[52]He has pulled the mighty down from their thrones,
>   and exalted the lowly.
[53]He has filled the hungry with good things,
>   and sent the rich away empty.
[54]He has come to the aid of his servant Israel,
>   remembering his mercy,
[55]as he spoke to our ancestors,
>   to Abraham and to his descendants forever.[56]

And Mary stayed with her about three months, and then returned home.

1:42 *Blessed are you among women* echoes blessings bestowed on Jael and Judith, Israelite heroines who killed powerful enemies of their people:

> Blessed among women be Jael, blessed among tent-dwelling women. (Judg 5:24)
> Blessed are you, daughter, by the Most High God, above all the women on earth. (Jdt 13:18)

Fruit of the womb is Old Testament language (see, for example, Gen 30:2).

Blessed is the fruit of your womb. It is to be expected in this Jewish culture that Mary is congratulated for the greatness of her son. Elizabeth also congratulates her for her own trust in God (1:45). Both of these characteristics of Mary are emphasized again in a brief scene later in the gospel.

> A woman raised her voice and addressed Jesus, "How privileged [literally, "congratulations to"] the womb that carried you and the breasts that nursed you." "Rather," Jesus replied, "congratulations to those who hear the word of God and keep it." (Luke 11:27–28)

1:43 This is the first time Jesus is called *lord* (*kurios*) in this gospel. In 1:45 and 1:46, *kurios* refers to God. While Luke and other New Testament authors apply the same title to Jesus as to God, this does not imply that Luke understands Jesus to be God. The Greek language used *kurios* as a standard title of respect for important people without any implication that such people were divine. For example, in the New Testament the term can refer to a slaveowner (Eph 6:5, 9; Col 3:22). There are several European languages in which modern Christians use the same title of respect for God, Jesus, and ordinary humans: for example, *Herr* in German and Swedish, *Herra* in Finnish, *Señor* in Spanish, *Signore* in Italian, and *Ur* in Hungarian. Although English-speaking Americans find such usage odd, in England there are still people who are properly addressed as "my lord."

1:46–47 *Soul* (*psuche*) and *spirit* (*pneuma*) are synonyms for the self. See, for example, their use in Isa 26:9 LXX:

> My *soul* yearns for you,
> at night my *spirit* keeps vigil for you.

1:48 is the only verse in the Magnificat that relates to Mary's situation. It contains two expressions that are distinctive of Luke's style: the *for behold* and the phrasing of *from now on*, each of which, it so happens, occurs six times in Luke's writings, but only once in the rest of the New Testament. Luke composed this verse to connect the Magnificat to the surrounding story by having Mary refer to herself as God's *slave* (as in 1:38) and by echoing the word *congratulate* (from 1:45).

That 1:48 was not originally part of the canticle is evident in Mary's reference to her *lowly status*. Characterizing her this way is appropriate within Luke's larger narrative because she is a young woman from a small village, but it fits badly with the specifics of the canticle. 1:52 tells of how the "lowly" (same word as in 1:48) are exalted through God's overthrow of the powerful, a description hardly appropriate to Mary.

1:51 God's *arm* is a symbol of his power, which he exerts to save his oppressed people. For example, "I will redeem you with an outstretched arm and with mighty acts of judgment" (Ex 6:6; see also Deut 4:34).

1:51–53 There are six verbs here in poetic parallelism, all of them in the past tense (*shown, put to rout; pulled down, exalted; filled, went away*). Though they do not apply to Mary's situation, they do reflect the perspective of the Jewish Christians responsible for this canticle. These folks remembered that Jesus congratulated the poor, hungry, and sorrowing, telling them that God was on their side. A verdict against this teaching, pronounced by the political and religious authorities, brought on the crucifixion of Jesus, in the estimation of the composers of the Magnificat. But the last word would be theirs. They believed that God had reversed that verdict by raising Jesus from the dead: Jesus was right about God.

For the Old Testament background to Mary's Canticle (see Boxes 2.8 and 2.9).

LUKE 1:57–80
The Birth and Presentation of John

The Benedictus

Like Mary's canticle, Zechariah's fits poorly into its narrative context. Only 1:76–77 refers specifically to John. Although Zechariah recites the canticle to praise God for the birth of his own son, it is primarily about the messianic role of Jesus.

- The *horn of salvation in the house of David* (1:69) can refer only to Jesus. (Zechariah's family is not Davidic.)
- From the perspective of the Christian understanding of John as a fore-runner of Jesus, *the Lord* (1:76) refers to Jesus (see 3:4).
- The obscure phrase *dawn from on high* (1:78) is also a reference to Jesus.

2.8   The Song of Hannah

Mary's song of praise and thanksgiving calls to mind an earlier woman's psalm-like response to her own miraculous conception of a son, the song of Hannah in the Hebrew Bible (1 Sam 2:1–10). The setting, tone, and subject matter of these two women's songs are so similar that Hannah's must be the literary model for the Magnificat, even if the individual verses of the Magnificat are modeled after quotations from various parts of scripture.

Hannah sings her prayer when she brings her young son Samuel—whose conception was a divine miracle—to live at the shrine of Yahweh in Shiloh. Like the Magnificat, the song of Hannah has very little to do with the specific circumstances of its singer (only v. 5b relates to Hannah's personal story, and that only symbolically). Rather, both Mary and Hannah sing on behalf of those in Israel who put their trust in the God of justice. Both songs are thanksgivings for God's mighty intervention on behalf of the lowly and the oppressed. Both celebrate the stark social and economic reversals through which God imposes justice on human society.

1 Sam 2:1–10

1 My heart exults in the Lord;
  my strength is exalted in my God.
My mouth derides my enemies,
  because I rejoice in your salvation.
2 There is no Holy One like the Lord,
  no one besides you;
  there is no rock like our God.
3 Boast no more,
    let no arrogance come from your
    mouth;
for the Lord is a God of knowledge,
  and by him actions are weighed.
4 The bows of the mighty are broken,
  but the feeble strap on strength.
5 The well-fed have hired themselves out
    for bread,
  but the hungry have grown fat on
    loot.
The infertile has borne seven,
  but she who has many children is
    forlorn.

6 The Lord kills and brings to life;
  he brings down to Sheol and raises up.
7 The Lord makes poor and makes rich;
  he humbles, he also exalts.
8 He raises up the poor from the dust;
  he lifts the needy from the rubbish
    heap,
  to seat them with princes and
  inherit a seat of honor.
For the pillars of the earth are the Lord's,
  and on them he has set the world.
9 He will guard the feet of his faithful ones;
  but the wicked shall be cut off in
    darkness;
  for not by might does one prevail.
10 The enemies of the Lord shall be
    shattered;
  against them he will thunder in heaven.
The Lord will judge the ends of the earth;
  he will give strength to his king,
  and exalt the power of his anointed.

The best explanation for all this is that the Benedictus was originally a Jewish-Christian canticle celebrating the fulfillment of God's covenant promises to Israel in the life of Jesus the Anointed. Luke loosely adapted the canticle to his story by inserting 1:76–77. Though the rest of the piece is built around phrases from the Old Testament, these two verses contain clear indications that Luke composed them himself. Yet 1:76 combines Mal 3:1 and Isa 40:3, the same blend of prophetic passages that Luke found in Mark's presentation of John (Mark 1:2–3). The phrase *knowledge of salvation* in 1:77 is not found in the Old Testament, but "salvation" is a distinctly Lukan term (ten times in Luke-Acts, only once in the rest of the gospels). And although the theme of forgiveness is common enough in the Old Testament, the abstract phrase *forgiveness of sins* never occurs there. It is, however, found in Luke 3:3 where Luke describes the purpose of John's baptism.

 2.9   Mary's Canticle and The Old Testament

The Magnificat	The Old Testament (LXX)
My soul extols the Lord,	My soul will rejoice in the Lord, it will delight in his salvation.[1]
and my spirit rejoices in God my Savior.	I will rejoice in the Lord, I will shout for joy in God my Savior.[2]
For he has looked on the lowly status of his slave;	If you will look on the lowly status of your slave[3] I will rejoice . . . for you looked on my lowly status.[4]
And so, look, from now on every generation will congratulate me.	All women will congratulate me.[5]
The Mighty One has done great things for me,	He is your God who has done great things in your midst.[6]
and holy is his name.	Holy and fearful is his name.[7]
His mercy will come to generation after generation of those who fear him.	The mercy of the Lord is from age to age on those who fear him.[8]
He has shown the strength of his arm, he has routed the arrogant, along with their private schemes.	You have brought down the arrogant as one who is slain, and with your powerful arm you have routed your enemies.[9] He overthrows the mighty of the earth.[10] He exalts the lowly and raises up the lost.[11]
He has pulled the mighty down from their thrones, and exalted the lowly.	The Lord makes poor and makes rich; he brings low and he lifts up.[12] He lifts up the poor from the earth . . . to seat them with the princes of the people and causes them to inherit the throne of glory.[13]

> The Lord has cast down the thrones of
> proud princes,
> and set up the meek in
> their place.[14]

He has filled the hungry with good
things,
and sent the rich away empty.
He has come to the aid of his servant
Israel,
remembering his mercy,
as he spoke to our ancestors,
to Abraham and to his
descendants forever.

> He fills the hungry with good things.[15]
>
> Israel, my servant, I have come to your
> aid.[16]
> He has remembered his mercy on
> Jacob.[17]
> You will show mercy to Abraham,
> as you swore to our ancestors,[18]
> to David and to his descendants for-
> ever.[19]

1. Ps 35:9 (In the Septuagint the psalms are numbered differently than in the Hebrew Bible. Here they are numbered according to the Hebrew Bible. For the Septuagint numbering subtract one). 2. Hab 3:18, 3. 1 Sam 1:11, 4. Ps 31:7, 5. Gen 30:13, 6. Deut 10:21, 7. Ps 111:9, 8. Ps 103:17, 9. Ps 89:10, 10. Job 12:19, 11. Job 5:11, 12. 1 Sam 2:7, 13. 1 Sam 2:8, 14. Sir 10:14, 15. Ps 107:9, 16. Isa 41:8–9, 17. Ps 98:3, 18. Mic 7:20, 19. 2 Sam 22:51

LUKE 1:57–80

1:57–58   John's birth
1:59–66   John's circumcision and naming
1:67–79   Zechariah's Canticle (the Benedictus)
1:80   Report on the boy's growth

[57]The time came for Elizabeth to give birth and she had a son. [58]Her neighbors and relatives heard that the Lord had shown her great mercy, and they rejoiced with her. [59]And so on the eighth day they came to circumcise the child; and they were going to name him Zechariah after his father.

[60]His mother spoke up and said, "No; he is to be called John."

[61]But they said to her, "No one in your family has this name." [62]So they made signs to his father, asking what he would like him to be called.

[63]He asked for a writing tablet and to everyone's astonishment he wrote, "His name is John." [64]And immediately his mouth was opened and his tongue loosened, and he began to speak, blessing God.

[65]All their neighbors became fearful, and all these things were talked about throughout the entire hill country of Judea. [66]And all who heard about these things took them to heart and wondered: "Now what is this child going to be?" You see, the hand of the Lord was with him.

[67]Then his father Zechariah was filled with holy spirit and prophesied:

> [68]Blessed be the Lord, the God of Israel,
> for he has visited and ransomed his people.

⁶⁹He has raised up for us a horn of salvation
   in the house of David his servant.
⁷⁰This is what he promised in the words of his holy prophets
   of old:
⁷¹deliverance from our enemies,
   and from the hands of all who hate us;
⁷²mercy to our ancestors,
   and the remembrance of his holy covenant.
⁷³This is the oath he swore to Abraham our ancestor:
⁷⁴to grant that we be rescued from the hands of our enemies,
   to serve him without fear,
⁷⁵in holiness and righteousness before him all our days.
⁷⁶And you, child, will be called a prophet of the Most High;
   for you will go before the Lord to prepare his way,
⁷⁷to give his people knowledge of salvation
   through the forgiveness of their sins.
⁷⁸In the heartfelt mercy of our God,
   the dawn from on high will visit us,
⁷⁹to shine on those sitting in darkness,
   in the shadow of death,
   to guide our feet to the way of peace.

⁸⁰And the child grew up and became strong in spirit. He lived in the desert until the day of his public appearance to Israel.

———————— ∼≫≪∼ ————————

1:58 The *rejoicing* here echoes the reaction of Sarah when she had given birth to Isaac (whose name comes from the Hebrew word for "laughter"): "God has brought laughter for me; everyone who hears will laugh with me" (Gen 21:6).

Luke tells the story as though Elizabeth's neighbors and relatives did not know that a baby was on the way. While their surprise makes the scene more dramatic, it is unrealistic to think that Elizabeth could keep her pregnancy secret in a village where everyone knows everyone else's business. Even if she had stayed at home for nine months and shunned visitors, her seclusion would have aroused curiosity and speculation. Once again we see that Luke is more interested in emphasizing the wondrous acts of God than in telling a realistic story.

1:59 Luke is poorly informed about Jewish naming customs. In his brief report there are three improbabilities.

1. Luke assumes that boys were named at circumcision, on the eighth day after birth. That custom began among Jews in the Middle Ages. The ancient Jewish practice was to name a child at birth. Non-Jews in the hellenistic world had a custom of naming a baby after seven days. Perhaps this is the source of Luke's confusion.
2. Contrary to what is presupposed in 1:59, neighbors and relatives (the only people that *they* can refer to) had no say in choosing a child's name.

3. The scene implies that it was standard practice to name a Jewish boy after his father, but that was actually quite unusual. For example, in the lengthy genealogies of Jesus in Matthew and Luke, there is not a single case of a father and son with the same name.

1:60–63 Everyone is *astonished* that Elizabeth and Zechariah agree on the boy's name. Astonishment is a standard reaction to a miracle (Luke 8:25, 9:43, 11:14). Luke implies that Elizabeth's choice of the name John was the result of divine revelation, as if Zechariah had not communicated with her about his experience with the angel. Zechariah could not speak, but he could write. Even if Elizabeth could not read, it is more plausible that someone would have helped Zechariah communicate with this wife in writing than that he would not have shared with her the angel's message. Here is yet another instance where Luke sacrifices plausibility in order to emphasize the miraculous.

1:62 Apparently Zechariah was deaf as well as mute. The same Greek word (*kophos*) has both meanings.

1:65 *Fear* is another typical reaction to a miracle, one that Luke usually combines with praise of God (Luke 5:26, 7:16; Acts 19:17)

1:66 In this expression, *hand* means guidance (2 Sam 3:12; Acts 11:21).

1:69 The *horn* is an Old Testament symbol of strength (Deut 33:17, Ps 89:17). The phrase *raise up a horn* calls to mind an ox or a bull shaking his head and so connotes a display of power (see Ps 148:14). A powerful champion can also be called a horn (Ps 132:17, Ez 29:21).

Luke's use of *raised up* carries a double meaning. In 7:16, after witnessing one of Jesus' miracles, the people "glorified God, saying, 'A great prophet has been raised up among us.'" To say that God "raised up" Jesus is also a description of his resurrection. A speech in Acts 4 connects Jesus' resurrection with the salvation he makes available (Acts 4:10, 12).

1:73 God's *oath* to Abraham concerned his ownership of the Promised Land (Gen 22:16–17), but the term could also be used more broadly, as it is here (see, for example, Deut 7:8).

1:77 In biblical language, knowledge of something means an intimate experience of it, not an intellectual grasp of it. Here *knowledge of salvation* is synonymous with *forgiveness of sins*.

1:79 *Sitting in darkness, in the shadow of death* calls to mind the image of prisoners in a dungeon waiting for execution (Isa 42:7, 49:9–10; Mic 7:8).

1:80 Luke describes John's growth in the same terms used in the stories of Isaac, Samson, and Samuel, boys born to infertile mothers through divine intervention.

- The boy [Isaac] grew up. (Gen 21:8)
- The boy [Samson] grew up and the Lord blessed him and the spirit of the
- Lord began to accompany him. (Judg 13:24–25 LXX)
- The boy Samuel grew in the presence of the Lord. (1 Sam 2:21)

Luke does not say how old John was when he moved to the *desert*, nor why. An intriguing theory, but one for which there is no corroboration, is that he went to live with the Essenes at Qumran. Josephus tells us that they would take in other people's children and raise them in the Essene way (*Jewish Wars* 2.8). As usual, Luke's characters act according to his theological and literary agenda, and John's move here prepares for his next appearance in the gospel, when "the word of the Lord" comes to him in the desert (3:2). Luke knew from both Mark and Q that John's public career took place in the desert (Mark 1:3–4 and Q 7:24), so his report that John also spent his youth there need not be based on any biographical information.

2.10   Zechariah's Canticle and The Old Testament

The Benedictus

Blessed be the Lord, the God of Israel,
　for he has visited and ransomed his
　　people.
He has raised up for us a horn of salva-
　tion
　in the house of David his servant.

This is what he promised in the words of
　his holy prophets of old:
　deliverance from our enemies,
　and from the hands of all who
　　hate us;
　mercy to our ancestors,
and the remembrance of his holy
　covenant.

This is the oath he swore to Abraham
　our ancestor:
　to grant that we be rescued from
　the hands of our enemies,
　to serve him without fear,
　in holiness and righteousness
　　before him all our days.

And you, child, will be called a
　prophet of the Most High;
　for you will go before the Lord to
　prepare his way,
　to give his people knowledge of
　salvation through the forgive-
　ness of their sins.

The Old Testament (LXX)

Blessed be the Lord, the God of Israel.[1]
He has ransomed his people.[2]

I will cause a horn to spring up for
　David.[3]
A horn will spring up for all the house
　of Israel.[4]
He will exalt the horn of his Anointed.[5]
He saved them from the hands of those
　who hated them
　and ransomed them from the hand of
　the enemy.[6]
You will show mercy to Abraham,
　as you swore to our ancestors.[7]
He remembered his covenant.[8]
God remembered his covenant with
　Abraham, Isaac, and Jacob.[9]
He has remembered his covenant forever,
　the word which he commanded for a
　　thousand generations,
　which he established as a covenant
　　with Abraham,
　and he remembered his oath to Isaac.[10]
that I may confirm my oath,
　which I swore to your ancestors,
　to grant them a land flowing with
　milk and honey.[11]

Prepare the way of the Lord.[12]
I will send out my messenger
　and he will survey the way before
　me.[13]

In the heartfelt mercy of our God,
   the dawn from on high will visit us,
to shine on those sitting in darkness,
   in the shadow of death,
to guide our feet to the way of peace.

You who live in the region and the
   shadow of death,
   a light will shine on you.[14]
those sitting in darkness,
   in the shadow of death[15]

1. Ps 41:3, 72:18, 106:48. (In the Septuagint the psalms are numbered differently than in the Hebrew Bible. Here they are numbered according to the Hebrew Bible. For the Septuagint numbering subtract one.) **2.** Ps 111:4, **3.** Ps 132:17, **4.** Ez 29:21, **5.** 1 Sam 2:10, **6.** Ps 106:10, **7.** Mic 7:20, **8.** Ps 106:45, **9.** Ex 2:24, **10.** Ps 105:8–9, **11.** Jer 11:5, **12.** Isa 40:3, **13.** Mal 3:1, **14.** Isa 9:2, **15.** Ps 107:10

LUKE 2

LUKE 2:1–20
The Birth of Jesus

This famous story has had enormous influence on the Christian imagination and is familiar even to people who have never read the gospels. For most Christians, this episode in Luke *is* the Christmas story. And justly so. It brings together imperial power, lowly shepherds, and angels from heaven—all around the birth of a baby in makeshift accommodations far from home. The humble physical setting and the supernatural splendor of a chorus of angels both testify to the kind of savior this infant will be.

Luke situates Jesus' birth against the backdrop of a worldwide exercise of Roman imperial power (2:1–5). The birth itself is only briefly narrated (2:6–7) and is not really the focus of the story, which is centered instead on the angelic announcement (2:8–14). The angel's solemn and joyful words in 2:10–11 convey the basic meaning, not only of this scene, but of Luke's whole infancy narrative. Then we see the various reactions to this good news (2:15–20).

The reference to the Emperor's census decree places Jesus' birth into the context of world history. The specific mention of Caesar Augustus is especially appropriate for Luke's agenda. Augustus (63 BCE–14 CE) had brought peace to the Roman Empire by ending a series of bloody civil wars. Rome dedicated the great "altar of the peace of Augustus" to him around 10 BCE. Many believed that he fulfilled the great poet Virgil's prophecy of a child who would grow up to rule over an era of world peace and abundance. Augustus was known as "savior of the world," and cities in Asia Minor adopted his birthday as New Year's Day. He was officially declared a god in 42 BCE. Coins bearing his image (for example, the *denarius* mentioned in the famous gospel scene about God and Caesar) proclaimed him "Son of God" (*divi filius* in Latin). Ancient readers would easily get the point of Luke's juxtaposition of Jesus and Augustus, divine bringer of world peace and salvation. There is delicious irony in Luke's story, for it is the decree of Augustus that sets in motion the events that lead to Jesus, the child who fulfills messianic hopes by being born in Bethlehem, city of King David.

The unhistorical requirement that subjects be counted in their ancestral cities (see p. 181) is Luke's device for explaining how it was that Jesus of Nazareth was born in Bethlehem. (In Matthew's gospel, by contrast, it is clear that Mary and Joseph live in Bethlehem and relocate to Nazareth with the child after staying in Egypt for an indefinite period.) Although Luke's description of the census is full of historical errors, theologically it is a brilliant stroke. Romans conducted censuses to ensure that everyone was being taxed. A census would generate widespread resentment among Rome's conquered subjects because it was an unmistakable reminder of who owned the empire in which they were forced to live. Jewish resistance to the first Roman census in Judea (the one under Quirinius to which Luke refers) was so severe that it turned into a rebellion. Luke's staging is therefore quite pointed. Jesus, the savior of the world, is born during a worldwide demonstration of Roman imperial might, under the oppressive authority of the "divine savior" Augustus.

LUKE 2:1–20

2:1–3   The census
2:4–5   The journey to Bethlehem
2:6–7   The birth of Jesus
2:8–14   Angels announce the birth to shepherds
2:15–20   Shepherds visit Jesus

2 In those days it so happened that a decree was issued by Emperor Augustus that a census be taken of the whole civilized world. ²This first census was taken while Quirinius was governor of Syria. ³Everybody had to go to his own town to be counted in the census. ⁴So Joseph too went up from Galilee, from the town of Nazareth, to Judea, to the town of David called Bethlehem, because he was a descendant of David, ⁵to be counted in the census with Mary, to whom he was betrothed; Mary was pregnant. ⁶It so happened while they were there that the time came for her to give birth; ⁷and she gave birth to a son, her firstborn. She wrapped him in strips of cloth and laid him in a feeding trough, because the travelers' shelter was no place for such things.

⁸Now in the same area there were shepherds living outdoors. They were keeping watch over their sheep at night, ⁹when a messenger of the Lord stood near them and the glory of the Lord shone around them. They became terrified. ¹⁰But the messenger said to them, "Don't be afraid: I bring you good news of a great joy, which is to benefit the whole nation; ¹¹today in the city of David, your Savior was born—he is the Anointed, the Lord. ¹²And this will be a sign for you: you will find a baby wrapped in strips of cloth and lying in a feeding trough."

[13]And suddenly there appeared with the messenger a whole troop of the heavenly army praising God:

> [14]Glory to God in the highest,
> and on earth peace to people whom he has favored!

[15]It so happened when the messengers left and returned to heaven that the shepherds said to one another, "Come on! Let's go over to Bethlehem and see what's happened, the event the Lord has told us about." [16]And they hurried off, and found Mary and Joseph, and the baby lying in a feeding trough. [17]And when they saw it they reported what they had been told about this child. [18]Everyone who listened was astonished at what the shepherds told them. [19]But Mary took all this in and reflected on it. [20]And the shepherds returned, glorifying and praising God for all they had heard and seen; everything turned out just as they had been told.

———— ∞⌒∞ ————

2:4 *went up to . . . the city of David*. In the Bible, to "go up" is the traditional terminology for a pilgrimage to Jeruslaem. And everywhere else in the Bible "the city of David" refers to Jerusalem, not Bethlehem (e.g., 2 Sam 5:7, 9). Luke's application of this terminology to Bethlehem is thus imprecise, but it does draw attention to Joseph's Davidic ancestry. However, unlike Matthew, Luke does not explain how Jesus can be Davidic if Joseph is not his natural father. See the comments on Matt 1:20–21 (p. 89).

2:5 *to be counted in the census with Mary*. Even in the historically inaccurate census procedure that Luke describes, women would not have been required to go in person to be counted. Husbands or fathers would have registered for them. So it makes no realistic sense for a woman to make the eighty-five mile trip from Nazareth to Bethlehem, much less a woman nine months pregnant! For Mary to accompany Joseph makes sense only in terms of Luke's need to explain how Jesus was born in Bethlehem.

2:7 *wrapped him in strips of cloth*. This was a customary feature of infant care and was done to keep newborns from moving their arms and legs, just as in the familiar confines of the womb.

The *feeding trough* does not signify poverty, but the haphazard circumstances of the time and place of the birth. The Infancy Gospel of James has Jesus born in a cave (InJas 18:1) and has Mary put him in a feeding trough, presumably under some hay, in order to hide him from Herod's soldiers (InJas 22:3–4). Luke's feeding trough is probably an allusion to Isa 1:3 LXX.

> The ox knows its owner
> and the donkey its lord's feeding trough;
> But Israel does not know me
> and my people does not understand me.

Although the ox and donkey are standard figures in popular presentations of the Christmas story, no animals are mentioned in Luke's scene. They appeared in later centuries as the Christian imagination used Isa 1:3 to fill in the details. The eighth-century Gospel of Pseudo-Matthew has the barnyard animals worshipping Jesus, in fulfillment of Isaiah's prophecy (Ps-Matthew 14, see p. 310).

The *travelers' shelter* was a caravansary, a large open shelter for people and animals. The sense of *no place* seems to be that the couple wanted privacy, not that there was no space for them. Luke may have in mind a verse from Jeremiah which laments that Israel treats its "savior" like a foreigner heading for a "travelers' shelter."

> O hope of Israel, Lord, a savior in time of troubles.
> Why should you be like a stranger in the land,
> > like a traveler on the way to a travelers' shelter? (Jer 14:8)

2:8 Luke casts *shepherds* in his narrative because it is only as a shepherd that the Old Testament connects David to Bethlehem, in a scene where Samuel anoints him king (1 Sam 16:1–13, especially v. 4 and v. 11. See also Ps 78:70–71.) Shepherds were among the lowly in society, though Luke does not portray them as outcasts or as poor. They apparently own *their sheep*.

2:10–11 The angel's announcement is in highly formal language which Luke probably modeled after the various civic proclamations of praise for the Roman emperor. One of them can still be read today in Priene, in the former Asia Minor. Priene's provincial assembly issued a decree, which was cut into a public inscription. Referring to Augustus, its last lines declare, "The birthday of the god marked the beginning of the good news for the world."

2:11 *Savior* was a common title for the Roman Emperor but the term is very rare in the gospels. It refers to God in Luke 1:47. 1:69 refers to Jesus as the "horn of salvation." In the four gospels the word "savior" refers to Jesus only twice: here in Luke and in John 4:42. Paul uses the term only once, to describe what Jesus will be at his second coming (Phil 3:20).

2:12 The *sign* is not meant to reveal anything about Jesus. Rather, their finding the baby in this odd place (a feeding trough) is meant to certify the truth of the angel's message.

2:13 The *heavenly army* is the gathering of spiritual beings who exist in the presence of God, like troops at the service of a king. For example, "I saw Yahweh sitting on his throne, with the whole heavenly army standing beside him" (1 Kgs 22:19).

2:18 *Everyone who listened.* When the shepherds arrive they tell those who are there what they heard from the angel. Luke wants there to be public amazement at this wondrous event, just as there was at the birth of John in 1:66. He thus presupposes that some sort of crowd has gathered at Jesus' birthplace, although he does not say how they got there or why they came.

LUKE 2:21–40
The Presentation of Jesus

This section begins with a brief report of the circumcision of Jesus. The next scene takes us to the temple for the public manifestation of the infant.

That scene opens by telling us that "they brought him up to Jerusalem to present him to the Lord," but the real purpose of the scene is to present him to the pious people of Israel, represented by Simeon and Anna. This scene is the counterpart to the presentation of the infant John at his circumcision (1:59–80), and Luke, as usual, has constructed the corresponding scenes in step parallelism to show that Jesus is superior to John. John is presented to neighbors and family friends, who are amazed and wonder who he will turn out to be (1:66). John's father prophesies (1:67) the boy's future greatness as the one "who will go before the Lord to prepare his way" (1:76). Jesus is presented in the temple to the representatives of faithful Israel, who, guided by the holy spirit (2:27) and by the gift of prophecy (2:36), publicly proclaim Jesus' future greatness as God's "salvation" (2:31) and the fulfillment of hopes for "the liberation of Jerusalem" (2:38).

The scene comes to its formal conclusion in 2:39, followed by a general conclusion for the whole infancy narrative in 2:40. (The story of the twelve-year old Jesus in the temple in 2:41–52 functions as an epilogue to the infancy narrative.) Luke's grand story thus comes full circle, beginning and ending in a temple scene featuring pairs of elderly men and women (Zechariah and Elizabeth; Simeon and Anna) who embody the ideals of Jewish faithfulness and piety . We have to admire Luke's literary skill here, for he brings his infancy narrative to conclusion in a scene in which Jesus' parents, in the course of their full obedience to the Law of God, come together with pious Israel for spirit-inspired prophecy about Jesus' destiny—and all of this in the temple in Jerusalem! It's almost as if the narrative has been designed for presentation on the stage.

The Setting

The center of 2:22–40 is the canticle and oracle of Simeon (2:29–32 and 34–35). That he happens to run into the family in the temple is a divinely arranged coincidence (2:27). Simeon's testimony about the infant Jesus is reinforced by Anna the prophetess, who also arrives on the scene by coincidence (2:38), though Luke does not report her words.

Simeon's Canticle

Simeon's canticle (2:29–32), known traditionally as the Nunc Dimittis (its first two words in Latin), lyrically celebrates Jesus as the fulfillment of Israel's hopes and the light of salvation for the gentiles. The canticle may have been a pre-existing piece that Luke spliced into his story by adding v. 28 at the beginning and v. 33 at the end, since the scene can go from v. 27 to v. 34 without disruption. Indeed, leaving out the canticle would make for a more even balance between the scene's two parts: a holy man and a holy woman greet the

family and speak about the baby's destiny. This suggests that Luke may originally have written the narrative without the Nunc Dimittis, only to insert this
poem later. If the canticle is pre-Lukan, presumably it comes from the same
source as the Benedictus and the Magnificat. Whoever composed it did so by
assembling various bits of scripture, mostly from Second Isaiah (see Box 3.1).

Simeon's Oracle

Simeon's words to Mary in 2:34–35 are not part of the canticle. 2:34–35
is rather an oracle, or cryptic prediction. Simeon foretells that Jesus and his
message will elicit antagonism and cause strife in Israel. His parenthetical
remark about Mary's future heartbreak has been traditionally taken as a prediction of the pain she endured watching her son die. However, this cannot
be what Luke intends, since in his gospel Jesus' mother is not present to see
the crucifixion. In the context of Luke's gospel, Simeon's ominous words foreshadow Mary's grief at the hostility and division that Jesus will provoke.

3.1   Simeon's Canticle and The Old Testament

The Nunc Dimittis	The Old Testament
Now, Master, you can dismiss your slave in peace, according to your word,	Now I am willing to die, for I have seen your face.[1]
now that my eyes have seen your salvation,	The whole human race will see God's salvation.[2]
which you have prepared in the sight of all the peoples,	The Lord has revealed his holy arm in front of all the gentiles and all the ends of the earth will see the salvation that comes from God.[3]
a light for revelation to the gentiles	That you may be a light for the gentiles, for salvation to the ends of the earth[4]
and glory for your people Israel.	I will put salvation in Zion for glory to Israel.[5]

1. Gen 46:30 2. Isa 40:5 LXX. See also Luke 3:6. 3. Isa 52:10 4. Isa 49:6 LXX 5. Isa 46:13 LXX

The Ceremonies

Luke 2:22–24 is told not for its own sake, but to set the scene for the encounter with Simeon and Anna. The way Luke describes Jewish rituals here shows how thoroughly he misunderstood them.

- There was a ritual of purification for a woman forty days after the birth of a son or eighty days after the birth of a daughter (see Lev 12:1–8 in Box 3.2). Luke mistakenly thinks that this ritual involved both parents,

---

 3.2   Ritual Texts

Purification after childbirth

Leviticus 12:1–8

[1]Yahweh said to Moses, [2]Say to the people of Israel, If a woman conceives and gives birth to a boy, she shall be ritually unclean for seven days; she shall be unclean as if she were menstruating. [3]And on the eighth day the flesh of his foreskin shall be circumcised. [4]The time of her blood purification shall be thirty-three days. She shall not touch any sacred thing, or enter the sanctuary, until the days of her purification are completed. [5]If she gives birth to a girl, she shall be unclean for two weeks, as if she were menstruating. Her time of blood purification shall be sixty-six days.

[6]When the days of her purification are completed, whether for a son or for a daughter, she shall bring to the priest at the entrance of the meeting tent a yearling lamb for a burnt offering, and a pigeon or a turtledove for a sin offering. [7]The priest shall offer it before Yahweh, and make atonement for her; then she shall be clean from her flow of blood. This is the law for a woman who give birth, either to a boy or to a girl. [8]If she cannot afford a lamb, then she shall take two turtledoves or two pigeons, one for a burnt offering and the other for a sin offering; and the priest shall make atonement for her, and she shall be clean.

Redemption of firstborn sons

Exodus 13:1–2, 12–15

[1]Yahweh said to Moses, [2]Consecrate to me all the firstborn; whatever is the first to open the womb among the people of Israel, of humans and animals, belongs to me. . . . [12]All the firstborn males of your livestock shall be Yahweh's. [13]Every firstborn donkey you shall redeem with a lamb; if you do not redeem it, you must break its neck. Every firstborn son you shall redeem. [14]And in the future, when your son asks you, "What does this mean?" you shall tell him, "By strength of hand Yahweh brought us out of Egypt, from the house of slavery. [15]When Pharaoh stubbornly refused to let us go, Yahweh killed all the firstborn in the land of Egypt, both humans and animals. That is why I sacrifice to Yahweh every male that first opens the womb; but every firstborn son I redeem."

Numbers 18:15–16

[15]The first issue of the womb of all creatures, human and animal, which is offered to Yahweh, shall be yours, but the firstborn of humans you shall redeem. [16]Their redemption price you shall fix at five shekels of silver.

for he refers to "their purification." ("Their" refers gramatically to the "they" who bring Jesus to Jerusalem.) Some ancient copyists of the New Testament even corrected Luke on this point by changing his "their" to "her."

- There was no ritual of "presenting" a child to God. The quotation from the Law in 2:24 refers to the ritual of redeeming the firstborn son, which did not involve bringing the boy to the temple.
- According to the Law every firstborn male, both human and animal, had to be dedicated to God, in memory of the Israelites' escape from Egypt when God killed all the firstborn males of the Egyptians (Ex 13:1–2,11–16). Firstborn sons, and some firstborn animals, could be "redeemed" (bought back) from God by paying a fee (Num 18:15–16). Luke does not mention anything about this.
- The sacrifice of the birds (Luke 2:24) was part of the ritual of purification for the mother, although Luke seems to connect it to the presentation/redemption of the baby.

Luke was probably confused or poorly informed about Jewish temple rituals. After all, he wrote at least two decades after the temple had been destroyed. It is also possible that he deliberately conflated three things: the ritual of maternal purification, the ritual of buying back the firstborn son, and the idea of presenting a baby boy to the Lord. The first gets the parents from Bethlehem to the temple, the second gets the infant Jesus there with them, and the third enhances the narrative echoes with the story of baby Samuel (see Box 3.3). Luke had to find a way to get the infant Jesus and his parents to the temple to meet Simeon and Anna, and what better way than to portray the family as fulfilling the Law while imitating Samuel and his parents?

LUKE 2:21–40

2:21	Circumcision of Jesus
2:22–24	Purification and presentation in the temple
2:25–35	Encounter with Simeon
2:29–32	Simeon's Canticle (The Nunc Dimittis)
2:34–35	Simeon's Oracle
2:36–38	Encounter with Anna
2:39	Return to Nazareth
2:40	Report on the boy's growth

[21]Now eight days later, when the time came to circumcise him, they gave him the name Jesus, the name assigned him by the heavenly messenger before he was conceived in the womb.

[22]Now when the time came for their purification according to the Law

of Moses, they brought him up to Jerusalem to present him to the Lord [23]as it is written in the Law of the Lord, "Every male that opens the womb is to be considered holy to the Lord," [24]and to offer sacrifice according to what is dictated in the Law of the Lord: "A pair of turtledoves or two young pigeons."

[25]Now there was a man in Jerusalem, named Simeon, a righteous and devout man who was waiting for the consolation of Israel, and the holy spirit was with him. [26]It had been disclosed to him by the holy spirit that he would not see death before he had laid eyes on the Lord's Anointed. [27]And so he was guided by the spirit to the temple area. When the parents brought in the

---

3.3   Samuel and Jesus

As in the story about John the Baptizer, Luke draws on Old Testament passages about the infancy of Samuel to shape his narrative in 2:22–40.

Both Samuel and Jesus are presented to God in a sacred place:
Samuel in the sanctuary at Shiloh; Jesus in the Temple in Jerusalem.

Hannah said, "As soon as the child is weaned, I will bring him, that he may appear in the presence of the Lord." (1 Sam 1:22)	Now when the time came for their purification according to the Law of Moses, they brought him up to Jerusalem to present him to the Lord. (Luke 2:22)

An appropriate sacrifice is offered for each boy:
a bull, grain, and wine for Samuel; two birds for Jesus.

When she had weaned him, she took him up with her, along with a three-year-old bull, a measure of flour, and a skin of wine. (1 Sam 1:24)	They offered a sacrifice according to what is dictated in the Law of the Lord: "A pair of turtledoves or two young pigeons." (Luke 2:24)

An elderly holy man blesses both sets of parents:
Eli blesses Samuel's; Simeon blesses Jesus'.

Eli would bless Elkanah and his wife, "May the Lord repay you with children by this woman for the gift she made to the Lord." (1 Sam 2:20)	Simeon blessed them and said to Mary his mother, "This child is linked to the fall and rise of many in Israel, and is destined to be a sign that is rejected. You too will have your heart broken—and the schemes of many minds will be exposed." (Luke 2:34–35)

child Jesus, to perform for him what was customary according to the Law, ²⁸he took him in his arms and blessed God:

> ²⁹Now, Master, you can dismiss your slave in peace,
>   since you have kept your word.
> ³⁰For my eyes have seen your salvation,
>   ³¹which you have prepared in the sight of all the peoples:
> ³²a light of revelation to the gentiles,
>   and glory for your people Israel.

³³His father and mother were astonished at what was being said about him. ³⁴Then Simeon blessed them and said to Mary his mother,

> This child is linked to the fall and rise of many in Israel,
>   and is destined to be a sign that is rejected—
> ³⁵you too will have your heart broken—
>   and the schemes of many minds will be exposed.

³⁶A prophetess was also there, Anna, daughter of Phanuel, of the tribe of Asher. She was well along in years, since she had married as a young girl and lived with her husband for seven years, ³⁷and then alone as a widow until she was eighty-four. She never left the temple area, and she worshiped day and night with fasting and prayer. ³⁸Coming on the scene at that very moment, she gave thanks to God, and began to speak about the child to all who were waiting for the liberation of Jerusalem.

³⁹And when they had carried out everything required by the Law of the Lord, they returned to Galilee, to Nazareth, their own town. ⁴⁰And the boy grew up and became strong, and was filled with wisdom; and God regarded him favorably.

———— ☙ ————

2:21 Luke mistakenly assumes that circumcision was a naming ceremony, an error he also makes regarding John's circumcision. See the comment on Luke 1:59 (p. 50).

2:23 This quotation does not match any one verse in the Old Testament. Luke borrowed the phrase *"every male that opens the womb"* from verses about the consecration and redemption of the firstborn son (Ex 13:1–2, 12, 15; 22:29; 34:19). The words *"is to be called holy to the Lord"* (lit.) are not from the Old Testament at all. Luke added them because they echo the words of the angel to Mary in 1:35, "The child to be born will be holy, and be called son of God."

2:24 The normal offering was a lamb and a bird (Lev 12:6). However, if a woman could not afford a lamb, she could substitute an extra bird (Lev 12:8). Although Luke here quotes Lev 12:8, he does not quote its exception clause. Even so, he portrays the family as one of modest means.

pigeons. In Mark's version of Jesus' temple demonstration, Jesus tried to drive out the moneychangers and the pigeon merchants from the temple (Mark 11:15). When Luke rewrote that scene in Mark, he says nothing about Jesus' objecting to the selling of pigeons (Luke 19:45–46), probably because in the present episode Jesus' family needs these birds to complete their obedience to the Law.

2:25 *watched and waited for the consolation of Israel.* Both Simeon (here) and Anna (in 2:38) exemplify Israel's eschatological expectation, and both of them proclaim the baby Jesus to be its fulfillment.

The phrase *consolation of Israel* may echo the dramatic introduction to the powerful prophecies of hope and deliverance in Second Isaiah: "'Console, console my people,' says the Lord" (Isa 40:1).

2:33 *his father and mother.* A good number of ancient copyists changed this to "Joseph and his mother" in order to pre-empt any confusion about the virgin birth. Similarly, the words of Mary in 2:48, "your father and I," were altered in some manuscripts to "we."

2:36–37 *Anna,* who has the same name as Samuel's mother (Anna is the Greek form of the Hebrew Hannah), is a *prophetess,* a *widow,* and a paragon of religious devotion. Her age, *eighty-four,* might be symbolic (7 x 12). If so, she represents expectant Israel encountering Jesus in the perfect fullness of time.

LUKE 2:41–52
The Finding of Jesus in the Temple

This episode is an anomaly in the New Testament, being the only biblical story about Jesus between his infancy and his adult life. It stands alone in Luke's gospel as well because it seems to be an independent story. It is not part of the elaborate parallelism between John and Jesus—there is no boyhood story about John—nor does it presuppose developments in the story that precedes it. The use of "his parents" in 2:44 and Mary's reference to "your father and I" in 2:48 do not presuppose the virgin birth. Mary and Joseph's failure to understand Jesus' reference to his heavenly father in 2:49 does not match up with what they should already know very well about him from Gabriel's announcement (1:32–33), the shepherds' report of the angel's revelation (2:8–17), and Simeon's prophecy (2:29–32).

The story also seems external to the larger narrative; we would not notice its omission. 2:40 would make a perfect conclusion to the whole infancy narrative, not the least because it forms a matched set with 1:80, which concludes the infancy story about John. 2:41–51 may well have been a traditional story that Luke appended to his infancy narrative at a second stage of his writing. If so, he rewrote this story in his own style, adapted its beginning to parallel the opening of the scene in 2:22, and added a second concluding summary about Jesus' growth (2:52) to match the one in 2:40.

Whether Luke picked up this story from others or created it himself, it works nicely as an epilogue to the scenes of Jesus' birth and infancy, and as a transition to Jesus' baptism, his first adult appearance in public (3:21–22). The narration builds up to Jesus' rhetorical questions in 2:49. Since these are his first words in this gospel, they are, according to the conventions of ancient biography, highly significant clues to his character. The structure of the scene thus spotlights Jesus' awareness that he is God's son, a declaration made about him earlier by Gabriel (1:32) and later by the voice from heaven at his baptism (3:22). Ancient biographies typically included one or more stories from the hero's childhood, the purpose of which was to show that his future greatness was already evident in his youthful behavior. In Luke's story, the young Jesus' presence among the teachers in the temple points to his own vocation as a teacher. His give-and-take with them looks forward to his hostile verbal exchanges with religious authorities. The precocious intelligence (2:47) of the boy presages the extraordinary wisdom of the man (see 4:22, 4:32, 20:26).

As in the other scenes in Luke 1–2, realism is subordinated to the larger religious and literary interests of the narrative. Is it likely that parents of a twelve-year-old boy would travel for a full day before asking where he was? What did Jesus eat and where did he sleep during the three days? How can his parents be baffled by his remarks, the meaning of which is perfectly clear to readers? Once again it is evident that among Luke's purposes in writing neither historical accuracy nor realistic storytelling has a high priority.

This assessment of Luke's motives helps us to make sense out of two puzzling features in 2:50–51. The first is his parents' inability to understand what Jesus says in v. 49. As odd as this is in light of what they are supposed to know about his origin, it prepares readers for other key failures to understand Jesus' divinely ordained mission.

- "Jesus said, 'Mark well these words: the son of Adam is about to be turned over to his enemies.' But they never understood this remark. It was couched in veiled language, so they could not get its meaning." (9:44–45)
- (After Jesus predicts his fate in detail in 18:31–33) "But they did not understand any of this; this remark was obscure to them, and they never did figure out what it meant." (18:34)
- "When Jesus got close enough to catch sight of Jerusalem, he wept over it: 'If you—yes, you—had only recognized the path to peace even today! But as it is, it is hidden from your eyes.'" (19:41–42)

The second puzzle is the statement that Jesus was obedient to his parents (2:51). This reinforces the theme of Jewish piety that suffuses Luke 1–2, but it is somewhat jarring after an episode that emphasizes the boy's divine vocation, his superior intelligence, and his parents' incomprehension. (We would be less surprised if instead there was a report to the effect that his parents always did whatever *he* told *them*.) Nevertheless, Jesus' obedience is virtually required by the shape of the larger gospel story, which assumes that Jesus appeared to be unexceptional until after his baptism at the age of thirty (3:23). His submission to his parents explains why this young man who knew himself to be God's son did not give his neighbors any reason to suspect his special status. When he later announces his mission in the synagogue at Nazareth, the people who had known him all his life are amazed at his eloquence and say, "Isn't this Joseph's son?" (4:22). (This reaction would be impossible if Jesus had behaved like the miracle-working brat in the Infancy Gospel of Thomas.)

Luke 2:51 concludes the scene. 2:52 is a stylized report that rounds off the entire infancy narrative and prepares for Jesus' next appearance in the gospel as an adult. It builds on the similar report in 2:40, which concludes the episodes about the baby Jesus and which in turn builds on the report in 1:80, capping the stories about the infant John. The two growth reports about Jesus are more elaborate than the one about John—another aspect of the step parallelism in these chapters that portrays Jesus as superior to John.

While it may seem repetitive to have two similar reports about Jesus in adjacent episodes, Luke included both in imitation of the story in 1 Samuel 1–2, which Luke used extensively in composing his infancy narrative. The story of the young Samuel ends with two growth reports, on which Luke has modeled 2:40 and 2:52.

Luke	1 Samuel
the boy grew up and became strong in spirit (1:80)	the boy Samuel grew in the presence of the Lord (2:21)
the boy grew up and became strong, and was filled with wisdom; and God's favor was on him (2:40)	
Jesus made progress in wisdom, age, and favor before God and the people (2:52)	the boy Samuel continued to grow in stature and in favor with the Lord and with the people (2:26)

LUKE 2:41–52

2:41–43   Jesus stays behind in Jerusalem
2:44–50   His parents find him
2:51   Return to Nazareth
2:52   Report on the boy's growth

[41]Now his parents used to go to Jerusalem every year for the Passover festival. [42]And when he was twelve years old, they went up for the festival as usual. [43]When the festival was over and they were returning home, the young Jesus stayed behind in Jerusalem, without his parents' knowing about it.

⁴⁴Assuming that he was in the traveling party, they went a day's journey, and then began to search for him among their relatives and acquaintances. ⁴⁵When they did not find him, they returned to Jerusalem to search for him.

⁴⁶And after three days it so happened that they found him in the temple area, sitting among the teachers, listening to them and asking them questions. ⁴⁷Everyone who listened to him was astounded at his understanding and his responses.

⁴⁸And when his parents saw him they were overwhelmed. "Child," his mother said to him, "why have you done this to us? Don't you see, your father and I have been worried sick looking for you."

⁴⁹"Why were you looking for me?" he said to them. "Didn't you know that it is my destiny to be in my Father's house?"

⁵⁰But they did not understand what he was talking about. ⁵¹Then he returned with them to Nazareth, and was obedient to them. His mother took careful note of all these things. ⁵²And Jesus, precocious as he was, continued to excel in wisdom and gain respect in the eyes of God and the people.

———— ⌒◡⌒ ————

2:41–52 For similar stories about other ancient heroes see Box 3.4.

2:41 Only men were expected to travel to Jerusalem for Passover. That the whole family goes every year shows their devout piety, a theme Luke emphasizes throughout the infancy narrative.

2:46 Here is the only place Luke calls such men *teachers*. Elsewhere he refers to them as "legal experts" or "scholars" and portrays them as hostile to Jesus.

2:47 Luke uses the verb *astounded* to describe reactions to miracles (e.g., Luke 5:26, 8:56; Acts 2:7, 8:11, 12:16).

2:48 See the comment on 2:33.

2:49 Jesus speaks of his presence in the temple as his *destiny*, a distinctly Lukan way of expressing the belief that Jesus' life was divinely directed.

- "This child is linked to the fall and the rise of many in Israel, and is destined to be a sign that is rejected." (2:34)
- "I am destined to declare God's imperial rule to the other towns as well; after all, that is why I was sent." (4:43)
- "The Son of Adam is destined to suffer a great deal, be rejected by the elders and ranking priests and scholars, and be killed and on the third day, be raised." (9:22)
- "Wasn't the Anointed One destined to undergo these things and enter into his glory?" (24:26)

3.4   The Precocious Child

The story of Jesus astounding the teachers in the temple is just the kind of story Luke's readers expected in the biography of a great man. It was a standard feature of ancient biographies to describe how the future greatness of the man could be seen in the extraordinary qualities of the boy.

Here are several examples from Israel, Persia, and Greece.

Abraham

How old was Abraham when he recognized his Creator? Rabbi Haniniah said, "He recognized his Creator when he was one year old." Rabbi Levi said, "When he was three." *(Midrash on Genesis* 95.3)   •

Moses

Teachers at once arrived from various places but he quickly advanced beyond their capacities. His gifted nature learned faster than they could teach, so much so that it seemed he was remembering rather than learning. What is more, on his own he devised problems that they could not easily solve. (Philo, *Life of Moses* 1.21)

Moses' growth in understanding, out of step with his physical growth, far surpassed the measure of his years. Its maturer excellence could be seen even in his games, and his early deeds held the promise of greater ones to come. When he was three years old, God gave him a wondrous growth spurt, and no one was so indifferent to beauty as not to be amazed at his charming appearance. (Josephus, *Antiquities* 2.230)

Zoroaster, Persian Prophet

It is recorded of only one person, Zoroaster, that he laughed on the very day he was born, and also that his brain throbbed so violently that it dislodged a hand placed on his head—which presaged his future knowledge. (Pliny, *Natural History* 7.72)

Cyrus, Emperor of Persia

When the child was ten years old, the following event took place and revealed Cyrus for who he really was. He was playing in the village with other children the same age. In one of their games they chose him to be their king—the one who was called the cowherd's son. He gave them different orders: these to build houses and those to be bodyguards, and one of them, I suppose, to be his chief of staff. To another he assigned the privilege of carrying messages to him. To each of them he gave a special function. One of the children, the son of a man of distinction among the Medes, refused to carry out one of Cyrus' orders. Cyrus ordered the other children to arrest him. They obeyed him, and he dealt with the rebel sternly, and had him whipped. (Herodotus, *History* 1.114)

Pythagoras, Greek Philosopher

Although he was still a child, people recognized that he already deserved honor and reverence, even from his elders. He captured the attention of everyone who saw him or heard him speak, creating the most profound impression. That is why many people reasonably inferred that he was a son of God. . . His great renown, even while still a child, reached not only men as famous for their wisdom as Thales of Miletus and Bias of Priene, but also extended to the neighboring cities. He was celebrated everywhere as the "long-haired Samian," and was generally thought to be under divine inspiration. (Iamblichus, *The Pythagorean Life* 10, 11)

Alexander the Great

He once entertained the envoys from the Persian king who arrived while Philip was away, and mingled with them freely. He charmed them with his friendliness, and by not asking childish or trivial questions, but by enquiring about the length of their roads and what it was like to travel into the interior of their country, about the king himself and what sort of warrior he was, and about the skill and power of the Persians. The envoys were astonished. (Plutarch, *Life of Alexander* 5.1)

Apollonius, Holy Man

When he was old enough to start learning his letters, he showed that he had an excellent memory and strong powers of concentration. He could speak pure Attic Greek and was not influenced by the local dialect. Everyone's eyes were constantly on him and he was admired by the hour.

(When Apollonius was fourteen, he began his formal study of philosophy.) He applied himself most to the teaching of Pythagoras, which he grasped with an indescribable wisdom. His teacher in Pythagorean philosophy was not very good, however, nor did he practice what he taught; instead he constantly indulged his desire for food and sex, modelling himself on Epicurus. This man was Euxenos from Herakleia in Pontus. He knew the doctrines of Pythagoras they way birds learn things from people. Birds can say "Hello" and "Do well" and "God bless you," and other such things, without understanding what they are saying and without feeling any concern for people, but simply because of their trained tongues.

Apollonius, however, was like the young eagles who fly beside their parents while their feathers are soft and are trained by them in flight. But as soon as they are able to climb in the air, they fly high above their parents, especially if they perceive them to be greedy, flying at ground level following the scent of prey. Like them, Apollonius stayed by Euxenos as long as he was a child and was led by him through the steps of reasoning, but when he reached the age of sixteen he rushed headlong toward the Pythagorean life, being "winged" for it by some Higher Power. (Philostratus, *Life of Apollonius*, 1.7)

Josephus, Jewish Historian

While I was still a child, about fourteen years old, I was commended by everyone for my love of learning. In fact, the leading men of the city often consulted me, asking my opinion about fine points of the Law. (Josephus, *Autobiography* 2.9)

THE GENEALOGIES OF JESUS

Genealogies were familiar to both Jews and pagans in the ancient world. They were a standard feature in the birth stories of Greek and Roman heroes, where they functioned to connect the hero to illustrious ancestors and/or deities. Jews used genealogies for various purposes, such as to secure a family's Israelite or priestly status. First and Second Chronicles, a history of Israel written after the return from the Babylonian Exile, begins with nine chapters of genealogies. These lists, as mind-numbing as they may be to us, were important to the post-exilic Jewish community as a documentary means of staking claims to continuity with the former Israelites, after the traumatic disruptions of their defeat and deportation to Babylon.

Ancient genealogies were often arranged into historical periods, allowing ancestors to be correlated with major events in national or world history. Names were sometimes grouped in numbered sets, seven and ten being favorite numbers, probably to aid memorization.[1] These two organizational features show that ancient people accepted stylization and artificiality in genealogies. And since written family records were quite scarce and seldom reliable, it would be unrealistic to assume that people in the ancient world understood genealogies to be historically accurate by our modern standards.[2]

---

1. For example, Josephus, relying on genealogical information from the Bible, points out that Moses was "the seventh from Abraham" (*Antiquities* 2.229). (Abraham, Isaac, Jacob, Levi, Kohath, Amram, Moses; see Ex 6:16–20). While this is symbolically appropriate, it is historically impossible because it spans the Israelites' four centuries in Egypt with only three generations (from Levi to Moses).

2. For a specific example in a biblical genealogy, see the cameo on Zadok's genealogy, p. 186.

Luke's Genealogy and the Old Testament

4.1

Luke	Old Testament
(3:23) Jesus	
Joseph	
•	
(18 names)	(not in the Old Testament)
•	
•	
(3:27) Zerubbabel	Zerubbabel (1 Chr 3:19) [?]¹
Shealtiel	Shealtiel (1 Chr 3:19)
•	
(19 names)	(not in the Old Testament)
•	
•	
(3:31) Nathan	Nathan (1 Chr 3:5)
David	David (2:15) *1 Chronicles 1–2*
(3:32) Jesse	Jesse (2:12)
Obed	Obed (2:12)
Boaz	Boaz (2:11)
Sala	Salma/Salmon (2:11)
Nahshon	Nahshon (2:10)
(3:33) Amminadab	Amminadab (2:10)
Arni	Ram (2:9)
²Admin	
Hezron	Hezron (2:9)
Perez	Perez (2:4)
Judah	Judah (2:1)
(3:34) Jacob	Jacob/Israel³ (1:34)
Isaac	Isaac (1:34)

Luke	Old Testament
Abraham	Abraham (1:34)
Terah	Terah (1 Chr 1:24; Gen 11:24)
Nahor	Nahor (11:22) *Genesis 11*
(3:35) Serug	Serug (11:20)
Reu	Reu (11:18)
Peleg	Peleg (11:16)
Eber	Eber (11:14)
Shelah	Shelah (11:12)
(3:36) ⁴Kenan	Kenan (11:13 LXX)
Arpachshad	Arpachshad (11:10)
Shem	Shem (11:0; 5:32) *Genesis 5*
Noah	Noah (5:29)
Lamech	Lamech (5:25)
(3:37) Methuselah	Methuselah (5:21)
Enoch	Enoch (5:18)
Jared	Jared (5:15)
Mahalalel	Mahalalel (5:12)
Kenan	Kenan (5:9)
(3:38) Enosh	Enosh (5:6)
Seth	Seth (5:3)
Adam	Adam (5:1)

1 Zerubbabel is the son of Shealtiel in the Septuagint. The Hebrew Bible contradicts itself on this matter. See the comment on Luke 3:27.

2 See comment on Luke 3:33.

3 Jacob is called Israel in 1 Chronicles.

4 Shelah is the son of Arpachshad in the Hebrew Bible. The Septuagint contradicts itself on this matter. See comment on Luke 3:35–36.

THE GENEALOGY OF JESUS
According to Luke

The genealogy of Jesus in Luke is not at the beginning of his gospel, where ancient readers would expect it to be. It is not even part of Luke's infancy narrative. It is found at 3:23–38, just after Jesus' baptism and just before the beginning of his public career. While such a location is unusual for a genealogy, it is not unique. The Book of Exodus, for example, does not give Moses' genealogy until after his first confrontation with Pharoah (Ex 6:14–27).

Luke arranges his genealogy in "ascending" order, from son to father, starting with Jesus and going back all the way to Adam. Luke lists the names in the format "A son of B, son of C" and does not mention any women or brothers, as does Matthew. Nor does Luke draw special attention to David or Abraham, as Matthew does.

Luke's list contains 77 names. Although this number hints at a deliberate arrangement, Luke does not draw attention to it the way Matthew does with his 3 x 14 arrangement. If we break Luke's list down into 11 x 7, no particular pattern is apparent, except perhaps in the cases of David, Abraham, and Enoch, each of whom begins a block of seven (the seventh, ninth, and eleventh).

Of the 77 names, 36 are otherwise unknown from the Old Testament or elsewhere. Between David and Jesus only four names are known to us (Nathan, Shealtiel, Zerubbabel, and Joseph). Twelve of the fourteen names between Abraham and David are found in 1 Chronicles 1–2 and ten of them in Ruth 4:18–22. The 21 names from Abraham to Adam are found in Genesis 5:1–32 and 11:10–26.

Luke's list has only 15 names in common with Matthew's (not counting Jesus and Joseph). The most striking difference between Matthew and Luke is that Matthew traces Jesus' lineage through the Davidic kings, while Luke does not. The only king in the family tree of Luke's Jesus is David himself.

LUKE 3:23–38

[23]Jesus was about thirty years old when he began his work. He was supposedly the son of Joseph, son of Eli, [24]son of Maththat, son of Levi, son of Melchi, son of Jannai, son of Joseph, [25]son of Mattathiah, son of Amos, son of Nahum, son of Hesli, son of Naggai, [26]son of Maath, son of Mattathiah, son of Semein, son of Josech, son of Joda, [27]son of Johanan, son of Rhesa, son of Zerubbabel, son of Shealtiel, son of Neri, [28]son of Melchi, son of Addi, son of Kosam, son of Elmadam, son of Er, [29]son of Jesus, son of Eliezer, son of Jorim, son of Maththat, son of Levi, [30]son of Simeon, son of Judah, son of Joseph, son of Jonam, son of Eliakim, [31]son of Melea, son of Menna, son of Mattatha, son of Nathan, son of David, [32]son of Jesse, son of

Obed, son of Boaz, son of Sala, son of Nahshon, [33]son of Amminadab, son of Admin, son of Arni, son of Hezron, son of Perez, son of Judah, [34]son of Jacob, son of Isaac, son of Abraham, son of Terah, son of Nahor, [35]son of Serug, son of Reu, son of Peleg, son of Eber, son of Shelah, [36]son of Kenan, son of Arpachshad, son of Shem, son of Noah, son of Lamech, [37]son of Methuselah, son of Enoch, son of Jared, son of Mahalalel, son of Kenan, [38]son of Enosh, son of Seth, son of Adam, son of God.

―――― ᘒᘖᘔ ――――

Peculiarities in Luke's Genealogy

Two sequences of names look curiously similar.

> Jesus, Eliezer, Jorim, Maththat, Levi (3:29)
> and Jesus, Joseph, Eli, Maththat, Levi (3:23–24)

Six names are so similar that they might be variations of the same name.

> Maththat (v.24)
> Mattathiah (v.25)
> Maath (v.26)
> Mattathiah (v.26)
> Maththat (v.29)
> Mattatha (v.31)

Historical Problems in Luke's List

3:27 *Zerubbabel, son of Shealtiel*

The Hebrew and Greek versions of 1 Chr 3:19 differ here. In the Hebrew text, Zerubbabel is the nephew of Shealtiel; in the Septuagint, he is his son, as in Luke and Matthew, as well as in notices in Ezra 3:2, Neh 12:1, and Hag 1:1.

3:27 *Shealtiel, son of Neri*

In Matthew, Shealtiel is the son of Jeconiah, as per 1 Chr 3:17. Neri is unknown.

3:29–30 *Levi, Simeon, Judah, Joseph*

These pre-exilic figures are named after the patriarchs of four of the twelve tribes of Israel. However, there is no evidence that Jews named their sons in this fashion until after the Exile.

3:32 *Sala*

The Old Testament calls him Salma and Salmon. Sala is another attested form of the same name.

3:33 *Amminadab, son of Admin, son of Arni, son of Hezron*

Admin and *Arni* are unknown. In the Old Testament there is only one ancestor, Ram, between Amminadab and Hezron (1 Chr 2:9–10). See also the comment on Matt 1:3–4, p. 78.

3:35–36 *Shelah, son of Kenan, son of Arpachshad*

In 1 Chr 1:18, 24 Shelah is the son of Arpachshad, as in the Hebrew text of

Gen 10:24 and 11:12–13. However, in the Greek text of Genesis, as in Luke, Shelah is the son of Kenan.

THE GENEALOGY OF JESUS
According to Matthew

Matthew's genealogy is arranged in the standard "descending" order, from father to son. It begins with Abraham and traces Jesus' lineage through the kings of Judah. In Matthew's format each name in mentioned twice: "A was the father of B, B of C, C of D," etc. The list is organized into three equal parts, each one opening and closing the important chapters in Israel's history: from Abraham to King David, from David to the time of the Babylonian Exile, and from the Exile to the Anointed One. These three pivotal figures are announced in 1:1: "This is the genealogy of Jesus the Anointed, who was a descendant of David and Abraham." At the end of the genealogy Matthew draws attention to the periodization: there are (supposedly) fourteen generations in each of the three epochs.

Like all ancient genealogies, this one traces Jesus' descent through the father's ancestral line, though Matthew is careful to note that Joseph is not the biological father of Jesus (1:16). Matthew interrupts the list of fathers seven times, three times to mention brothers not in the direct lineage (vv. 2, 3, 11), and four times to mention women who were among Jesus' ancestors: Tamar (v. 3), Rahab and Ruth (v. 5), and Bathsheba, referred to as "Uriah's wife" (v. 6).

Genealogical data figured in Jewish debates over whether the Anointed One would be royal (descended from David) or priestly (descended from Aaron). Each side criticized the other by identifying ancestors who were thought to taint the lineage of their rivals' type of messiah. Particularly relevant to Matthew's genealogy is the fact that advocates of the priestly messiah theory used precisely the four women mentioned in Matthew—who were probably gentiles and whose sexual histories were burdened by different degrees of scandal—to show that David's line was compromised. The royal messiah partisans in turn glorified these same women and considered them converts to Judaism.

MATT 1:1–17

[1]This is the record of the origin of Jesus the Anointed, son of David, son of Abraham.

[2]Abraham was the father of Isaac, Isaac of Jacob, Jacob of Judah and his brothers, [3]and Judah and Tamar were the parents of Perez and Zerah. Perez was the father of Hezron, Hezron of Aram, [4]Aram of Amminadab, Amminadab of Nahshon, Nahshon of Salmon, [5]and Salmon and Rahab were the parents of Boaz. Boaz and Ruth were the parents of Obed. Obed was the father of Jesse, [6]and Jesse of David the king.

4.2

Matthew's Genealogy and The Old Testament

Matthew	Old Testament
	1 Chronicles 1–3
(1:2) Abraham	Abraham (1:34)
Isaac	Isaac
Jacob	Jacob
Judah	Judah (2:1)
(1:3) Perez	Perez (2:4)
Hezron	Hezron (2:5)
Aram	Ram (2:9) Aram (LXX)[1]
(1:4) Amminadab	Amminadab (2:10)
Nahshon	Nahshon
Salmon	Salmon/Salma[2] (2:11)
(1:5) Boaz	Boaz
Obed	Obed (2:12)
Jesse	Jesse
(1:6) David	David (2:15)
Solomon	Solomon (3:5)
(1:7) Rehoboam	Rehoboam (3:10)
Abijah	Abijah
Asaph	Asa
(1:8) Jehoshaphat	Jehoshaphat
Joram	Joram (3:11)
	Ahaziah
	Joash
	Amaziah (3:12)
Uzziah	Uzziah/Azariah[3]
(1:9) Jotham	Jotham
Ahaz	Ahaz (3:13)
Hezekiah	Hezekiah
(1:10) Manasseh	Manasseh

Matthew	Old Testament
Amos	Amon (3:14)
Josiah	Josiah
	Jehoiakim (3:15)
(1:11) Jeconiah	Jeconiah/Jehoiachin[4] (3:17)
(1:12) Shealtiel	Shealtiel
Zerubbabel	Zerubbabel (3:19) [?][5]
(9 names)	*(not in the Old Testament)*
(1:16) Joseph	
Jesus	

[1] In the Hebrew Bible the father of Amminadab is Ram. In the Septuagint the father of Amminadab is Ram's brother, Aram. See comment on Matt 1:3–4.

[2] The same man is named Salma in 1 Chronicles and Salmon elsewhere.

[3] Kings sometimes took a new name at their coronation. This king was born Azariah; Uzziah was his throne name.

[4] Jeconiah was this man's birth name, Jehoiachin his throne name.

[5] Shealtiel is the father of Zerubbabel in the Septuagint. The Hebrew Bible contradicts itself on this matter. See the comment on Matt 1:12.

David and Uriah's wife were the parents of Solomon. [7]Solomon was the father of Rehoboam, Rehoboam of Abijah, Abijah of Asaph, [8]Asaph of Jehoshaphat, Jehoshaphat of Joram, Joram of Uzziah, [9]Uzziah of Jotham, Jotham of Ahaz, Ahaz of Hezekiah, [10]Hezekiah of Manasseh, Manasseh of Amos, Amos of Josiah, [11]and Josiah was the father of Jeconiah and his brothers at the time of the exile to Babylon.

[12]After the Babylonian exile, Jeconiah was the father of Shealtiel, Shealtiel of Zerubbabel, [13]Zerubbabel of Abiud, Abiud of Eliakim, Eliakim of Azor, [14]Azor of Zadok, Zadok of Achim, Achim of Eliud, [15]Eliud of Eleazar, Eleazar of Matthan, Matthan of Jacob. [16]And Jacob was the father of Joseph, the husband of Mary, who was the mother of Jesus. Jesus is known as the Anointed.

[17]In all, the generations from Abraham to David come to fourteen, those from David to the Babylonian exile number fourteen, and those from the Babylonian exile to the Anointed amount to fourteen also.

———— ~⃝~ ————

Omissions in Matthew's Genealogy

1:8 *Joram, father of Uzziah*

This leaves out three generations. According to the Bible (e.g., 1 Chr 3:11–12), the list of kings is as follows:

> **Joram**
> Ahaziah ⎫
> Joash   ⎬ *missing from Matthew*
> Amaziah ⎭
> **Uzziah**

Matthew may have been confused by the similarity in the Greek names for Ahaziah (spelled variously as *Ochozia, Ozeia,* or *Ozias*) and Uzziah (spelled as *Azariah* or *Ozias*). All these variant spellings exist in ancient copies of the Septuagint, so it is possible that Matthew was using a list in which Ahaziah and Uzziah had identical names in Greek.

It was a common copying error to omit material between two identical or very similar words. The copyist looked away from the page to write a phrase or two; when he looked back his eye would catch the second word and continue forward, inadvertently omitting the words in between. Whole lines could disappear in this fashion. If the two above names were spelled the same in the list Matthew was copying, he may have looked away when he got to the first *Ozias* (Ahaziah), looked back and spotted the second *Ozias* (Uzziah) without noticing that he had missed three names. It is also possible that Matthew intentionally deleted the three kings between Joram and Uzziah, so as not to have more than fourteen generations in this section of the genealogy.

1:11 *Josiah, father of Jeconiah and his brothers*

This leaves out one generation. Josiah was actually the father of Jehoiakim and the *grand*father of Jeconiah, who had only one brother.

Josiah
Jehoiakim } *missing from Matthew*
Jeconiah (= Jehoiachin)

Perhaps Matthew deliberately skipped a generation, in order to keep the number of kings at fourteen. Or perhaps he confused Jeconiah (usually known as Jehoiachin) with Jehoiakim, his father. Jehoiakim had two brothers, Jehoahaz and Zedekiah, who were kings in the tumultous years before Babylon destroyed Jerusalem. Zedekiah was put on the throne by the Babylonians to replace his nephew Jehoiachin, whom they took into exile in Babylon (2 Kgs 24:17). It would have been easy for Matthew to mistake Jehoiachin for Jehoiakim because the Septuagint, which Matthew used, oddly calls both of them *Ioakim*. To make matters worse, both of them had brothers named Zedekiah. Confused? So was the author of 2 Chronicles, who mistakenly lists Zedekiah, brother of Jehoiachin, as a king (2 Chr 36:10). This error was easy to make, especially since King Zedekiah, Jehoiachin's *uncle*, was only two or three years older than the nephew he succeeded (compare 2 Kgs 24:8 and 24:18).

Historical Problems in Matthew's List

1:3–4 *Hezron was the father of Aram, Aram was the father of Amminadab*
These two generations cover 400 years. Hezron lived in the time when Jacob's sons moved to Egypt (Gen 46:12), Amminadab in the time of Moses (Num 1:7). (For the figure of 400 years, see Gen 15:13 and Ex 12:40).
In the Hebrew Bible, Hezron was the father of Ram and Ram was the father of Amminadab (1 Chr 2:9–10 and Ruth 4:19). Matthew here relies on 1 Chr 2:9–10 LXX, in which Hezron is father of Ram *and Aram*, and Aram, not Ram, is the father of Amminadab. To complicate matters further, Ruth 4:19 LXX lists "Arran" as the son of Hezron and father of Amminadab.
1:5 *Boaz, whose mother was Rahab*
Rahab lived in the time of Joshua's conquest, 200 years before Boaz.
1:12 *Shealtiel was the father of Zerubbabel*
The Hebrew and Greek versions of 1 Chronicles differ on this point. In the Hebrew text, Shealtiel's brother, Pedaiah, is the father of Zerubbabel (1 Chr 3:18). In the Septuagint (1 Chr 3:19), as in Matthew and Luke, and according to notices in Ezra 3:2, Neh 12:1, and Hag 1:1, Zerubbabel's father is Shealtiel.
1:13 *Zerubbabel was the father of Abiud*
Abiud is not mentioned among Zerubbabel's eight children in 1 Chr 3:19–20.

Mistaken Identities

1:7 *Asaph* (a psalmist, to whom Psalms 50 and 73–83 are ascribed) should be "Asa," a king (1 Kgs 15:9). Several ancient New Testament copyists corrected Matthew's mistake.
1:10 *Amos* (a prophet) should be "Amon," a king (2 Kgs 21:19; 1 Chr 3:14).

Three Times Fourteen?

Matthew claims that the genealogy has three sets of fourteen generations. A simple count show this to be inaccurate (see Box 4.3).

- From Abraham to David there are 14 names, in 13 generations (i.e., 13 begettings).
- From David to the Exile there are 14 generations (although four historical generations of kings are missing from Matthew's list).
- From the Exile to Jesus there are 13 generations (12 if we don't consider Jesus' birth to be the result of a begetting).

Is this an honest mistake? Probably. Matthew points to the 3 x 14 as a sign of divine providence. So it's unlikely that he deliberately miscounted, especially when readers can so easily spot his mistake. If he were trying to deceive, he would have added a name to the third set; after Zerubbabel they are all unknown, so no one would be the wiser. There is no miscount in the second set of names. There the numbers come out right, but only because the list is historically erroneous. Did Matthew rig the numbers by deliberately

---

4.3 Counting the Generations in the Genealogy in Matthew

from Abraham to David 1:2–6a	from David to the Babylonian Exile 1:6b–11	from the Babylonian Exile to the Anointed 1:12–16
Abraham	David	Jeconiah
1. Isaac*	1. Solomon	1. Shealtiel
2. Jacob	2. Rehoboam	2. Zerubbabel
3. Judah	3. Abijah	3. Abiud
4. Perez	4. Asaph	4. Eliakim
5. Hezron	5. Jehoshaphat	5. Azor
6. Ram	6. Joram	6. Zadok
7. Amminadab	7. Uzziah	7. Achim
8. Nahshon	8. Jotham	8. Eliud
9. Salmon	9. Ahaz	9. Eleazar
10. Boaz	10. Hezekiah	10. Matthan
11. Obed	11. Manasseh	11. Jacob
12. Jesse	12. Amos	12. Joseph
13. David	13. Josiah	13(?)** Jesus
	14. Jeconiah	

*From Abraham to Isaac is two names but one generation, i.e., one begetting.
**It is uncertain whether Matthew intends the step from Joseph to Jesus to count as a generation, since Joseph did not beget him.

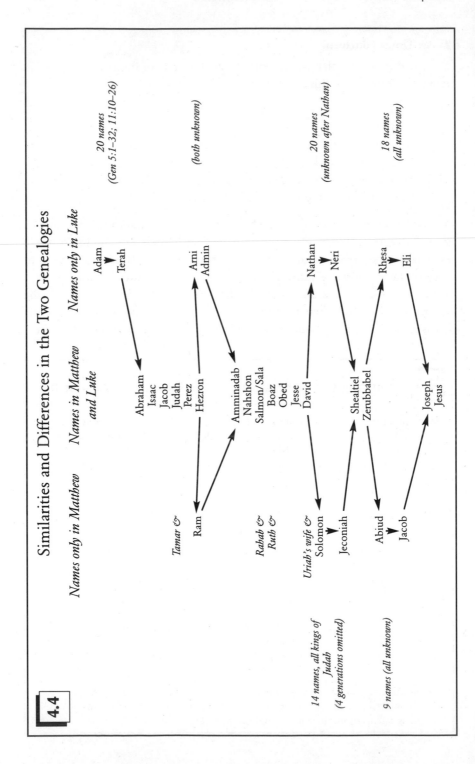

Similarities and Differences in the Two Genealogies

4.4

deleting four generations? Or did he omit them accidentally (see notes on 1:8 and 1:11)? How can we tell?

What's special about 14? That's hard to say. There is no evidence that 2 x 7 was a special number. Some think that it has to do with the "number" of David's name, which in Hebrew is 14. The ancient Hebrew language had no numerals in its writing system; it used letters to represent numbers. This means that every word had a number, the sum of the numerical value of its letters. In Hebrew the name "David" is spelled דוד (dwd). The numerical value of ד is 4 and ו is 6. So, ד + ו + ד = 14. It might not be a coincidence, therefore, that David's name is fourteenth on Matthew's list. Also, since David's name (in Hebrew) has three letters that add up to 14, this theory can also explain why David's name is mentioned three times (in 1:1 and twice in 1:17) and why Matthew emphasizes both 3 and 14.

4.4 *continued*

The two lists diverge and come back together three separate times. In all three cases, Matthew and Luke disagree on the number of generations between the same ancestors, most strikingly in the last set where Luke has twice as many names as Matthew. The most contradictory result of the discrepancies between the two genealogies is that there are three men (Amminadab, Shealtiel, and Joseph), each of whom has a different father in Matthew than he does in Luke. Matthew and Luke do not agree even on the identity of Jesus' grandfather.

How many names?

Matthew		Luke
40	total number of Jesus' male ancestors	76
4	women in genealogy	0
41	names from Abraham to Jesus	57
13	names from Abraham to Jesse	14
16	names from David to Shealtiel	22
12	names from Zerubbabel to Jesus	21

The problem with this theory is that Matthew wrote in Greek, and in Greek the number of David's name is 419. (In Greek the name is spelled *Dauid*. D [4] + a [1] + u [400] + i [10] + d [4] = 419.) According to this theory, then, Matthew wrote in Greek but expressed a meaning that only someone who knew Hebrew could get. This sounds implausible but we should not rule it out. Matthew's explanation of the meaning of Jesus' name in 1:21 is based on a pun that works only in Hebrew (see p. 89). Matthew may have indulged in bilingual word play also in formulating the mysterious "quotation" in 2:23 (see pp. 117–18). Since Matthew could work in both Greek and Hebrew, perhaps he hid a few "bonus points" in his Greek gospel that only bilingual readers could appreciate.

The 14 is probably less important than the fact that there are three equal sets of generations. Apocalyptic writings frequently divide history into periods of equal length, creating scenarios in which the age of fulfillment will begin after a fixed number of these periods have elapsed. Thus Matthew probably saw eschatological significance in the 3 x 14: Jesus was born at precisely the right time for the appearance of the messiah. In this way, the genealogy makes the same point that Jesus will make in his first public pronouncement, "Heaven's reign is closing in" (Matt 4:17).

THE FOUR WOMEN IN MATTHEW'S GENEALOGY
Tamar, Rahab, Ruth, and Uriah's wife (Bathsheba)

Because the listing of women in a genealogy is unusual, Matthew's decision to add them indicates that they are important to his purposes. Their presence in this genealogy is noteworthy not only because they were women but also because of the kind of women they were. All of them were probably gentiles. Rahab was a Canaanite, and Tamar was probably one as well. Ruth was a Moabite. Bathsheba's husband, Uriah, was a Hittite; she may have been from that ethnic group too. The presence of foreigners in the family tree of the house of David fits in with Matthew's theme that Jesus is for all people, Jews and gentiles. Matthew makes this point symbolically at the beginning of his gospel when the foreign magi visit the infant Jesus (2:1–12), and it becomes explicit at the very end of the gospel, when the risen Jesus commissions his followers to teach his commandments to "all peoples" (28:18–20).

The four women have something else in common. They all have something irregular or scandalous in their sexual histories—though none of them was considered a sinner in Jewish tradition—and they all took unusual initiatives that ended up serving God's plans for Israel.[3]

Tamar (Matt 1:3) was the childless widow of two of Judah's sons. Judah

---

3. What follows is strongly influenced by *The Illegitimacy of Jesus* by Jane Schaberg, pp. 20–34.

promised her his third son in marriage but broke his word. Determined to have a child in Judah's family, Tamar seduced her father-in-law by disguising herself as a prostitute. She became pregnant by him and bore twin sons, one of whom became an ancestor of David (Genesis 38). The Bible and the Jewish tradition make it clear that Tamar did nothing wrong (Gen 38:26). Judah was the one at fault because he had denied Tamar her family rights.[4] Her extraordinary initiative righted a wrong and restored the family line that led to David.

Rahab (Matt 1:5) was a prostitute working in Jericho. When Israelite spies came on a reconnaissance mission to the city, Rahab put herself at risk to hide and protect them and to engineer their escape (Josh 2:1–21). She thus played a vital role in the Israelites' entrance into the Promised Land. In return for her courageous assistance, the conquering Israelites spared her and her household (Josh 6:25). Matthew names her as the wife of Salmon, although the Hebrew Bible never mentions that she was married. The Christian tradition looked past Rahab's prostitution and held her up as a model of faith (Heb 11:31) and an example of justification by good works (James 2:25).

Ruth (Matt 1:5) was a childless widow from Moab. She accompanied her mother-in-law Naomi to the land of Israel, where she established a home for herself and Naomi by taking the risky initiative of approaching their rich relative Boaz to sleep with him. This scene is delicately written and uses double meanings which hint that Ruth and Boaz were intimate (Ruth 3:1–9, 14). At any rate, the author does not rule out the impression that sex was part of their night together. (Later Jewish authorities went to great lengths to interpret this scene in such a way that readers would doubt that Ruth and Boaz had sex. All this effort was an implicit admission that this scene was regularly understood to be a sexual encounter.) Whatever did or did not happen under the blanket, Ruth charmed and impressed Boaz, who married her as soon as the Law allowed (Ruth 4:10). The Book of Ruth ends by telling us that she was David's great-grandmother (Ruth 4:17).

This is no insignificant fact. Ruth was a Moabite, and the Torah specifically prohibits Moabites and their descendants from joining Israel's covenant:

> No Ammonite or Moabite, nor their descendants, not even to the tenth generation, shall become a member of the community of Yahweh. (Deut 23:4).

Ruth's ethnicity was thus a matter of great concern to the later Jewish tradition because it jeopardized David's Israelite status. That David was on friendly terms with the king of Moab and sent his parents to him for safekeeping (1 Sam 22:3–4) hints that he had family connections there.

---

4. See the discussion of levirate marriage on pp. 91–92.

The Rape of Bathsheba

2 Samuel 11:2–4

[2]Late one afternoon, when David woke up from his nap and was walking around on the roof of the palace, he saw from the roof a woman bathing. The woman was very beautiful. [3]David sent someone to inquire about the woman. He was told, "That is Bathsheba, daughter of Eliam and wife of Uriah the Hittite." [4]So David sent messengers and took her; and she came to him, and he lay with her.

Traditional interpretations of the sordid story of David and Bathsheba inevitably treat it as a story of adultery and typically portray Bathsheba as seducing David. Not only is this a blatantly male interpretation, but it reads into the scene something that is not actually in the text. The Bible only says that David saw her, liked what he saw, and "took her" by sending his men to pick her up. The Hebrew word for "take" in v. 4 connotes the use of force and the Hebrew grammar makes it clear that it was David who took her, something which seldom comes through in English translations.

The Bible is silent about whatever Bathsheba may have thought about this because that was beside the point. When the king's men show up at your door to take you to the king, your consent is irrelevant. When a powerful man has sex with a vulnerable woman under circumstances in which her consent is irrelevant, it is rape.

Bathsheba (Matt 1:6) was raped by King David while her husband was off fighting in David's army (2 Sam 11:2–4; see the cameo). When David learned that she was pregnant, he engineered her husband's death and married her (2 Sam 11:5–17, 26–27). In David's old age, Bathsheba manipulated him into naming her son Solomon heir to the throne, in the place of David's oldest surviving son (1 Kgs 1:5–31).

Matthew evokes the memory of these four women to establish precedents for the unusual circumstances of Jesus' birth. Mary is pregnant out of wedlock, but her scandalous situation turns out to be part of God's plan for Israel. Like the four women in the genealogy, the mother of Jesus is an unlikely instrument of divine providence.

The circumstances of Tamar, Rahab, Ruth, and Bathsheba are quite different from one another, and it is not obvious what their situations have in common. Furthermore, while these four women all take unusual initiatives, Mary does not. In fact she does nothing at all in Matthew's story; it is Joseph who receives the angelic communications and follows through on them. However, this may be an important clue to Matthew's purpose in mentioning the four women. One scholar who follows this clue suggests that what all four women have in common is that they "find themselves outside patriarchal family structures" and "are wronged or thwarted by that world."

The situations of all four are righted by the actions of men who acknowledge guilt and/or accept responsibility for them, drawing them under patriarchal protection, giving them an identity and a future within the patriarchal structure, and legitimating them and their children-to-be.[5]

Since the very next verse after the genealogy tells of Mary being pregnant (Matt 1:18), it is clear that Matthew wants his readers to understand her situation to be in some sort of continuity with those of the four women whom he added to the genealogy. Seen in this light, Mary is a victim of circumstances, at risk because of her irregular pregnancy, who is nonetheless gathered up into God's plans and, along with her child, made legitimate by the actions of a righteous man.[6]

5. Schaberg, "A Cancelled Father," p. 63, n. 18.
6. See the further discussion of the four women on pp. 200–201.

MATTHEW 1-2

MATT 1:18–25

The Announcement of the Birth of Jesus

To understand Matthew's purpose in 1:18–25, we must read this passage in light of the genealogy that precedes it. At the very end of the genealogy the list swerved away from its pattern of father-to-son. It pointedly declined to state that Joseph was the father of Jesus. Instead, Joseph was said to be the husband of Mary the mother of Jesus (1:16). Matthew said nothing about Mary's genealogy, and for good reason. Israelite descent was reckoned in the Torah through the male line. A woman of royal or priestly blood did not convey her status to her offspring unless she married someone of similar status.[1] In 1:18–25 Matthew will explain how Jesus can rightly be said to be a descendant of David (1:1), even though Joseph was not his natural father.

Matthew 1:18 announces that the following paragraph is the story of Jesus' birth. Yet Matthew does not actually narrate the birth. It is implied in 1:25 and then mentioned as a past event in the next verse (2:1). Instead, 1:18–25 focuses on Joseph and the resolution of his dilemma over Mary's pregnancy.

Bethrothal and Marriage

There were two formal stages in the making of an ancient Jewish marriage. The first was the *betrothal*, in which the woman, usually in her early teens, was transferred from the authority of her father to that of her husband-to-be. We should not compare betrothal to our custom of engagement because the betrothal was considered part of the marriage, not a state prior to it. A betrothal was legally binding and the couple were considered legally married—note that in 1:19 Matthew calls the betrothed Joseph "her husband." Sex between a betrothed woman and another man was treated as adultery, that is, as the violation of a marriage. If a betrothed man died, the woman became a widow.

---

1. In later centuries, Jewish custom changed in regard to reckoning whether someone was Jewish by birth: if the mother was Jewish, so was the child.

Breaking off a betrothal required a formal divorce. A betrothed woman continued to live with her family, usually for a year or so. The second step in the marriage took place when the woman moved into her husband's home and he began to support her.

Were betrothed couples permitted to have sex? The only direct information on this comes from late second-century texts in the Mishnah, which show that Judeans and Galileans were divided on this question. Betrothed couples in Judea (where Matthew sets the story) were allowed to have sex; those in Galilee were not.[2] Whether this distinction reflects customs from the first century is not known.[3] At any rate, in both Galilee and Judea, a child conceived during the betrothal period was considered a legitimate child of the marriage.

5.1	Sex and Betrothal

Here is a second-century Jewish law dealing with one aspect of a betrothed couple's sexuality.

> If a man in Judea ate in the house of his father-in-law [and had an opportunity to be alone with his betrothed wife] and had no witnesses [to prove that he did not have sex with her], he may not lodge a virginity suit against her, since he had [already] spent time alone with her. (Mishnah, Ketubot 1.5)

This law assumes that it was normal and socially acceptable for betrothed couples to be alone together and that it took special legal requirements to overcome the presumption that such couples were sexually active.

MATT 1:18–25

[18]The origin of Jesus the Anointed is as follows: While his mother Mary was betrothed to Joseph, but before she moved into his house, she was found to be pregnant by a holy spirit. [19]Her husband Joseph was a righteous man, but did not want to expose her publicly; so, he planned to break off their betrothal quietly.

[20]While he was thinking about these things, a messenger of the Lord surprised him in a dream with these words: "Joseph, son of David, don't hesitate to take Mary as your wife, since a holy spirit is responsible for her pregnancy.

---

2. For Judea, Mishnah, Kebubot 1.5, Mishnah, Yebamot 4.10; for Galilee, Babylonian Talmud, Ketubot 9b, 12a. See also Box 5.1.

3. We cannot tell whether the differences between Judea and Galilee on this matter go back to the first century or whether the differences developed after the time of Matthew. Either way, it seems that the stricter standard in Galilee was imposed to discourage an existing practice. It is most unlikely that the more lenient Judean custom represents the loosening of an earlier prohibition, since the tendency in the Mishnah is to make regulations stricter.

²¹She will give birth to a son and you will name him Jesus, because he will save his people from their sins." ²²All this happened in order to fulfill the prediction of the Lord through the prophet:

> ²³Look, a "virgin" will conceive a child
> and she will give birth to a son,
> and they will name him Emmanuel

(which means "God is with us").

²⁴Joseph got up and did what the messenger of the Lord told him: he took Mary as his wife. ²⁵He did not have sex with her until she had given birth to a son. Joseph named him Jesus.

———— ❧ ————

1:18 *Origin* translates the Greek word *genesis*—which can also mean "birth"— echoing Matthew's use of the same word in the heading of the genealogy (1:1) and recalling the Greek name of the first book of the Bible.

1:20–21 The angel assures Joseph that God is responsible for Mary's pregnancy.[4] The angel directs him to do two things: complete his marriage and name the child who will be born. By taking Mary into his house and thus finalizing the marriage, Joseph assumes responsibility for her and the child. By naming the infant, Joseph publicly acknowledges paternity. Joseph thus adopts Jesus and becomes his legal father. This is crucial for Matthew because that is the only way that Jesus can be a "son of David"—notice that the angel addresses Joseph as *son of David* in v. 20— without having Joseph be the biological father of Jesus. An adopted son had full rights of inheritance and so Jesus is legally entitled to Joseph's genealogy.

1:21 The name *Jesus* is the Latin form of *Iesous*, which is the Greek form of Joshua, the Old Testament hero after whom Jesus was named. In Hebrew Joshua (*Yehoshu'a*) means "Yahweh helps." In its shortened Aramaic form (*Yeshua'*, ישׁוע), the name sounds nearly the same as the word for "rescue" or "salvation" (*yeshu'ah*, ישׁועה).

he will save his people from their sins. Throughout Matthew's gospel *the people* means Israel. It was generally believed that the Messiah, by definition, would *save his people.* But the Jewish people of the time had some very different understandings of what that salvation would be. Among these notions was the hope that the Messiah would remove sinners from the land of Israel (Ps Sol 17:21–25; see Box 5.2). However, there was no Jewish expectation that the Messiah would *forgive* sins, which is how Matthew takes it (see 26:28). That notion is a Christian innovation and was, in effect, a radical re-definition of the meaning of messiah.

Joseph's Dilemma (1:18–19)

The situation portrayed here is a delicate one. Since Mary's pregnancy is discovered after she had been betrothed to Joseph, only Mary and Joseph know

---

4. See the cameo, "a holy spirit," pp. 40–41.

5.2   The Messiah in the Psalms of Solomon

The Psalms of Solomon are Jewish prayers from the first century BCE. Here is
one passage that expresses hopes for what the Messiah will accomplish.

> Look on them, Lord, and raise up for them their king,
>   the son of David, to rule over your servant Israel
>   in the time known to you, O God.
> Provide him with your strength to destroy the unrighteous rulers,
>   to purge Jerusalem from Gentiles
>   who trample her to destruction;
>   in wisdom and righteousness to drive out
>   the sinners from the inheritance;
> To smash the arrogance of sinners
>   like a potter's jar.
> To shatter all their substance with an iron staff;
>   to destroy the unlawful nations
>   with the word of his mouth;
> At his warning the nations will flee from his presence
>   and he will condemn sinners
>   by the thoughts of their hearts. (Ps Sol 17:21–25)

---

that the child is not his. No one else could know unless Joseph were to make a
public issue of it. Matthew describes Joseph as *righteous*, which for Jews meant
someone who lived in obedience to God's Law, the Torah. Because he is righteous, he cannot bring himself to finalize a marriage with a girl carrying someone else's child. And if Mary had become pregnant prior to her betrothal—v.
18b is unclear as to when Mary became pregnant—then the righteous Joseph
would be barred from marrying her, even if he was willing to do so. Under
Mosaic law, if a man had intercourse with an unbetrothed girl—regardless of
whether he had seduced her or raped her—he was required to marry her (Deut
22:28–29). So if Joseph learned that Mary had already been pregnant at the time
of their betrothal ceremony, it would mean that their betrothal was invalid,
since Mary would have already belonged to the father of the child whom she
carried. Matthew doesn't tell us anything about Joseph's emotional condition
in this poignant situation, but v. 19 shows that he felt mercy for the young and
vulnerable Mary.

Because Matthew is so focused on his christological agenda, he passes over
details relating to the human dimension in the story. How did Joseph discover
that Mary was pregnant? Did they speak to one another? If so, what did she tell
him? Questions like these were just not important to Matthew.

Unwilling to complete his marriage, Joseph decides on a prudent and compassionate course: a quiet divorce. What this means is a bit unclear because a divorce was a formal legal process. Besides, Mary's pregnancy would eventually expose her in any case. What Matthew probably means here is that Joseph planned to terminate the marriage without making a public accusation of adultery. The Torah allowed him to present her with a written notice of divorce (Deut 24:1) signed by two or three witnesses. The other legal alternative would be a public inquiry to determine whether Mary was pregnant by rape or by consent (Deut 22:23–27). Technically, adultery carried the death penalty (Deut 22:22, 24), though we have no evidence that this punishment was actually carried out in this period in history.

By opting for a quiet divorce, Joseph chooses a path that spares everyone, especially Mary, extreme humiliation. Matthew's narration here is skillful. In a few sentences he brings us into Joseph's dilemma and leads the reader to admire this just man, an admiration which will increase as we watch him take public responsibility for a child not his own.

But what of Mary's feelings? What did this young teenager make of her pregnancy? Was she full of hope or regret, or a mixture of both? What were her fears as she waited for a man to decide her fate? Unfortunately for our interests, Matthew chose to tell the story solely as a man's story. He doesn't care what the reader thinks about Mary.

Legal Paternity

To appreciate the strength of Matthew's case for the Davidic ancestry of Jesus, we must understand the notion of legal paternity in Jewish law. Christian tradition usually treats Joseph as Jesus' stepfather, but that falls short of the relationship Matthew describes. From his perspective Joseph was Jesus' legal father and a legal father was a father in every way that mattered.

To see how seriously this notion was taken in Judaism, we can consider the arrangement called "levirate marriage" (from the Hebrew word *levir*, "brother-in-law") prescribed in Deut 25:5–10 (see Box 5.3). If a man died without a male heir, his oldest brother was required to have intercourse with the widow (his sister-in-law) until she had a son. A boy born from this union was considered the dead man's son, with full inheritance rights to the property and authority of his deceased father. The living brother who was the biological father lost all legal claims to his brother's estate. (Note that this is all about property, not about sex.) Since some men were reluctant to relinquish designs on their dead brother's assets, Deuteronomy provided enforcement means by which the widow could go to court and publicly shame her brother-in-law into fulfilling his sexual duty to her.

The story of Onan (Gen 38:6–10; see Box 5.4) is a cautionary tale on this

---

5.3 Levirate Marriage

[5]When brothers reside together, and one of them dies and has no son, the wife of the deceased shall not be married outside the family to a stranger. Her husband's brother shall have intercourse with her, taking her in marriage, and performing the duty of a husband's brother, [6]and the firstborn whom she bears shall succeed to the name of the deceased brother, so that his name may not be blotted out of Israel. [7]But if the man has no desire to marry his brother's widow, then his brother's widow shall go up to the elders at the gate and say, "My husband's brother refuses to perpetuate his brother's name in Israel; he will not perform the duty of a husband's brother." [8]Then the elders of his town shall summon him and speak to him. If he persists, saying, "I do not want to marry her," [9]then his brother's wife shall go up to him in the presence of the elders, pull his sandal off his foot, spit in his face, and declare, "This is what is done to the man who does not build up his brother's house." [10]Throughout Israel his family shall be known as "the house of him whose sandal was pulled off." (Deut 25:5–10)

---

topic. Onan was required to father a son for his dead brother with his widowed sister-in-law Tamar, the same woman mentioned in Jesus' genealogy (Matt 1:3). Onan had intercourse with Tamar, but refused to inseminate her because "he knew the offspring would not be his" (Gen 38:9), a sin for which God killed him. The story makes it clear that Onan's sin was not one of sex, but of injustice toward Tamar.

Matthew 1:23/Isaiah 7:14

Matthew breaks into his narrative to tell us that a prophecy was fulfilled. This is one of the twelve instances in his gospel where he does so; five of them occur in chapters 1–2. The quotation of Isa 7:14 is crucial to the meaning of the whole infancy narrative. How did Matthew understand this ancient prophecy and its relevance to Jesus? Since a proper understanding of Matt 1:23 is so important for our overall interpretation of Matthew 1–2, we need to be thorough here. We must examine the meaning of Isaiah 7 in its historical context: the question of whether Isa 7:14 is about a virgin birth, Isaiah's understanding of when the promised boy will be born, and the significance of his symbolic name.

In its own context, Isaiah's prophecy is not about events beyond Isaiah's own immediate future. The prophecy has nothing do with either a virginal conception or the coming of the Messiah. Matthew, following the exegetical practices of his day, applies this prophecy to his own time by lifting it out of context.

The Sin of Onan

⁶Judah took a wife for Er his firstborn; her name was Tamar. ⁷But Er, Judah's firstborn, was evil in the sight of Yahweh, and Yahweh put him to death. ⁸Then Judah said to Onan, "Have intercourse with your brother's wife and perform the duty of a brother-in-law; raise up off-spring for your brother." ⁹But since Onan knew that the offspring would not be his, he spilled his semen on the ground whenever he had intercourse with brother's wife, so that he would not give offspring to his brother. ¹⁰ What he did was displeasing in the sight of Yahweh, and he put him to death also. (Gen 38:6–10)

Onan's behavior earned him an unenviable notoriety: a sin was named after him. The sexual practice described in this passage, now known by its latinized name, "coitus interruptus," is traditionally called "onanism" in Christian moral theology and was condemned because it was a form of contraception.

Isaiah 7 in its Historical Context

In its own literary and historical context, and in its original language, the meaning of Isa 7:14 is clear enough, even if the poetical style, foreign names, and complex geopolitical setting of Isaiah 7 make the scene obscure for modern readers (see Box 5.5). The year is 735 BCE. The powerful Assyrian empire is threatening to conquer the smaller nations in Syria-Palestine. Kings from two of these minor states, King Rezin of Syria and King Pekah of the northern king-dom of Israel (Isa 7:1), formed a military alliance in the hope of defending themselves against Assyria. Rezin and Pekah badly needed the southern king-dom of Judah, ruled by the house of David, to join them. But Ahaz, the king of Judah, figured that it was suicidal to resist a superpower like Assyria, and so he refused to join the alliance. Pekah and Rezin sent their armies to invade Judah, depose Ahaz, and install a king who would join their anti-Assyrian coalition (7:6). With those two armies advancing on Jerusalem, Ahaz was planning to save his throne by making a covenant with Assyria, exchanging Israel's inde-pendence for Assyrian military protection. But Isaiah is opposed to any covenant with Assyria because it would obligate Israel to worship the Assyrian gods and because Israel already has a covenant with Yahweh. So Isaiah con-fronts Ahaz, challenging him to put his trust in Yahweh rather than in the Assyrian army (7:7–9), and offering to provide a sign of Yahweh's reliability (7:10–11). When Ahaz refuses (7:12), Isaiah tells him that God will give him a sign anyway: "the young woman" (someone known to Ahaz, presumably one of his wives) is or will soon be pregnant (the verb can be either present or future)

5.5   Isaiah 7:1–16

[1]In the days of Ahaz son of Jotham son of Uzziah, king of Judah, King Rezin of Aram and King Pekah son of Remaliah of Israel went up to attack Jerusalem, but could not mount an attack against it. [2]When the house of David heard that Aram had allied itself with Ephraim, the heart of Ahaz and the heart of his people shook as the trees of the forest shake before the wind. [3]Then Yahweh said to Isaiah, "Go out to meet Ahaz, you and your son Shear-jashub, at the end of the conduit of the upper pool on the highway to the Fuller's Field, [4]and say to him, 'Pay attention, be quiet, do not be afraid, and do not let your heart be faint because of these two smoldering stumps of firebrands, because of the fierce anger of Rezin and Aram and the son of Remaliah. [5]Because Aram—with Ephraim and the son of Remaliah—has plotted evil against you, saying, [6]"Let us go up against Judah and cut off Jerusalem and conquer it for ourselves and make the son of Tabeel king in it." [7]Therefore thus says the Lord Yahweh: "It shall not stand, and it shall not come to pass. [8]For the head of Aram is Damascus, and the head of Damascus is Rezin. (Within sixty-five years Ephraim will be shattered, no longer a people.) [9]The head of Ephraim is Samaria, and the head of Samaria is the son of Remaliah. If you do not stand firm in faith, you shall not stand at all."'" [10]Again Yahweh spoke to Ahaz, saying, [11]"Ask a sign of Yahweh your God; let it be deep as Sheol or high as heaven." [12]But Ahaz said, "I will not ask, and I will not put Yahweh to the test." [13]Then Isaiah said: "Listen, O house of David! Isn't it enough that you take mortals for fools? Do you take my God for a fool too? [14]Therefore Yahweh himself will give you a sign. Look, the young woman is pregnant and will give birth to a son, and will name him Immanuel. [15]He will eat curds and honey by the time he knows how to refuse evil and choose good. [16]For before the child knows how to refuse the evil and choose the good, the land before whose two kings you are in dread will be deserted."

and will have a son with the aptly symbolic name Immanuel (7:14). Before that boy is old enough to know right from wrong, the two nations worrying Ahaz will have been destroyed (7:16). The birth of this boy is thus a sign to Ahaz that God will stand by his promise to protect the throne of the house of David.

Is there a virgin in Isa 7:14?

The Hebrew text of Isa 7:14 refers simply to "the young woman" (*almah*). The Septuagint, a Greek translation of the Hebrew Bible for hellenistic Jews, translates the Hebrew *almah* with the Greek word *parthenos*, which also means "young woman" but in specific contexts can mean "virgin."[5] Other ancient Greek translations of the Hebrew Bible use the common word for girl (*neanis*) in Isa 7:14, but it is the Septuagint that Matthew quotes.

5. The ranges of meaning for all the relevant ancient words are discussed in Chapter 10.

Isa 7:14 (Hebrew)
Look, the young woman is/will be pregnant and will have a son
and she will name him Immanuel.
Isa 7:14 (Greek)
Look, the *parthenos* will conceive and will have a son
and you will name him Emmanuel.
Matt 1:23
Look, the *parthenos* will conceive and will have a son
and they will name him Emmanuel.

The Hebrew text clearly has nothing to do with virginity. There is no reason to think that the Septuagint does, either. Certainly no Jewish source takes Isa 7:14, in any language, to refer to a virgin. But *parthenos* can mean "virgin" and it's possible—though unlikely—that Matthew saw that meaning in the Greek version of Isaiah's prophecy (see pp. 203–4). Nevertheless, "the *parthenos*/virgin will conceive and will have a son" does not describe a virginal conception. Even if we take *parthenos* to mean "virgin," Septuagint Isa 7:14, understood in its normal sense—apart from Christian theological concerns that were read into this passage centuries after it was written—means only that a woman who is now a virgin will become pregnant. No miracle is intended. (*Every* woman who gets pregnant was once a virgin.) The key to the meaning here lies in the tense of the verb "be pregnant." The Hebrew language does not have different verb forms for future and present; that has to be determined from context. But Greek does distinguish these tenses and in the Septuagint the verb is future. A miracle would be in view if the text said that the virgin *has* conceived or *is* pregnant. In Isa 7:14, in both Hebrew and Greek, the divine sign is the timing of the conception, not its manner.

Christianity has misunderstood Isa 7:14 because it has interpreted this prophecy from the perspective of the traditional Christian understanding of Matt 1:23. This led older English Bibles (e.g., the King James Version) mistakenly to render the Isaiah verse with the word "virgin" so that it would match Matthew's wording. When in 1952 the Revised Standard Version properly translated Isa 7:14 with "young woman," many Christians were surprised and misinterpreted this correction to be a denial of Jesus' virgin birth. Some fundamentalists were so upset that they sponsored public burnings of the RSV. The official Catholic translation, the New American Bible, uses "virgin" in Isa 7:14 because bishops overruled the Catholic scholars and demanded that it be mistranslated.

An Imminent Birth

Because Hebrew does not have different forms for present and future verbs, the Hebrew word for "conceive" here can mean either *is pregnant* or *will become pregnant.* Thus the Septuagint's future tense, "will conceive," is a legitimate translation. But it makes no real difference to the meaning of Isaiah's message whether we construe the verb as present or as future.

To see just how little difference the tense of this verb makes, we can observe how this same Hebrew phrase is used in other passages that announce a coming birth. The exact same Hebrew words "(will) conceive and give birth to a son" (*harah vyoledeth ben*) that describe the unnamed young woman in Isa 7:14 are also used in two other birth announcements (see Box 5.6). One is to the mother of Samson (Judg 13:3, 5, 7), who conceives soon afterward—the angel's instructions in 13:7 assume that she could become pregnant at any time. The other place we see the Hebrew phrase *harah vyoledeth ben* is when an angel announces the birth of Ishmael to his mother Hagar (Gen 16:11). Hagar is already pregnant when she hears these words. These two passages show that the same verb, in the same form, can describe both a woman who is pregnant and one who will soon be so.

Whether the conception of Immanuel has already happened or will occur in the immediate future is beside the point for Isaiah. It is the imminent *birth* of the baby that is the point, and that birth is coming soon enough to be a sign to Ahaz that God will protect the throne of David during the current military crisis. The providential birth of which Isaiah speaks can be a sign for Ahaz only if it is imminent. Isaiah could not possibly have intended to predict the birth of Jesus, for the obvious reason that a birth over seven hundred years in Isaiah's future could not be a sign to Ahaz. Respect for the Bible requires us to understand Isaiah as someone speaking to his own time, with a message that he and his audience understood in relation to their situation in the eighth century BCE.

Respect for the Bible also requires us to understand Matthew on his own

---

5.6	Harah vyoledeth ben
	הרה וילדת בן

said to the mother of Samson (3 times)
"You will conceive and give birth to a son." (Judg 13:3, 5, 7)
(13:7 adds: "So then drink no wine or strong drink, and eat nothing unclean, for the boy shall be a nazirite to God from birth to the day of his death.")

said to Hagar
"You are pregnant and will give birth to a son." (Gen 16:11)

said about the mother of Immanuel
"The young woman is (*or* will be) pregnant and will give birth to a son." (Isa 7:14)

terms. Matthew, and all Jews in his era, treated the words of the prophets as coded messages beyond the prophets' own understanding. This view of prophecy originated among the Greeks and was absorbed into Judaism during the hellenistic period. The ancient Greeks believed that their prophets spoke under the influence of a "spirit of prophecy" that overrode the speaker's own rational capacities. As a result, sometimes neither the prophets nor their audiences could understand the true significance of their words. Thus the real meaning of some of those pagan prophecies could be discerned only after the predicted events had already occurred. First-century Jews applied these Greek beliefs about prophecy to the biblical prophets, and so came to believe that God had planted throughout their writings cryptic clues about his plans for the future.

Many Christians hold this same belief today. They think that prophets such as Isaiah and Ezekiel, as well as New Testament authors such as Paul, Peter, and John, unwittingly wrote about events happening in our own time or about to happen in the near future, in the 21st century. Today you can find books in the "End Times Prophecy" sections of Christian bookstores that claim to understand the prophets better than the prophets understood themselves. Inevitably these books explain that we are living in the last generation, a time of unparalleled evil from which only a few will be saved. Since this issue is taking us away from the infancy narratives, I will not pursue it further, but ask only that you to pause for a moment to consider three interrelated premises of that view of prophecy:

- the belief that all of history has been building up to our own lifetime
- the assumption that the prophets did not understand their own messages but that we do
- the outlook that we are among the "saved" and that the rest of humanity is therefore "unsaved," awaiting its eternal damnation

What human needs are answered by such self-centered beliefs? What kind of God is worshiped by a religion that caters to those needs?

"Emmanuel"

Matthew explains the meaning of the name Emmanuel for his Greek-speaking readers. No significance should be attached to the variant spellings of the Greek and Hebrew names, a common phenomenon when moving between languages. Matthew understands the name symbolically, not literally: Joseph is not told to name the boy Emmanuel. That is why Matthew slightly alters the prophecy as he quotes it, changing "*you* will name him Emmanuel" to "*they* will name him Emmanuel." The fact that Jesus is nowhere (in Matthew or any New Testament writing) called by this name is beside the point.

In Matthew's theology Jesus' birth, his ministry of teaching and healing, his saving death, and his resurrection are all signs of God's eschatological presence with his people. That is how Matthew understands Jesus to be "God is with us." He does not mean by this that Jesus himself is God. That would be to read into Matthew the later metaphysical definitions in the Christian doctrine of the Trinity. This is one place where we can badly misunderstand Matthew if we forget that his frame of reference was Jewish. Matthew understands the symbolism of this name in the same way Isaiah did. Isaiah surely did not mean that Ahaz's son would be God. He meant that the boy's presence would be a living sign that God was protecting his people (see Isa 8:8, 10). For Isaiah, "God is with us" is a reassurance that God is faithful to his promises and that the divine purposes in human history will be fulfilled. Another valid translation of "Immanuel" is "God is on our side," which nicely expresses the meaning that Isaiah, and Matthew, intended in this symbolic name.

We can see how important the symbolism of this name was for Matthew by looking at the end of his gospel. The last words of Jesus, in the very last line of the gospel, echo the meaning of the name Emmanuel.

> Teach all people to observe everything that I have commanded you. And be assured, *I am with you* every day until the end of time. (Matt 28:20)

This dramatic declaration is further evidence for how Matthew understands the "with" in "God is with us." Jesus' promise in 28:20 does not mean that Jesus will be physically present on earth. For Matthew that will happen only at Jesus' Second Coming. But in the meantime Jesus will still be "with" his disciples in their work. And that is the sense in which Matthew means that Jesus is Emmanuel: God is with us in the words and deeds of Jesus' ministry in the same way that the risen Jesus is with his disciples in their mission to carry his teaching to all people.

The (In)significance of Jesus' Conception for Matthew

It is possible—though unlikely—that Matthew happened to agree with Luke that Jesus was born to a virgin. If Matthew did understand Jesus' conception to be a miracle, however, he had a perfect opportunity to dwell on its miraculous nature and to emphasize the power of God. But Matthew shows no interest in this dimension of Jesus' conception. If he saw Mary's pregnancy as a miracle, that is not how he treats it in his narrative. Judging from how the pregnancy actually functions in Matthew's story, we can see two reasons why it was important to him.

1. It fulfills prophecy. Even if Matthew understood Jesus' conception to be a miracle, that would still be irrelevant to the fulfillment of prophecy, as we see from the other prophecies that Matthew quotes in the infancy narrative. There

is nothing miraculous about being born in Bethlehem (2:6), leaving Egypt (2:15), or being from Nazareth (2:23).

2. The point of having the angel tell Joseph that Mary has conceived by a holy spirit is to assure the young husband that he is not offending God by finalizing his marriage. (Remember, it was because Joseph was righteous that he was unwilling to take Mary into his home.) Within the plot of Matthew's narrative, therefore, the conception by a holy spirit is not important for its own sake, not even if it is meant to be a miracle. Nor is it important for what it signifies about Mary. For Matthew the "spirit conception" is important because it is a vital link in the story of how Jesus came to be the son of Joseph and thus a rightful descendant of David. For Luke, the virginal conception is what makes Jesus son of God (Luke 1:35). Matthew, by contrast, focuses on Jesus as son of Joseph, and thus son of David. Matthew notes in passing that Jesus is son of God (in his quotation of the prophecy of Hosea in Matt 2:15), but he does not connect this to the manner of Jesus' conception.

My reading of the evidence leads me to the conclusion that Matthew probably thought that Jesus had a human father other than Joseph.[6] Yet I am also acutely aware that few biblical scholars read Matthew the way I do. Because so many scholars understand Matthew to be narrating a virginal conception, and because that interpretation is taken for granted in the tradition of the church—and because I believe there is some chance that interpretation might be correct—I want to offer an answer to a question that comes up within the traditional interpretation. *If Matthew believed in the virgin birth, why did he do so little with it?* Why does he focus on Joseph as Jesus' legal father and not on Mary as his virgin mother?[7] The first relationship does not exclude the second; Matthew could have focused on both. Yet he does not use the virginal conception as a basis for making any theological or christological point at all. In fact he never mentions or even alludes to it elsewhere in his gospel, not even in the rest of the infancy narrative. For Matthew the virginal conception is, as it were, theologically inert. Why would he make so little out of a miracle that later Christians made so much of? In a way this question is unfair because it amounts to asking why Matthew does not meet the expectations of later generations, something he was obviously under no obligation to do. Even so, the question is worth asking because it forces us to pay close attention to Matthew's own agenda.

Determining why an author did not do something is inherently specula-

6. I argue this position at length in Chapter 11.

7. Other early Christians were extremely interested in the significance of Mary's virginity. A florid example of that interest is the second-century Infancy Gospel of James (see Chapter 17), which contains a lengthy story of Mary's birth and girlhood. This gospel elaborately describes her life of physical purity, makes Joseph her guardian rather than her husband, and emphatically asserts that she remained anatomically "intact" after giving birth to Jesus. Matthew, however, is completely uninterested in Mary's life as a virgin.

tive. The best we can do is make educated guesses. Assuming, then, for the sake of the argument, that Matthew believed there was a virgin birth, here are two suggestions as to why he still gave it so little attention.

1. All through chapters 1 and 2, Matthew was trying to show that Jesus' birth and infancy fulfilled prophecy and thus that Jesus met Israel's expectations for the Messiah. However, there was no Jewish expectation that the Messiah would be born of a virgin mother. On the other hand, there was a popular, though not universal, expectation that the Messiah would be from the house of David. That is Matthew's focus in 1:18–25.

2. Matthew was uneasy with the whole notion of virginal conception. He and his readers surely knew about the stories of the births of Greco-Roman heroes, most of which told of sex between gods and humans. As a Jew, it was impossible for Matthew to imagine God physically impregnating Mary, so the evangelist had to walk a fine line here. He wanted to say that God was responsible for Mary's pregnancy without saying that God literally took the male role in causing it (see p. 241). Since Matthew did not want his readers to start wondering about the details of how Jesus was conceived without a human father, he made little of its miraculous aspect, and quickly moved the narrative forward.

These suggestions arise from imagining the difficulty Matthew would have faced while trying to communicate his Jewish sensitivities on this matter in the Greek language. But in the end it's guesswork. What do you think?

MATT 2:1–12
Magi Visit Jesus

The magi scene follows one that centered on Joseph and the prediction of Jesus' birth. But Joseph is temporarily out of the picture now, and Mary is mentioned only in passing. Worth noting is the fact that Matthew has not narrated Jesus' birth. The event happens, as it were, offstage and between scenes. Matthew is not interested in the birth itself, but in the different responses to it. Foreigners come from far away to worship Jesus while his own people ("all Jerusalem" in 2:3) side with the wicked ruler bent on killing the baby. This anticipates the situation of Matthew's own day, when gentiles were steadily joining the Jesus movement while all but a few Jews wanted nothing to do with it. Matthew's somber focus on the Jewish rejection of Jesus stands in stark contrast to Luke's narrative, which resounds with rejoicing. In Matthew there is only one joyful response to Jesus' birth, and it comes from the foreign magi (2:10).

The visit of the magi is surely not historical. These learned men are meant to represent the gentile world. Their search for and worship of Jesus portends a future in which gentiles will come to believe in him. The story makes little sense apart from its religious symbolism. It is most implausible that real-life astrologers from Mesopotamia would undertake a long, expensive, and dangerous journey simply on the hope of paying their respects to the infant king of a small and unimportant foreign country.

The Magi

The term *magi* has had different connotations at different times in history. (The plural "magi" is the Latin spelling of the Greek word *magoi*; the singular form is *magus* in Latin or *magos* in Greek.) According to the ancient historian Herodotus, the magi originally were Medean priests who specialized in interpreting dreams.[8] After Medea was invaded by the Persians, the magi adopted the religion of their conquerors and became Zoroastrian priests. By the first century, "magi" referred in a general way to experts in Eastern wisdom and science, which included astronomy, astrology, and divination. Our word "magic" comes from them.

Early Christians were supposed to shun astrology and the other occult arts because these were considered to be traffic with pagan gods and demonic powers. The Book of Acts portrays magi as charlatans and enemies of the gospel (see the cameo), and makes it clear that the magical arts are incompatible with belief

8. In the Septuagint version of the Book of Daniel, the Babylonian king Nebuchadnezzar summons magi to interpret his troubling dreams. (Dan 2:2, 10 LXX)

Magi in the Book of Acts

Magi and magic (*mageia* in Greek) are mentioned in three scenes in the Acts of the Apostles. These scenes reflect the early Christian attitude that the practice of magic was a serious and spiritually dangerous matter.

- A magus named Simon had won the admiration of the people of Samaria by working wonders with his magic. When he witnessed the superior miracles worked by the apostle Philip, he believed and was baptized (Acts 8:9–13). When he later saw that Peter and John could bestow the holy spirit on people by laying hands on them, he offered to buy this power from them. Peter bitterly rebuked him and Simon asked for forgiveness (Acts 8:18–24). Simon has the dubious distinction of having a sin named after him. In Christian moral theology the buying and selling of religious benefits is called "simony."
- A sinister Jewish magus named Bar Jesus was a false prophet who opposed the preaching of Paul and Barnabas. Paul cursed him and he was struck blind (Acts 13:6–11).
- In Ephesus, many who became believers in Jesus confessed that they had been practicing magic. In a public display of their repentance, they burned their very expensive books of magic (Acts 19:18–19).

in Jesus. Yet there is nothing but approval for the magi in Matthew's story. He portrays them as wise, righteous, and religiously elite gentiles. He has no trouble assuming that astrology helped them find their way to Jesus. Matthew neither reports nor implies that these gentiles gave up their native religion or their occult craft after worshiping Jesus.

In 66 CE the Armenian king Tiridates journeyed to Rome from the East, accompanied by magi, to do homage to the Emperor Nero. Tiridates made a grand show out of this politically shrewd gesture and it was reported by several ancient historians. Perhaps the memory of this event influenced Matthew's story.

The Star

Christians have long been fascinated by the star in this story. Scholars and astronomers have searched extensively for a scientific basis for Matthew's star. Planetarium shows about "the star of Bethlehem" are still popular in the Christmas season. The three most common theories identify the star with a supernova, a comet, or an unusual conjunction of planets. While there are no historical descriptions of what we would call a supernova from any time around the birth of Jesus, ancient Chinese astronomers noted a bright comet around 4 BCE and modern astronomers know that Halley's comet appeared in 12 BCE. Astronomical calculations also indicate that there was a rare conjunction of Jupiter, Saturn, and Mars in 7 or 6 BCE, although these planets were not close enough together to look like a single star. It is possible that Matthew's story preserves a memory of an unusual celestial phenomenon in the years close to the birth of Jesus, even though Luke shows no awareness of it.

Speculations about a possible natural basis for the story may interest us today, but they are foreign to the spirit of Matthew's narrative. He clearly intends to describe a miraculous star, one that leads the magi some great distance to Jerusalem, then apparently disappears, then reappears to lead them south five miles to Bethlehem, and finally stops over a specific house. More relevant to Matthew's purpose than theories from modern astronomy is the ancient belief that new stars and comets broadcast messages from the heavens (see the cameo on comets). The appearance of a new star was thought to herald the birth of a new ruler, a belief Matthew's story endorses. Comets were taken as omens of disaster, which also fits Matthew's story inasmuch as the star sets in motion a chain of events that leads to the slaughter in Bethlehem.

Something else that seems to have influenced Matthew here is the Old Testament story of Balaam (Numbers 22–24). The king of Moab, Balak, hired a foreign seer, Balaam, to pronounce a curse on the people of Israel who were preparing to invade his land. Balaam, however, was led by God to pronounce a

---

5.7

The Star of Bethlehem

Ignatius of Antioch was a bishop in the early second century. In one of his letters he describes the star.

> How was Jesus revealed to the ages?
> A star shone in heaven
> brighter than all the stars,
> and its light was indescribable,
> and its novelty caused astonishment.
> All the other stars
> together with the sun and moon
> formed a ring around it,
> and yet it outshone them all with its light. (Ephesians 19:2)

As far as we can tell from his seven letters, Ignatius did not know Matthew's gospel. His description of the star is not based on any work known to us. In the very next verse in his Letter to the Ephesians, Ignatius writes, "From that time on all magic (*mageia*) was annulled" (9:13). It's difficult to imagine how he could say this if he knew the story of the magi.

---

blessing on Israel, thus reversing the king's hostile intent. Balaam's eloquent blessing builds up to a cryptic prophecy about a star rising out of Israel, a prophecy understood in first-century Judaism as a reference to the coming messiah.

> I see him, though not now;
>> I behold him, though he is not near.
> A star will come forth from Jacob,
>> and a scepter will rise from Israel. (Num 24:17)[9]

The first-century Jewish philosopher Philo identified Baalam as a magus whose "magical arts" leave him when he was possessed by the "spirit of true prophecy" (*Life of Moses* 1.50). Though Matthew does not cite Num 24:17, the story of Balaam has the same plot as Matthew 2:1–12. An evil king, Herod, tries to enlist foreign magi against Jesus, his newly-arrived rival. Instead, the magi worship the child and leave unnoticed, frustrating Herod's murderous designs.

9. In the second century CE, a rebel military leader, Simeon ben Kosibah, was proclaimed the messiah by the leading rabbi of the day. Ben Kosibah was nicknamed "Bar Kochba" (Aramaic for "son of the star") to connect him with Balaam's prophecy.

MATT 2:1–12

2:1–8   The magi in Jerusalem
    2:1–3 The magi arrive
    2:4–6 Herod consults with religious experts
    2:7–8 Herod meets with the magi
2:9–11 The magi visit Jesus
2:12   The magi go home

¹Jesus was born at Bethlehem, Judea, when Herod was king. Magi from the East showed up in Jerusalem just then. ²"Tell us," they said, "where to find the one born to be king of the Judeans. We have observed his star at its rising and have come to pay him homage."

³When this news reached King Herod, he was visibly shaken, and all Jerusalem along with him. ⁴He assembled all the ranking priests and local experts, and pressed them for information: "Where is the Anointed supposed to be born?"

⁵They replied, "At Bethlehem, Judea. This is how it is put by the prophet:

      ⁶And you, Bethlehem, in the land of Judah,
        in no way are you least among the leaders of Judah.

Comets

The appearance of anything new or unusual in the heavens was taken as a portent. New stars, especially comets—our word comes from the Greek *kometes*, meaning "long haired," describing a comet's fiery tail—were thought to announce heaven's choice of a new ruler.

> A comet blazed into view, which in common opinion portends a change in the monarchy. Therefore, acting as if Nero has already lost his throne, people began to speculate about who would be the next choice. (Tacitus, *Annals* 14.22)

> A comet began to appear several nights in a row, a phenomenon commonly believed to portend the death of great rulers. This worried Nero. However, he learned from the astrologer Balbillus that kings usually averted such omens by arranging for the death of some distinguished man, thereby turning that fate away from themselves onto the heads of the nobility. And so Nero decided to put to death all the eminent men of the State. (Suetonius, *Nero*, 36.1)

> A few months before Augustus was born a public portent was observed in Rome [presumably in the sky], which warned the people that Nature was about to give birth to their king. (Suetonius, *Augustus*, 94.3)

A Comet for Caesar

A few months after the death of Julius Caesar in 44 BCE, his son and successor Octavian (later named Augustus) sponsored a week of athletic competition in his memory. A comet appeared the very day the games began and passed into popular lore as the soul of Julius ascending to heaven. Two years later the great poet Virgil wrote, "Behold, the star of Caesar appeared as a sign." Augustus later issued a silver coin—a denarius, a denomination in common use—with his own name and face on one side and a comet on the other, with the Latin inscription *divus Iulius*, "divine Julius."

A Christian Perspective

The fourth-century church historian Eusebius used accepted beliefs about comets as his context for explaining the meaning of the moving "star"–the ancients often called comets stars–that guided the magi to Jesus in Matthew's gospel.

> In the case of remarkable and famous men we know that strange stars have appeared, what some call comets, or meteors, or tails of fire, or similar phenomena that are seen in association with great or unusual events. But what event could be greater or more important for the whole universe than the spiritual light coming to the human race with the arrival of the savior, bringing to human souls the gift of holiness and the true knowledge of God? For this reason the herald star gave the great sign. (Eusebius, *The Demonstration of the Gospel*, 9.1)

> Out of you will come a leader
>   who will shepherd my people, Israel."

⁷Then Herod called the magi together secretly and ascertained from them the precise time the star became visible. ⁸Then he sent them to Bethlehem with these instructions: "Go make a careful search for the child. When you find him, report back to me, so I can also go and pay him homage."

⁹They listened to what the king had to say and continued on their way.

And there guiding them on was the star that they had observed in the East: it led them until it came to a standstill above where the child lay. ¹⁰Once they saw the star, they were beside themselves with joy. ¹¹And they arrived at the house and saw the child with his mother Mary. They fell down and paid him homage. Then they opened their treasure chests and presented him with gifts: gold, frankincense, and myrrh. ¹²And because they had been advised in a dream not to return to Herod, they journeyed back to their own country by a different route.

──────── ⚭ ────────

2:2 The magi come *from the East*, just like Balaam (Num 23:7).

at its rising. The Greek word *anatole* usually means "rising" but can also mean "east," because that is the direction of the sunrise. Some translations have the magi report seeing the star "in the east," but "at its rising" is preferable. Since the magi are from the East, they would have seen the star in their west. Furthermore, astrologers attributed great significance to the time of a heavenly body's first appearance, its "rising."

2:3–4 That *all Jerusalem* would be upset to hear about a new king makes little sense historically because Herod was a very unpopular ruler. Matthew is foreshadowing the end of the gospel, in which the people of the city side with their leaders against Jesus. (See the chilling scene in 27:20–25, which climaxes with: "All the people said, 'Smear his blood on us and on our children.'")

The same dynamic is behind Herod's *assembling* the ranking priests and scholars. Matthew portrays them as cooperating with Herod, but they were actually his bitter opponents and would have welcomed a new king. Matthew is again pointing ahead to the end of the gospel, where every time Jewish leaders "assemble" (*synagagein*), they do so to plot against Jesus (22:34, 41; 26:3, 57; 27:62; 28:12). Perhaps Matthew's choice of verbs to describe these hostile gatherings is meant to play on the word "synagogue" (*synagoge*, literally "assembly"), which had become a hostile place for Matthew's community.

The Magi in Christian Legend

The exotic magi have intrigued the Christian imagination, which over the centuries has filled in details missing in Matthew's story and elaborated on the magi's lives both before and after their encounter with Jesus. Our culture is so familiar with Christmas images of "the three kings" that most Christians are unaware that the Bible neither tells their number nor identifies them as kings. They were eventually counted as three because of the three kinds of gifts. (However, Syrian Christians have a tradition about twelve magi.) The magi became kings on the force of the suggestions in Isa 60:3, 6 and Ps 72:10–11, passages that Christians often associated with this story, and ones that Matthew himself may have had in mind.

> Nations shall walk by your light
>   and kings by your shining radiance. . . .
> Caravans of camels shall fill you,
>   dromedaries from Midian and Ephah;
> All from Sheba shall come
>   bearing gold and frankincense,
>   and proclaiming the praises of the Lord. (Isa 60:3, 6)

> The kings of Tarshish and the Islands shall offer gifts;
>   the kings of Arabia and Seba shall bring tribute.
> All kings shall pay him homage
>   all nations shall serve him. (Ps 72:10–11)

The gifts of the magi were interpreted as symbolic tributes to Jesus: gold because he was a king, incense used in worship because he was divine, and myrrh used in burial because he would die as the redeemer. The magi were anonymous until the Middle Ages, when they were given a variety of names. Eastern Christians named them Hormizdah,

Yazdegerd, and Perozadh. In Ethiopia they were identified as Hor, Basanter, and Karsudan. The most popular tradition in the West calls them Caspar, who was young and shaven, Melchior, a bearded old man, and Balthasar, who was black—physical descriptions that are standard in all nativity displays and Christmas pageants. The alleged relics of these kings were widely revered. Today they are kept in a splendid shrine in the cathedral of Cologne, Germany. Elaborate legends grew up around the magi, one of them reported by Marco Polo in the 13th century. He had visited the tombs of the three kings in Persia, where he heard the following tale:

> The three kings brought gifts of gold, frankincense, and myrrh in order to learn whether the new child was a king, a god, or a healer. If he accepted the gold, he was an earthly king; if he accepted the frankincense, he was a god; if he accepted the myrrh, he was destined to be a healer. The baby Jesus accepted all three. In return, Jesus gave the three kings a small closed chest. They later opened it and found that it contained a stone. Jesus had evidently given them the stone to indicate that they would be firm and constant in their new faith. Since the kings did not know this, they threw the stone into a well. As soon as the stone fell into the well, fire descended from heaven and filled the well. The kings took some of the fire and carried it to their own country where they worshiped it as god. This is how they came to be fire worshipers.*

Zoroastrians use fire as their sacred symbol of the presence of God. This tale reflects the ancient association of the magi with Zoroastrianism. It is a good example of how myths take on a life of their own.

* This paraphrase of Polo's report is borrowed from *The Acts of Jesus*, p. 508.

2:5-6 In Josephus' version of the story of Moses' birth, Pharoah's scholars (scribes) predict the birth of Moses (see p. 130). In other popular Jewish retellings of the Exodus story, it is magi who foretell for the Pharoah the birth of a rival (Targum Jonathan on Ex 1:15; Exodus Rabbah on Ex 1:22).

Later in the Book of Exodus a similar group of experts assists Pharoah in his first showdown with Moses. The Bible describes them as "scholars, sorcerers, and magicians" (Ex 7:11). Josephus calls them priests (*Antiquities* 2.285) and Philo calls them magi (*Life of Moses* 1.16). First-century Jews thus could imagine the evil Egyptian king advised by scholars, priests, and magi, just as Matthew pictures Herod conferring with scholars, priests, and magi.

Matthew uses this scene to make two points that relate to larger themes in his gospel. 1) The magi know about the birth of a Jewish king from their astrology. Their knowledge is true, but incomplete. To find Jesus these gentiles need to receive additional instruction from the Jewish scriptures. 2) The Jewish authorities, even though they correctly interpret the scriptures, do not heed them. They do not even go looking for Jesus, much less acknowledge him as Israel's messiah.

2:6 This prophecy is analyzed on pp. 112–13.

2:7 Matthew portrays Herod's cunning by having him meet *secretly* with the magi, not allowing them to talk directly with the priests and scholars.

2:9 Here the coherence of the story breaks down. The magi did not know where to look for the new king until they learned about Bethlehem from the Bible, via Herod. But now Matthew makes that scriptural knowledge superfluous by having the star lead them to the town.

2:11 *The house* presupposes that the family lives in Bethlehem. In Luke's gospel the family lives in Nazareth and does not stay in a house during their visit to Bethlehem.

Frankincense and myrrh were expensive luxury items. There is no apparent religious symbolism to these two gifts or to the other one, gold. No Old Testament text lists them together.

Christian sermons on this story sometimes claim that myrrh is associated with Jesus' passion and thus interpret this gift as a symbolic foreshadowing of Jesus' destiny on the cross. But this is not the case for Matthew. Myrrh is used for Jesus' burial in John 19:39. In Mark 15:23 the crucified Jesus is offered "wine mixed with myrrh." However, Matthew changes this to "wine mixed with gall" (Matt 27:34) and mentions myrrh only in the magi scene.

2:12 *by a different route.* The Tiridates story might be in the background here. After paying homage to Nero, Tiridates and his entourage, which included magi, took a different route on their return trip home.

MATT 2:13–23
Herod Tries to Kill Jesus

This episode has three scenes, each telling how an event in the infancy of Jesus fulfills prophecy. Each scene builds up to a quotation of the scripture that has been fulfilled. The impression Matthew creates with this arrangement is that nothing in the early life of Jesus is accidental or unforeseen. Though it might look like the family's flight to Egypt and later relocation to Nazareth were movements made in response to the danger posed by hostile kings, Matthew makes it clear that Jesus' travels were actually predicted by prophets and directed by angels. Matthew thus assures us that these events unfolded according to divine providence. Even the horrifying atrocity of a massacre of babies should be understood in the light of prophecy.

The atmosphere of this episode is grim, dominated by the threat of death and the mass murder of children. There are no miracles to glorify Jesus or to dramatize God's protection of him. It is enough that his family slip away and later return unnoticed. The only supernatural interventions are the dreams that guide Joseph. Matthew finds no bright side in any of this, nothing to cause any rejoicing. Jesus' escape from death is not accompanied by any expression of relief or gratitude to God, but rather by the bitter grief of a mother weeping for her dead children.

The most prominent aspect of Matthew's theological agenda is revealed in the way he associates Jesus with Israel's history. At one level, the story of Moses is recalled by the focus on Herod. The barbarous spectacle of a king who orders the murder of baby Jewish boys puts Herod in the role of the Pharoah in the story of Exodus. In Exodus and in Matthew, the death of the king is the signal that it is safe to return from the place of refuge (see note on Matt 2:20). That Moses flees *from* Egypt and Jesus flees *to* Egypt is but a minor mismatch between the stories. At a second level, the movements of the infant Jesus (out of Israel and then out of Egypt back to Israel) correlate with the three divinely-directed journeys of the people of Israel: the Exodus (emphasized by the prophecy quoted in 2:15), the Exile (mentioned three times in the genealogy of Jesus and alluded to by the prophecy quoted in 2:18), and the Return from exile (an association Matthew does not develop, but one that easily comes to mind when Jesus' story is mapped against the pivotal events in Israel's history). Matthew thus structures his narrative and marshalls quotations from prophecy to show that the child Jesus recapitulates and fulfills the history of his people.

The similarities between Herod and Pharoah and between Jesus and Moses leave no doubt that Matthew intended to recall the story of the Exodus as the background for the infancy of Jesus. However, we need to look further than the biblical Book of Exodus to see how extensive and precise the similarities are. The story of Moses' infancy had been embellished in Jewish storytelling into a much more elaborate narrative that developed the dramatic potential of the biblical story. Matthew's story of the birth and infancy of Jesus has so many points of contact with this legendary story, known as the Moses Haggadah (see Chapter 6), that we can be certain that Matthew has used it as the basis for designing his own narrative.

MATT 2:13–23

2:13–15   The family flees to Egypt
2:16–18   Herod massacres the babies
2:19–21   The family returns to Israel
2:22–23   The family relocates to Nazareth

[13]After the magi had departed, a messenger of the Lord appeared in a dream to Joseph, saying, "Get up, take the child and his mother and flee to Egypt. Stay there until I give you instructions. You see, Herod is determined to hunt down the child and destroy him."

[14]So Joseph got up and took the child and his mother under cover of night and set out for Egypt. [15]There they remained until Herod's death, in order to fulfill the prediction of the Lord through the prophet:

I called my son out of Egypt.

[16]When Herod realized he had been duped by the magi, he was outraged. He then issued instructions to kill all the children two years old and younger in Bethlehem and the surrounding region. This corresponded to the time of the star that he had learned from the magi. [17]Then the prediction of Jeremiah the prophet was fulfilled:

> [18]In Ramah the sound of mourning
> and bitter grieving was heard:
> Rachel weeping for her children.
> She refused to be consoled:
> They were no more.

[19]After Herod's death, a messenger of the Lord appeared in a dream to Joseph in Egypt: [20] "Get up, take the child and his mother, and go to the land of Israel; those who were seeking the child's life are dead."

[21]So he got up, took the child and his mother, and went to the land of Israel. [22]He heard that Archelaus was the king of Judea in the place of his father Herod; as a consequence, he was afraid to go there. He was instructed in a dream to go to Galilee; [23]so he went there and settled in a town called Nazareth, in order to fulfill the prediction of the prophets:

> He will be called a Nazorean.

━━━━━ ∽∾∽ ━━━━━

2:13–15 In v. 13 Joseph receives instructions from an angel and in vv. 14–15 he follows them to the letter: he gets up, takes the child and his mother, goes to Egypt, and stays there until he receives further instructions (see v. 19). That the family fled by night underlines the danger of the situation.

2:16 It is utterly unrealistic that the cunning and paranoid Herod would put himself in the position where his only way to find a rival to his throne was to trust foreign magi. He knew they were going to Bethlehem, so why didn't he have them tailed? Following these highly visible strangers in a small town would have been a simple task. Besides, if a moving star had parked itself over the very house where Jesus lived, anyone could have followed it and found the house.

2:17 Matthew's standard formula for introducing a quotation from the prophets uses terminology that indicates God's intention in its fulfillment: an event occurs *in order to* fulfill prophecy (see the wording in 1:22, 2:15, and 2:23). In this case, however, Matthew substitutes the Greek word "then" for his usual "in order to." This minor change in diction signals a major theological distinction: the massacre fulfills scripture, but it does not happen for that purpose. Matthew thus deliberately avoids saying that God intended this atrocity. Matthew makes the same substitution in 27:9 when he introduces a prophecy fulfilled by the suicide of Judas.

Nevertheless, it does not seem to trouble Matthew that God intervened to save Jesus and left the rest of the babies, in effect, to die in his place.[10] The Catholic

10. For an assessment of the historicity of this massacre, see p. 184.

church considers them martyrs and commemorates their death on the feast of the Holy Innocents on December 28.

2:19–21 is closely modeled on Ex 4:19–20 and is also nearly identical to Matt 2:13–14 (see Box 5.8). Matthew's formulaic wording creates an almost exact symmetry between Jesus' two journeys to Egypt and back to Israel. It looks like Matthew wrote 2:19–21 in careful imitation of Ex 4:19–20 and then used it to clone 2:13–14, making the necessary adjustment in the reference to Herod in v. 13b.

2:20 This verse is a nearly verbatim quotation from Ex 4:19. Matthew has copied it so closely that he seems not to have noticed that "*those* who were seeking the child's life" makes no sense in the context of his own story. Herod was the only one who wanted to kill Jesus and it is Herod's own death (not the death of a group) that makes it safe to return to Israel.

2:22 Herod the Great was a client king in the Roman Empire. After his death the Romans divided his kingdom among his three surviving sons. Herod Antipas, who later murdered John the Baptizer, was given Galilee. *Archelaus* was assigned Judea. Why Joseph thought it would be safer to live under Antipas than under Archelaus is baffling. Strictly speaking, Archelaus was not a king; the Romans commissioned him to be an "ethnarch," literally, a ruler of a race of people. Matthew similarly calls Antipas a king in 14:9, though he was technically a "tetrarch," liter-

---

5.8   Moses, Jesus, and Egypt

Moses Returns to Egypt **Exodus 4:19–20 LXX**	*Jesus Returns to Israel* **Matt 2:19–21**	*Jesus Flees to Egypt* **Matt 2:13–14**
[19]After these many days the king of Egypt died. The Lord said		
	[19]After Herod's death, a messenger of the Lord appeared in a dream to Joseph in Egypt and said to him,	[13]After they had departed, a messenger of the Lord appeared in a dream to Joseph and said to him,
	[20]"Get up, take the child and his mother,	"Get up, take the child and his mother,
to Moses in Midian,		
"Go back to Egypt,	and return to the land of Israel,	and flee to Egypt,
for all those who were seeking your life are dead."	for those who were seeking the child's life are dead."	for Herod is determined to seek out the child and destroy him."
	. . .	
[20]Moses took his wife and children and put them on donkeys and returned to Egypt.	[21]So he got up, took the child and his mother and returned to the land of Israel.	[14]So he got up, took the child and his mother and left for Egypt.

ally, a governor of one-fourth of a region. Matthew is either misinformed or else uses the term "king" loosely.

THE PROPHECIES IN MATTHEW 2

Matt 2:6 (Mic 5:2 + 2 Sam 5:2)

The Old Testament quotation here is a combination of a free rendering of Micah 5:2 and a phrase from 2 Sam 5:2. The wording of the verse from Micah is not based on any known ancient version. In addition to the difference in wording, Matthew has made at least two alterations in the quotation. First, he replaces "Ephrathah" with "land of Judah," probably to make the geographical reference more intelligible to his audience. Second, he adds one Greek word that means "not at all" or "in no way" to the beginning of the second line, emphatically contradicting Micah's assertion that Bethlehem is "least among the clans of Judah."

This second modification is striking evidence that Matthew felt free to change the scriptures to suit his purposes. The specific way he altered this prophecy reveals one aspect of how early Christians understood the relationship between the scriptural prophecies and Jesus' life. From Matthew's perspective, Jesus had changed the status of Bethlehem. Although it had been a town of no significance, it had become great because it was the birthplace of the Messiah. Analyzing Matthew's use of Micah here lets us see how a prophecy can be changed by the event it "foretells." That is the opposite process from the one presupposed by the traditional Christian understanding: that the utterances of the prophets were designed by divine inspiration to be predictions that were later fulfilled in the life of Jesus. Matt 2:6 is an especially obvious example of how Christians' reflection on the life of Jesus could influence the way they quoted a prophecy, even to the point of using their perception of a gospel event to *correct* the words of a prophet.

Micah 5:2	Matthew 2:6
But you, O Bethlehem of Ephrathah,	And you, Bethlehem, in the land of Judah,
who are the smallest of the clans of Judah.	*in no way* are you least among the leaders of Judah.
Out of you will come for me one who is to rule in Israel.	Out of you will come a leader
2 Samuel 5:2	
It is you who will be shepherd of my people, Israel	who will shepherd my people, Israel.

The last line of the quotation in 2:6 shows a different aspect of the freedom with which early Christians quoted the Old Testament. Here Matthew has attached a line from 2 Sam 5:2 to the "quotation" from Micah. Such composite quotations are fairly common in the New Testament. Matthew blends in this line from 2 Samuel because it refers to the kingship of David. This works nicely because Bethlehem was the home of David the shepherd and because Matthew takes such care to underline Jesus' status as David's rightful heir.

Matt 2:15 (Hos 11:1)

The quotation is from the prophet Hosea (Hos 11:1). Matthew interprets it as a prediction of an event in the life of Jesus. In its original context it refers to the Exodus and "my son" means Israel. The full passage from which Matthew takes this quotation (Hos 11:1–7) is about God's plans to punish Israel (see Box 5.9). God even threatens to drive them back to Egypt (Hos 11:5). Matthew has lifted out the only words in the whole passage that could possibly be reinterpreted to apply to Jesus. He could not even quote all of 11:1, since the mention of "Israel" in the first half of that verse would make it impossible for him to use "my son" as a reference to Jesus.

5.9

Hosca 11:1–7

¹When Israel was a child, I loved him,
    and I called my son out of Egypt.
²The more I called them,
    the further they went from me;
they kept sacrificing to the Baals,
    and offering incense to idols.
³Yet it was I who taught Ephraim to walk,
    I held them in my arms;
        but they did not know that it was I who healed them.
⁴I led them with cords of human kindness,
    with bands of love.
I was to them like those who lift infants to their cheeks.
    I bent down to them and fed them.
⁵They shall return to the land of Egypt,
    and Assyria shall be their king,
        because they have refused to return to me.
⁶The sword rages in their cities,
    it consumes their oracle-priests,
        and devours because of their schemes.
⁷My people are determined to turn away from me.
    To the Most High they call,
        but he does not raise them up at all.

Matthew's quotation follows the Hebrew text of Hosea rather than the Greek translation, which reads, "I called his children out of Egypt." The Hebrew singular "my son" refers to the people of Israel and so can legitimately be translated with the Greek plural "his children." In fact, the Hebrew text immediately switches to plural pronouns, referring to "my son" (Israel) in 11:1 as "they" in the rest of 11:1–7. The Septuagint correctly conveys the sense of the Hebrew original. However, the Septuagint version was not useful to Matthew and so he made his own, more literal, translation. The result is an interesting paradox: the Septuagint version of Hos 11:1 is a looser translation of the original, but faithful to its meaning, while Matthew's translation is more precise grammatically, but he gives it a meaning quite foreign to its original sense.

"Out of Egypt" does not mesh with the movement in the story because Jesus is fleeing *toward* Egypt. Strictly speaking, the Hosea prophecy is not fulfilled until 2:21 when the family leaves Egypt to return to Israel, so it is puzzling why Matthew puts it at 2:15 rather than after 2:21. His arrangement makes sense when we note the different geographical orientations of 2:13–14 and 2:19–21. The latter is pointed toward Israel, the former toward Egypt. Putting the prophecy after 2:21 would blur the focus on the land of Israel. In its present location at 2:15 the quotation reinforces the Egypt theme of 2:13–14 and anticipates the movement in 2:21.

Matt 2:18 (Jer 31:15)

This quotation is from Jer 31:15. Rachel was the wife of Jacob and the ancestral mother of the tribes of Joseph. Ramah was a town that the conquerors of Israel had used as a staging area for assembling Israelites whom they were deporting into exile. After Israel's defeat by the Babylonians, Jeremiah was himself taken in chains to Ramah to be processed for deportation to Babylon (Jer 40:1). In Jer 31:15, the prophet imagines Rachel's spirit to be haunting her tomb, still weeping for Israelites who had been deported by the Assyrians a century before Jeremiah's time. God then tells Rachel to stop crying because the exiles will return (Jer 31:16–17; see Box 5.10). For Jeremiah, then, 31:15 is part of a message of hope. But Matthew uses it to express hopeless and inconsolable grief.

There were two competing traditions about the location of Rachel's tomb. The earlier one locates it in Zelzeh, near the city of Bethel, about five miles north of Ramah (1 Sam 10:2). A later (and almost certainly mistaken) tradition has her buried in Bethlehem (Gen 35:19, 48:7), about twelve miles south of Ramah. Matthew relies on the Bethlehem tradition. This makes his mention of Ramah a bit of a geographical problem—Rachel's crying in Bethlehem is heard twelve miles away—but it suits his christological agenda because of Ramah's historical connection with the Exile. By quoting this particular prophecy Matthew

---

| **5.10** | Jeremiah 31:5–7 |

[15]Thus says Yahweh:
A voice is heard in Ramah,
    lamentation and bitter weeping.
Rachel is weeping for her children;
    she refuses to be comforted for her children,
    because they are no more.
[16]Thus says Yahweh:
Keep your voice from weeping,
    and your eyes from tears;
for there is a reward for your work,
             says Yahweh:
    they shall come back from the land of the enemy;
[17]there is hope for your future,
             says Yahweh:
    your children shall come back to their own country.

---

associates an event in the early life of Jesus with the Exile, even if the relationship of the prophecy to the event is indirect (Rachel's weeping is over the babies' death, not their deportation).

Matt 2:23 (?)

"He will be called a Nazorean" is not a quotation from the Old Testament. Matthew signals this by ascribing this statement to "the prophets" rather than to "the prophet" (as in 1:22, 2:5, 2:15) or to a named prophet (such as Jeremiah in 2:17 or Isaiah in 3:3). This is Matthew's way of admitting that he is giving us a paraphrase of the sense of more than one passage rather than a quotation of a specific verse.

Matthew is not alone in using the Bible this way. At least three other New Testament authors claim to be quoting scripture when they are actually offering what seems to be a paraphrase of their interpretation of one or more passages (see Box 5.11).

The gospels call Jesus both "Nazorean" and "Nazarene" (Greek *Nazoraios* and *Nazarenos*). Mark uses "Nazarene;" Matthew and John use "Nazorean;" Luke uses both. The two terms mean the same thing and there is no significance in the different spellings. The name of the village is also variously spelled: *Nazareth, Nazaret,* and *Nazara* all occur in the gospels.

Which Old Testament texts does Matthew have in mind? Since Nazareth is never mentioned in the Old Testament, he cannot be alluding to a prophecy about someone from there. So it must be that the place name "Nazorean" reminds Matthew of another scriptural word that sounds like it. Scholars nomi-

5.11

Other Unattributable Quotations

Matthew is not the only New Testament author with an alleged quotation from scripture that cannot be found in any biblical book. Here are three more examples.

> On the last and most important day of the festival, Jesus stood up and shouted, "Anyone who's thirsty must come to me and drink. The one who believes in me—just as scripture says—'*rivers of life-giving water will flow out of him.*'" (John 7:37–38)

> Israel failed to obtain what it was seeking. The chosen obtained it, but the rest became obstinate, as it is written,
>
> > *God gave them a sluggish spirit,*
> > *eyes that would not see*
> > *and ears that would not hear,*
> > *until this very day.* (Rom 11:7–8)

> Whoever wants to be a friend of the world makes himself an enemy of God. Do you think that it's for nothing that the scripture says, "*God jealously longs for the spirit that he has made to dwell in us*"? (James 4:4–5)

None of these quotations can be found in the Old Testament or anywhere else.

> Another mysterious quotation is featured in 1 Corinthians.

> As it is written,
>
> > *What eye has not seen, and ear has not heard,*
> > *and what has not entered the human heart,*
> > *what God has prepared for those who love him,*
>
> this has been revealed to us through the Spirit. (1 Cor 2:9–10)

1 Cor 2:9 has the quotation formula ("it is written") that Paul regularly uses to introduce quotations from the Old Testament. Although the first line resembles phrases in Isa 64:3, the rest of the quotation is nowhere to be found in the Jewish scriptures. However, the saying is remarkably similar to one in the Gospel of Thomas:

> Jesus said, "I will give you what no eye has seen, what no ear has heard, what no hand has touched, what has not arisen in the human heart." (Thomas 17)

Whether Paul is freely quoting from this gospel or whether both Paul and Thomas are quoting some undiscovered third writing is unknown.

nate two Hebrew words as likely suspects: *nazir* and *netser*. 1) A *nazir* (adopted into English as "nazirite") was someone consecrated to the service of God by a special vow.[11] The public signs of a nazirite's consecration were abstaining from

---

11. See Num 6:1–21 for the details.

alcohol and never shaving or cutting the hair. The most famous nazirite was Samson, whose strength came from his long hair, the sign of his dedication to God. 2) *Netser* means "branch" and the prophecy in question is about the Davidic king who will be the next on the throne: "A shoot will grow from the stump of Jesse,[12] and a branch (*netser*) will spring from his roots" (Isa 11:1). In Isaiah's context this coming king is probably the mysterious child earlier named Immanuel (Isa 7:14). Later Jewish interpretation applied Isa 11:1 to the future messiah. A further clue that Matthew had his eye on this verse is that the very next line in Isaiah reads, "The spirit of the Lord will rest upon him," which could easily remind Matthew of Jesus' baptism (see Matt 3:16).

If we assume that Matthew heard in "Nazorean" the echoes of "nazirite" and Isaiah's messianic Davidic "branch" (*netser*), we still are left to guess how he came up with "he will be called a Nazorean." Our only two options here are that he either made it up out of thin air or that he used some line from scripture as a model. The first option may be the right one, but before we choose it we need to explore the second. Unfortunately, the only scholarly theory that is even slightly plausible is quite complicated. It pictures Matthew moving between two alternative Greek translations of a line from the Book of Judges, using a pun that works only in Hebrew to focus on a verse in Isaiah, and taking a cue from a verse in Mark's gospel that Matthew deleted from his own.

Here's the theory, put as simply as I can explain it, in three parts.

1. In the Hebrew text of Judg 16:17 Samson says, "I am God's nazirite" (*nazir*). Different copies of the Septuagint have two very different versions of the Book of Judges. One of them simply transliterates the Hebrew word *nazir* into Greek: "I am God's *naziraios*." The other translates *nazir* by giving it a meaning: "I am God's holy man" (*hagios* in Greek). Let's assume that Matthew is aware of these alternate Greek renderings of Samson's statement.

2. Isa 4:2 reads, "On that day the branch that the Lord has grown will become glorious in its beauty." The Hebrew word for "branch" here is *tsemach*, a synonym for the *netser* of Isa 11:1. The next verse (Isa 4:3), in Greek translation, reads, "He who is left in Zion and remains in Jerusalem will be called holy" (*hagios* in Greek). Let's assume that Matthew is interested in Isa 4:3 because it follows on Isa 4:2 which mentions a branch which he associates with the other branch in Isa 11:1 and which triggers for him the pun between *netser* and *nazir*.

3. In Mark 1:24 a demon shouts out, "Jesus! What do you want with us, you Nazarene? Have you come to destroy us? I know you, who you are: God's holy man!" Note that the demon calls Jesus both "Nazarene" (*Nazarenos*) and "holy man" (*hagios*). We know that Matthew studied Mark carefully, even though he decided not to use this particular line in his own gospel.

---

12. Jesse was David's father.

Let's put these three pieces together. Matthew learns from Mark 1:24 that "God's holy man" and "Nazarene" work as paired titles for Jesus. He knows (we assume, for the sake of the argument) that "God's holy man" and "God's nazirite" are equivalent Greek translations of Judg 16:17. We further assume that the messianic *netser*-branch in Isa 11:1 raises Matthew's interest in the branch in Isa 4:2 and that reading down to the next verse he sees "he will be called holy" in 4:3. So, using Isa 4:3 as his starting point, and knowing that "nazirite" can substitute for "holy," Matthew tweaks "nazirite" (*naziraios*) into "Nazorean" (*Nazoraios*). Presto: "He will be called a Nazorean."

Is this too farfetched? You decide. In the end it matters little. Whether we imagine Matthew as devising this prediction by creatively rewriting a verse from Isaiah, or simply as fabricating it from his own imagination, the fact remains that there is no scripture predicting anything about Nazareth. Matthew obviously knew this, which is why he had to supply one himself.

Why did Matthew go to this trouble? Why did he need a non-existent prophecy about a Nazorean? It was common knowledge that Jesus was from Nazareth. Why was it so important for Matthew to "prove" this from scripture? The most likely supposition is that he was responding to Jewish arguments that used the well-known Nazareth origins of Jesus against his followers. We can surmise from John's gospel that some Jews argued that Jesus could not have been the messiah precisely because he was from Nazareth in Galilee.

Check for yourself: no prophet has ever come from Galilee. (John 7:52)

Surely the Anointed is not to come from Galilee? Doesn't Scripture teach that the Anointed is to be descended from David and come from the village of Bethlehem, where David lived? (John 7:41–42)

John is also alluding to this objection in 1:45–46, when a future disciple first hears about Jesus.

Philip finds Nathanael and tells him, "We've found the one Moses wrote about in the Law, and the prophets mention too: Jesus, Joseph's son, from Nazareth."

"From Nazareth?" Nathanael said to him. "Can anything good come from that place?"

Galilee was full of Gentiles.[13] Jews from Judea looked down on Galilean Jews with a prejudice that assumed that their religion was compromised by the influence of their pagan environment. Nazareth was an obscure place with no Davidic or messianic associations. Jews who debated with Matthew and his peo-

13. Matt 4:15 quotes Isaiah, who calls the region "pagan Galilee." See also the reference to "pagan Galilee" in 1 Maccabees 5:15.

ple undoubtedly rubbed it in: no way could Israel's messiah come from Galilee, much less from Nazareth.

One of Matthew's purposes in writing his infancy narrative was to get all this right. He designed his story of Jesus' early life, in part, to pre-empt Jewish objections to Jesus' origins. According to Matthew, Jesus had actually been born in Bethlehem, David's city. He was moved to Galilee by his (adoptive) father, an observant Jew (1:19) and descendant of David (1:16), in obedience to a dream sent by God (2:22). In between Bethlehem and Galilee Jesus had relived the Exodus and the Exile, fulfilling prophecy both times. And it was no accident that Jesus was a Nazorean. This too fulfilled prophecy.

The Moses Haggadah

The episode in Matt 2:13–16 implies that Jesus is like Moses in two ways. The first is hard to miss: the infant Jesus, like the infant Moses, providentially escapes a king's massacre of baby boys. The second is a little more subtle: God arranges for Jesus to leave Egypt. Since the primary purpose of an infancy narrative is to foreshadow the adult character of the hero, even those ancients who encountered the story of Jesus for the first time would understand from these allusions that they should expect more comparisons with Moses as Matthew went on to narrate Jesus' adult career. Matthew did not disappoint his readers, for the portrait of Jesus as a new Moses is a prominent theme in this gospel.

An ancient Jewish audience would have noticed a Moses-Jesus comparison at several places in Matthew 1–2, not just at 2:13–16. By the first century, the folklore about baby Moses had become much more elaborate than the account in the Book of Exodus. Centuries of Jewish storytelling had built the brief biblical narrative into a richly detailed drama that sharpened its theological message and emphasized Moses' heroic stature. Most religions tend to embroider the birth of their founders with legends, a tendency which expresses the conviction that the coming into the world of the founder was as significant as the message he would preach. Moses was a founder par excellence. He led Israel out of slavery. He was Israel's first and greatest prophet, as well as the mediator of its covenant with God. It was only natural for Israel to expand and embellish the story of Moses, for he was, in short, the founder of the nation. This legendary expansion is known as the Moses "Haggadah" (the Hebrew word for "narrative"). There was no one way to tell this narrative. Storytellers would imaginatively mix and match details to create distinctive

---

This chapter is largely based on "From Moses to Jesus," by John Dominic Crossan.

versions of it. Most have not survived in writing, but two that we do have from first-century Jewish authors show beyond question that Matthew drew on the Moses Haggadah in composing his infancy narrative.

Sources for the Moses Haggadah

Our two first-century sources are both contemporary with the Gospel of Matthew. The first is a creative rewrite of the narrative portions of the Hebrew Bible, a work called the *Book of Biblical Antiquities* (known to scholars by its Latin title *Liber Antiquitatum Biblicarum*). It was written probably around 75 CE by an unknown author whom we call Pseudo-Philo because he poses as the famous philosopher and biblical scholar Philo of Alexandria. The second source is the *Antiquities of the Jews* written in 94 by the Jewish historian Flavius Josephus. These two versions of the Moses Haggadah are rather different from one another, and scholars theorize that each of them selectively borrowed from a longer story that was circulating among Jewish storytellers. A third version is found in a later work, the *Book of Memory* (also known by its Hebrew title, *Sefer ha-Zikronot*). It survives only in a twelfth-century manuscript, and we do not know when it was originally composed. Nevertheless, since a few of its details about Moses are nicely parallel to details about Jesus in Matthew, some of the story recorded in the *Book of Memory* may well come from the first century.

Improving the Story

In both the Gospel of Matthew and the Book of Exodus, a wicked king's massacre of baby boys puts the infant heroes in mortal danger, and in both stories extraordinary measures are taken to save them from the general slaughter. A major difference between Matthew and Exodus is that Herod is out to kill Jesus specifically, while Pharoah has never heard of Moses. Jesus is in danger because Herod, informed by the magi, wants to eliminate a future rival. Moses is in danger because he happens to be born at the time when the Pharoah is trying to kill all the newborn Israelite boys. Apparently, Jewish storytellers were dissatisfied with this aspect of the Exodus narrative. It makes for a poor story if the newborn Moses is in danger simply out of bad luck. The Moses Haggadah remedies this weakness by putting the spotlight where it belongs: on Moses himself. In Josephus and the *Book of Memory*, Pharoah learns, either from a dream or from a prophecy, that a mighty leader has been born to the Hebrews, one who will overthrow Egyptian power. Pharoah doesn't know which Hebrew boy this is, so he orders that all of them be killed. This, of course, is precisely the plot in Matthew's story as well.

Another haggadic improvement on the Exodus story parallels a plot device in Matthew. In Pseudo-Philo and the *Book of Memory* Israelite men decide to divorce their wives rather than stay married and father sons for Pharoah to murder. In the *Book of Memory*, Amram, the father of Moses, goes along with this plan and divorces his wife. In Pseudo-Philo, Amram refuses. In Josephus, Amram's wife is already pregnant. In all three versions, God intervenes (through either a dream or a prophecy) to reassure Amram that his future son will be protected from danger and will grow up to be the savior of Israel. The story in the *Book of Memory* is especially pertinent to Matthew: reassured by the message in his dream, Amram remarries his wife Jochebed, who then conceives Moses. The parallel to Matthew is not exact: Joseph's dream directing him to complete his marriage to Mary does not come in the context of Herod's decision to kill the baby boys. Nevertheless, a combination of a dream and a prophecy overcomes Joseph's anxiety in circumstances

---

 6.1

Pharoah's Attempted Genocide

Exodus 1:6–22

[6]Then Joseph died, and all his brothers, and that whole generation. [7]But the Israelites were fruitful and prolific; they multiplied and grew exceedingly strong, so that the land was filled with them.

[8]Now a new king arose over Egypt, who did not know Joseph. [9]He said to his people, "Look, the Israelite people are more numerous and more powerful than we. [10]Come, let us deal shrewdly with them, or they will increase and, in the event of war, join our enemies and fight against us and escape from the land."

[11]Therefore they set taskmasters over them to oppress them with forced labor. They built supply cities, Pithom and Rameses, for Pharoah. [12]But the more they were oppressed, the more they multiplied and spread, so that the Egyptians came to dread the Israelites. [13]The Egyptians became ruthless in imposing tasks on the Israelites, [14]and made their lives bitter with hard service in mortar and brick and in every kind of field labor. They were ruthless in all the tasks that they imposed on them.

[15]The king of Egypt said to the Hebrew midwives, one of whom was named Shiphrah and the other Puah, [16]"When you act as midwives to the Hebrew women, and see them on the birthstool, if it is a boy, kill him; but if it is a girl, she shall live." [17]But the midwives feared God; they did not do as the king of Egypt commanded them, but they let the boys live. [18]So the king of Egypt summoned the midwives and said to them, "Why have you done this, and allowed the boys to live?" [19]The midwives said to Pharoah, "Because the Hebrew women are not like the Egyptian women; they are vigorous and give birth before the midwife comes to them." [20]So God dealt well with the midwives; and the people multiplied and became very strong. [21]And because the midwives feared God, he gave them families. [22]Then Pharoah commanded all his people, "Every boy that is born to the Hebrews you shall throw into the Nile, but you shall let every girl live."

when the fate of the woman and her son-to-be is in question—here we see Matthew borrowing elements of the Moses Haggadah and refashioning them to serve the needs of his own story.

The two expansions of the Exodus story that we have analyzed, making Moses the direct target of Pharoah's program to kill the male infants and exploring the men's anxiety over whether to continue in their marriages, show that storytellers had skillfully analyzed the Exodus story and noticed its short-comings. The Moses Haggadah contains interesting solutions to these prob-lems. These imaginative retellings of the Moses story were aimed at improving it, not only to make it more engaging as a story, but also to let its religious message come through with more clarity and power. Matthew stands in this tradition of Jewish storytelling, doing for Jesus what the Haggadah did for Moses.

More Similarities

Three more features of Matthew's story are parallel to items that the Moses Haggadah added to the Exodus story.

1. A revelation predicts that the boy to be born will grow up to be the savior of his people.

"He will save the Hebrew people
from their bondage in Egypt"
(God to Amram, Josephus 2:216).

"I will work signs through him and
save my people" (an angel to
Miriam and told to her parents,
Pseudo-Philo 9:10).

"He will save his people from
their sins" (an angel to Joseph,
Matt 1:21).

"A son will be born to my father
and mother who will save Israel
from the power of Egypt" (Miriam
prophesying after the spirit of God
descends on her, the *Book of
Memory*).

2. Information crucial to the unfolding of the story is communicated in dreams.

God tells Amram in a dream
of the future destiny of his
son-to-be (Josephus
2:212–216).

Joseph is told not to divorce Mary
(Matt 1:20–23).

Miriam, Moses' older sister, has a dream in which an angel tells her that her parents will have a boy who will save his people (Pseudo-Philo 9:10).	The magi are warned not to report to Herod (Matt 2:12).
Pharoah's daughter is prompted by a dream to bathe in the river, at just the right time and place to discover baby Moses (Pseudo-Philo 9:15).	Joseph is warned to flee with the family to Egypt (Matt 2:13).
Pharoah has a symbolic dream which is interpreted as a premonition of the birth of an Israelite who will destroy Egypt (*Book of Memory*).	Joseph is told to return to Israel (Matt 2:19). Joseph is instructed to resettle in Galilee (Matt 2:22).

Except for the dream of Pilate's wife later in the gospel (Matt 27:19), the five dreams in Matthew 1–2 are the only dreams in the New Testament gospels. In Matthew's infancy narrative, dreams direct all the decisions that affect the life of the infant Jesus. Perhaps it was the Moses Haggadah that gave Matthew the idea of using dreams as a major literary device in his narrative.[1]

3. The king learns about the future savior from religious specialists.

Pharoah learns about the imminent birth of a future savior of the Israelites from a "priest-scholar" (Josephus 2:205).[2]	Herod learns about the birth of the future king from magi (Matt 2:2–3)[3] and about the birthplace of the messiah from chief priests and scholars (2:4–6).

Escape to/from Egypt

Matthew further enhances his comparison of Jesus to Moses in his narration of Jesus' escape to Egypt and return to Israel. Three details in Matthew's story call to mind the scenes in Exodus when Moses flees from and later returns to Egypt.

---

1. The dreams in Matthew's gospel establish another connection with the story of Israel in Egypt, though the connection is indirect. Four of the five dreams in Matthew 1–2 come to Joseph, who has the same name as the man whose gift for interpreting dreams in Egypt led to saving his family from famine and thus enabled God's plan for his people to go forward.

2. The term for this official, *hierogrammateus*, combines the standard words for priest and scholar (*heiros* and *grammateus*) that occur in Matthew's story.

3. Besides the Moses Haggadah there were other types of Jewish retellings of biblical stories called targums and midrashes. In two of these works (Targum Jonathan on Ex 1:15 and Exodus Rabbah on Ex 1:22), it is magi who warn Pharoah that a Hebrew deliverer is about to be born.

1. Jesus is taken from his native land in order to save him from Herod's attempt to kill him. The young (but not infant) Moses leaves his homeland, fleeing Pharoah's effort to kill him (Ex 2:15).

2. Matthew's report of the divine message that it is safe to go home again is almost an exact quotation from Exodus.

> "for those who were seeking the life of the child are dead" (Matt 2:20)
> "for all those who were seeking your life are dead" (Ex 4:19)

Note the mismatch in Matthew's scenario here: although only Herod has died, the angel refers to the death of *those* who were out to kill Jesus. Apparently for Matthew it was more important to echo the Moses story than to keep his own plot strictly coherent.

3. Matthew's report of the return journey closely follows Exodus, though here the parallel is between Moses and Joseph.

> Joseph took his wife and his son and returned to the land of Israel (Matt 2:21).
> Moses took his wife and his sons and returned to the land of Egypt (Ex 4:20).

6.2   Baby Moses

Exodus 2:1–10

[1]Now a man from the house of Levi went and married a Levite woman. [2]The woman conceived and bore a son; and when she saw that he was a fine baby, she hid him three months. [3]When she could hide him no longer she got a papyrus basket for him, and plastered it with bitumen and pitch; she put the child in it and placed it among the reeds on the bank of the river. [4]His sister stood at a distance, to see what would happen to him.

[5]The daughter of Pharaoh came down to bathe at the river, while her attendants walked beside the river. She saw the basket among the reeds and sent her maid to bring it. [6]When she opened it, she saw the child. He was crying, and she took pity on him, "This must be one of the Hebrews' children," she said. [7]Then his sister said to Pharaoh's daughter, "Shall I go and get you a nurse from the Hebrew women to nurse the child for you?" [8]Pharaoh's daughter said to her, "Yes." So the girl went and called the child's mother. [9]Pharaoh's daughter said to her, "Take this child and nurse it for me, and I will give you your wages." So the woman took the child and nursed it. [10]When the child grew up, she brought him to Pharaoh's daughter, and she took him as her son. She named him Moses, "because," she said, "I drew him out of the water."

Moses in a Basket

The final section of the baby Moses narrative is the famous story where his mother places him in a little basket, floats him down the river, and entrusts him to the humanity of whatever stranger might accidentally discover him. Here the Moses Haggadah makes no significant elaborations and so we assume that the Jewish tradition saw no need to improve on the Exodus version. Indeed the story in Ex 2:1–10 is skillfully plotted, with two "coincidences" which signal that the hand of God is silently guiding events: Moses is found by none other than the daughter of Pharoah, and the baby ends up being nursed and raised by his natural mother.

Moses and Sargon

At this point we leave the Moses Haggadah and the Jesus-Moses comparison for a brief but interesting detour that has to do with the Exodus scene of Moses in the basket. This ancient story is an adaptation of an even more ancient one about a famous Mesopotamian king, Sargon of Akkad. Sargon's rise to imperial power was extraordinary because he was not born into a rul-

---

6.3   The Birth of Sargon

Call me Sargon. The child of a priestess and an unknown pilgrim from the mountains, I now rule a Mesopotamian empire from my capital in Agade.

Because my mother was a priestess who was supposed to offer her children as sacrifices, she did not want anyone in the city of Asupiranu to know that she had conceived and given birth to me. So she hid me along the bank of the Euphrates River, in a basket woven from rushes and waterproofed with tar.

The river carried my basket down to an irrigation canal where Akki, the royal gardener, lifted me out of the water and raised me as his own. Akki trained me to become his assistant in the royal gardens.

With the help of Ishtar, goddess of love and war, I rose to the position of king of the black-headed people in just over four years. I then campaigned in every land from the Armenian mountains west to the Mediterranean sea, from the land of Dilmun on the Persian Gulf to the port of Dor on the Mediterranean coast. Three times I marched from the Persian Gulf to the Mediterranean blazing trails through the mountains with bronze-headed axes; scaling peaks, crossing valleys, conquering ports like Dor and cities like Kazallu.

To my successors I leave this as a legacy.

Quoted from *Old Testament Parallels*, by Victor Matthews and Don Benjamin (New York: Paulist Press, 1991), pp. 55–56. Used with permission.

ing family. The only thing we know about his pedigree is that his father was a peasant. Eventually a story developed in which this child of obscure and lowly origin comes to be raised in a royal environment. The similarities between the stories of Sargon and Moses are so striking that they cannot be coincidental. Since Sargon lived twelve centuries before Moses, we can safely assume that the Akkadian king's story was widely known throughout the ancient Middle East when the Book of Exodus was taking shape.

The story of Sargon's birth is relevant to our concerns because it helps us to see an ongoing process in the art of ancient storytelling. Sargon's story is recycled and adapted in the Exodus narrative about Moses, which is in turn improved and expanded by the Moses Haggadah, which in turn is adapted by Matthew as the template for his story about baby Jesus. And it doesn't stop there. Matthew's story (like Luke's) is, in turn, the subject of much imaginative elaboration and embellishment by Christian storytellers, a tradition richly documented by the infancy gospels.

PSEUDO-PHILO
Book of Biblical Antiquities 9

[1]After Joseph passed away, the children of Israel multiplied and greatly increased. A king who had not known Joseph came to power in Egypt. He said to his people, "Look, that people has multiplied more than we have. Let us make a plan against them so they will not multiply more." And the king of Egypt ordered all his people, "Every son born to the Hebrews must be thrown into the river; but let their girls live." The Egyptians answered the king, "Let's destroy their males and keep their females to give to our slaves as wives. Their children will be slaves and will serve us." All this was evil in the eyes of the Lord.

[2]Then the elders of the people gathered them in lamentation. As they lamented, they said in their grief, "The wombs of our wives have miscarried; our offspring is handed over to our enemies. Now we are doomed. This is where we should draw the line: men should not go near their wives lest the fruit of their wombs be defiled and our offspring serve idols. For until we know what God is going to do we'd be better off dying without sons."

[3]But Amram answered them, "This age will fade away forever, or the world will collapse in catastrophe, or the heart of the abyss will touch the stars before the race of the children of Israel will fade away. . . . [4]Therefore I will no longer go along with your plan, but I will go in and take my wife and father sons so that we may increase on the earth. For God will not stay angry, nor will he forget his people forever, nor will he throw the race of Israel out helpless into the world. Not for nothing did he establish a covenant with our fathers. And God spoke of these matters before we even existed. [5]So I will go and take my wife, and I will not comply with the king's command. If this seems right to you, let's all do the same. . . . [6]And when the time of child-

birth comes, if we can possibly avoid it, we will not throw out the fruit of our womb. And who knows? Perhaps this will provoke God to free us from our humiliation."

[7]And God was pleased with the plan that Amram devised. . . .

[9]And Amram from the tribe of Levi went out and married a wife from his own tribe. When he had taken her, others followed his example and took their own wives. And this man had one son and one daughter, Aaron and Miriam. [10]The spirit of God descended on Miriam one night and she had a dream. She reported it to her parents the next morning, saying, "Last night I had a vision. A man dressed in linen stood there and told me, 'Go and tell your parents, "Look, your next son will be thrown into the water, just as through him the water will be dried up. I will work signs through him and save my people, and he will always be their leader."'" But when Miriam reported her dream, her parents did not believe her.

[11]Meanwhile, the plan of the king of Egypt intensified against the children of Israel, and they were ground down by being forced to make more bricks. [12]Now Jochebed conceived by Amram and concealed the child in her womb for three months. She could not keep him secret any longer, because the king of Egypt appointed officials who, when the Hebrew women gave birth, would immediately throw their boys into the river. So she took her infant and made him a basket out of pine bark and put it on the bank of the river. [13](Now that boy was born in the covenant of God and the covenant of the flesh.) [14]When they had abandoned him, all the elders got together and argued with Amram, saying, "Didn't we say, 'We'd be better off dying without sons than have the fruit of our womb thrown in the water'?" But Amram ignored them.

[15]Now Pharoah's daughter, acting on what she had seen in her dreams, came down to bathe in the river. Her maids saw the basket, so she sent one to fetch it and open it. When she looked at the boy and saw the covenant (that is, the covenant of the flesh), she said, "This is one of the Hebrew children." [16]And she took him home and nursed him. He became her own son and she named him Moses. . . . And the child was nursed and became more glorious than any other man, and through him God freed the children of Israel, just as he had said.

———— ∂ಞಌ ————

10 *through him the water will be dried up.* The author makes a clever connection between Moses' being saved from the water as a baby and his later splitting of the sea as the leader of the people.

11 *Being forced to make more bricks* refers to the slave labor imposed on the Israelites (see Ex 5:6–19). The author assumes that his audience is familiar with the biblical story. ·

12 *Concealed the child in her womb for three months* is confusing. In the biblical story, as well as in Josephus' version of the Haggadah, Jochebed hides Moses for three months after he is born (Ex 2:2 and Josephus 2:218).

She could not keep him secret any longer. This makes sense in its context in Exodus, but here it is puzzling, since the narrative jumps abruptly from Jochebed's third month of pregnancy to her efforts to save the life of her newborn.

13 The *covenant of the flesh* is circumcision. The author thus claims that Moses was born circumcised.

15 The Bible does not tell how Pharaoh's daughter knew that the baby was Hebrew. Pseudo-Philo explains that she deduced this from his circumcision. The author seems not to know that Egyptians also circumcised their baby boys.

JOSEPHUS
Antiquities of the Jews, Book 2

[205]One of the Egyptian priest-scholars—people who can predict the future with great accuracy—announced to the king that there would soon be born among the Israelites someone who, if he reached adulthood, would bring down the dominance of the Egyptians and build up the Israelites, and would surpass everyone in virtue and win everlasting fame. [206]The king was alarmed at this news, and on the advice of the scholar, ordered that every newborn Israelite boy should be done away with by being drowned in the river. He also ordered that pregnant Hebrew women should be watched when they went into labor, and that the Egyptian midwives should watch out for their deliveries. [207]The king insisted that this assignment be given to women who were loyal to him and therefore unlikely to disobey his will. He also ordered that parents who defied this decree and dared secretly to save their children would be executed along with their offspring.

[208]This put the victims in a terrible situation. Not only were they going to be deprived of their children, but the parents themselves were expected to participate in the destruction of their own offspring. This plan to eliminate their race by slaughtering the babies and the thought of their own imminent extermination made their circumstances cruel and hopeless. [209]They were in a miserable situation. But no one can defeat the will of God, no matter how many plans he may devise with that in mind. For this child, the one the priest-scholar had foretold, did grow up, escaping the king's surveillance. Everything that was said about what he would accomplish turned out to be true. This is how it happened.

[210]Amram, a Hebrew of noble birth, feared that the whole race would disappear because there would be no new generation. He was seriously anxious about his own situation because his wife was pregnant. [211]In his desperation he prayed to God, begging him finally to have compassion on those who had in no way transgressed in worshiping him, and to rescue them from their present distress and from the prospect of their extermination as a people. [212]God had mercy on him and, moved by his petition, appeared to him in his sleep and told him not to despair about the future. . . . [215]He said, "This child, whose birth so terrifies the Egyptians that they have decided to destroy all the offspring of the Israelites, will be yours. He will escape those

who are standing by to kill him. [216]After an amazing childhood he will save the Hebrew people from their bondage in Egypt, and be remembered as long as the universe exists, by Hebrews and foreigners alike."

[217]Amram woke up and told his wife Jochabel what had been revealed to him in his vision. But the prediction in the dream only increased their fear, for they were anxious not only about their child, but about the great happiness that was his destiny. [218]However, the way the woman's delivery went confirmed their trust in God's promises, for she escaped surveillance because her labor was mild and she was not beset by violent pains. For three months they raised the child in secret. [219]Amram grew afraid that he would be detected and that the king's wrath would come down on him, in which case he would perish along with the baby and thus undermine God's promise. So he decided to turn over the child's safety and protection to God, rather than run the risk of trying to hide him and thus endangering not only the child who was being raised in secret, but also himself. [220]He was certain that God would guarantee that nothing he had promised would turn out false. Having made this decision, they got some papyrus reeds and wove a basket shaped like a cradle, big enough to give the infant plenty of sleeping room. [221]They coated it with pitch, which prevents water from leaking through the wicker. Then they put the baby inside and set it adrift on the river, entrusting his safety to God. The river carried along what it received while Miriam, the boy's sister, at her mother's urging, kept pace with it along the bank to see where the basket would end up.

——— ❧❧❧ ———

206 *Egyptian midwives.* In the Bible the midwives are Hebrew (Ex 1:5). The Haggadah, or Josephus—whoever altered this detail—saw that it makes more sense for Egyptians to be assigned to kill the Hebrew newborns, as the next sentence (207) explains.

216 *amazing childhood.* See the descriptions of Moses in Box 3.4, p. 69.

217 *Jochabel.* In the Bible the name of Moses' mother is Jochebed (Ex 6:20). The spelling of her name here is probably the result of a copyist's error. The Greek equivalent of D (Δ) can easily be mistaken for that of L (Λ).

218 The story implies that God enabled Jochabel to *escape surveillance* by granting her a mild labor, which helped her keep quiet during that time of maximum danger.

ANONYMOUS
The Book of Memory (excerpt)
In the 130th year after Israel went down to Egypt, Pharoah dreamed that he was sitting on the throne of his kingdom. He looked up an saw an old man standing before him holding a balance like those used by merchants. The old man took hold of the scales and held them up before Pharoah. Then he took all the elders of Egypt, her princes, and her nobles and put them on

one scale of the balance. After that he took a tender lamb and put it on the second scale. The lamb outweighed them all. Then Pharoah wondered at this amazing sight, how the lamb outweighed them all. Pharoah woke up and realized it was only a dream. Next morning, Pharoah got up, summoned all his courtiers, and narrated his dream. They were all extremely frightened. Then one of the royal princes answered, "This can only mean that a great disaster will come on Egypt at the end of days." "And what is that?" the king asked the eunuch. So the eunuch replied to the king, "A child will be born in Israel who will destroy the whole land of Egypt. If it pleases the king, let a royal statute be written here and distributed throughout the land of Egypt to kill every newborn male of the Hebrews so that the disaster will be averted from the land of Egypt." The king did so and sent for the midwives of the Hebrews. . . .

When the Israelites heard Pharoah's decree that their male children be thrown into the river, some of the men divorced their wives but the rest stayed married to them . . . .

There was a man of the tribe of Levi in the land of Egypt whose name was Amram, son of Qahat, son of Levi, son of Jacob. This man married Jochebed, a daughter of Levi and his own aunt, and the woman conceived and gave birth to a daughter and called her Miriam . . .

One day the Spirit of God descended on Miriam and she prophesied in the center of the house saying, "Behold, a son will be born to my father and my mother at this time who will save Israel from the power of Egypt." When Amram heard the words of the child he remarried his wife whom he had divorced after the decree of Pharoah ordering the destruction of every male of the house of Jacob. He slept with her and she conceived by him. Six months later she gave birth to a son and the house was filled with brightness like that of the sun and moon at their rising.

HELLENISTIC INFANCY NARRATIVES

Matthew and Luke were influenced in various ways by certain Old Testament stories about the births and infancies of Israelite heroes. But there are other ancient birth stories that can help us to understand the ones in the gospels. These come from the biographies of ancient hellenistic heroes, great men who achieved unusual excellence, whether as conquerors, kings, athletes, philosophers, or holy men. Accounts of their births and childhoods are integral features of their biographies.

Ancient biographies were shaped by two beliefs that were universally held and taken for granted. The first was that the extraordinary accomplishments of heroes so surpass the achievements of ordinary people that these figures cannot be merely human. Greatness on such a scale has to have a divine quality about it. The second belief was that human life is determined by Fate. Wherever one's life leads, the path was laid out all along, even if it can be seen only in hindsight. This means that the greatness of heroes is no accident. A great man had been destined for greatness from his birth.

These two beliefs come through in two claims that are standard features of hellenistic biographies: 1) the hero is the son of a god; 2) the greatness of the hero can be seen early in his life.

1. The ancient perception that there was something divine at work in the extraordinary life of a hero could be expressed in more than one way. For example, it could be supposed that the gods had bestowed supernatural abilities on the hero. However, biographies nearly always explain the divine element in a hero's life otherwise: heroes live these extraordinary lives because

---

The selection of texts in this chapter is indebted to that of David Cartlidge and David Dungan in *Documents for the Study of the Gospels*, pp. 129–136. Much of the information about the ancient authors and subjects of these stories comes from the *Oxford Classical Dictionary*.

they are the sons of gods. While ancient people understood this belief in different ways, the biographies express it in story form: these heroes were physically fathered by gods. They had divine fathers and human mothers. (There were a very few heroes who had divine mothers and human fathers. For example, Aeneas, the mythical founder of Rome, was the son of the Trojan prince Anchises and the goddess Venus. See the Appendix).

2. An essential function of ancient biographies is to tell how the greatness for which a hero is famous was revealed early in his life. This is expressed in two ways. First, there may be omens or portents at the child's birth, highly unusual or miraculous events that announce the arrival of a god's son. Second, the deeds of the child show the kind of greatness for which he is destined. The significance of these deeds is usually not appreciated by other characters in the story, but readers, who already know what the hero is famous for, can see the destiny of the man revealed in the boy.

Hellenistic biographies move rapidly from the hero's miraculous birth to the account of his adult life. The gap between birth and adulthood was often spanned by a single event from childhood. These childhood stories have the same function in every biography: presaging the specific kind of greatness the hero will achieve. The purpose of ancient biographies was not to tell the full story of a life but rather to describe the person's character. For this, one childhood story was usually sufficient.

People in the ancient world believed that heroes were the sons of gods because of the extraordinary qualities of their adult lives, not because there was public information about the intimate details of how their mothers became pregnant. In fact, in some biographies the god takes on the physical form of the woman's husband in order to have sex with her. This plot device is a transparent admission that there was no information, not even any rumors, about an unusual conception. Stories like these allow a god to physically father a child without the woman's realizing that a deity was involved or even suspecting that anything unusual occurred. This indicates that stories about divine paternity were purely interpretive, not informational. They were not based on knowledge about heroes' biological origins. They were created to account for the "superhuman" achievements of extraordinary men. Needless to say, such stories could emerge only after the heroic quality of their lives had become apparent.

This has one implication that is crucial for our understanding of ancient infancy narratives, whether Christian or pagan: ancient readers, before they even opened the biography of a hero, could expect to find a story about his divine begetting. When they read the gospels of Matthew and Luke, they found just what they assumed they would, modified of course in accordance with Jewish sensibilities. Ancient readers might be puzzled by Mark's gospel because it lacks an infancy narrative. Still, Mark's first sentence announces that Jesus was "the son of God," which would make readers feel they were in familiar biographical territory. As for the Gospel of John, although readers would notice the absence of a birth story, they would understand John's intention in proclaiming that Jesus was the divine Logos come to earth.

Along with some story about how the hero was fathered by a god, ancient biographies drew on three other narrative elements to reinforce the hero's divine paternity. These elements supplemented the central theme and so were not necessary to the formula, but most biographies with infancy narratives featured one or more of the three. The first, found at the beginning of some infancy narratives, is a genealogy. These tend to be brief—no other ancient genealogy even comes close to the length of those in the gospels—and typically trace the family lineage back to some deity. (Occasionally the god who is the ancestor of the family is also the father of the hero.) The second element is an account of a message from a god, or a dream or vision, in which one or both parents learn about the divine nature of their future son. The third element, already mentioned above, is a description of supernatural signs that herald the birth and sometimes symbolize the heroic character of the child. In some biographies seers can discern the general meaning of these signs, but of course their full significance can be appreciated only by the readers, who have the benefit of hindsight.

Following the infancy narrative, readers would also expect to find a report from the hero's childhood, usually about some precocious achievement of the boy that points to his future career.

Comparisons with the Gospels

Luke and Matthew, each in his own way, made use of these elements of hellenistic biographies in telling their stories about Jesus. Both gospels express the universal Christian belief that Jesus was God's son, though two differences between them should be noted. First, this theme is much more important to Luke's infancy narrative that it is to Matthew's. Second, Matthew's understanding of divine sonship is more deeply rooted in Jewish tradition than is Luke's, which is more grounded in hellenistic ideas.

Both gospels include lengthy genealogies of Jesus, though Luke's is not integrated into his infancy narrative. Both gospels narrate angelic messages that reveal Jesus' coming birth: Luke tells of Mary's vision, Matthew of Joseph's dream. Finally, both gospels report celestial signs announcing the birth. In Matthew, a miraculous moving star guides magi to Jesus; in Luke, a glorious radiance in the night sky and a chorus of angels bring the good news to shepherds.

The last element in a hellenistic infancy narrative, a childhood incident illustrating the boy's precociousness, shows up in Luke's story about Jesus' impressing the teachers in the temple. No such story is found in Matthew, who was less influenced by hellenistic literature than Luke was.

THEAGENES: OLYMPIC CHAMPION

This very brief account of the life of Theagenes lacks most of the standard elements of hellenistic biographies. Nevertheless, it is instructive for two reasons. First, it shows how extraordinary excellence in any field could be attributed to divine paternity. Theagenes was not a philosopher, conqueror, emperor, or holy man. He was an athlete, surely one of the greatest of the ancient world. He is reported to have won 1,400 career gold medals in competition at the Olympic games. Second, this story shows how easily a hero cold be "promoted" to divinity. Theagenes' only accomplishments were athletic. Nothing in his biography hints that he was extraordinary in any way we might consider religious. He left no teaching, was not known for his ethical example, worked no miracles, had no disciples, and died an ordinary death. Yet after his passing he was widely honored as a god and revered for curing diseases.

This story of the life of Theagenes is a tiny section in the sprawling *Description of Greece* by Pausanius, a traveller and geographer from the mid-second century CE.

PAUSANIUS
Description of Greece, Elis II.11.2–9

[2]The Thasians say that Theagenes was not the son of Timosthenes, who was a priest of Herakles. They say that Herakles appeared to the mother of Theagenes looking like her husband and had intercourse with her. They also say that one day, when he was eight years old, he was on his way home from school when he was attracted by a bronze statue of some god or other in the marketplace. He picked up the statue, put it on his shoulders, and carried it home. [3]The citizens were enraged at what he had done, but one of them, a respected man of advanced years, urged them not to kill the boy, and ordered him to carry the statue from his home back to the marketplace. He did this, and instantly became famous for his strength. His feat caused an uproar all throughout Greece.

The biography next goes on to summarize Theagenes' amazing athletic accomplishments, especially at the Olympic games. It concludes thus:

[5]The total number of gold medals that he won was one thousand four hundred.

The rest of the biography goes beyond the topic of infancy narratives, but is included here because it is so interesting.

[6]When he departed this life, a man who had been one of his enemies visited the statue of Theagenes every night and whipped the bronze as if he were abusing Theagenes himself. The statue put an end to this outrage by falling on him, but the sons of the dead man filed charges against the statue for murder. So the Thasians dumped the statue into the sea, in compliance with the ruling of Draco, the jurist who had codified the Athenian laws dealing with homicide and had prescribed the sentence of exile even for inanimate objects, if one of them should fall and kill a man.

[7]Now there came a time when the earth yielded no crops for the Thasians. They sent delegates to Delphi to find out why and the god instructed them to allow their exiles to return home. They followed this instruction and allowed their exiles to return, but this did not put a stop to the famine. So they went back to the Pythian priestess, saying that although they had obeyed her instructions, the wrath of the gods still hung over them. [8]The Pythian priestess then replied, "But you have forgotten your great Theagenes."

They say that when the Thasians could not come up with a device for retrieving the statue of Theagenes, some fishermen put out to sea to fish, caught the statue in their net, and hauled it back to land. The Thasians set it up in its original position, and it became their custom to offer sacrifice to him just as if he were a god. [9]I know of many other places, both among Greeks and among barbarians, where they have set up statues of Theagenes, and he cures diseases and is honored by the local people.

—————— ∽◦∾ ——————

2 *Thasia* was Theagenes' home town.

There was nothing unusual about Theagenes' birth. There is no story, for example, about his mother or father receiving a dream or vision of a god. Nor were there any omens at his birth. For all anyone knew, Theagenes' father was Timosthenes, a priest of the deified Herakles (see p. 152). It was only in view of his adult achievements that people figured that Theagenes must have been fathered by a god. Evidently, however, there was no story in circulation about Theagenes' miraculous conception. The best his fans could come up with is that Herakles had appeared in the form of Timosthenes and impregnated Theagenes' mother. Neither Timosthenes nor his wife had any reason to suspect that a god was involved.

The one childhood story about Theagenes signifies the kind of greatness he will achieve as a man. Even a small bronze statue weighs hundreds of pounds. This one weighed enough to make the boy famous for his strength all throughout Greece.

6 *Draco*'s strict code of laws was notorious for the harshness of the punishments it prescribed, a memory that lives on in the English word "draconian."

7 The oracle at *Delphi* gave answers from Apollo to questions brought by pilgrims seeking divine guidance. Here the oracle indicates that the Thasian crop failure is due to divine displeasure at their having banished someone favored by the gods.

The *Pythian priestess* was the one through whom Apollo spoke at Delphi.

8 Theagenes' statue is recovered miraculously, i.e., "by coincidence."

ALEXANDER THE GREAT: CONQUEROR

Alexander of Macedonia, known to history as Alexander the Great, was the most renowned military leader of the ancient world. He inherited the throne from his father Philip and went on to conquer an empire that stretched from Greece to Egypt to India. He died in 323 BCE at the age of thirty-three.

Plutarch was an Athenian who held office in the Roman empire. His writings include numerous philosophical works, especially in ethics, and over fifty biographies, which he wrote in the early second century CE.

PLUTARCH
Life of Alexander, 2.1–6; 3.1–9

2.1Alexander was a descendant of Herakles through Caranus on his father's side; on his mother's side he was a descendant of Aeacus through Neoptolemus. Everyone believes this to be the case. 2.2They say that his father Philip was initiated into the mysteries at Samothrace with his mother Olympias. At that time Philip was still young and Olympias was an orphan. He fell in love with her and married her, with the consent of her brother Arybbas.

2.3Now prior to the night they were to be united as husband and wife in the bridal suite, the bride had a dream. There was a peal of thunder and a bolt of lightning struck her womb. The lightning touched off a big fire, which broke into flames that danced about until they died out. 2.4Some time later, after they were married, Philip dreamed that he put a seal on his wife's womb, a seal that he thought bore the image of a lion. 2.5Some seers became suspicious as a result of this dream and thought Philip should keep a closer watch on his wife. Another seer, Aristander of Telmessus, said that Olympias was pregnant, since no one puts a seal on something that is empty, and that the son to be born would be courageous and lion-like.

2.6On another occasion, a snake appeared stretched out at Olympias' side while she slept. They say this greatly dampened Philip's desire and enthusiasm for his wife. He no longer slept with her as frequently, either because he was afraid she might cast a spell or work some magic on him, or because he thought she had mated with a higher being. . . .

3.1After his vision, Philip sent Chairon of Megalopolis to Delphi to learn its meaning. Chairon returned with an oracle from Apollo, who instructed him to sacrifice to Zeus-Ammon and to hold that god in special reverence. 3.2Chairon also told Philip that he was to lose one of his eyes—the eye he used to spy on the god through a crack in the door, the god who had slept with his wife in the form of a snake.

^{3.3}Eratosthenes tells us that Olympias, when she sent Alexander off to war, revealed to him the secret of his conception and instructed him to aim only for things worthy of his birth. ^{3.4}But others claim that she denied the whole thing and said, "Alexander should stop spreading rumors about me to Hera."

^{3.5}Alexander was born early in the month of Hecatombaeon, the Macedonian name of which is Loüs, on the sixth of the month, the same day the temple of Artemis in Ephesus burned to the ground. . . . ^{3.6}Hegesias the Magnesian said of this coincidence, "It's no wonder the temple of Artemis burned down—the goddess was too busy bringing Alexander into the world." ^{3.7}But all the magi who were in Ephesus at the time interpreted the temple disaster as a portent of further calamities. They went around punching themselves in the face and shouting that Asia's ruin and great misfortune had been set in motion that very day. ^{3.8}In contrast, Philip, who had just conquered Potidea, received three messages at the same time: the first was that Parmenio had defeated the Illyrians in a great battle; the second was that his racehorse had won a victory at the Olympic games; and the third was that Alexander had been born. ^{3.9}He was delighted with the news, and the seers gave him more to cheer about by declaring that the son whose birth coincided with three victories would be unconquerable.

2.3 Olympias' dream.

The *bolt of lightning* was a symbol of Zeus, the supreme God of the Greek pantheon. Her dream means that Zeus will impregnate her and that her child will have Zeus-like qualities.

2.5 Philip's dream.

Philip consulted seers and received two different interpretations of his dream.

2.6 *a snake appeared.* The term *appeared* is the word used to describe appearances of supernatural beings. Philip takes the *snake* to be a manifestation of a god. In the ancient Mediterranean world the snake was a symbol of immortality because it periodically shed its skin and so seemed never to grow old or die. (One remnant of this symbolism in our own culture is the caduceus, a depiction of two snakes entwined on a winged staff, the ancient insignia of the medical profession still in use today.) Since the gods were immortal, snakes were sometimes believed to represent the physical presence of a deity.

3.3–4 Plutarch reports two contradictory accounts of the origin of the popular belief that Alexander was the son of Zeus. In the first, it is Alexander's mother who tells him the *secret of his conception.* In the second, she denies ever having said this, for fear of provoking the jealousy of the goddess Hera, wife of Zeus. His numerous extramarital affairs, her fearsome jealousy, and her hostility toward his illegitimate children are recurrent themes in Greek mythology. The second story is revealing. It shows that Alexander was himself claiming to be fathered by Zeus and that this was believed despite the fact that Olympias herself denied the story.

3.5–7 Omens at Alexander's birth.

The temple of Artemis at Ephesus burns down. At the time this was interpreted as a portent of future disaster, which, as ancient readers knew, turned out to be Alexander's conquest of Ephesus. (Ephesus was in *Asia*, the ancient name for what is now called Turkey.) Later, an astrologer attributed the fire to the fact that Artemis was so involved (somehow) in assisting at the birth of Alexander that she neglected to look after her own temple.

3.8–9 On the day of Alexander's birth, his father had three victories: his own conquest of Potidea, another military victory by his general Parmenio, and an Olympic gold medal won by his horse.

AUGUSTUS CAESAR: EMPEROR

Augustus was born Gaius Octavius in 63 BCE. His father, also named Octavius, died when the future emperor was four. Julius Caesar, his mother's uncle, eventually adopted young Octavius and made him his heir. Caesar was assassinated in 44 BCE and officially deified in 42, after which Octavius was known as *divi filius* (son of God). Although Caesar had designated him his successor, Octavius had to fight long and hard with other generals for power. Those civil wars ended with his victory in Egypt over the forces of Antony and Cleopatra in 31 BCE. The Senate bestowed the title *Augustus* (meaning "the sanctified one".) on Octavius in 27. He acquired absolute power over Rome and its empire in 24 BCE. Augustus figures in Christian history because Jesus was born during his reign. The Gospel of Luke (mistakenly) reports that Augustus ordered an empire-wide census, during which Jesus was born in Bethlehem. Augustus died in 14 CE.

Selections from two biographies of Augustus are included here. These two infancy narratives of the emperor show the kind of diversity often seen in the New Testament gospels: they have different versions of the same events; they are of very different lengths; and the longer one reports events not found in the shorter one.

The first selection is from a biography written in Greek by Dio Cassius, a senator who held high office in Rome. He worked on his *History of Rome* for over twenty years, completing it around 240 CE. The second selection, more than twice as long as the first, is from *The Twelve Caesars*. This work was written in Latin and published in 121 CE by Suetonius, a Roman historian who wrote over one hundred biographies.

DIO CASSIUS
History of Rome, 45 1.2–2.4

[1.2]Attia (the mother of Augustus) emphatically asserted that her child had been fathered by Apollo. She said that once, while she was sleeping in his temple, she thought she had intercourse with a snake, and that because of this she had given birth at the end of her term. [1.3]Before her child came to the light of day, she dreamed that her womb was lifted to the heavens and spread out over all the earth. That same night her husband Octavius thought that the sun rose from between her thighs.

Shortly after the boy was born, Nigidius Figulus, a senator, immediately prophesied that the child would attain absolute power. [1.4]This man was unrivaled at discerning the order of the celestial sphere and the differences among the stars, what they accomplish when on their own and when together, by their conjunctions and by their intervals; because of this he had been accused of practicing some forbidden craft. [1.5]On the day the baby was born, Nigidius ran into Octavius, who was late getting to the Senate, which was meeting that day. When Nigidius asked him why he was late and learned the cause, he shouted, "You have fathered a master over us." Octavius was alarmed at this and wanted to destroy the infant, but Nigidius restrained him, saying that it was impossible for it to suffer any such fate.

[2.1]While the child was being raised in the country, an eagle once snatched a loaf of bread from his hands, soared off, and then flew down and gave it back to him. Later, when he was still a boy and was staying in Rome, [2.2]Cicero dreamed that the child had been lowered from the sky to the Capitol on golden chains and had been given a whip by Jupiter. He did not know who the boy was, but when he met him the next day on the Capitol, he recognized him and told the vision to the people who were there. [2.3]Catulus, who had never seen Octavius either, thought in his sleep that all the boys from the nobility had marched in a solemn procession to Jupiter on the Capitol and that during this ceremony the god threw what seemed to be an image of the goddess Roma into that boy's lap. This frightened him, so he went up to the Capitol to pray to the god, where he found Octavius, who had come there for some reason or other. [2.4]He realized that Ocatvius looked like the boy in his dream and convinced himself of the truth of the vision.

1.2 Because of their associations with immortality and thus with the gods, *snakes* were welcome in some temples and it was considered good luck to encounter one there.

while sleeping in the temple. People sometimes slept in temples in the hope of being visited by the temple deity in a dream or nocturnal vision.

She thought she had intercourse with a snake. That *she thought* this had happened means that this was how she interpreted her dream. She takes the snake to be a manifestation of Apollo.

1.3 Both parents have dreams that symbolize the worldwide authority of the boy who is still in his mother's womb.

1.4–5 *Nigidius*, a senator and the most competent astrologer of the time–his predictions were so accurate that he had been accused of witchcraft–prophesies that the newborn boy will become a king. The story implies that Nigidius had observed some astrological indications that a ruler had been born.

Roman aristocrats jealously guarded their political power. The Romans designed their system of government to ensure that long-term power could not be concentrated into the hands of one man. Senators would therefore be very concerned over supernatural signs that might indicate the coming of a future king. This explains why Octavius would think of killing his newborn son when he heard Nigidius' prophecy. Nigidius intervenes to save the child. The similarities to Matthew's infancy narrative are striking.

• Astrologers discover that a future king has been born.
• Those who fear his future rule want to kill him.
• The astrologers take steps to avert the threat to the baby.

2.1 The *eagle* symbolized Roman power. This event is an omen that Rome will submit to Augustus.

2.2 Cicero's dream signifies that Augustus will receive authority over Rome from Jupiter, Rome's supreme God (the Roman equivalent to the Greek Zeus).

2.3–4 Catulus' dream has the same meaning as Cicero's.

SUETONIUS
The Twelve Caesars, Augustus 94:1–11

[1]This seems to be the right place to describe the omens that occurred before Augustus was born, on the day of his birth, and afterwards. From these one could foretell his future greatness and continual good fortune.

[2]A long time ago, a part of the city wall of Velitrae was struck by lightning, and this was interpreted to mean that a citizen of that town would one day rule the world. The people of Velitrae were so confident in this prediction that they immediately went to war against the people of Rome and kept fighting until they themselves were nearly wiped out. This proved, a long time later, that the omen had foretold the reign of Augustus.

[3]According to Julius Marathus, a few months before Augustus was born, a public portent was observed in Rome, which warned the people that Nature was about to give birth to their king. The Senate was so alarmed at this that they issued a decree prohibiting the raising of any boy born that year. However, senators who had pregnant wives saw to it that the decree was not filed in the treasury, since each of them hoped the prophecy was about his own son.

[4a]I found the following story in the book of Asclepias of Mendes called *Theologumena.* Atia attended a solemn service of Apollo in the middle of the night. She had her litter set down in the temple and fell asleep, as did the other married women. A snake crawled up to her and left a little while later. When she woke up, she purified herself as if she had slept with her husband. A snake-colored mark immediately appeared on her body. She could never get rid of it and so stopped going to the public baths. When Augustus was born nine months later he was therefore considered to be the son of Apollo.

[4b]Atia herself, before she gave birth to him, dreamed that her womb was carried up to the stars and spread over all lands and seas. His father Octavius dreamed that the sun rose from Atia's womb.

5aOn the day he was born the Senate was debating the conspiracy of Catiline. Octavius arrived late because of his wife's childbirth. Everyone knows that when Nigidius Figulus learned the reason for his tardiness and the hour of the birth, he declared that the ruler of the world had been born.

5bLater, when Octavius was leading an army through the remote parts of Thrace, he consulted the priests in the grove of Father Liber about his son. After performing foreign rituals they made the same prediction, because when the wine was poured on the altar a pillar of flame shot up so high over the roof of the temple that it touched the sky. A portent like that had never happened except when Alexander the Great had offered a sacrifice at the same altar.

6aThe next night Octavius dreamed that his son appeared in superhuman splendor, with the lightning bolt, scepter, and insignia of Jupiter Greatest and Best, wearing a solar crown and riding in a laurel-wreathed chariot pulled by twelve dazzling white horses.

6bAccording to Gaius Drusus, when Augustus was an infant, one evening his nurse put him in his cradle on the ground floor. The next morning he had disappeared. After a long search he was found lying at the top of a very high tower with his face towards the rising sun.

7aOnce, when he was just starting to talk, the frogs at his grandfather's country home were making a big racket and he told them to be quiet. They say that no frog has ever croaked there since.

7bOnce, when he was having lunch in a grove at the fourth milestone on the Campanian road, an eagle surprised him and snatched the bread right out of his hand. It flew to a great height and surprised him even more by gliding down again and giving it back to him.

8aAfter Quintus Catulus had dedicated the Capitol, he had dreams two nights in a row. The first night he dreamed that Jupiter Greatest and Best called aside one of the boys of the noble families who were playing near his altar and slipped an image of the goddess Roma into the folds of his toga. The next night he dreamed that he saw this same boy sitting in the lap of Jupiter of the Capitol. When he tried to have him removed, the god warned him off because the boy was being raised to be the savior of his country. The next day Catulus met Augustus, whom he had never seen before. He was quite surprised and said that he looked just like the boy in his dream.

8bThere is another version of Catulus' first dream. A crowd of children from noble families were asking Jupiter for a guardian. He pointed to one of them and told them to ask him for whatever they needed. Then he put his fingers on his own lips and lightly touched them to the boy's mouth.

9Once, when Cicero was escorting Julius Caesar to the Capitol, he told his friends his dream from the night before: a boy of noble appearance was let down from heaven on a golden chain, stood at the door of the temple, and was given a whip by Jupiter. Just then Cicero caught sight of Augustus, who had been brought to the ceremony by his uncle Caesar but who was still unknown to most of the people there. Cicero claimed that the boy was the very one who had appeared in his dream.

[10]When Augustus was celebrating his coming of age, his senatorial gown split down the seams and fell at his feet. Some interpreted this as a sure sign that the Order of Senators signified by this gown would one day be made subject to him.

[11]Once, when the Deified Julius was cutting down some woods at Munda to clear a site for his camp, he noticed a palm tree and ordered it to be spared as an omen of victory. The tree then suddenly put out a new shoot. In a few days it had grown so tall that it overshadowed the parent tree. What was more, many doves began nesting in the fronds, despite the fact that doves dislike hard and rough foliage. They say that it was that omen in particular that led Caesar to choose his sister's grandson, and no one else, to succeed him.

---

1 *This seems to be the right place.* Suetonius puts this infancy narrative towards the end of Augustus' biography, as the 94th chapter out of 101. This positioning shows that Suetonius figured that the significance of the portents and dreams he reports here could best be appreciated in hindsight, after the narration of Augustus' adult accomplishments.

2 *Velitrae* was Augustus' home town. The Velitraeans interpret the omen correctly, but misunderstand to whom it refers, with disastrous consequences. Note how long it took—several centuries—for the precise meaning of the omen to become apparent. This story is a particularly vivid example of how the true significance of omens can be fully understood only in hindsight.

3 *prohibiting the raising of any boy born that year.* Since the Roman Senate strongly opposed being ruled by a king, they tried to pre-empt the fulfillment of the portent by ensuring that no boys born that year would grow up to become rulers. The Latin *educare* can mean either "to raise" or "to educate," so it is not clear whether the Senate was prohibiting these boys from being trained for public life or was ordering that they be exposed and left to die.

A decree that *was not filed in the treasury* did not become law. In this way senators with pregnant wives took political steps to defeat this measure.

4a *She purified herself as if she had slept with her husband.* Ancient religions required those who went to temples to be in a state of ritual purity. This included bathing after sexual activity. Atia thus behaves as if her visitation by the snake (in a dream?) had been a sexual encounter with the god.

4b These two dreams of Augustus' future authority are also reported by Dio Cassius (1.3).

5a–6a Augustus' destiny as ruler of a worldwide empire is foretold by prophecy (through the astrologer Nigidius in 5a), by a ritual portent (5b), and in a symbolic dream (6a).

6b This incident symbolizes his exalted destiny: literally, he will have a lofty position and will tower over everyone else.

7a This infancy story portends his future authority: even nature obeys him.

7b See comment on Dio Cassius 2.1 (p. 142).

8a The goddess *Roma* was the divine personification of the Roman state.

Catulus has two dreams with the same meaning. The first one is also reported by Dio Cassius (2.3), though with slightly different details.

8b Suetonius reports a second version of Catulus' first dream; each has the same meaning.

9 Cicero's dream is also reported by Dio Cassius (2.2).

10 *senatorial gown*. Roman senators wore a toga with a purple stripe to designate their status.

11 *his sister's grandson*. Augustus was the son of Julius Caesar's niece.

PLATO: PHILOSOPHER

Plato was a student of Socrates and became the most influential philosopher of the ancient world. He wrote some twenty-five books, all in dialogue form, on a broad range of philosophical topics, especially cosmology, epistemology, metaphysics, political philosophy, and ethics. Plato's philosophy promotes a purely spiritual notion of God and insists on the supreme importance of living according to reason, justice, and other spiritual values. Plato founded a philosophical college in Athens known as the *Academy* (the source of our word "academics"), which flourished intermittently until it was shut down by the Christian emperor Justinian in 529 CE. Plato died in 347 BCE.

Nothing is known about Diogenes Laertius except that he lived in the first half of the third century CE and that he wrote a compendium of ancient philosophies along with short biographies of the men who developed them. His *Lives of Eminent Philosophers* is the source of most of our biographical information about ancient philosophers.

DIOGENES LAERTIUS
Lives of Eminent Philosophers, 3.1–3, 45

[1]Plato was the son of Ariston and Perictione (or Potone) and a citizen of Athens. His mother traced her lineage back to Solon. Solon had a brother, Dropides, who was the father of Critias. Critias was the father of Callaeschrus. Callaeschrus was the father of Critias, one of the Thirty, and of Glaucon, who was the father of Charmides and Perictione. Plato was the son of Perictione and Ariston, six generations removed from Solon. Solon, for his part, traced his lineage back to Neleus and Poseidon. They say his father was also a descendant of Codros, son of Melanthus, both of whom were descendants of Poseidon, according to the account of Thrasylus.

[2]In his work entitled *Plato's Wake*, Speusippus, together with Clearchus in an encomium on Plato, and Anaxilaides in the second volume of his work *On Philosophers*, all report a story circulating in Athens to this effect: Ariston made passionate love to beautiful Perictione but did not succeed in getting

her pregnant. When he stopped assaulting her, Apollo appeared to him in a dream. From then on he left her unmolested until she gave birth.

[3]In his chronology, Apollodorus says that Plato was born in the 88th Olympiad, on the seventh day of Thargelion, which is the day the Delians say Apollo himself was born. He died, according to Hermippus, at a wedding party, in the first year of the 108th Olympiad, when he was eighty-one. Neanthes says, however, that he died when he was eighty-four.

[45]If Phoebus did not father Plato in Greece,
How did Plato heal the souls of mortals with words?
Asclepius, you will recall, also the son of the god,
    heals the body,
While Plato makes the soul immortal.

Phoebus fathered Asclepius and Plato
    for the benefit of humankind,
the one to save their bodies,
the other to save their souls.
From a wedding banquet Plato was taken up to
    the city he had founded for himself
    and established in the heavenly realm of Zeus.

―――――― ∾⌘∾ ――――――

1 This genealogy traces Plato's descent on his mother's side six generations back to the family of *Solon*, the great statesman of Athens. His father's lineage is traced back only two generations. Both sides of his family claimed descent from the great god *Poseidon*. Unlike the genealogies of Jesus in the gospels, Plato's does not emphasize that the human father was not the biological father (see Matt 1:16 and Luke 3:23).

2 *assaulting her.* The Greek word connotes a violent attack. It is not clear whether this wording is meant to characterize Ariston's ardor for his wife or whether it means that he was forcing himself on her.

Apollo appears to Plato's father in a dream, from which he somehow learns that the god has made his wife pregnant. No details are given on how Perictione conceived. This brief narrative shares some key elements with Matt 1:18–25.

- The story is told entirely from the husband's perspective. The woman's experience is not reported.
- It is clear that the husband is not the biological father.
- The husband learns about the miraculous conception in a dream.
- Once he realizes that his wife is pregnant by divine power, the husband abstains from intercourse until the child is born.

3 The year of Plato's birth is related to the history of Greece (*in the 88th Olympiad*), which is similar to Luke's relating Jesus' birth to Roman history (Luke 2:1–2; see also Luke 3:1–2). The date of Plato's birth, *the seventh day of Thargelion,* was the day of an agricultural festival dedicated to Apollo, and according to one tradition, Apollo's birthday.

45 At the end of this biography are two memorial poems for Plato.

Phoebus was another name for Apollo.

Asclepius was a famous physician with legendary powers. He too was believed to be a son of Apollo, and after his death he became the most beloved god in the ancient world. People flocked to his temples to be healed, and hundreds of cures were attributed to him. His temples were places of pilgrimage for eight centuries, until they were forcibly closed by Christian authorities in the fourth century.

Plato *heals the souls of mortals with words, makes the soul immortal,* and *saves souls.* Plato's philosophy taught that the soul was an immortal and immaterial substance. He taught that after death the souls of those who had lived morally and dedicated their lives to spiritual values would live forever in spiritual bliss. Many of Plato's followers considered him a savior because he had given the world the teachings that enabled people to attain eternal life. The words of Peter to Jesus could easily have been applied by Plato's disciples to their master: "You have the words of everlasting life" (John 6:68).

Note the reasoning: how could Plato have taught such powerful and salvific truth unless he had been fathered by a god?

APOLLONIUS OF TYANA: HOLY MAN

Apollonius of Tyana was born around 20 CE. For most of his adult life he travelled from city to city, going as far as India, spreading the teachings of Pythagoras and preaching strict morality. He was known as an ascetic, a healer, and a clairvoyant. His disciples attributed many miracles to him, including raisings of the dead. They also claimed that he never died, but was instead taken directly to heaven, and even appeared afterward to prove to a skeptical disciple that he was still alive. Devotion to Apollonius the savior spread around the Mediterranean world and persisted even after Christianity was made the official religion of the Roman empire. One fascinating indication of his religious importance comes from the palace of the Roman emperor Severus Alexander (222–245 CE). In his private shrine were statues, not of the traditional gods of Rome, but of Orpheus, Abraham, Alexander the Great, Jesus, and Apollonius.

Philostratus is known to us only as the author of the *Life of Apollonius of Tyana*, which he wrote around 220 CE at the request of the Emperor's wife.

PHILOSTRATUS
Life of Apollonius, 1.4–7

[4a]Apollonius' hometown was Tyana, a Greek city located in the territory of the Cappodocians.

Apollonius' father had the same name; he came from an old family descended from the original settlers. His family was wealthier than others, although the region was well off generally. [4b]As his mother was about to give birth, she had a vision of Proteus, an Egyptian deity, who, according to Homer, changes his form at will. She was not in the least afraid, so she asked him, "To whom will I give birth?"

> He replied, "to me."
> "And who are you?" she asked.
> "Proteus," he said, "the god of Egypt."

I do not have to explain to those who have listened to the poets how wise Proteus is, how mercurial, now appearing as this, now that, how elusive, apparently having both knowledge and foreknowledge of everything. [4c]We need to keep Proteus in mind as the story unfolds, since it will show that Apollonius possessed even greater foreknowledge than Proteus. Apollonius proves that he can rise above any number of dangerous and impossible situations, especially when he seems trapped.

[5a]It is rumored that he was born in a meadow, close to which now stands a temple built to his honor. We should also not fail to mention how he was born. Just as the time was approaching for his mother to give birth, she was told in a dream to go to this meadow and pick flowers. She had no sooner arrived than she fell asleep on the grass, while her maids spread out over the meadow to pick flowers. There were some swans there who got their food from the meadow. These swans danced around her as she slept and, as they often do, flapped their wings and honked all at the same time, for there was a light breeze on the meadow at the time. At this sound she jumped up and gave birth since any sudden shock can cause a premature delivery. [5b]Those who lived around there claim that a bolt of lightning appeared to strike the earth but then was carried aloft where it vanished. It seems to me that the gods used this sign to reveal and predict that Apollonius would transcend all earthly standards and rival the gods.

[6] . . . The people of Tyana say that Apollonius is a son of Zeus; the sage himself says that he is the son of Apollonius.

[7a]When he was old enough to start learning to read, he showed that he had an excellent memory and strong powers of concentration. He could speak pure Attic Greek and was not influenced by the local dialect. Everyone's eyes were constantly on him and he was admired by the hour.

Apollonius began his formal study of philosophy at age fourteen, studying the systems of Plato, Chrysippus, Aristotle, and Epicurus.

[7b]He applied himself most to the teaching of Pythagoras, which he grasped with an indescribable wisdom. His teacher in Pythagorean philosophy was not very good, however, nor did he practice what he taught; instead he constantly indulged his desires for food and sex, following the example of Epicurus. [7c]This man was Euxenos from Herakleia in Pontus. He knew the teachings of Pythagoras the way birds learn things from people. Birds can say

"Hello" and "Do well" and "God bless you," and other such things, without understanding what they are saying and without feeling any concern for people, but simply because of their trained tongues. Apollonius, however, was like the young eagles who fly beside their parents while their feathers are soft and are trained by them in flight. But as soon as they are able to climb in the air, they soar above their parents, especially if they perceive them to be greedy, flying at ground level following the scent of prey. Like them, Apollonius stayed by Euxenos as long as he was a child and was led by him through the steps of reasoning, but when he reached the age of sixteen he rushed headlong toward the Pythagorean life, being "winged" for it by some Higher Power.

4b There is no story of a supernatural conception for Apollonius. Instead, his very pregnant mother has a vision in which she learns that her son will be the incarnation of the shape-shifting god Proteus. Nothing in this implies that there was anything unusual about how Apollonius was conceived. This shows that the ancient imagination accepted the notion that someone could be a god incarnate and yet be conceived in the natural way.

4c This explains why Apollonius was believed to be divine: his uncanny knowledge of the future and his ability to triumph over extreme adversity.

5a This strange and beautiful scene of dancing and singing swans depicts nature welcoming Apollonius at the moment he is born.

5b The *bolt of lightning* at the time of his birth is a portent, for which the author offers his own interpretation.

6 This statement demonstrates that a hero could be acclaimed a son of God during his own lifetime, even though he has made no such claim for himself and even though he affirmed his physical descent from his human father.

7a Apollonius' extraordinary intellectual talents are evident at a very early age. This summary is equivalent to the brief report about Jesus in Luke 2:52.

7b The young Apollonius' *indescribable wisdom* reflects his precocious ability, a standard feature in hellenistic infancy narratives.

7c Philostratus uses different kinds of birds as metaphors for two different ways of learning philosophy. He compares Apollonius to the noble eagle, in order to tell how he surpassed his teacher while still a teenager. Stories of young heroes who outshine their elders are common in ancient biographies; see the scene of the twelve-year old Jesus in the Temple (Luke 2:41–51).

PYTHAGORAS: PHILOSOPHER

Pythagoras was a Greek who lived in the sixth century BCE. As far as we know, he wrote nothing. His fundamental teaching was that the soul is a divine being trapped in a physical body and that it is successively reincarnated until it recovers its original spiritual purity. Pythagoras' philosophy emphasized the study and mystical contemplation of music, astronomy, and mathematics—everyone has heard of the Pythagorean theorem. It also prescribed a strict lifestyle that included vegetarianism and periods of silent self-examination. Nothing certain is known about Pythagoras' life, but his disciples circulated a collection of detailed stories about him, including reports of numerous miracles.

Iamblichus was a Syrian philosopher who lived between 250–325 CE. He belonged to a school of philosophy called Neoplatonism, which combined the traditions of Plato and Pythagoras. Among Iamblichus' writings are explanations of Pythagorean philosophy and *The Pythagorean Life*.

What is most important about this excerpt about the early life of Pythagoras is the stance its author takes toward the belief that Pythagoras was the son of Apollo. Iamblichus, a sophisticated intellectual, defends the truth of this belief, even while denying that it is *literally* true.

IAMBLICHUS
The Pythagorean Life, 3–5, 7–10

³It is said that Ankaios, who lived in Samos in Kephallenia, was fathered by Zeus. Perhaps this reputation came from his virtue or from a certain greatness of soul. In any case, he was wiser and more renowned than the rest of the Kephallenians. Ankaios was directed by the Pythian oracle to establish a colony made up of people from Kephallenia, Arcadia, and Thessaly. . .

⁴ . . . They say that Pythagoras' parents, Mnemarchos and Pythia, were from this house and were descendants of Ankaios, the founder of the colony.

⁵On one occasion when the citizens were celebrating Pythagoras' noble birth, a certain poet from Samos claimed that Pythagoras had been fathered by Apollo.

> Pythia, most beautiful of the Samians
> By Apollo bore Pythagoras, the friend of Zeus.

It seems worth our while here to explain how this report came to be so widely accepted. Mnemarchos had gone to Delphi on a business trip and left his wife before her pregnancy had become apparent. He consulted the oracle about his return trip through Syria and learned that it would be profitable and would turn out to be exactly what he wished for. He was also told that his wife was already pregnant and would give birth to a boy who would surpass everyone who has ever lived in beauty and wisdom and who would do more than anyone else to make life better for the human race.

⁷The child was born soon afterwards in Sidon in Phoenicia. Mnemarchos named him Pythagoras, because he had been foretold by the Pythian Apollo. Now Epimenides, Eudoxos, and Xenocrates claim that at that time Apollo had already had intercourse with Pythia and had impregnated her, and that he had straightened out the situation by predicting the boy's birth through the prophetess. But there is not the slightest truth in this assertion.

[8]Nevertheless, no one can deny that the soul of Pythagoras was sent down among us humans from the realm of Apollo, having been there either a companion of the god or associated with him in some more intimate way. This can be inferred both from his origins and from the wide-ranging wisdom of his soul.

[9]Mnemarchos made a fortune on his trip, returned home to Samos from Syria, and built a temple to Apollo. He saw to it that his son had a superb education in a variety of subjects. He studied with Creophilus, and then under Pherecydes the Syrian, and then under nearly all the leading authorities in sacred topics to whom Mnemarchos entrusted him, so that he would acquire the best possible expertise in theological matters. And so by education and good fortune, Pythagoras became the most handsome and godlike of anyone mentioned in the history books.

[10]After his father died, Pythagoras developed a great dignity and self-control. Although he was still a child, people recognized that he already deserved honor and reverence, even from his elders. He captured the attention of everyone who saw him or heard him speak, creating the most profound impression. That is why many people reasonably inferred that he was a son of God. Being blessed with such a reputation, with such an education from his earliest years, and with such a godlike appearance, he showed that he deserved all these advantages by the adornment of his religious observance and learning, by his disciplined way of life, and by his firmness of soul and bodily moderation. He spoke and acted with tranquillity and a certain inimitable serenity, and he was never overcome by violent emotion or laughter or rivalry or contentiousness, or by any other disorder or rash behavior. It was as if a benign deity had made his home in Samos.

———— ∽∾ ————

3 *Ankaios* was the ancestor of Pythagoras (see 4).

Note how the author accounts for the tradition (*It is said*) that Ankaios was *fathered by Zeus*. People believed this about him, not because they had information from his mother about the manner of his conception, but because of the man's *virtue or greatness of soul*, i.e., his outstanding moral and spiritual qualities. Iamblichus here provides us with clear evidence that some ancient people knew full well that stories about a god who fathers a child were created to explain a man's extraordinary achievements.

5 According to Iamblichus, Pythagoras was conceived naturally by his two human parents.

7 The author, who is a devoted admirer of Pythagoras and a proponent of his teachings, and who affirms the belief that Apollo was the father of Pythagoras, still emphatically denies that this belief is true in a literal, physical sense.

the Pythian Apollo. The site of Apollo's oracle at Delphi was originally called Pytho. According to the myth, Apollo killed the serpent—named Python—who guarded the site. Pythagoras' mother, Pythia, was named in honor of the oracle.

The *prophetess* refers to the priestess through whom Apollo delivered his oracles at Delphi.

8 Although Apollo was not Pythagoras' father in the physical sense, *the soul of Pythagoras was sent from the realm of Apollo*. The philosopher's soul pre-existed his body in the heavenly realm, where he was an equal to Apollo. Iamblichus interprets Pythagoras' birth as the sending of his soul to earth. Iamblichus is confident that *no one can deny* this. How else to explain *the wide-ranging wisdom of his soul*, i.e., the lofty truth of his teachings?

10 Here is the familiar theme that the greatness of the man was already evident in the outstanding qualities of the boy. The young Pythagoras' personal virtues were so impressive that it was thought reasonable to consider him *a son of God*. For this author, who was an astute philosopher in his own right, to say that something can be *reasonably inferred* is to say that it is true in the highest sense.

HERAKLES: SAVIOR

Herakles (known in Latin as Hercules) was the most popular and widely revered hero of the ancient world. He was hugely famous for his courage and feats of strength, many of which he performed for the benefit of others, e.g., slaying monsters. He was promoted to divinity by being granted immortality after his death. He was worshiped as a savior, and people often prayed to him to ward off evils. Although there may well have been a historical person named Herakles who was remembered for his strength, nothing is known of his life because the facts about him were long ago swallowed up in myth. Strictly speaking, then, the story of his life is not a biography like that of a real person. The legend about his infancy and birth is included here because it has several of the standard elements of infancy stories in hellenistic biographies. It thus is a good example of what the ancient world expected in a story about the birth of an extraordinary figure, whether historical or mythical.

Nothing is known of Diodorus of Sicily except that he lived in the mid-first century BCE. His story about Herakles is probably based on a lost work from the second century BCE.

DIODOROS OF SICILY
Library of History, IV 9.1–3, 6; 10.1

9.1They say that Perseus was the son of Zeus and Danae, daughter of Akrisios. Perseus had intercourse with Andromeda, daughter of Kepheos, and she bore Elektryon. Then Elektryon and Euridike, daughter of Pelops, lived together and she gave birth to Alkmene. Alkmene was tricked into intercourse with Zeus and bore Herakles. 9.2So the root of his family tree, through both of his parents, is said to go back to the greatest of the gods, in the way just explained.

The excellence bred into Herakles not only is seen in his deeds, but also was known before his birth. When Zeus slept with Alkmene, he made the night last three times as long as usual, and the length of time spent in making the baby prefigured the excessive strength of the one who was conceived. 9.3Zeus had intercourse with her, not so much out of sexual desire—as was the case with other women—but more out of generosity, in order to make the baby. Because he wanted to make this intercourse lawful, he did not want to force Alkmene into it. But since her self-control left him no hope of seducing her, he decided to trick her by making himself look exactly like her husband Amphitryon. That is how he deceived Alkmene.

9.6When Alkmene gave birth she was afraid of Hera's jealousy and so she exposed the baby in a place that is still called the Field of Herakles. At just that time Athena was going by with Hera. Athena was amazed at the nature of the child and convinced Hera to offer him her breast. The child sucked on her breast much more violently than a baby usually does. This caused Hera extreme pain and she threw the infant down. So Athena carried him to his mother and encouraged her to raise him.

10.1Some time later Hera sent two snakes to kill the infant. The boy did not panic, but instead grabbed each snake around the neck and strangled it with his bare hands.

———— ⌒⌒⌒ ————

9.1 The story begins with a genealogy. Zeus was the father of Danae, who was the mother of Perseus, who was the father of Elektryon, who was the father of Alkmene, the mother of Herakles.

9.2 Herakles' future greatness is foreshadowed in the "triple strength" of his conception.

9.3 Here is another example of a divine begetting that escapes the awareness even of the mother.

9.6 The story doesn't explain how Alkmene knew that Zeus was the father of her child. On her fear of *Hera's jealousy*, see the comment on the *Life of Alexander* 3.3–4 (p. 139.).

Two goddesses "coincidentally" find the exposed child and unknowingly give him back to his mother to be raised. The parallel to the story of Moses is noteworthy.

The child sucked on her breast more violently than a baby usually does. Herakles' extraordinary strength is evident on the very day of his birth.

10.1 The courage and fighting skill of the adult is foreshadowed in the manner in which the baby escapes Hera's attempt on his life.

Did Jesus fulfill prophecy?

HOW MATTHEW USES PROPHECY

Twelve times in his gospel, Matthew interrupts the story to tell us that the event he is narrating fulfilled a specific prophecy, which he then quotes. Five of these twelve are found in chapters 1–2, where they are the focal points of the five episodes of the infancy narrative, each showing how an event connected to Jesus' birth and infancy happened in fulfillment of prophecy. Three of these fulfillment scenes are correlated to the pivotal events in the history of Israel: the Exodus, the Exile, and the Return (see p. 109). By beginning his gospel in this way, Matthew creates the powerful impression that all of Israel's history has been building up to Jesus, in whom God's plans for Israel are reaching their fulfillment.

Before examining the five prophecies in Matthew's infancy narrative, it will help to consider three other prophecies quoted in this gospel. In these three examples it is relatively simple to track the particular ways Matthew uses prophecy to help tell the story of Jesus.

Prophecies Outside the Infancy Narratives

Matt 4:15–16

In recounting the start of Jesus' public career, Matthew follows Mark's outline: Matt 4:12 = Mark 1:14 and Matt 4:17 = Mark 1:15 (see Box 8.1). Between Mark 1:14 and 1:15 Matthew inserts a detailed geographical elaboration of Jesus' movements in Galilee (Matt 4:13), followed by Matthew's fulfillment formula (Matt 4:14) and his quotation of Isa 9:1–2 (Matt 4:15–16). The prophet cited, Isaiah, mentions Galilee along with the old Israelite tribal names Zebulun and Naphtali and locates them on the way to the sea and across the Jordan River (Isa 9:1). In Matt 4:13, Matthew uses the geographical markers from Isa 9:1 to fill out the description of Jesus' movements that he

found in Mark. Matthew knows from Mark that Jesus had a house in
Capernaum, on the Sea of Galilee. (Mark refers to "his house" there in Mark
2:1 and 2:15.) So Matthew reports that Jesus moved from Nazareth to
Capernaum, which allows Matthew to work the word "sea" from the Isaiah
verse into 4:13. He also describes Capernaum (somewhat inexactly) as "in the
territory of Zebulun and Naphtali." He cannot work in Isaiah's "across the

---

8.1	The Move to Galilee	

Mark 1:14–15	**aMatthew 4:12–17**	**Isaiah 9:1 (Septuagint)**
¹⁴After John was locked up, Jesus came to Galilee	¹²When Jesus heard that John had been locked up, he headed for Galilee. ¹³He took leave of Nazareth to go and settle down in Capernaum-by-the-sea, in the territory of Zebulun and Naphtali, ¹⁴so that the word spoken through Isaiah the prophet would come true:	
	¹⁵Land of Zebulun and land of Naphtali, the way to the sea,	Region of Zebulun, land of Naphtali, the way to the sea, and those survivors who live on the coast
	across the Jordan, pagan Galilee.	and across the Jordan, pagan Galilee, the remnant of the Judeans.
	¹⁶The people who sat in darkness have seen a great light, and those who sat in the region and shadow of death, for them a light has dawned.	The people who walked in darkness, look, a great light. Those who live in the region and shadow of death, a light will shine on you.
proclaiming God's good news. ¹⁵His message went: "The time is up! God's imperial rule is closing in. Change your ways and put your trust in the good news."	¹⁷From that time on Jesus began to proclaim: "Change your ways because Heaven's imperial rule is closing in."	

Jordan" because Jesus never crosses that river. All of Galilee is on the west side of the Jordan, and Capernaum is several miles around the lakeshore from the point where the river enters the Sea of Galilee. To be geographically precise, Nazareth is in Zebulun and Capernaum in Naphtali. Strictly speaking, then, Matthew describes Jesus leaving Zebulun to move to Naphtali. But this is to pick nits: Matthew is focused on the phrase "pagan Galilee." For Matthew, that is what brings out the religious point of this prophecy about geography. By portraying Jesus as fulfilling this prophecy, Matthew shows that he was sent for both Jews and Gentiles.

Matt 21:4–5

In this scene Jesus rides into Jerusalem to the cheers of a crowd. Matt 21:1–9 follows Mark 11:1–10 closely, except for two features.

1. Matthew interrupts the narrative to announce the fulfillment of a prophecy (21:4), which he then quotes (21:5). 21:5 begins with a phrase from Isa 62:11 and then selectively quotes Zech 9:9 (see Box 8.2). Mark's scenario, in which Jesus rides a donkey into Jerusalem while a crowd cheers for the "coming kingdom," apparently reminded Matthew of Zechariah's prophecy. Zech 9:9 seems to mention two animals, a "donkey" and a "colt, the foal of a donkey." In the Hebrew text of Zech 9:9 it is clear that these are two descriptions of the same beast. Parallel phrasing like this is quite common in Hebrew poetry. But in the Septuagint version of Zechariah the Greek word for "and" appears: "a pack animal *and* a young colt." Matthew's "quotation" of Zech 9:9 blends elements from the original Hebrew with the Greek version: the gentle king is "mounted on a donkey and on a colt, the foal of a pack animal" (Matt 21:5).

8.2   A King on a Donkey

Hebrew Bible	*Matthew*	*Septuagint*
Isaiah 62:11	**Matt 21:5**	**Isaiah 62:11**
Tell daughter Zion	Tell the daughter of Zion,	Tell the daughter of Zion
Zechariah 9:9		**Zechariah 9:9**
Look, your king is coming to you, triumphant and victorious, mounted on a	Look, your king is coming to you	Look, your king is coming to you, righteous and rescuing,
	in gentleness, mounted on a donkey	in gentleness, mounted on a pack ani-
donkey, on a colt, the foal of a donkey.	and on a colt, the foal of a pack animal.	mal and a young colt.

2. Matthew takes the Septuagint wording of this prophecy quite literally, as if it describes a king riding two animals. Accordingly, Matthew rewrites Mark's story so that now the disciples bring a donkey *and* a colt to Jesus and, sure enough, he sits on both of them (21:7). For consistency, Matthew also

---

8.3   How many animals did Jesus ride?

Mark 11:1–10

[1]When they get close to Jerusalem, near Bethphage and Bethany at the Mount of Olives, he sends off two of his disciples [2]with these instructions: "Go into the village across the way, and right after you enter it, you'll find *a colt* tied up, one that has never been ridden. Untie it and bring it here. [3]If anyone questions you, 'Why are you doing this?' tell them, '*Its* master has need of *it* and he will send *it* back right away.'"

[4]They set out and found a colt tied up at the door out on the street, and they untie it. [5]Some of the people standing around started saying to them, "What do you think you're doing, untying that colt?" [6]But they said just what Jesus had told them to say, so they left them alone.

[7]So they bring *the colt* to Jesus, and they throw their cloaks over *it*; then he got on *it*. [8]And many people spread their cloaks on the road, while others cut leafy branches from the fields.

[9]Those leading the way and those following kept shouting,

> Hosanna! Blessed is the one who comes in the name of the Lord!
> [10]Blessed is the coming kingdom of our father David!
> Hosanna in the highest!

Matt 21:1–9

[1]When they got close to Jerusalem, and came to Bethphage at the Mount of Olives, then Jesus sent two disciples ahead [2]with these instructions: "Go into the village across the way, and right away you will find *a donkey* tied up, *and a colt* alongside her. Untie them and bring them to me. [3]And if anyone says anything to you, you are to say, '*Their* master has need of *them* and he will send *them* back right away.'" [4]This happened so the word spoken through the prophet would come true:

> [5]Tell the daughter of Zion,
> Look, your king is coming to you in gentleness,
> mounted on a donkey and on a colt, the foal of a pack animal.

[6]Then the disciples went and did as Jesus instructed them,

[7]and brought *the donkey and colt* and they placed their cloaks on *them*, and he sat on top of *them*. [8]The enormous crowd spread their cloaks on the road, and others cut branches from the trees and spread them on the road. [9]The crowds leading the way and those following kept shouting,

> Hosanna to the son of David!
> Blessed is the one who comes in the name of the Lord!
> Hosanna in the highest.

goes back earlier in the scene and adds a second animal to the report of the finding the donkey by the disciples (Mark 11:2//Matt 21:2). He also changes the two pronouns in the next verse so that Mark's "it" becomes "them" (Mark 11:3//Matt 21:3).

By way of comparison, note that the Gospel of John also quotes Zech 9:9 in connection with its much briefer version of this scene (John 12:12–15). John's version of the prophecy sensibly mentions only one animal.

Matt 27:9

Mark 14:10–11 tells of Judas' approach to the high priests and his offer to betray Jesus, for which the priests promise to pay him. When Matthew rewrites this brief scene, he has Judas demand the money up front. Matthew also specifies the amount of money agreed on by Judas and the priests: thirty silver pieces (Matt 26:14–15; see Box 8.4). Mark never mentioned the amount, nor do Luke or John. From what source has Matthew obtained this inside information? Answer: the prophets.

Later in the story Judas, overwhelmed by guilt, flings the money back at the priests and then commits suicide (Matt 27:3–5). When the priests use the money to buy some land, Matthew informs us that this fulfills a prophecy of Jeremiah about thirty pieces of silver (Matt 27:6–10). The prophecy in question is actually from Zechariah, not Jeremiah. Matthew's mistake shows that here at least he is quoting from memory and not from a text.

A close comparison of Zech 11:12–13 and Matt 27:3–10 (a scene unique to Matthew's gospel) also reveals where Matthew discovered that Judas had returned the money and had done so by throwing it into the temple.

What these three examples show about Matthew's use of prophecy.

Matt 4:14–16

To position Jesus as fulfiller of prophecy, Matthew chooses descriptive details from Isaiah and crafts them into elaborations on the reports and clues that he found in Mark. The reason why Jesus' movements match the words of prophecy so closely—though not exactly—is that Matthew has derived Jesus' itinerary from those very words.

Matt 21:4–5

Matthew creates a ludicrous scene: Jesus stunt-rides two animals into Jerusalem. The only possible purpose Matthew could have had in changing Mark's straightforward narrative into such a spectacle is to demonstrate that Jesus fulfilled prophecy to the letter. Obviously, Matthew's Jesus can fulfill this prophecy in this odd manner only because Matthew rigs the story with details cribbed from the "fulfilled" prophecy. This bizarre scene shows to what extremes Matthew was prepared to go to portray Jesus as the fulfiller of prophecy. It should also raise a serious question about Matthew's competence as an interpreter of Hebrew scripture.

Matt 26:15 and 27:9

With the thirty silver coins, Matthew again inserts a detail from a prophecy into a story that he borrowed from Mark. A chapter later, Matthew relies on the readers' memory of that detail to confirm that that prophecy was fulfilled to the letter.

Matthew's specification of thirty silver pieces, and his report that Judas returned the money, are small but lucid examples of how Matthew uses the

---

 8.4   Thirty Silver Pieces

Mark 14:10–11

[10]And Judas Iscariot, one of the twelve, went off to the ranking priests to turn Jesus over to them. [11]When they heard, they were delighted, and promised to pay him in silver.

Matt 26:14–15

[14]Then one of the twelve, Judas Iscariot by name, went to the ranking priests, [15]and said, "What are you willing to pay me if I turn him over to you?" They agreed on *thirty silver pieces*.

Matt 27:3–10

[3]Then Judas, who had turned him in, realizing that he had been condemned, was overcome with remorse and returned the *thirty silver pieces* to the ranking priests and elders [4]with this remark, "I have made the terrible mistake of turning in this blameless man."

But they said, "What's that to us? That's your problem!"

[5]And hurling the silver into the temple he slunk off, and went out and hanged himself.

[6]The ranking priests took the silver and said, "It wouldn't be right to put this into the temple treasury, since it's blood money."

[7]So they devised a plan and bought the Potter's Field as a burial ground for foreigners. [8]As a result, that field has been known as the Bloody Field even to this day. [9]So the prediction Jeremiah the prophet made came true:

> And they took the *thirty silver pieces*, the price put on a man's head (this is the price they put on him among the Israelites), [10]and they donated it for the Potter's Field, as my Lord commanded me.

Zechariah 11:12–13

[12]They counted out my wages: *thirty silver pieces*. [13]Then the Lord said to me, "Throw it into the treasury"—the handsome price at which they valued me. So I took the *thirty silver pieces* and threw them into the treasury in the house of the Lord.

Old Testament as a source of information for the story of Jesus. It is not the case that Matthew knew a factually accurate account of the life of Jesus and then realized, from his knowledge of scripture, that the life of Jesus fulfilled prophecy. Rather, the process worked in the opposite direction. *Matthew started with the conviction that Jesus' life must have fulfilled scripture, and then went back to read (or remember) the Old Testament with the intention of finding out more about what had happened in Jesus' life.* That is how he, alone out of the four evangelists, "knows," for example, that Jesus rode two animals into Jerusalem and that Judas was paid thirty silver pieces.

The Prophecies in the Infancy Narratives

Having taken this detailed and, I trust, instructive detour through some prophecy fulfillment scenes outside Matthew's infancy narrative, we now turn to the five that are found in chapters 1 and 2. While much of this material was discussed earlier, a more detailed analysis of these Matthean quotations is in order. Since Matthew's claim that Jesus fulfilled prophecy has had such far-reaching influence on Christianity, the extra effort required for a critical assessment of that claim is well worthwhile.

Matthew believes that prophecies were fulfilled in:

1. The salvific symbolism of Jesus' name and/or his birth to a virgin mother (Matt 1:23).

   Look, a "virgin" will conceive a child
   and she will give birth to a son,
   and they will name him Emmanuel (Isa 7:14)
   (which means "God is with us").

2. Jesus' birth in Bethlehem (Matt 2:6).

   And you, Bethlehem, in the land of Judah,
   in no way are you least among the leaders of Judah.
   Out of you will come a leader
   who will shepherd my people, Israel. (Mic 5:2 + 2 Sam 5:2)

3. Jesus' journey as an infant to and from Egypt (Matt 2:15).

   I called my son out of Egypt. (Hos 11:1)

4. Herod's slaughter of baby boys in Bethlehem (Matt 2:18).

   In Ramah the sound of mourning
   and bitter grieving was heard:
   Rachel weeping for her children.
   She refuses to be consoled:
   They were no more. (Jer 31:15)

5. Jesus' having Nazareth for his hometown (Matt 2:23).

He will be called a Nazorean. (*nowhere in the Old Testament*)

The meanings found by Matthew in the quoted prophecies become plausible only when the texts in question are isolated from their original contexts. What each of them meant in its own context is summarized here. (For a full analysis of each prophecy see the comments on pp. 92–98 and 112–19.)

1. Isaiah's prophecy is about a boy born to a young woman in the natural manner seven centuries before the time of Jesus.
2. Micah's prophecy about Bethlehem is a prediction that the Davidic monarchy will be restored in Israel after the return from Exile. (Historically, this expectation turned out to be a false hope.)
3. "I called my son out of Egypt" refers to the Israelites' escape from Egypt under Moses, and is part of Hosea's condemnation of Israel for its sinfulness.
4. Jeremiah imagines the ghost of Rachel weeping over the deportation of the tribes of northern Israel by the Assyrians. This is part of a message of hope, in which Jeremiah conveys God's promise that these tribes will return to the land of Israel. (Historically, this expectation also turned out to be a false hope. The northern Israelite tribes, sometimes called the "lost tribes," were scattered by the Assyrians and vanished from history.)
5. This statement, which Matthew attributes to "the prophets," is not an actual quotation from any biblical prophet, and so has no scriptural context.

PROPHECY AND POLEMIC

It is a deeply rooted belief in Christianity that Jesus fulfilled prophecy. In its most common version, this belief entails that:

• the Old Testament contains a number of prophetic predictions about the coming messiah;
• these prophecies were, in effect, waiting to be fulfilled;
• people would know the messiah when he finally came because he would fulfill these prophecies.

That is how most Christians understand the term "Old Testament prophecy," and Matthew's gospel has been instrumental in fostering this notion. Matthew's method of quoting specific prophecies and pointing out how they were fulfilled gives the impression that it should have been fairly clear to people who knew the scriptures that Jesus was the long-awaited messiah. So effective has Matthew's gospel been in this regard, that Christianity has long puzzled over why the Jews of Jesus' time "rejected" him. Matthew gives the impression that the Jewish leaders knew (or at least should have known) that Jesus was the messiah but opposed him because of their hypocrisy and hard-heartedness. At the very end of the gospel, Matthew makes his accusation explicit: these authorities knew that Jesus had risen from the dead but con-spired to deceive their own people about the truth of his resurrection (28:11–15; see Box 8.5).

8.5   Matthew 28:11–15

[11]Some of the guards [at the tomb] returned to the city and reported to the ranking priests everything that had happened. [12]They met with the elders and hatched a plan: they bribed the soldiers with an adequate amount of money [13]and ordered them: "Tell everybody that his disciples came at night and stole his body while we were asleep. [14]If the governor should hear about this, we will deal with him; don't worry." [15]They took the money and did as they had been instructed. And this story has been passed around among the Jews until this very day.

We should pause to examine this brief story because Matthew's attitude toward the Jewish leaders bears directly on his proof-from-prophecy theme. The first thing to be said about this scene is that there is not a shred of histor-ical evidence for the conspiracy Matthew describes. Besides, if it had happened just the way Matthew says it did, he could not have known about it: if the sol-diers really "took the money and did as they had been instructed" (Matt 28:15), no one could have known about the alleged bribery and the lying. It isn't dif-ficult to conclude that Matthew made this story up. It is fiction. Now the gospels contain many fictions that express truth—stories that while not histori-cally true communicate truths that are more important than historical facts. (Jesus' parables and the stories that he multiplied bread and fish are good exam-ples.) But the story about Jewish leaders who covered up Jesus' resurrection is not like those benign fictions. This story is a malicious lie. That Matthew told it to counteract the accusation that the disciples stole Jesus' body helps us understand the motivation for the lie, but does not excuse it.

Matthew's proof-from-prophecy argument is intertwined with his polemic against official Judaism. He asserts not only that his people are right to follow Jesus as the Jewish messiah, but also that Jews who do not follow Jesus are unfaithful to Judaism. In its simplest form, Matthew's message to his people is:

   a. "We" have a right to exist as a Jewish community, despite the fact that "they" say we don't; and
   b. "We" are the only real Jews.

The debate between Matthew's people and the keepers of official Judaism at that time (i.e., the Pharisees) must have been fierce, to judge from the polemical rhetoric in Matthew's gospel. See, for example, the way Matthew's Jesus rips into the Pharisees in chapter 23. We don't expect cool logic in heated debates, which too often end up with each side even more convinced of its own rightness. And that is precisely the sort of framework in which Matthew's use of prophecy must be placed. Matthew's rhetoric was not designed to win over the Jewish opponents of his community. Nor was Matthew's manipulation of scripture meant to persuade the open-minded, if in that situation there were any such people. It was intended to reinforce the belief of Matthew's own people that all of Jewish history had been building up to Jesus, and thus up to them.

EVALUATING MATTHEW'S CLAIMS

There are two distinct tasks involved in evaluating Matthew's claim that five specific prophecies were fulfilled by the events in chapters 1 and 2. The first is to determine whether the statements Matthew quotes are actually prophecies about the coming of the messiah. The second is to weigh the evidence and decide whether the events Matthew narrates are historical. In other words:

1. Do the five quoted statements qualify as messianic prophecies?
2. Did the five narrated events actually happen?

These two questions are not mutually dependent; the answer to one does not affect the answer to the other. By asking them separately we can, in effect, run two independent analyses of Matthew's use of prophecy.

1. Are these messianic prophecies?

Our first task is to analyze each of the five quotations in order to determine what type of statement it is. Not every quotation from the words of the prophets is a "prophecy" in the sense we mean when we speak of the fulfillment of prophecy. For example, when the prophets speak the word of the Lord about Israel's past history, there is no prophecy to be fulfilled. So we can ask of Matthew's five quotations whether they are about the prophets' past, present, or future. If a prophecy is about the future, we can then ask if it can be imagined as a prediction about a messianic figure or the messianic age.

Matt 1:23 (Isa 7:14)

As we saw earlier, Isa 7:14, at least in the Greek form in which Matthew quotes it, is indeed a prediction (see pp. 95–97). However, Isaiah's prediction is about his immediate future: Isaiah expects the boy to be born within the next year or so. Jewish interpretations of this prophecy understood it to have been fulfilled in the birth of Hezekiah, son of Ahaz. (Christians defending Matthew's interpretation cannot dispute this Jewish interpretation on the grounds that Hezekiah was not named Immanuel, because neither was Jesus.) Furthermore, the Jewish tradition has never understood Isa 7:14 to be a prophecy about the messiah.

Matt 2:6 (Mic 5:2 + 2 Sam 5:2)

Micah 5:2 foresees the birth of a Davidic king in Bethlehem. Many Jews of Matthew's time, though by no means all, hoped for a messiah who would be a powerful king and restore Israel to the political greatness it had under King David. Since David was from Bethlehem, those who looked for a David-like military messiah understood Micah 5:2 to be a messianic prophecy. However, Jews who longed for a priestly (Aaron-like) messiah or a messiah who would be a prophet like Moses (Deut 18:15, see John 6:14) did not expect the messiah to be from Bethlehem because they did not expect him to be Davidic.

Matt 2:15 (Hos 11:1)

"I called my son out of Egypt" is not a prediction. Hosea refers to the Exodus, an event that had already occurred long before his time. So Hosea 11:1 was not a prophecy waiting to be fulfilled: it does not say "I *will* call my son out of Egypt."

Matt 2:18 (Jer 31:15)

Jeremiah's depiction of Rachel's grief is not a prediction. Jeremiah is imaginatively describing the present consequences of a traumatic event from his past. This was not a prophecy waiting to be fulfilled. It does not say that Rachel *will* weep for her children. In fact, the very next verse in Jeremiah tells Rachel to stop weeping because her children will be returned to her (Jer 31:16; see Box 5.10 on p. 115).

Matt 2:23 (?)

Strictly speaking, "He will be called a Nazorean" is a prediction because it uses the future tense. But it is not an authentic prophecy. Matthew wrote it himself and attributed it to "the prophets." Needless to say, any prophecy can be guaranteed fulfillment if it is formulated *after* the event it "predicts." And even if, contrary to the facts, there were an actual Old Testament passage that read, "He will be called a Nazorean," such a prophecy would be irrelevant to Matthew's purpose unless it were evident that the "he" refers to the messiah, or the ideal Davidic king, or the son of God, or some such role which, even taken out of context, could fit Jesus.

Summary

Of the five prophecies in Matthew 1–2 only three are predictions. One of these (2:23) is not actually from scripture. Another (1:23) is a prediction, but not one about a messiah-like figure. Only one out of five, Micah's prophecy about Bethlehem, was considered a messianic prophecy by some first-century Jews.

2. Are these historical events?

Matthew claims that certain events or facts in the birth and early life of Jesus fulfilled prophecies. Our second task in evaluating this claim is to determine whether the events Matthew narrates actually happened. Specifically, we have to ask:

a. Was Jesus conceived by a virgin?[1]
b. Was he born in Bethlehem?
c. Did he depart from Egypt?
d. Did Herod massacre babies in Bethlehem?
e. Was Jesus from Nazareth?

From our brief examination of Matthew's use of prophecy elsewhere in his gospel, we know that in some cases he draws on prophecies to shape the story. For each of these five cases, then, we have to take seriously the possibility that Matthew created the story out of the prophecy. That means we have to ask whether, apart from Matthew's saying so, there is enough evidence for us to conclude that the event in question is historical.

A. *Was Jesus conceived by a virgin?* The short answer is No. The more nuanced answer is that since there is no good historical (i.e., public) evidence for the virgin birth, it cannot count as an historical truth (see p. 210). Responsible historians, regardless of their theological commitments, have to hold that it is not an historical fact that Jesus was conceived without a human father. Of course, millions of Christians might acknowledge that there is no public evidence that Mary became pregnant while still a virgin, and nonetheless believe in the virgin birth solely on religious grounds. However, even within this approach to belief in the virgin birth, the alleged facts of the case do not amount to a fulfillment of prophecy. This is an important point. Even if Mary's virginity was a physical fact, her miraculous pregnancy would not accomplish what a fulfilled prophecy is supposed to do: furnish evidence that Jesus was the messiah. *The purpose of fulfilling a prophecy is defeated if it is fulfilled*

---

1. I think it unlikely that Matthew believed in the virgin birth (see Chapter 11). Nevertheless, because the entire Christian tradition and the vast majority of biblical scholars understand Matthew to be implying that Jesus had no biological father, I will, for the sake of the argument, assume that interpretation here.

in secret. And Mary's sexual status at the time of Jesus' conception is just that: a secret, something about which there is no public knowledge, and even more, *can* be no public knowledge.

Even if Mary had publicly claimed that Jesus was conceived without a human father—and there is no evidence to suggest that she did—there is no way her claim could be verified. Thus, since no one else knew that Mary conceived virginally, the miraculous manner of her conception cannot serve as evidence that it fulfilled prophecy. (Keep in mind that for the sake of the argument we are assuming something that is not true: that Isaiah's prophecy is about a virginal conception.)

So, even if it were literally true that Jesus was conceived by a virgin, this fact still would not show that prophecy was fulfilled in the way Matthew implies.

B. *Was Jesus born in Bethlehem?* This is possible, but highly doubtful (see pp. 181–183). To be sure, Luke agrees with Matthew that Jesus was born in Bethlehem; yet this coincidence indicates merely that neither of them invented this notion. In light of their contradictory stories to explain it, and in light of the very strong evidence that Jesus was always known as "Jesus of Nazareth," prudence favors the conclusion that the tradition of a Bethlehem birth was based on the belief that Jesus was the Davidic messiah, and not on any factual biographical data.

C. *Did Jesus depart from Egypt?* No. Since no other Christian source shows any knowledge of this event, and since it fits perfectly into Matthew's symbolic agenda of showing how Jesus recapitulated the key moments of Israel's history, we cannot overcome the suspicion that Matthew was prompted by the prophecy to invent the story.

D. *Did Herod massacre babies in Bethlehem?* No (see p. 184). Matthew invented the story in order to create for the baby Jesus an escape from a mass murder that parallels the one from which the baby Moses escaped.

E. *Was Jesus from Nazareth?* Yes.

Summary

Of the five events that, according to Matthew, fulfilled prophecy, only one of them is historically true. Ironically, that is also the only one for which Matthew could find no specific prophecy.

Conclusion

Combining the findings of our two independent analyses of the alleged fulfillment of prophecy in Matthew 1–2, we obtain a dismal result. Out of the five cases in which Matthew claims that an event or fact about Jesus fulfills prophecy, there is not a single case in which the established facts of history match an actual prophecy from the scriptures.

MATTHEW'S SELECTIVITY

One more dimension to Matthew's handling of Old Testament prophecies remains to be examined: his *selectivity* in quoting them. In a strict sense, quotations are always selective whenever we quote some, but not all, of what someone said or wrote. Since it is seldom practical or appropriate to quote in full, we select what is relevant to our purpose. Since the meaning of any statement depends on its context, the ethical responsibility of a writer who quotes is to include or explain enough of the context so that the meaning of the citation in its original setting is accurately conveyed. Quoting out of context can severely distort someone's meaning. As schoolchildren some of us thought we could shock family and friends by reporting that the Bible says, "There is no God." The full verse is, "Fools say in their heart, 'There is no God'" (Ps 14:1 and 53:1). Checking the original contexts of Matthew's quotations enables us to compare the meanings that he finds in them with what the prophets themselves meant to say.

Another aspect of Matthew's selectivity has to do with translation. It goes without saying that when translating a passage, there is a responsibility to translate accurately. If more than one correct translation of a key word or phrase is possible, the one selected should be the one that best represents the sense of the original. These assumptions are basic to honest interpretive practice today. Matthew could read Hebrew and Greek, for his quotations of the prophets are in some cases based on the original Hebrew and in other cases based on a Greek translation. Therefore it is important to gauge what effect his choice of either the Hebrew or the Greek version has had on the meaning he has found in the words that he quotes.

Selectivity in Translation

Let's take up the translation issue first. There are two passages where the meaning Matthew wants is available in one version of the Old Testament text but not in the other.

1. *Matt 1:23: "The 'virgin' will conceive."*[2] There is no reference to a virgin in the Hebrew original of Isa 7:14. The Greek translation of Isaiah uses the word which means "young woman," but which can, under special circumstances have the meaning of "virgin" (see pp. 189–90). Matthew will be able to read the meaning he wants into Isaiah only by choosing to quote this prophecy from the Septuagint and not from the Hebrew Bible.

2. *Matt 2:15: "I called my son out of Egypt."* Here Matthew makes the opposite choice. The Hebrew text of Hos 11:1 has "my son" while the Septuagint

---

2. As before (see note 1 above), I am assuming, only for the sake of the argument, that Matthew intends his story to be about a virginal conception.

has "his children" (see Box 8.6). Both versions refer to the people of Israel, but only in the Hebrew wording will it be possible for Matthew to see a prophecy about Jesus. So here, Matthew chooses the Hebrew.

In both the passages just discussed (Matt 1:23 and 2:15), Matthew is able to connect a prophecy to Jesus only by selecting the version that was right for his purpose. Isaiah 7:14 works for Matthew only in Greek, Hosea 11:1 only in Hebrew.

8.6   Hosea 11:1–2

Hosea 11:1–2 (Hebrew)
[1]When Israel was a child,
  I loved him,
  and I called my son out of Egypt.
[2]The more I called them,
  the more they went from me;
  they kept sacrificing to the Baals,
  and offering incense to idols.

Hosea 11:1 (Septuagint)
[1]Because Israel was childish,
  I loved him
  and called his children out of Egypt.

Quoting Out of Context

Now we turn to the issue of Matthew's practice of quoting the prophets out of context. By "context" here I do not mean *historical* context. All of Matthew's quotations are taken out of their historical contexts, as we saw above. Here I am interested in the immediate *literary* context of the lines Matthew quotes. What happens to the meanings Matthew sees in these prophecies when we take into account the lines just before or after the ones Matthew selects for quotation?

1. In 1:23 Matthew applies to Jesus the prediction that "the 'virgin' will conceive and give birth to a son" from Isa 7:14. Matthew includes the next line about naming the boy Emmanuel. Though Jesus was not called by that name, Matthew nonetheless believes that Jesus fulfills its symbolic significance. However, the next line in the prophecy (Isa 7:15) has no possible application to Jesus. The same is true for the verse preceding the one Matthew quotes (Isa 7:13). Matthew can read Jesus into Isa 7:14 only if he isolates it from the verses immediately before and after it (see Box 8.7).

2. Matt 2:6 combines lines from Micah and 2 Samuel. Although Matthew alters Micah's wording to contradict part of the prophet's meaning (see pp. 112–13), the literary context of Micah 5:2 supports Matthew's purpose, which is to identify Bethlehem as the birthplace of the future ruler of Israel.

3. In 2:13–15 Matthew correlates "I called my son out of Egypt" (Hos 11:1) to the family's escape to and return from that country. Here Matthew

Isaiah 7:14–16

[14]Therefore Yahweh himself will give you a sign. Look, the young woman is pregnant and will give birth to a son, and will name him Immanuel. [15]He will eat curds and honey by the time he knows how to refuse evil and choose good. [16]For before the child knows how to refuse the evil and choose the good, the land before whose two kings you are in dread will be deserted.

quotes only the second half of Hos 11:1. It's easy to see why. Hos 11:1a makes it clear that "my son" in 11:1b is a collective reference to Israel. Quoting the full verse would wreck the correlation to Jesus. This is doubly true for the next verse (Hos 11:2). Not only does that verse refer to the Israelites in the plural; it also speaks of their idolatry (see Box 8.6). Both features of that verse make it impossible for Matthew to read Jesus into it.

4. In 2:16–18 Matthew judges Jeremiah's poetry about "Rachel weeping for her children" because "they are no more" (Jer 31:15) to be fulfilled in Herod's massacre of the babies in Bethlehem. The verse that Matthew quotes is the beginning of a short poetic unit that ends at Jer 31:17. Jer 31:16–17 comforts Rachel with the promise that her children will come back to her (see Box 5.10, p. 115). No wonder Matthew selects only 31:15.

5. Since "He will be called a Nazorean" is not a quotation from the Old Testament, it is irrelevant to ask about its original context.

Conclusion

Of the four scriptural quotations in Matthew's infancy narrative, only one (Matt 2:6) comes from a context amenable to his interpretation. The other three prophecies have immediate literary contexts that make Matthew's meanings impossible. Matthew can connect these prophecies to Jesus only by taking carefully chosen lines out of their surrounding contexts. In their own literary settings these prophecies wreck Matthew's project.

JUDAISM AND MATTHEW'S USE OF PROPHECY

How would Jews in Matthew's day respond to his attempt to show that Jesus fulfilled prophecy? The ancient world assumed that prophets sometimes spoke about future realities beyond their own understanding (see p. 97). For example, some of the Dead Sea scrolls from Qumran claim that certain prophecies had been or were about to be fulfilled in the experiences of the Qumran community. So there would be no objection to the general approach Matthew takes to the prophets. But first-century Jews would surely reject

Matthew's specific interpretations of the prophecies, especially where his interpretations go against the clear meanings those prophecies have in their own contexts. Anyone who knew or looked up Hosea could tell that "my son" obviously refers to Israel. If Jewish readers took Matthew's story to be about a virgin birth, they could easily tell that Isaiah was not predicting anything of the sort. And when Matthew asserted that the prophets had said "He will be called a Nazorean," all anyone had to do was ask where this was written to realize that something was wrong. These brief observations are enough to show why, far from accepting Matthew's interpretation of those prophecies, Jews who knew the scriptures might well conclude that he was deliberately distorting their sense.

Besides rejecting the way Matthew used scripture, his Jewish contemporaries had no reason to believe that the events Matthew points to as fulfillments of prophecy were real. No one would doubt that Jesus was from Nazareth, but that fact was irrelevant because there was no genuine prophecy about that village. When told about Herod's mass murder of children, Jews might well reply that they had never heard about that before. As for Jesus having been born in Bethlehem and having been in Egypt, why should they take Matthew's word for it? And if Matthew really was claiming that Jesus had no human father, he would naturally be met with total skepticism.

In short, it seems most unlikely that anyone who was not already inclined to believe that Jesus was the messiah would be persuaded by Matthew's presentation to change his or her mind. Perhaps some people did not know what the prophets really said, or did not question whether Matthew's stories were literally true; those people might be convinced that Jesus had fulfilled prophecies. While this may well have been the effect of Matthew's gospel on a few, we need not conclude that Matthew's purpose was to trick the gullible. A more responsible line of inquiry into Matthew's purpose in correlating prophecies with stories about Jesus is to imagine the circumstances which would allow Matthew and his audience to honestly believe in his presentation of Jesus fulfilling prophecy.

Scholars generally agree on what those circumstances were. We have to try to see things the way Matthew and his people did, regardless of whether people see things that way today. Matthew and his audience already believe that Jesus is the messiah. They also believe that God must have been dropping hints about the messiah in the scriptures, especially in the books of the prophets. So Matthew goes back to the scriptures and studies them carefully, looking for clues about Jesus the messiah. For Matthew, the recognition of Jesus as the messiah is the newly revealed key that can unlock the hidden meaning of prophecy. When Matthew finds a prophetic statement that *could* be about Jesus, he tries to match it up with something he already knows—or believes—

about Jesus' life. That is how Matthew can take Isaiah's declaration about the providential birth of a boy with a wondrously symbolic name to be a prophecy about Jesus. Furthermore—and this is crucial—*whatever a prophet says about the messiah, or the future Davidic king, or God's son, Matthew can take to be information about Jesus not previously recognized as such.* Hosea said that God's son came out of Egypt, so surely Jesus must have spent some time there. Micah predicted that the ruler of Israel will be born in Bethlehem, which confirms that Jesus was born there. And since Jesus was from Nazareth, in Matthew's mind it stands to reason that this was also predicted somewhere by the prophets. No one expected the messiah to come from that obscure village, but God knew that he would, and surely God must have revealed this somewhere in the prophets. Even if they didn't exactly *say* that the messiah will be a Nazorean, they have must *meant* it.

What all this means is that *the early Christian belief that Jesus fulfilled prophecy arose after and because of the belief that he was the promised messiah.* This very important finding needs to be emphasized. The belief that Jesus was the messiah was the basis for the belief that he was the fulfillment of prophecy. It was not the case that people noticed that Jesus had fulfilled a series of prophecies and so concluded that he must be the messiah. The process worked the other way around. It was because Christians were convinced that Jesus was the messiah that they went searching through the scriptures to discover which prophecies Jesus had fulfilled. In other words, the proclamation that Jesus fulfilled prophecy is a testimony to Christian faith, not a description of its origin.

With this in mind, we can easily see why Matthew's Jewish contemporaries were not persuaded by his "proof from prophecy." It had nothing to do with their having hard hearts or closed minds, or their being deceived by their leaders. All of that is Matthean caricature. It had to do with the fact that Matthew's presentation of prophecy makes sense only from the perspective of prior belief in Jesus. Outside of that perspective, Matthew's use of prophecy has no persuasive power, and can even look like a deliberate distortion of the scriptures aimed at deceiving those who are uninformed and easily impressed.

Matthew knew that he was not going to change minds with his fulfillment of prophecy theme. He designed it to support the faith of his own Christian-Jewish community, not to convert outsiders. Matthew's message is that since the prophets confirm that Jesus is the messiah, his followers are the true heirs of Israel and children of Abraham, despite what the vast majority of other Jews may say. This message would have offered encouragement to a tiny Jewish sect like Matthew's community, at a time when the belief that Jesus was the messiah could make you an outcast in Jewish society. Believing that Jesus was the fulfillment of prophecy helped to reassure his Jewish followers of the rightness of their cause, at a time when the prestige of Jewish authority made this cause seem religiously illegitimate.

But that time no longer exists. It has not existed for nineteen centuries. The viability of Christian belief is not even remotely threatened by Judaism. Today there is not the slightest possibility that Christians will stop following Jesus because Jews do not regard him as the messiah. In the first century perhaps it was necessary for followers of Jesus to believe that the Hebrew Bible pointed to Christ, that Jews did not understand the true meaning of their own scriptures, and that therefore they properly belonged only to Christians (who eventually made them into the "Old Testament"). Christian history is marred with the ugly consequences of the anti-Judaism fostered by those beliefs. In view of the horrifying price that Christians have forced Jews to pay for keeping their covenant with God, isn't it about time to stop insisting on Matthew's mistaken premise? Do not Christians now have the moral obligation to let go of the notion that if Jews truly understood the scriptures they would become Christians?

Millions of Christians still hold this belief, but it seems that few have carefully considered what it really takes to be persuaded by Matthew that Jesus fulfilled prophecy. Our study of Matthew's presentation of prophecy has shown us that:

- He attributes meanings to the prophets' words that they did not intend.
- He interprets their words in ways that are impossible in their own contexts.
- He relates prophecies to events that never happened.
- He invents a prophecy that did not exist.

Let's make this specific by reconsidering just one example: Matthew's claim that the infant Jesus fulfilled Hosea's prophecy, "I called my son out of Egypt." We have seen that:

- Hosea was referring to an event in the past (the Exodus), not in the future.
- "My son" can be taken to refer to an individual, Jesus, only when carefully removed from its own context.
- There is no historical evidence that the infant Jesus was ever taken to Egypt.

Therefore, in order for Matthew to convince you that Jesus fulfilled prophecy, you must approach Matthew's gospel with three assumptions firmly in place:

1. The prophets did not understand the real meaning of their words, but we do.

2. In order to understand the true meaning of a scriptural passage, we must sometimes isolate it by ignoring its original scriptural context.
3. Every story in the gospels reports an actual historical event and can be taken as sufficient evidence that the event occurred.

Is anyone really able to defend these assertions? If you have doubts about *any one* of them, and if you care enough about this issue to study the prophecies for yourself, you will not be persuaded by Matthew.

Let me reiterate: if you have doubts about even *one* of the above statements, you will not be persuaded that Jesus fulfilled prophecies.

Doesn't common sense tell us to doubt not just one of those assumptions, but all three of them? And not just to doubt them, but to deny them outright? Isn't it more responsible to replace them with the following set of principles?

1. The prophets (and all biblical authors) knew what they were talking about—otherwise we are in danger of reading our own meanings into what they said.
2. Scripture must be understood in its own context—hence we need to be skeptical about any quotation taken out of context.
3. Historical judgments about gospel stories have to be based on historical evidence—therefore we must hold open the possibility that some of the stories are not literal history.

Conclusion

In light of all these considerations, the notion that Jesus was the fulfillment of prophecy seems irretrievably flawed.

• It is untenable, unless one is willing to embrace three extremely doubtful presuppositions about the Bible.
• It fosters a demeaning and distorted view of Judaism, inasmuch as it denies that someone could truly understand the Hebrew Bible and also remain a Jew in good faith.
• It discourages Christians from thinking honestly about the Bible.

The belief that the prophets were pointing to Jesus may have been helpful at the time Matthew wrote his gospel, but it has long since outlived its usefulness. It is a belief that distorts the scriptures and has had ugly consequences in history. Therefore, out of respect for Judaism, and out of respect for the Bible, I maintain that Christians have an intellectual and moral duty to relinquish this obsolete, self-serving, and dangerous belief. What do you think?

Are the infancy narratives Historical?

THE UNHISTORICAL NATURE OF THE INFANCY NARRATIVES

After our study of the Lukan and Matthean infancy narratives, the Moses Haggadah, and Matthew's theme of the fulfillment of prophecy, we are left with little reason to think that Luke and Matthew recorded actual history. Rather, we have strong reasons to think that they freely created their stories to express theological, not historical, truth.

That assessment would not have been alarming, nor even especially interesting, to the gospels' original readers. For them, the truth of this kind of story did not depend on its historicity. Our deep concern for historical accuracy and our attendant distrust of theological fiction are distinctly modern phenomena. In the 21st century we expect biographies to be factually true. Though we admit that fiction can be an effective vehicle for religious truth—after all, no one dismisses the parables of Jesus because he made them up—we nonetheless are much more comfortable believing that our religious truths are based on factual events. It matters greatly to us what happened. That is why *we* need to ask whether the infancy narratives are historically true, even while recognizing that this is not their most important dimension, and even while understanding that Luke and Matthew and their ancient audiences would have shrugged off that concern as beside the point.

There are four major reasons why scholars regard the infancy narratives as a whole to be non-historical.

1. These stories are relatively late and isolated pieces of the New Testament. While it is impossible to date Matthew and Luke precisely, scholars all but unanimously accept the educated guesswork that puts their composition between 85 and 100. At the earliest, that is about fifty-five years after Jesus' death and around ninety years after his birth. Nothing in either of the infancy narratives (except for the claim that Jesus was a descendant of David) turns up elsewhere in the New Testament, not even in the rest of the Gospels of Matthew and Luke.

2. Unlike the traditions about the words and deeds of the adult Jesus, there are no plausible candidates for eyewitnesses to whom the material in the infancy narratives could be traced. The words and deeds of the historical Jesus were witnessed by his followers, who had some reason to remember them and pass them on to others. No similar audience can be imagined for the events surrounding his birth and infancy. Of the figures who appear in the two narratives, it seems Mary was the only one alive when Jesus became a public figure and people began to take an interest in his life. Since Luke makes Mary the central character in his narrative, the Christian tradition has imagined that Luke must have interviewed her in later life so that he could base his first two chapters on her recollections. This scenario is suggested by Luke's two assurances that Mary carefully observed and remembered what was taking place (Luke 2:19, 51).

However, the theory that Mary's personal memories are the source for Luke's story is untenable in light of the errors in the description of the temple rituals in which she supposedly participated (Luke 2:22–24). That scene has the family going to the temple for "their purification" and to present the infant to the Lord. But as we have noted, the purification after childbirth was for the mother alone, and there was no such ritual as the presentation of a child. Luke 2:23 quotes the law mandating the redemption of the firstborn, but that law required neither a visit to the temple nor a sacrifice of birds—that was part of the ritual of maternal purification—but rather a payment of money, of which there is no mention. That the gentile Luke could have been mistaken about rituals he had most likely never seen is understandable. But it's asking too much to believe that Mary—whom Luke describes as a thoughtful observer—could have been so confused about such important ceremonies that she experienced firsthand.[1]

3. The narratives of Luke and Matthew are mutually contradictory and irreconcilable. This was discussed earlier (see pp. 11–13) and there's no need to review the discrepancies here. While it is logically possible that one narrative could be historically true and the other historically false, I am not aware of any actual theories arguing this case. Those who want to defend the literal truth of the Bible are not going to argue that Luke is right and Matthew is wrong, or vice-versa. Critical scholars, who rely on evidence in making historical judgments, understand the contradictions between Luke and Matthew to be an example of what can happen when two authors independently create narratives in the absence of historical information.

4. The final reason for thinking that the infancy narratives do not record historical events is that, as best we can tell, their authors did not intend them to

---

1. This is especially true if Mary was kin to a priestly family. The caste of priests were the hereditary ritual experts, and Luke identifies Mary as a relative of Elizabeth, a woman of priestly caste (Luke 1:5, 36).

be historical accounts, nor did their audiences expect it. In Luke's hellenistic culture, biographies were expected to convey a plausible picture of the man's life and times and, more important, a true sense of the man's character. Stories of the man's birth and childhood were not evaluated on whether they preserved reliable memories from those who knew his early years. Instead, they were evaluated on how effectively they introduced the known abilities and character of the man by making them evident in the manner of his origin and in his childhood behavior.

The Jewish culture in which Matthew wrote was familiar with several styles of creative elaborations on biblical stories, of which the Moses Haggadah is just one example. Our selection about Moses from Pseudo-Philo is but a single chapter in that author's complete retelling of the story of Israel in the Hebrew Bible. And Pseudo-Philo was not unique; a number of Jewish works aptly described as "rewritings of the Bible" are known to us from antiquity. Translations of the Hebrew Bible into Aramaic, the targums, went far beyond strict translation and included a mass of material that altered or supplemented the original biblical text. These expansions in the written targums were based on oral storytelling during public worship. Other kinds of writings could be introduced here but the point should be clear enough: Jewish audiences were accustomed to creative fiction based on biblical themes and characters. Matthew's readers would easily have seen that his infancy narrative recycled the story of baby Moses and showed Jesus recapitulating the high points of Israel's religious history. The original readers would have evaluated the truth of Matthew's rendition accordingly. They would have asked whether Jesus truly was the new Moses and the fulfillment of Israel's hopes, not whether Matthew's stories reported actual events.

That there are no identifiable witnesses to whom the stories in the infancy narratives can be plausibly traced (#2) and that nearly all the material about Jesus in Luke contradicts Matthew's narrative (#3) weigh heavily against the historicity of the infancy narratives. That the themes and stories in them are isolated and relatively late phenomena in the New Testament (#1) means that we

---

The Parents of Jesus

The names Mary and Joseph are so familiar that it might be surprising how seldom they appear outside of the infancy narratives. Jesus' mother is mentioned several times in the gospels, but outside the infancy narratives she is named only in Mark 6:3 (copied in Matt 13:55) and Acts 1:14. Joseph is mentioned in the genealogies and infancy narratives, but beside there only in Luke 4:22 and John 1:45 and 6:42. Despite this slender attestation for the names of Jesus' parents, there is no reason to doubt their accuracy.

have no evidence that they were circulating in the oral tradition. For all we know, Luke and Matthew were the first ones to tell any of these stories. All of this means that if we go looking in the infancy narratives for reliable history we will have little to show for our effort. And since there are strong indications that neither Luke, nor Matthew, nor their first readers considered the infancy narratives to be factual accounts (#4), there's little reason for us to do so.

Nevertheless, the infancy narratives are not necessarily devoid of any historical information. Although they were not intended to be factual, this doesn't mean that everything in them is fiction. Some of the information there might be true, even if it cannot be confirmed and therefore count as historical knowledge. For example, only Luke tells us that John the Baptizer's parents were named Zechariah and Elizabeth and that both of his grandfathers were priests (Luke 1:5, 36). That would make John a priest as well. There is nothing implausible about this information and it is not contradicted by any other source. There is no apparent motive for Luke to have made up those details. They just might be true. (If, on the other hand, Luke had reported that John's elderly parents were named Abraham and Sarah, we would be justifiably skeptical.) Still, we need to emphasize that this information *might* be true. We'll never know. The most that responsible historians can say is that *according to Luke*, John's mother was named Elizabeth, whose father was of Aaron's line, while John's father, Zechariah, was a also a priest.

If we are looking for nuggets of information that can qualify as historical, we must start by sifting the narratives for items that are capable of confirmation, either because they turn up independently in both Luke and Matthew or because they involve historical figures known to us from other sources. This process leaves us with a short list of candidates because nearly all the material in the infancy narratives fails to meet either of those initial criteria. Our analysis of the narratives in Chapter 1 found only five items common to both Luke and Matthew.

- Mary became pregnant after she and Joseph were betrothed but before they lived together.
- Joseph was not Jesus' biological father.
- Jesus was a descendant of King David.
- Jesus was born during the reign of Herod the Great.
- Jesus was born in Bethelehem and grew up in Nazareth.

The first two items should be evaluated in the context of a full discussion of the virgin birth and so are dealt with in Chapter 12. The last three are treated below in the present chapter.

In addition to the five items above, there are three incidents in the infancy narratives involving known historical figures, all of which are assessed below:

- The Roman census conducted by the governor Quirinius (Luke 2:1–2).
- Herod's meeting with the magi (Matt 2:1–8).
- Herod's murder of the babies (Matt 2:16).

WHEN WAS JESUS BORN?

In what year was Jesus born? At first sight the answer seems as obvious as the one to "Who's buried in Grant's Tomb?": Jesus was born in 1 CE (= 1 AD). Unfortunately, the calibration of the Christian calendar was flawed at the outset. The convention of numbering years from the birth of Jesus began in the sixth century, following a proposal by the scholar Dionysius the Short. Relying on Matthew's gospel, he put Jesus' birth in the same year as the death of Herod the Great. However, Dionysius got the date of Herod's death wrong by four years—Herod actually died in 4 BCE (= 4 BC). Correcting for this mistake creates the paradox that Jesus was born four years "Before Christ."

Dionysius' numbering was off, but was he correct in thinking that Jesus was born the year Herod died? Both Matthew and Luke have Jesus born during Herod's reign. This is stated directly in Matt 2:1 and indirectly in Luke 1:5 (which associates Herod with the birth of John the Baptizer, placing Jesus' birth about six months later.)

In Matthew's story the baby is born at some indefinite time before the magi arrive.[2] Herod's calculation of two years (Matt 2:16) reflects his paranoid willingness to murder every baby who could possibly fit the time frame described by the magi. Jesus' family flees to Egypt and remains there until they get word of Herod's death. Their stay in Egypt cannot have been too long because Matthew still calls Jesus a "little child" (*paidion*, Matt 2:20) when the family returns to Israel. According to Matthew's narrative, then, Jesus was born a year or two before 4 BCE.

Luke's infancy narrative does not contain any such clues to the year of Jesus' birth. However, Luke 3:23 says that Jesus was "about thirty" when he began to teach in public. Other historical indications put the start of Jesus' career between 27 and 29 CE. So, if we assign a range of 27 to 33 to Luke's "about thirty," we can infer that Luke thought Jesus was born somewhere between 7 BCE and 2 CE.

Matthew and Luke basically confirm each other's clues about the approximate year of Jesus' birth, a mildly surprising agreement for two gospels written toward the end of the first century. Unless they were both guessing—which is possible—they must have had information that Jesus was born sometime around

---

2. Some English Bibles miss the mark here with the translation "newborn king of the Jews" (Matt 2:2). The Greek is less specific: the magi simply ask, "Where is the one born to be king of the Jews?".

the end of Herod's life. Whether that information is accurate is beyond confirmation. Still, the rough arithmetic based on Luke's approximation, which gives us a date between 7 BCE and 2 CE, is a safe and reasonable guess. Our meager evidence does not allow us to be any more precise.

WAS JESUS BORN DURING A CENSUS?

Only Luke reports that Jesus was born during a Roman census. As Luke describes it, the census had three features.

1. Its purpose was to count everyone in the Roman Empire (2:1).
2. It took place while Quirinius was governor of Syria (2:2) and during the reign of King Herod: John is born in the days of Herod (1:5) and Mary's pregnancy is linked to Elizabeth's (1:36, 43).
3. It required people to travel to the cities of their ancestors to be counted (2:3–5).

Luke's information about the census is confused and mistaken on all three points. Let's take them up one at a time.

1. There is no evidence of any empire-wide census under Augustus and no evidence that Romans ever tried to count everyone in their empire in one census.

2. Quirinius began governing Syria in 6 CE. He oversaw one (and only one) census, which included Judea (where Bethlehem is located) but not Galilee (where Nazareth is located), since Galilee was not in his jurisdiction. This census took place in 6 or 7 CE, *ten years after* the death of Herod the Great, in whose reign Luke situates the births of John and Jesus (1:5). Luke refers to this census again in Acts 5:37, where he correctly associates it with a rebellion led by Judas the Galilean. However, Luke mistakenly places this 6 CE census and rebellion after another uprising led by someone named Theudas, which actually occurred around 45 CE.

How did Luke get it so wrong? Remember, he is writing at least ninety years after Jesus' birth. A mistake of ten years or so is easy enough to make from that far away. But there may be a specific reason for his mistake. Both the death of Herod in 4 BCE (which Matthew places shortly after the birth of Jesus) and Quirinius' census ten years later sparked Jewish uprisings. Both uprisings provoked Roman military responses, the first involving widespread death and destruction in Galilee, the second ending in the imposition of direct Roman rule and taxation in Judea. Luke could easily have confused these two tumultuous events, especially from his standpoint nearly a century later.

Scholars who defend Luke's historical accuracy have used the phrase "first census" in 2:2 to argue that Luke is referring to an earlier census than the one in 6 CE. However, we know that Quirinius was not in Syria before 6 CE, and there is no evidence that he conducted more than one census. The "first census" does not mean the first of two under Quirinius, but the first Roman census in the area. Other defenders of Luke's historical accuracy point out that the Greek word for "first" can sometimes mean "prior," which would make 2:2 refer to a census prior to Quirinius'. That meaning, however, violates the Greek grammar of 2:2. Besides that, it does not fit Luke's context, in which the census is a Roman one, ordered by the emperor (2:1). But Judea was not under direct Roman rule until Quirinius took it over and so any census prior to his term as governor would not have been a Roman one.

3. There is no evidence that any Roman census required people to travel to their ancestral cities to be counted. Romans counted people where they lived because that is where they were taxed. People in small villages might be sent to a nearby town that served as an administrative center (rather like a rural county seat), but that is not what Luke envisions. The process described by Luke would create major disruptions in farming and business, the very activities that generated Roman taxes. It would miss those who had immigrated from distant lands or who did not know exactly where their ancestors had lived. Besides, many ancestral towns had been destroyed in the centuries of warfare and not rebuilt. Where would people with roots in those vanished places go? Finally, Quirinius' census was for Judea and did not include Galilee, so it makes little sense for Joseph to travel from Galilee to be counted in a jurisdiction where he did not reside.

Conclusion

There was a census in Judea under Quirinius, but it did not require people to travel and it took place far too late to have anything to do with the birth of Jesus. Either Luke relied on faulty information or he invented the census to create a setting for his narrative. In either case, there is no historical basis for Luke's explanation of how Jesus happened to be born in Bethlehem.

WHERE WAS JESUS BORN?

The infancy narratives of Luke and Matthew agree that Jesus was born in Bethlehem, something mentioned nowhere else in the New Testament—not even in the rest of Luke or Matthew—where Jesus is always "Jesus of Nazareth." In Mark's gospel, when Jesus visits his "hometown" (*patris* in Greek),[3] he goes to Nazareth (Mark 6:1–6). Matthew takes over this scene from Mark without changing the word "hometown" (Matt 13:55). Although Luke's version of the visit to Nazareth is quite different from Mark's, it still refers to the village as Jesus' *patris* (Luke 4:23, 24). In John's gospel, Jesus' *patris* is the region of Galilee (John 4:44).

---

3. The Greek word literally means something like "father place" and designates one's native land or birth place. It can refer to a town, a region, or a country. *Patris* is the root of our word "patriot."

Outside of Luke 2 and Matthew 2, the word "Bethlehem" occurs only once in the New Testament, in John 7:42, in a scene describing a difference of opinion about Jesus.

> Some in the crowd said, "This man has to be the Prophet." Others said, "He's the Anointed." But some objected: "Is the Anointed supposed to come from Galilee? Doesn't scripture teach that the Anointed will be a descendant of David and come from the village of Bethlehem, where David lived?" (As you can see, the crowd was split over who he was.) (John 7:40–43)

Some interpretations of this passage take the mention of Bethlehem to be an ironic twist: John and his readers know that Jesus is from Bethlehem, but the objectors in the crowd are misled by their ignorance and thus misunderstand Jesus' true identity. There are two major problems with this interpretation. First, there is no evidence that John or his readers knew that Jesus was from Bethlehem. This interpretation assumes what it needs to demonstrate. Second, John clearly supposes that Jesus is from Nazareth. This is evident when the new disciple Philip shares his enthusiasm with a friend.

> Philip finds Nathanael and tells him, "We've found the one Moses wrote about in the Law, and the prophets mention too: Jesus, Joseph's son, from Nazareth." "From Nazareth?" Nathanael said to him. "Can anything good come from that place?" (John 1:45–46)

John often breaks into his story to pass on information that he thinks his readers need, especially in contexts where they might misunderstand something.[4] That he does not do so here, when Jesus' Nazareth origins make it hard for people to take him seriously, is a strong indication that John assumes that Jesus was born there.

There is irony in John 7:42, but not because John thinks the people are wrong in saying that Jesus was not born in Bethlehem. From John's perspective the irony is that they are right about the earthly facts, but wrong about the spiritual truth: Jesus' true origin is heaven—where he was physically born is irrelevant—and this is what they do not understand. Later Jesus will explain why they do not recognize who he really is: "You are from below; I am from above" (John 8:23).

So the only support for a Bethlehem birth is in the infancy narratives of Luke and Matthew. As we have seen, however, those two narratives contain very different explanations of how Jesus of Nazareth happened to be born in Bethlehem. In Luke, Jesus is born in Bethlehem while his parents are away from

---

4. See, for example, John 2:21, 6:6, 8:27, 11:13, 12:13.

their home in Nazareth, whereas in Matthew the family lives in Bethlehem and later relocates to Nazareth. These contrived and contradictory scenarios suggest that Luke and Matthew were dealing with a Bethlehem birth tradition that had no story associated with it. Each of them had to devise his own narrative scenario for Jesus' birth and then reconcile it with the fact that Jesus was actually from Nazareth.

If there was no story associated with the tradition that Luke and Matthew inherited, how did it originate? The reasoning reported above in John 7:42 provides a valuable clue:

- The Anointed (the Messiah) would be a descendant of King David.
- The Anointed would come from Bethlehem, the birthplace of David.
- Jesus was the Anointed.
- Therefore, Jesus must have been born in Bethlehem.

The conclusion is derived solely from theological premises. No historical data are involved.

Matthew has his own version of this reckoning of the birth place of the Anointed, one that is backed up by scripture (Matt 2:4–6). Luke is careful to point out that Joseph was a descendant of David and—mistakenly—that Bethlehem was the "city of David" (Luke 2:4, 11).[5] And both Luke and Matthew furnish genealogies for Jesus that, despite their massive discrepancies, trace his ancestry back to King David.

In the face of the solid countervailing evidence that Nazareth was Jesus' "father place" (*patris*), and the strong probability that the minority tradition that Jesus was born in Bethlehem is based on christological reasoning rather than historical memory, we should endorse the nearly unanimous conclusion of historical-critical scholars that Jesus was born in Nazareth.

DID HEROD MEET WITH THE MAGI?

No source other than Matthew reports that Herod met with magi. Normally the silence of other sources is not very meaningful, but in this case such silence is a strong clue that the event did not happen. The arrival at Herod's court of exotic visitors whose inquiry about a new king spread fear all over Jerusalem (Matt 2:1–3) is not the kind of event to go unmentioned by an attentive historian like Josephus. But Josephus says nothing about a visit from magi in his detailed chronicle of Herod's reign. Besides, Matthew's report that Herod consulted with the Jewish religious authorities during the magi's visit is quite implausible (see the comment on Matt 2:4, p. 106). Finally, the magi who find Jesus by following a star are themselves almost certainly a creation of Matthew (see pp. 100 – 101). All the indications are that Herod's meeting with the magi is fictional.

5. See the comment on Luke 2:4, p. 57.

DID HEROD MASSACRE BABIES IN BETHLEHEM?

Apart from Matthew, no ancient source refers to a slaughter of children ordered by Herod. The Jewish historian Josephus, who meticulously recorded Herod's atrocities, does not mention this event. If he knew about it he would have reported it. But would this event have been well enough known to come to his attention? Perhaps not. A murder of babies would be lurid enough to be long remembered in the area, but the number of victims would be relatively low. If the population of Bethlehem was around one thousand—a safe guess—there would have been about twenty boys below two years of age. The murder of twenty peasant boys might not be remembered beyond the immediate locality. It's not inconceivable that it might escape the notice of Josephus a century later. By itself, therefore, the absence of corroboration for the story is historically inconclusive.

Yet there are three considerations that weigh decisively against the historicity of the story.

1. The story cannot stand on its own apart from Matthew's narrative. Herod orders the slaughter because of the information brought to him by the magi about the timing and meaning of their new star. Since the star and the magi are fictions, there is no motive for Herod to kill the boys.
2. The story could be historical only if Jesus was actually born in Bethlehem, which he almost certainly was not.
3. The scene meshes seamlessly with Matthew's strategy of modeling the infancy of Jesus after the story of baby Moses in the Moses Haggadah. Herod's monstrous act exactly mirrors Pharoah's attempt to kill Moses by ordering the mass murder of Hebrew infants.

Conclusion

This story in inextricably rooted in Matthew's literary agenda, not in historical remembrance.

The massacre in Matt 2:16 may be fictitious, but it is realistic fiction, for it rings true to the historical character of Herod. He murdered with impunity. He was especially ruthless when dealing with anyone he feared would become a rival. He murdered his brother, several of his wives and in-laws, and three of his own children. A bad joke of the day, a Greek pun attributed to Caesar Augustus, was that it was safer to be Herod's pig (*hus*) than his son (*huios*). This alludes to Herod's futile attempt to be accepted as a Jew by keeping a kosher, pork-free table. Herod was well aware how deeply he was hated by his subjects. As a final act of calculated viciousness, he pre-arranged for a number of popular Jewish leaders to be assassinated as soon as he died, to ensure that there would be weeping in his kingdom on the day of his death.

WAS JESUS DESCENDED FROM DAVID?

One of the few points of agreement in the two genealogies is that Jesus was a descendant of David. Does that reflect a historical memory about Jesus' family?

That the genealogies agree on this is not in itself historical evidence, since both genealogies could have been constructed precisely to "document" an existing belief that Jesus was Davidic. This seems quite likely in view of the fact that the two genealogies diverge immediately after David and do not agree even on the identity of Joseph's father (see Box 4.4, p. 80).

The title "son of David" was a standard designation for the messiah, one that Matthew emphasizes (Matt 1:1). So it may well be that the belief that Jesus was Davidic arose from theological reasoning: since Jesus was the messiah, he must have been a son of David. That a genealogy could be invented to supply someone with a religiously necessary lineage can be seen in the case of Zadok, the high priest (see the cameo). Nothing is known of Zadok's family origins, but because high priests had to be from the house of Aaron, a biblical genealogy suspiciously lists him as a tenth(!)-generation descendant of Aaron (1 Chr 6:3–8; see the cameo).

On the other hand, Jews were by no means agreed that the Anointed One would be Davidic[6] and so it is possible that the assertion of Jesus' ancestry comes from family tradition rather than from logical deduction from the belief that he was the messiah. Eusebius, a fourth-century church historian, reports a story from the second-century author Hegesippus that grandsons of Judas (Jesus' brother, see Mark 6:3) acknowledged their Davidic ancestry before the Roman emperor.

> Now there still survived of the family of the Lord grandsons of Judas, who was said to have been his brother according to the flesh. Someone informed on them to the Romans, saying that they were of the family of David. The officer brought them before Domitian Caesar,[7] who, like Herod, feared the coming of the Christ.[8] He asked them if they were of the house of David, and they admitted it. He then asked them how much property they had, or how much money they controlled. They said that all they owned was nine thousand denarii between them, half belonging to each, and they stated that they did not own this in money but that that was the value of the small

6. In Mark's gospel (a source for Luke and Matthew), Jesus is called son of David (Mark 10:47–48), but Jesus himself argues against calling any son of David the messiah. In fact, he confounds the Jewish opponents with this argument (Mark 12:35–37; Matt 22:41–46; Luke 20:41–44).

7. Domitian was emperor from 81 to 96 CE. It is extremely unlikely that the grandsons would have been questioned by the emperor himself. If there is any historical basis to this story, it is almost certainly an exaggerated account of an interrogation by a local Roman official.

8. This means that the Romans were worried that descendants of David might consider themselves potential messiahs and thus pose problems for Roman rule.

amount of land on which they paid taxes and on which they lived by their own labor. . . . Domitian did not condemn them at all, but took them for simple folk and looked down on them. He released them and decreed an end to the persecution of the church. After their release they became the leaders of the churches, both because of their testimony and their being related to the Lord. They lived on during the peace which lasted until Trajan. (Eusebius, *Ecclesiatical History* III 30.1–6)

Zadok's Suspicious Genealogy

According to 1 Chr 6:8 Zadok was the son of Ahitub, a descendant of Aaron. This agrees with 1 Chr 18:16 and 2 Sam 8:17, which refer to two priests, "Zadok son of Ahitub and Ahimelech son of Abiathar." If that were the whole story there would be no problem. What casts this genealogical configuration under suspicion is the contradictory information in 1 Sam 22:20 that Ahitub was the father of Ahimelech (not of Zadok) and that Ahimelech was the father (not the son) of Abiathar.

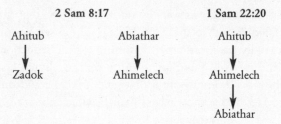

The confusion is increased by two conflicting notices about Zadok's priestly partner under king David: according to 2 Sam 20:25 and 1 Chr 5:11, Zadok and Abiathar were David's priests, while 2 Sam 8:17 and 1 Chr 18:16 tell us that Zadok and Ahimelech played that role.

The suspicion deepens because of Zadok's unusual name, which might be the name of a Canaanite god. Zadok, then, may well have been a Canaanite priest in Jerusalem who prudently switched to the worship of Yahweh after David captured the city. If so, it would have been David who appointed him to the priesthood, probably to help win over his new Canaanite subjects in Jerusalem. We do know that Zadok remained loyal to David during the rebellion of Absalom (2 Sam 15:24–29). In the struggle for the throne after David's death, Zadok sided with Solomon against his older brother Adonijah and anointed Solomon king (1 Kgs 1:39). In reward for his loyalty, Solomon appointed him high priest in place of Abiathar, who had supported Adonijah (1 Kgs 2:35). If Zadok, high priest of Israel, was a Canaanite, his descendants would need to acquire an Aaronite pedigree to defend their legitimacy as priests. Hence the genealogy in 1 Chr 6:3–8.

This story might have some historical basis, or it might have been created for the purpose of supporting the belief that Jesus came from a Davidic family.[9]

There is no evidence that any Jews questioned Christian claims that Jesus was a son of David, even though there were hostile questions raised about the legitimacy of his birth (see pp. 215–20). This silence can be interpreted in more than one way. It could mean that the Jewish opponents were simply not aware of Jesus' alleged ties to David. Or, perhaps there were Jewish objections, but they were not recorded in any extant source. Or, the silence could mean that Jesus' Davidic descent was accepted even by those who rejected the claim that he was the messiah. After all, by the first century there must have been tens of thousands of people who could plausibly claim to be descended from David. So the Jewish silence on this matter is too ambiguous to warrant any historical inferences.

Finally, Paul states that Jesus "was descended from David according to the flesh" (Rom 1:3). Paul makes no theological point of this; he simply states it as a fact. Although Paul can hardly be considered an authoritative source for the historical Jesus, there is no obvious reason why he would invent this notion. And it is reasonable to assume that an expert in Judaism like Paul would have verified information like this with those who were in a position to know.

Conclusion

While there are some indications that Jesus was Davidic, the evidence is too slender for us to say that it is historically probable. The Jesus Seminar voted gray on the question of whether Jesus was descended from David. That is an appropriate judgment in cases where there is guesswork and weak evidence on both sides of the question.

9. Eusebius also relies on Hegesippus for a report that the head of the church in Jerusalem, Symeon—said to be a son of Joseph's brother and thus Jesus' first cousin—was put to death during the reign of Trajan (98–117) because he was a descendant of David (*Ecclesiastical History* III 32.6). According to Hegesippus, Symeon was 120 when he was martyred, a number so unrealistic and so symbolic that it makes the whole story look like a legend.

WHAT IS A "VIRGIN"?

The doctrine of the virgin birth is so well known, and Christmas references to the virgin Mary are so familiar, that raising the question of what "virgin" meant might seem fatuous. We know exactly what the word means. But that is in English. What did the word "virgin" mean in the world of the New Testament? What would ancient Christians or Jews or pagans think when they heard that word?

That's a trick question because the ancient languages did not have a word for virgin. (If this surprises you, keep in mind that, given any two languages, one will have numerous words for which there are no single-word translations in the other. For example, what is the English word for "chili" or "smorgasbord" or "karaoke"?) More exactly, there are no terms in ancient Hebrew, Greek, or Latin that mean precisely what "virgin" means in English. Ancient people obviously knew what sexual intercourse was. They had words for discussing it. They could say whether or not someone had yet had his or her first sexual encounter. But being sexually inexperienced was not a significant enough characteristic for the ancients to need a special word dedicated to meaning just that. When we say "virgin" we mean that the person has not yet experienced intercourse. But in the ancient languages, no single word always carried that meaning. When ancient speakers wanted to convey that concept they either had to imply it by the context or else use additional words to clarify their meaning.

GREEK

The Greek word in Matthew and Luke is *parthenos* (παρθένος). In classical Greek it meant a mature young woman, either married or unmarried. Classical authors could use it to refer to a young wife or a young widow. In other contexts it refers to unmarried girls who we would assume are virgins, but that is seldom the point of the reference. In the Greek Old Testament *parthenos* has a range of meaning. It often means "young woman," with nothing more specific implied. In some contexts it has the connotation of being unmarried. In a few places, the woman's virginity is important to the sense of the passage—for example, in the law that priests can marry only women who are virgins (Lev 21:13–14)—but that has to be inferred from the context. In those rare passages which specifically draw attention to the woman's virginity, *parthenos* is qualified with an added phrase: "a *parthenos* who has not known a man," using the well-known biblical euphemism for sexual intercourse (as in Gen 24:16 and Judg 21:12). In one passage where virgins are clearly meant, the sense is conveyed by the phrase "uncorrupted girls" (*korasia aphthora*),[1] without using the word *parthenos* (Esther 2:2). As in other Greek literature, *parthenos* in the Septuagint did not by itself connote what we mean by virginity. In one passage, this term refers to a rape victim after she has been attacked (Gen 34:3). In another, the term refers to a young widow.

> Lament like a *parthenos* dressed in sackcloth
> for the husband of her youth. (Joel 1:8)

Our literary data show that in the centuries in which the Septuagint and the New Testament were produced, the normal sense of *parthenos* was a young woman of childbearing age who had not yet had a child. In Isa 7:14 LXX, then, the clear connotation of "the *parthenos* will conceive and give birth to a son" is that this will be her first child. A woman is a *parthenos* during her time of transition to full fertility. What completes her transition is having her first child. She stops being a *parthenos*, in other words, after having a baby, not after having intercourse. That is why the second-century bishop, Ignatius of Antioch, can refer to certain *parthenous* (a plural form of *parthenos*) in the congregation who qualify as widows:[2] they are young women who have lost their husbands and have no children.

HEBREW

In the Hebrew Bible the relevant words are *betulah* (בתולה) and *almah* (עלמה). Neither word means virgin, though *betulah* occurs in contexts where virginity is included in the sense of the passage (as in Lev 21:13–14, mentioned above). It is also the word that is modified by "who has not known a man" when

---

1. In the New Testament the adjective *aphthoros* is used to refer to teaching that shows "integrity" (Titus 2:7).
2. "I send greeting to the households of the brothers with their wives and children, and to the *parthenous* who are called widows" (Letter to the Smyrneans 13:1).

the woman's virginity is emphasized. *Betulah* usually means a young, never-married woman, although it is the word for the grieving widow in Joel 1:8.

Almah occurs only nine times in the Hebrew Bible. It means a young woman old enough for marriage, but by itself does not connote whether or not she is actually married. English translations render it "young woman" or "girl," except at Isa 7:14, where Christian doctrinal concerns override linguistic accuracy in some English Bibles (see p. 95).

LATIN

The Latin language is of interest to us here only because our English word "virgin" comes from the Latin *virgo*, which simply means "young woman" and can be used for a wife. Our word "virginity" is from *virginitas*, which is the state of being a *virgo*, and so means something like "girlhood." The later Christian tradition gave this word the sexual (or non-sexual) meaning it has in English. When Latin speakers wanted to refer to someone whom we would call a virgin, they used the phrase *virgo intacta* (an "untouched" *virgo*).

IMPLICATIONS FOR TRANSLATION

Given what we know about the meaning of the Greek word *parthenos*, how should we translate this word in the infancy narratives? The word occurs in only two verses: Matt 1:23 and Luke 1:27, where it is found twice.

Matthew 1:23

Matthew does not call Mary a *parthenos* except indirectly when he applies to her the words of Isaiah's prophecy. Since the term occurs in words that Matthew quotes, we have to ask whether he understood *parthenos* in its usual general sense of "young woman" or in the more specific sense of "virgin." Remember, either can be an accurate translation depending on the context. The ancient scholars who produced the Septuagint thought that *parthenos* meant "young woman" because they consistently used it to translate the Hebrew *almah*. (Some Christian scholars argue that the Jewish translators used *parthenos* to mean "virgin," but there is no evidence that the Septuagint saw a virgin birth in Isa 7:14. Not a single Jewish source reads the text that way.)

What Isaiah meant, however, is not the issue. Nor is what the Jewish Greek translators of Isaiah meant. We are asking what Matthew thought the *parthenos* in Isaiah meant. The only honest answer is that we're not sure, and that leaves the modern translator with a dilemma. There seem to be only two choices and both are bad ones.

A. "The virgin will conceive."
B. "The young woman will conceive."

My judgment is that Matthew probably meant B, but he might have meant A.[3] A is a bad choice because it would stack the deck against the argument that Matthew probably meant "young woman." It would sound as though we were reading an unusual meaning into the word rather than taking it in its normal sense, when in fact the opposite is true. Using "virgin" in the translation and then arguing that Matthew meant "young woman" may even give some readers the false impression that we were twisting the plain sense of scripture. But B is a bad choice too. In the unlikely case that Matthew believed in the virgin birth—please suspend your judgment on this matter until you read Chapter 11—the translation "young woman" would suggest a certain dishonesty in Matthew's application of Isa 7:14 to the virgin birth, and that would be unfair. The basic problem is that *parthenos*, although usually meaning "young woman," can sometimes mean "virgin," and no English word or expression conveys that range of meaning.

Both translations are therefore mistranslations. Having no good option, I've decided on the following bad one: go with choice A, but flag the word with quotation marks to recall the uneasy fit between this English term and the original ambiguity of the words that Matthew had available to him.

Luke 1:27

The only time Luke uses *parthenos* in his gospel is in the opening lines in Mary's first scene. There he introduces her as

> a *parthenos* betrothed to a man named Joseph, of the house of David. The *parthenos'* name was Mary.

When the angel tells her that she will conceive and bear a son, Mary discretely asks, "How can this be, since I don't know a man?" (a literal rendering of Luke 1:34). As we noted before (p. 37), her question is a strange and artificial one for a betrothed woman looking forward to starting a family with her husband. The question is there solely to inform the audience that she and Joseph were not yet sexually active, as betrothed couples sometimes were. Mary's illogical question in 1:34 is therefore essential to Luke's story about the virgin birth.

Luke knew that simply calling Mary a *parthenos* was not enough to ensure that his readers would understand this point. Luke 1:27 tells us that Mary was a *parthenos* and 1:34 clarifies what kind of *parthenos* she was: a *parthenos* who was also a virgin. The question at 1:34 shows us that Luke uses *parthenos* in its normal sense in the descriptive introduction at 1:27.

This makes the task of translation much easier than in Matthew. In Luke 1:27 parthenos means "young woman" or "girl." Since Mary is probably less

---

3. See my lengthy argument for this conclusion in the Chapter 11.

than fifteen years old in the story, "girl" is the better choice. Then in 1:34, instead of reproducing the biblical euphemism "I don't know a man," or inelegantly translating it "I'm not having sex with anyone," the sense in English is perfectly conveyed by "I'm still a virgin."

Not So Original

When I decided on these translations for Luke 1:27 and 1:34, I thought I had broken some small new ground in Bible translation. I congratulated myself for getting the sense of the verses just right, although I was a bit worried that some readers might think it flippant to call Mary a girl instead of a virgin. I later discovered that what I thought were innovative translations of these two verses had been in print since 1966 in the popular Today's English Version and since 1961 in the New English Bible, which is sponsored by all the mainstream churches of the U.K. and Ireland, including the Roman Catholic church. On a whim I also checked Luke 1:27 in my 1981 Swedish language Gideon's Bible and, sure enough, found *ung flicka*, "young girl."

Is there a virgin birth in Matthew?

Before taking up this question, let's clarify the terminology. By "virgin birth" I mean the claim that Jesus was born to a virgin because Mary had conceived him without intercourse. Some who discuss this topic have drawn a distinction between virginal conception and virgin birth, reserving the latter term for a post-biblical belief: Mary miraculously gave birth to Jesus without rupturing her hymen. But since no such claim is ever in view in the New Testament, I do not make this distinction. I follow the common understanding of the term "virgin birth" as defined above, and therefore I use the terms "virgin birth" and "virginal conception" interchangeably. When it comes time to discuss the additional claim that Mary remained anatomically intact after childbirth, the context will make clear that that is what is meant.

The issue under discussion in this chapter is whether Matthew describes a virgin birth. Please note that this is a literary question, not an historical one. We are asking whether Matthew intended to tell a story in which Jesus had no biological father, not whether what Matthew reported actually happened. (We'll get to that later.)

Christianity has unanimously understood Matthew's infancy narrative to be about a virgin birth. And I presume that virtually all of you who are reading this have always taken Matthew that way, whether or not you believe in the virgin birth yourself. After all, Matthew proclaims that Jesus' birth fulfilled the prophecy about a virgin who conceives and gives birth to a son. Besides, Matthew's scene of the angel's revelation to Joseph inevitably reminds us of Luke's scene of the angel's revelation to Mary, which plainly affirms that Mary will conceive while still a virgin. Since Matthew's and Luke's infancy narratives are blended together in the Christian imagination into one composite Christmas story, it is only natural for us to assume that the annunciations in Matthew and Luke are, in effect, different scenes in the same story and that therefore they mean the same thing.

But Matthew did not know Luke's story. And neither did his original readers. One big reason why we take Matt 1:18–25 to be announcing a virgin birth is that we assume the annunciations in Matthew and Luke mean the same thing. For the sake of the argument, let's pretend that all traces of Luke's gospel have been lost and the only Christmas story we have is Matthew's. What happens if we read Matthew on his own terms, without presupposing Luke's narrative?

If we do that, it is not apparent that Matthew is talking about a virgin birth. When I began work on this book I assumed that Matthew believed that Jesus had no human father. My initial research strengthened that assumption. In the first draft of my comments on Matt 1:18–25 I said that Matthew affirms the virgin birth and I explained why. However, while preparing to write a chapter on the virgin birth I studied the issue further and discovered evidence that I hadn't fully considered earlier. Now I'm not sure. I wish I could reach a firm decision one way or the other, but my analysis of all the evidence allows me only a probable conclusion. My judgment is that Matthew probably did *not* intend to describe a virginal conception, but I'm not willing to say for sure that he did not. (If the question, "Does Matthew describe a virgin birth?" were put to the Jesus Seminar, I would vote gray, by which I would mean "probably not, but I can't rule it out.") Perhaps Matthew meant to be ambiguous on this point. More likely, he knew what he meant and figured that his audience would too. But we can read only Matthew's story, not his mind, and his story leaves me in some doubt about his intentions.

The rest of this chapter will lay out both sides of the issue so that you can see the strengths and weaknesses of each. Because the issue is complex, this will be the most closely argued section in the book. If you want to cut to the chase, you can skip the details and go right to the summary of the results at the end of the chapter. But because the virgin birth is such an important topic, you may want to consider the full range of the evidence, think through the arguments, and judge for yourself which position makes more sense.

THE CASE FOR A VIRGINAL CONCEPTION IN MATTHEW

There are four reasons to conclude that Matthew's story is about a virginal conception.

1. Matthew and Luke both know a tradition that Jesus was conceived before Mary and Joseph completed their marriage.
2. Matthew makes it clear that Joseph was not Jesus' natural father.

3. The two reports that Mary was "pregnant by a holy spirit" (Matt 1:18, 20) indicate that God, not a human male, is responsible for Mary's pregnancy.

4. Matthew sees in Jesus' conception the fulfillment of the prophecy, "The 'virgin' will conceive" (Matt 1:23).

Taken together these make an impressive case that Matthew does not think that Jesus had a human father. Let's consider them in turn.

1. The infancy narratives of Matthew and Luke agree on very little, but they do agree that Mary became pregnant while she was betrothed and that Joseph was not the father. It's unlikely that Matthew and Luke independently made up a scenario in which Mary became pregnant without Joseph's involvement; it's doubly unlikely that both evangelists then coincidentally placed this scenario during the betrothal period. We can safely conclude, therefore, that this information came to Matthew and Luke from an earlier tradition. (This does not necessarily mean that this information is historically accurate. It only means that neither Matthew nor Luke invented it.) Luke certainly thinks that Jesus was born to a virgin (see pp. 192–193). Since Matthew agrees with Luke that Mary's pregnancy began during her betrothal and that Joseph was not involved in the conception, it seems a fair assumption that he also agrees with Luke in understanding these circumstances as a virginal conception.

2. The way Matthew describes Joseph's dilemma in 1:18–19 presupposes Joseph's certainty that he is not the father of Mary's child.

3. Matt 1:18 reports that Mary was pregnant "by (*ek*) a holy spirit." In 1:20 the angel tells Joseph, "That which is begotten in her is of (*ek*) a holy spirit." In descriptions of conception or pregnancy, the preposition *ek* (which literally means "out of") is a common way in Greek of denoting the natural father, as in "A was fathered by (*ek*) B." While Matthew is careful to avoid implying that there was any physical contact between God and Mary, his double use of *ek* signals that God, through his holy spirit, is responsible for the conception of Jesus.

4. According to Matthew, Jesus' conception fulfills Isa 7:14, "The virgin will conceive" (Matt 1:23). Matthew's quotation differs from Isaiah's original at a key place: Isaiah speaks in Hebrew of a "young woman" while Matthew refers in Greek to a "virgin." Matthew uses this word because he found it in the Greek translation of the Hebrew Bible, the Septuagint. Now it would be one thing if Matthew took all of his Old Testament quotations from the Septuagint, but he doesn't. Sometimes he makes his own translation when the Septuagint doesn't have the nuance that he needs (for example, in quoting Hos 11:1 in Matt 2:15, see pp. 113–114). As we have previously concluded, Matthew knew both the Hebrew original and the Greek translation of

Isa 7:14 and chose to use the one that can mean "virgin." Leaving aside all the questions this raises about the validity or integrity of Matthew's use of prophecy (see Chapter 8), his choice of the Septuagint version here indicates that he is telling a story about a virgin birth.

THE CASE AGAINST A VIRGINAL CONCEPTION IN MATTHEW

Since it seems counter-intuitive to hold that Matthew had no intention of asserting that Jesus was born to a virgin, and since the opposite position is so deeply ingrained in the Christian tradition, we will go into much greater detail on this side of the argument. Three topics require our attention: Matthew's and Luke's shared tradition, the use of the preposition *ek*, and the role of the four women in Matthew's genealogy.

A Shared Tradition

The assumption that Matthew and Luke both knew a tradition about a virgin birth is just that: an assumption. It is a reasonable assumption, but not a necessary one. What Matthew and Luke actually learned from tradition is that Mary conceived while she was betrothed to Joseph. It might be that both evangelists construed that scenario to imply a virgin birth, but it might also be that Luke understands it that way and Matthew some other way. Which of these two possibilities is more likely remains to be seen.

The Preposition *ek*

Matthew's use of the Greek preposition *ek* in his two references to Mary's being pregnant "by a holy spirit" is not necessarily an indication that Jesus has no human father. It is true that *ek* is a grammatically correct way to name the man responsible for a pregnancy, but that is not the only way the expression functions in Greek. Moreover, there are good reasons to think that Matthew is *not* using this phrase to exclude a biological father for Jesus.

Here we need to go slowly and examine several texts in detail. This may seem like a lot of trouble over a two-letter word. But understanding the precise nuance of the *ek* is crucial to discerning the meaning of Matt 1:18–25, and the meaning of that passage is crucial to a critical investigation of the virgin birth.

There are four considerations that support the conclusion that Matthew's use of "begotten by (*ek*) a holy spirit" does not imply a virginal conception.

1. The Johannine writings repeatedly assert that Christians are "begotten by (*ek*) the spirit" or "fathered by (*ek*) God" (see pp. 226). Obviously, neither usage of *ek* connotes the absence of biological fathers.

2. The Old Testament has several references to individuals who are called

"sons of God" and one passage in which God tells the newly-crowned king, "Today I have fathered you" (Ps 2:6–7, see p. 223). Several other passages name God as the direct cause of specific pregnancies, when it is clear that the woman has had intercourse with her husband (see p. 225). This Jewish way of thinking shows through in the New Testament when Paul describes Isaac as "begotten according to the spirit" and distinguishes him from Abraham's other biological son, Ishmael, who was "begotten according to the flesh" (Gal 4:29).

These examples from the Jewish Bible and Paul the Jew are the appropriate context for understanding the claims in the Gospel and First Letter of John that Christians are divinely begotten, for these writings evince a thoroughly Jewish mentality. All these texts show us that Jews (including Jewish-Christians) could freely refer to people who are fathered by God or begotten by the spirit without ever imagining that they were born to virgin mothers. Matthew is the most thoroughly Jewish author in the New Testament. It is clear that in his Jewish world the concept of divine begetting had nothing to do with the physical circumstances of conception. Being fathered by God was never understood to exclude being fathered by a human male. In light of this, there is no reason for thinking that Matthew's description of the unborn Jesus as begotten by a holy spirit (Matt 1:18, 20) implies that he had no human father. If Matthew is referring to the virgin birth in 1:18 and 1:20, he is using the language of divine begetting to mean something very different from what it means *in every other passage in the Bible*.

3. The annunciation scene in the Infancy Gospel of James contains a fascinating bit of dialogue that sheds light on our topic. The angel tells Mary that she will conceive "by (*ek*) the word of God." Mary is puzzled and asks, "Am I going to conceive by the Lord, the living God, the way every woman does who gives birth?" (InJas 11:5–6). Mary believes what the angel says, but asks whether she will conceive the way all women do. The angel then explains, in words copied from Luke's gospel, that she will conceive without a man (InJas11:7).

The Infancy Gospel of James was written in a non-Jewish setting long after Matthew's gospel. Yet the author was aware that the expression "to conceive by the word of God" was ambiguous enough, even to gentile Christians who believed in the virgin birth, that he needed to narrow its meaning. He has Mary ask her question so that he can have the angel supply further clarification. The author knew that by itself the phrase "to conceive by the word of God" did not exclude a human biological father.

4. There is one more biblical passage that is directly relevant to understanding what Matthew means when he writes that Mary was pregnant by a holy spirit. That passage is in the book of Genesis, toward the end of the story

of Tamar, one of the four women that Matthew inserts into his genealogy of Jesus (Matt 1:3).

Tamar, in order to obtain the marital rights that her father-in-law had unjustly denied her (see pp. 82–83), became pregnant by disguising herself as a prostitute and luring him into incestuous intercourse. When her pregnancy is discovered, Tamar is accused of being "pregnant by (*ek*) fornication" (Gen 38:24 LXX). Her father-in-law, Judah, has no idea that he is the father of her child and he orders that she be put to death. Tamar successfully defends herself by proving that she is "pregnant by (*ek*)" Judah, who then declares, "Tamar is on the side of justice, not I." (Gen 38:25–26). Here we see two uses for the preposition *ek*, the second one to identify the man who participated in the conception, the first one to characterize its moral/spiritual *quality*.

We can be sure that Matthew knew Tamar's story because he mentions her in the genealogy immediately preceding the annunciation to Joseph. The suspicion that a woman is "pregnant by fornication" is exactly what readers have to imagine is weighing on Joseph's mind—what else was he supposed to think? The revelation from the angel directly addresses his anxiety: Mary's pregnancy is not "*ek* fornication," as Joseph fears, but "*ek* a holy spirit." Neither *ek*-phrase is meant to exclude male sexual complicity; rather, both phrases describe *what kind of* conception this is: either sinful or holy. The angel tells Joseph, in effect, that regardless of how Mary became pregnant, her condition is now sacred. God has stepped in, has put this pregnancy under his protection, and plans to use it to serve his will. Joseph, a man of justice (Matt 1:19), is instructed to do justice (i.e., make things right)[1] for the woman and her child, for God has chosen this child to be Israel's savior.

The Four Women

Along with Tamar, as we have noted, three other women appear in Matthew's genealogy of Jesus: Rahab the prostitute, Ruth the seductress, and Bathsheba the rape victim (Matt 1:5, 6, see p. 84). Since women were rarely included in ancient genealogies, we know that Matthew was making a point by adding them and that he could bank on his readers noticing their presence in the list of Jesus' ancestors. Readers who knew the Old Testament would wonder why Matthew had gone out of his way to mention four women, all of whom had sexual histories marked by scandal or shame, hardly the kind of women one expects to be highlighted in the lineage of the Messiah.

As soon as the genealogy is finished, Matthew opens the episode of the

---

1. In biblical terms, a "just" man (*dikaios* in Greek, often translated as "righteous") is not only one who observes the Law. He is a righter of wrongs. In biblical language, to "do justice" is to intervene on behalf of the oppressed and the vulnerable and to make things right for them, as God did in freeing the Israelites from their slavery in Egypt.

annunciation by describing a situation fraught with the potential for scandal and shame: Mary is pregnant, but not by Joseph. The relevance of the women in the genealogy now becomes apparent.

> Mention of the four women is designed to lead Matthew's reader to expect another, final story of a woman who becomes a social misfit in some way; is wronged or thwarted; who is party to a sexual act that places her in great danger; and whose story has an outcome that repairs the social fabric and ensures the birth of a child who is legitimate or legitimated.[2]

On the other hand, if Matthew means that Mary's pregnancy was the result of a virginal conception, it is very difficult to discern what connection he saw between Mary and the women in the genealogy. Their stories feature no divine interventions, and certainly no miracles. If Matthew had wanted to prepare readers for a miraculous birth, he could have mentioned Sarah, mother of Isaac, and Rachel, mother of Jacob—both of whom conceived through miracles—instead of Tamar, Rahab, Ruth, and Bathsheba.

MATTHEW 1:23

The greatest difficulty for the argument that Matthew does not assume a virginal conception is posed by Matt 1:22–23:

> All this happened so the prediction of the Lord given by the prophet would come true:

> > Look, the "virgin"[3] will conceive a child
> > and she will give birth to a son,
> > and they will name him Emmanuel

> (which means "God is with us").

If Matthew does not think that Jesus was born to a virgin, why would he quote this prophecy? Its meaning is so traditional and so uncontested that it might seem wrongheaded even to question it. But we are not asking what this verse means to the Christian tradition. We are asking what it meant to Matthew and his original audience. Here it is especially important to remind ourselves of that distinction.

It would help if we put the shoe on the other foot. Instead of asking what else Matt 1:23 could intend besides the virgin birth, let's ask whether 1:23 by itself would make us think that Jesus was virgin born. In other words, if we read 1:23 without assuming that we already know what it means, would we think that it was about the virgin birth?

2. Schaberg, *Illegitimacy*, 33.
3. For an explanation of the quotation marks, see pp. 191–92.

I think we would, but only if two conditions were met:

1. The word "virgin" in Matthew would have to mean exactly what we mean by it today.
2. "The 'virgin' will conceive" would have to mean that she would conceive *and still remain a virgin.*

How well do these conditions hold up under critical scrutiny?

1. Matt 1:23 says, "the *parthenos* will conceive." As we have seen, *parthenos* can, but usually does not mean in Greek what virgin means in English (see pp. 189–190). (Luke is well aware of this, and therefore has Mary tell the angel that she is not sexually active, so as to specify for the reader what kind of *parthenos* she is.) The only other time Matthew uses *parthenos* is in the parable of the ten "maidens" in Matt 25:1–13, which has nothing to do with virginity. Indeed, the word could refer to someone in her first pregnancy without stretching its normal meaning. Is Matthew using *parthenos* in its usual sense (young woman) or in a special sense (virgin)? Unfortunately, the word itself doesn't help us answer that question. Since it could legitimately be used in either way, its meaning here must be inferred from something else.

2. Even if Matthew gave *parthenos* the special meaning of "virgin," the meaning of "the virgin will conceive" is still not clear. The key to the puzzle here is the sense of the "will" in the future tense verb "will conceive." Does Matthew mean that the woman remains a virgin *after* the conception, that she conceived without sexual intercourse? (That is certainly not what Isaiah had in mind, but that is beside the point. We are trying to discern what meaning *Matthew* saw in these words.)

The normal sense of "the virgin will conceive" connotes nothing miraculous. Someone who is now a virgin will conceive, but then she will no longer be a virgin. We effortlessly understand numerous expressions like this.

> The bachelor will get married.
> The candidate will win the election.
> The rich man will go bankrupt.

You can easily think of a dozen more examples. In all of them the "will" marks the event after which the description of the person can no longer apply.

Again, is Matthew using these words in their normal sense or is he describing a miracle? As before, the words by themselves can carry either meaning and so our decision about what Matthew means has to be made on other grounds.

What all this shows is that *nothing in the ordinary meaning of the prophecy indicates that Matthew had to understand it to be a prediction of a virgin birth.* The quotation *could* carry that meaning for Matthew, but only if he read that meaning into it, by 1) taking *parthenos* in a specialized sense, and 2) construing "will conceive" to point to a miracle. In short, Matthew could find a virgin birth in this prophecy only if he already knew what he was looking for.

Is it likely that Matthew would treat the words of the prophets this way? Yes. Judging from how he handles other prophetic passages, he was quite willing to find special—even hidden—meanings in them. He was even willing to alter the prophet's words if that's what it took to bring out the meaning he was looking for (see p. 112). It's possible that Matthew believed that the words of Isaiah in Matt 1:23 were about a virgin birth, and if he did it's easy to see why he quotes them: to show that Jesus' miraculous birth fulfills prophecy. Remember that Matthew's audience is comprised largely of Jewish followers of Jesus, people for whom a story about a virgin birth would be unsettling because it would sound distinctly pagan. By adducing Isaiah's prophecy Matthew was sending a strong signal of reassurance that Jesus' virgin birth, far from being some pagan innovation, was in the plan of Israel's God all along.

We may therefore conclude that although the wording of the prophecy as quoted in Matt 1:23 does not in itself point to a virgin birth, it is plausible that Matthew could have read that meaning into it, and easy to see why he would quote it in support of a narrative about Jesus' virgin birth.

A More Likely Proposal

When we look at the story the other way, that is, as a story that is not about a virgin birth, it is less clear why Matthew quoted Isa 7:14. After all, "the young woman will conceive and give birth to a son" is fulfilled every time a boy is born to a young mother. So if Matthew understood those words in their normal sense, they do not point to anything special about the birth of Jesus. In that case something else in Isa 7:14 must have caught Matthew's attention and fired his imagination, something else that highlighted for him how God was at work in the life of Jesus. I think we can discover what that was by looking at the context Matthew designed for the prophecy: he introduced it immediately after the explanation of Jesus' name in 1:21. Notice the precise symmetry between 1:21 and the quotation of the prophecy in 1:23.

Matt 1:21	Matt 1:23
She will give birth to a son	She will give birth to a son
and you will name him Jesus,	and they will name him Emmanuel,
for he will save his people from	which means "God is with us."
their sins.	

The verbatim similarities in the first two clauses of each verse—the Greek words are identical except for the "you" and the "they"—shows that Matthew

---

Can they all be wrong?

Every early Christian author who mentions Matthew's infancy narrative treats it as a virgin birth story. Is it credible that all of them could have misunderstood Matthew's intent?

Yes it is, for two reasons. First, all these authors were gentiles. The pagan cultures in which they lived were familiar with stories about heroes who had one divine and one human parent. Even if Christians did not believe those stories, their culture disposed them to think of a son of God as someone without a human father, a concept foreign to Jews like Matthew. While it is possible that Matthew adopted an alien concept, the point is that the idea of a virgin birth came naturally to gentile Christians, and so explains why they would interpret Matthew that way.

Second, early Christians who had access to more than one gospel believed that they all were telling the same basic story. They knew there were differences among them, but reasoned that because all the gospels had the same Author they all had the same meaning. Christians therefore assumed that Matthew and Luke were telling about the same thing. Since Luke's narrative is clearly about a virgin birth, they had no reason to suspect that Matthew's was not. As we have seen for ourselves, if we expect Matthew's story to be about a virgin birth, that is what we will see there.

So it is not difficult to understand why early Christian writers unanimously saw a virgin birth in Matthew's gospel: 1) they read Matthew with gentile pre-suppositions, and 2) they read Matthew in light of Luke. Since Matthew himself was a Jew who had not read Luke, Matthew's later Christian readers read his gospel from a distinctly different perspective than the one from which he wrote it. We should not be surprised that they misunderstood him on the topic of Jesus' divine begetting.

---

wrote 1:21 to mirror the words of Isaiah in 1:23 and then added explanations of the meanings of "Jesus" and "Emmanuel" to ensure that his Greek-speaking audience understood the symbolism of these Semitic names. This is a strong clue that Matthew's primary interest in Isa 7:14 was the rich symbolism of the name Emmanuel, not the word *parthenos*.[4]

It is also evidence that Matthew was not foisting an alien meaning onto the words of Isaiah, but rather that he saw in Jesus a significance similar to what Isaiah saw in Immanuel. For Isaiah the birth and unexpected survival of the child Immanuel in the "house of David" would be a sign that God was protecting his people and keeping faith with his promises (see pp. 93–94). Similarly, for Matthew the birth of Jesus and his unlikely adoption by Joseph into the lineage of David was the sign that God's saving will for Israel was reaching its ultimate fulfillment.

4. This position is not a novel one. There is wide agreement among scholars who have studied this passage carefully that for Matthew the cash value of Isa 7:14 has to do with the name Emmanuel.

CONCLUSION

If we let Matthew's infancy narrative stand on its own and if we read it without using our knowledge of Luke, it becomes difficult to take it as a story about a virgin birth:

- The genealogy prepares us for a sexual irregularity and a woman whose plight is set right, not for a miraculous birth.
- In a Jewish context generally, and in biblical usage specifically, the language of divine begetting *never* suggests a virgin birth.
- Conception "by a holy spirit" does not connote the absence of a human father.
- Nothing in the normal sense of Isaiah's prophecy points to a virgin birth. The context in which Matthew quotes Isa 7:14 indicates that he sees its prophetic significance focused on the symbolism of Emmanuel's name, not on the circumstances of his conception.

All this adds up to a strong case that Matthew did not have a virgin birth in mind when he wrote his gospel. Why then do I think that this reading of Matthew is only probable? What stands in the way of an unqualified rejection of the possibility that Matthew implies the virgin birth? (In the terms of the Jesus Seminar's conventions for voting, why a gray vote instead of a black one?)

There are two reasons for my hesitation. First, nothing in Matt 1:18–25 positively rules out a virgin birth, and if you take up the passage expecting a virgin birth, nothing there will lead you to think otherwise.[5] That is why Christian interpreters all through history have read it that way (see the cameo "Can they all be wrong?"). Second, a Jewish Christian wishing to write a story about a virgin birth, while still making the other theological points that Matthew makes, would be hard put to write anything much different from what Matthew actually wrote. Perhaps this hypothetical author would have inserted different women into the genealogy (see above), but 1:18–25 would stand pretty much as written.

To understand Matthew's perspective on all this, we need to keep in mind that the concept of a virgin birth was foreign to his Jewishness. The thought of Jesus being born without a human father would strike Matthew as a dangerously pagan notion. It is unlikely that Matthew could have brought himself to imagine that Jesus was virgin born, even if he knew that other Christians held and taught this belief. Nevertheless, the possibility remains that Matthew accepted this innovation and then did his best to counteract its pagan overtones by expressing it in the traditional Jewish language of divine

---

5. I also insist that if you come to Matt 1:18–25 *without* expecting a virgin birth, nothing is there to suggest it. See above.

begetting[6] and by buttressing it with the quotation from Isaiah. I think this is unlikely, but I can't see how to rule it out.

6. As we have seen, that traditional language never points to a virgin birth. There would thus be a strong internal tension in Matthew's expressing a non-Jewish idea in traditional Jewish language. But Matthew is not immune to internal tensions. For instance, he includes several examples of Jesus altering the Law of Moses (Matt 5:31–32, 38–39, 43–44), even as he reports Jesus insisting that not even the slightest detail in the Law can ever be changed (Matt 5:17–19).

Is the virgin birth historical?

Is the virgin birth an historical fact? Can we say, as a matter of historical knowledge, that Jesus was conceived without a human father? I phrase the question that way in order to distinguish it from the question that asks for a statement of religious faith. My answer to the historical question is no. Because this topic is a sensitive one theologically, I need to point out that this is a widely held position among biblical scholars. I am not aware of any critical scholars who argue that the virgin birth can be historically demonstrated to be even probably true. The most that some will claim is that its literal truth cannot be excluded by historians. I disagree, but we'll get to that in a few pages.

The Evidence

First we need to assess the evidence. The most striking thing about the evidence is how little there is. Only in Luke 1, and possibly—but not probably—in Matthew 1 do we find attestation for the virgin birth. No other New Testament book refers to it, and neither Luke nor Matthew mentions it outside of their opening chapters.[1]

How far back does belief in the virgin birth go? Since the earliest parts of the New Testament (Paul, Q, and Mark) show no trace of it, the belief is unlikely to have existed long before Luke wrote his gospel. None of the New Testament gospels hints that Jesus' contemporaries, or his disciples, or even his family believed that he was virgin born.[2] Some scholars argue that the silence of the rest of the New Testament does not preclude other authors or

1. This fact has made scholars wonder if, and some to argue that, the virgin birth was added to these two gospels in a second draft.
2. Except, of course, Mary in Luke's gospel.

other Christians from knowing about that belief.[3] While it's theoretically true that silence doesn't prove what people don't know, appealing to this principle in this case is special pleading. It strains the imagination to wonder why so many Christian writers would keep silent about such a distinguishing miracle if they had heard of it; the near-total silence of the New Testament is not a neutral silence.

In short, the evidence for the virgin birth is both 1) very meager (probably in only one passage, possibly two), and 2) absent from the earliest (pre 70 CE) parts of the tradition.

The virgin birth first appears in a written gospel no earlier than fifty years after the death of Jesus, by which time early Christianity was a predominately gentile religion. Gentiles in a pagan culture expected a man whose life embodied divinity to have a divine father and a human mother. The virgin birth thus corresponds to what gentile Christians expected in a biography of Jesus. The only feature of the belief that stands out from its pagan parallels is that Jesus was conceived without divine intercourse with his mother, a distinction in keeping with the theological sensibilities of Jews, Christians, and philosophically minded pagans, for whom it was out of the question to associate sexuality, or any human passion, with God.

The only evidence we have for the virgin birth is evidence that some Christians believed it. That belief was neither early nor widespread, and even if it had been, we would still have to ask whether it was based on historical fact. And that is where historical investigation reaches a dead end. There are two reasons for this, either of which by itself is enough to rule out considering the virgin birth to be an historical fact. The first has to do with the philosophical problem of allowing reports of miracles into the historical record. The second has to do with the very definition of history.

History and Miracles

Thinking about alleged miracles like the virgin birth inevitably raises the question of how philosophical views influence historical judgments. If your understanding of reality is such that you don't believe that a miracle like the virgin birth is possible, then you cannot even consider taking the virgin birth literally. On the other hand, if your world view makes room for the possibility of a human life beginning without a biological father, then you can approach the historical question more neutrally. In debates about these mat-

---

3. For instance: "We have no way of knowing how widespread in New Testament times was a belief in the virginal conception." Brown, *Birth of the Messiah*, 521.

ters, those who believe in the possibility of such miracles may try to claim the higher philosophical ground, arguing that they are more open minded[4]—as if indecision about what is possible in our world were always a virtue. Those who advocate this perspective on principle—and not just as a convenient rhetorical strategy—would have to concede that it was also intellectually virtuous to keep an open mind about such things as channeling and alien abductions.[5]

But this open mindedness comes at a steep price. If you believe that it was possible for Jesus to have no human father, you also have to hold open the same possibility for Plato, Pythagoras, Augustus, and the other hellenistic heroes. And remember, you don't have to believe that the stories about them are actually true, only that they could be true. Of course, we discount those stories today, not so much because of philosophical considerations, but because we no longer believe in the Greek and Roman gods. This is a simple observation, but it has very important implications. It shows that those who believe in the virgin birth of Jesus but not in the hellenistic stories are using religious criteria to make this distinction. (Our God exists; their gods don't.) There is nothing wrong with that, of course, as long as everyone understands that this is a religious belief. It becomes a problem, however, when this religious belief is mistakenly treated as an historical conclusion—that is, a belief about what happened in the past based on critical consideration of public evidence. If that sounds like splitting hairs, think about the Islamic teaching that Jesus did not die on a cross. Muslims believe this because the Qur'an says so (4:157). But the fact that the Qur'an says so is not by itself historical evidence against Jesus' crucifixion. I hope even Muslim historians would agree that the Qur'an's denial of Jesus' death on a cross is persuasive only if one accepts the religious authority of that holy book.

4. An extreme example of this rhetorical strategy is N. T. Wright's explanation for why he believes in a literal virgin birth. "There are indeed more things in heaven and on earth than are dreamed of in post-Enlightenment metaphysics. The 'closed continuum' of cause and effect is a modernist myth. . . It is all very well to get on one's high metaphysical horse and insist that God cannot behave like this, but we do not know that ahead of time. . . Such positions produce a cartoon picture: the mouse draws itself up to its full height, puts its paws on its hips, and gives the elephant a good dressing down." (*The Meaning of Jesus*, 172–73.) This kind of rhetoric masquerades as intellectual humility, but is unmistakably intended to belittle people with the opposite view by making them look foolish.

5. Unfortunately, those who urge us to keep an open mind about miracles seldom seem to apply that principle to reports about miracles that, if true, would undermine their own religious beliefs. I wonder, for example, how many of those who are open minded about the biblical accounts of angelic appearances take seriously the story about the angel Moroni revealing the Book of Mormon to Joseph Smith.

History as Public Knowledge

Historical knowledge is by definition public knowledge, and so must be based on public evidence.[6] By its very nature a virgin birth is the kind of phenomenon for which there can be no public evidence. Suppose a woman claimed that her child was not fathered by a man (and leave aside any possibility of cloning). You either take her word for it or you don't. Public evidence is the kind of thing that should influence fair minded people who aren't content simply to take someone's word for it. But what evidence could possibly support the woman's claim? Even if she were to pass a lie detector test, that would show only that she herself believed her claim, not that it was objectively true. Moreover, in our hypothetical case we are dealing with a first-person claim by the woman in question; we have no indication that Mary ever made such a claim. In short, since a virginal conception cannot be an object of public knowledge, the virgin birth of Jesus cannot be historical knowledge.

This does not prove that it did not happen. After all, many things happen that are not, or cannot be, known to history. History is a partial account of the past. Those who choose to believe that Jesus had no biological father will not be contradicted by historical knowledge. (Nor for that matter will Muslims who believe that it was a Jesus look-alike, not Jesus himself, who was crucified.) Now here is where it can get sticky. Scholars who are careful not to let historical criticism of the Bible undermine traditional dogma hold the door open for the virgin birth by arguing that historians cannot say anything either for *or against* its historicity. This is misleading[7] because it gives the impression that the historical issue is a toss-up. If we accept the principle that historical knowledge has to be public knowledge, however, consistency requires us to close that door on the virgin birth. Its ineligibility as historical knowledge means that it cannot be used in any account of the life of the historical Jesus. A properly historical account of his life must proceed on the assumption that Jesus' life began as naturally as anyone else's.

6. For an extended discussion of this point, see my "Back to Basics," expanded in *The Jesus Seminar and its Critics*, chapter 2.

7. Dominic Crossan argues that this position is not only misleading, but that it poses a serious ethical problem for historians. See his trenchant remarks in *The Birth of Christianity*, pp. 26–29.

Was Jesus illegitimate?

Matthew and Luke agree that Joseph was not Jesus' biological father. Luke assumed that Jesus had no human father at all. Matthew probably thought that Jesus was fathered by a man other than Joseph. From our perspective, then, Matthew's story implies, discretely and respectfully, that Jesus was illegitimate. From Matthew's perspective, however, Jesus was not illegitimate. He was properly adopted by Joseph (see p. 89) and hence his lawful (i.e., legitimate) son.

Other than Matthew, no Christian writer states or implies that Jesus was illegitimate. And no Christian commentator on Matthew's gospel read his story that way.[1] There are, however, a number of ancient insinuations and accusations of Jesus' illegitimacy that call for historical analysis.

In this chapter we take up passages from the Gospels of Mark and John, the Acts of Pilate, an anti-Christian treatise called *The True Doctrine*, and later Jewish literature.

ALLUSIONS IN THE GOSPELS?

"Son of Mary" (Mark 6:3)

> Isn't this the carpenter, the son of Mary? (Mark 6:3)
> Isn't this the carpenter's son? Isn't Mary his mother? (Matt 13:55)
> Isn't this the son of Joseph? (Luke 4:22)
> Isn't this Jesus, the son of Joseph? Don't we know both his father and his mother? (John 6:42)

A good deal of the information presented in this chapter comes from Jane Schaberg's *The Illegitimacy of Jesus*.

1. But see the cameo, "Can they all be wrong?" on p. 204.

In Mark 6:1–6 Jesus visits Nazareth accompanied by his disciples.

¹He comes to his hometown and his disciples follow him. ²When the sabbath day arrived, he started teaching in the synagogue; and many who
heard him were astonished and said so: "Where's he getting this?" and
"What's the source of all this wisdom?" and "Who gave him the right to
perform such miracles?" ³"Isn't this the carpenter, the son of Mary? And
who are his brothers, if not James and Judas and Simon? And who are his
sisters, if not our neighbors?" And they resented him. (Mark 6:1–3)

Identifying Jesus as "son of Mary" is unique in the New Testament and identifying a man solely by referring to his mother is highly unusual in Jewish culture. Were the people of the village where Jesus grew up insinuating that his
father was unknown, i.e., that Jesus was illegitimate? Or were they implying
only that Jesus was fatherless, the son of a widow? Mark has no birth story,
never mentions Joseph, and shows no interest in Jesus' origins, so we cannot
turn to any other passage in Mark for help in discovering how he understood
this odd description. Nor do we pick up any clues from ancient Jewish language customs. We just don't know whether "son of Mary" by itself would
have been derogatory. In later centuries, it was Jewish legal practice to refer to
a man solely as the son of his mother only if he was illegitimate, but there is
no evidence that this was the custom in the first century, nor should we
assume that any expression means the same in everyday speech as it does in
technical legal language.

Since nothing outside of Mark 6:1–6 helps us interpret what is implied
by "son of Mary," the only thing we have to go on is how this term functions
within the context of the scene itself. *If* Mark understood it to be a snide reference to Jesus' illegitimacy, we could safely infer that this was something he
found in his tradition, since it is extremely unlikely that he would create such
a stinging insult on his own. That would be a significant finding because it
would indicate that rumors of Jesus' illegitimacy predated our earliest gospel.
However, in the context of Mark 6:1–6 no insult seems intended. The point
of all the rhetorical questions in 6:2–3 is to contrast Jesus' new reputation as a
miracle worker and teacher of wisdom with his ordinary roots. That is surely
the point of mentioning that he used to ply the lowly trade of carpentry. It is
also the point of naming his brothers and sisters—to underline that he belongs
to an ordinary family that everyone knows, not that he is the one illegitimate
member of an otherwise respectable family. Therefore, the way Mark uses "son
of Mary" does not indicate that he intends it to be taken as a slur on Jesus'
legitimacy.

Matthew, however, was uneasy with the phrase[2] and took care to exclude

2. So were some early Christian scribes. See the cameo, "Mark 6:3 Censored."

it from his gospel. In editing Mark's scene, he changed "Isn't this the carpenter, the son of Mary?" to "Isn't this the carpenter's son? Isn't Mary his mother?" (Matt 13:55). With a deft touch Matthew both replaced a phrase that might be taken as an insult and obscured the memory that Jesus had

---

Mark 6:3 Censored

Not all ancient copies of the Gospel of Mark read "son of Mary" at 6:3. Several of them, including the oldest manuscript that we have, changed "the carpenter, the son of Mary" to "the son of the carpenter and Mary." A few other manuscripts read "son of Mary and Joseph." Since scholars agree that "son of Mary" is the original reading, these textual variants show only that some Christian scribes felt it was more prudent to change Mark's text than to run the risk of upsetting their Christian readers.

---

made a living working with his hands, a social position Matthew apparently deemed too lowly for the Messiah.

Luke's version of Jesus' visit to his hometown (Luke 4:16–30) has no mention of either Mary or carpentry. The neighbors simply ask, "Isn't this Joseph's son?" (Luke 4:22). Luke's scene is so different from Mark 6:1–6 that the question in Luke 4:22 might not be the result of rewriting Mark 6:3 and so cannot tell us whether Luke was worried about the connotation of "son of Mary."

John's gospel also reports a hostile question that involves Jesus' parentage:

Isn't this Jesus, the son of Joseph? Don't we know both his father and his mother? (John 6:42)

These lines, however, have no bearing on our question because John does not borrow them from Mark.

Conclusion

"Son of Mary" in Mark 6:3 does not help to make the case that rumors of Jesus' illegitimacy existed prior to the writing of the gospels.

"We're not bastards!" (John 8:41)

In an especially rancorous exchange between Jesus and "the Judeans" in the Gospel of John, they assert that Abraham is their father and Jesus retorts that this is not so. They then fire back,

We're not bastards! We have only one father: God. (John 8:41)

The syntax of the Greek sentence puts emphasis on the "we," a semantic feature that can be communicated in English by using italics ("*We* are not illegitimate") or by adding words ("We are not the ones who are illegitimate").

Actually, "bastards" captures the insulting tone here much better than the more polite "illegitimate." The unmistakable implication of their comeback is, "We're not bastards—you are."

Does this stray bit of intemperate dialogue indicate that John knew that some Jews were saying that Jesus was illegitimate? That's highly doubtful. This insult occurs in the middle of a long verbal slugfest (John 8:12–59). Shortly after the insinuation that Jesus is illegitimate, he returns the favor by calling the Judeans children of the devil (8:44). The ugly episode ends only when they try to kill him and he escapes (8:59). In this context the insults are hurled for their own sake and have no necessary connection to reality. A few insults later, Jesus' opponents call him a Samaritan (8:48). No one should stop to wonder

---

13.1   Acts of Pilate 2:2–4

The Acts of Pilate is an elaborate account of Jesus' trial before Pilate, his crucifixion and burial, events at the empty tomb, and a discussion of Jesus' resurrection by a council of Jewish elders. The prologue to this work claims that it was written in Hebrew by Nicodemus soon after Jesus' death. It was actually written in Greek sometime in the second or third century. Here is the excerpt relevant to our concerns. It comes from chapter 2.

> [2]Pilate summoned Jesus and said, "What do these men testify against you? Don't you have anything to say." Jesus answered, "If they had power, they would say nothing; for each man has control over his own mouth, to speak good and evil. They will see to it."
> [3]Then the Jewish elders answered and said to Jesus, "What do we have to say? First, you were born of fornication. Second, your birth meant the death of the children in Bethlehem. Third, your father Joseph and your mother Mary fled to Egypt because their reputation among the people was ruined." [4]Then some bystanders who were devout Jews spoke up. "We deny that he comes from fornication because we know that Joseph was betrothed to Mary. So he was not born of fornication." Pilate then said to the Jews who said that he had come from fornication, "What you say is not true, for there was a betrothal, as your fellow countrymen say." Annas and Caiaphas say to Pilate, "We, this whole crowd, assert that he was born of fornication, and we are not believed. These men are proselytes and disciples of his." And Pilate summoned Annas and Caiaphas and asked them, "What are proselytes?" They answered, "Their parents were Greek, but now they have become Jews." Then those who testified that he was not born of fornication—namely Lazarus, Asterius, Antonius, Jacob, Amnes, Zeras, Samuel, Isaac, Phineas, Crispus, Agrippa, and Judas—said, "We are not proselytes, but are children of Jews and speak the truth: we were there in person at the betrothal of Joseph and Mary."

whether this reflects a rumor that Jesus was not Jewish. There is no more reason to think that calling him a bastard reflects a rumor about his birth.

Conclusion

Even if John 8 were an exact transcript of an actual argument—instead of a fictitious exchange that John himself created—8:41 is no indication that there was an accusation circulating among Jews that Jesus was illegitimate.

SECOND-CENTURY ACCUSATIONS

"Born of Fornication" (Acts of Pilate 2:2–4)

In this scene from the Acts of Pilate, written by a second- or third-century Christian, Jesus is on trial before Pilate, who is hearing the charges brought against him by the Jewish authorities. Among their accusations is one that Jesus was "born of fornication."[3] Other Jews, "devout men," defend Jesus: "We know that Joseph was betrothed to Mary and that he was not born of fornication." They go on to testify that they witnessed the betrothal of Joseph and Mary.

The scene describes an argument between some Jews who say that Jesus was illegitimate and other ones who say that he was the son of Joseph, legitimately conceived after the betrothal. The Acts of Pilate opens with "the chief priests and scholars" coming to Pilate and saying, "We know that this man is the son of Joseph the carpenter and was born of Mary; but he says that he is the Son of God and a king" (1:1).

The Acts of Pilate is dependent on the Gospels of Matthew and John and tells us nothing about the historical Jesus. It shows only how a Christian author imagined an intra-Jewish debate over the circumstances of Jesus' birth. Whether it reflects actual opinions among second-century Jews is impossible to determine.

"Son of Panthera:" Jesus according to Celsus

In his anti-Christian treatise, *The True Doctrine*, written around 178, Celsus paraphrases a Jewish story about the birth of Jesus.

> Let us imagine what a Jew might put to Jesus: "Isn't it true, good sir, that you made up the story of your birth from a virgin to quiet rumors about the real and unsavory circumstances of your origins? Isn't it the case that when your mother's deceit was discovered—that is, that she was pregnant by a Roman soldier named Panthera—she was driven out by her husband, the carpenter, and convicted of adultery? In fact, isn't it true that in her disgrace, wandering far from home, she gave birth to a boy in silence and

3. The Greek phrase for "of fornication" uses the preposition *ek*. See the discussion of this important little word on pp. 198–200.

humiliation? Isn't it also true that you hired yourself out as a laborer in Egypt, learned there the arts of magic, and used them to make a name for yourself, which now you flaunt among your kinsmen?" (*The True Doctrine* 2)

Here is a direct accusation that Jesus was illegitimate, one that names his biological father. This account is explicitly designed to rebut Christian claims about the virgin birth. Is it a fanciful attack, or does it include a nugget of historical information? To put the question more bluntly: is this charge of illegitimacy a fabricated reaction to the Christian claim that Jesus had no biological father, or is the Christian story a creative response to rumors that Jesus was born out of wedlock?

It is unlikely that Celsus himself invented the whole story. He implies that he heard it from a Jew, a claim that squares with later Jewish sources that call Jesus "son of Pantera" and with a reference by the North African theologian Tertullian in 197 to Jewish accusations that Jesus was the son of a prostitute (*De Spectaculis* 30.6). Although Celsus' narrative is quite different from anything in the gospels, three of its elements line up with details unique to Matthew: Joseph's being a carpenter, his consternation at Mary's pregnancy, and Jesus spending time in Egypt. It seems that Celsus, or his Jewish source, knew Matthew's gospel. This was also Origen's impression. In his refutation of Celsus, he accuses him of using Matthew selectively, leaving out things inconvenient to his case, especially the proof from prophecy that "a virgin will conceive." It seems likely, therefore, that all this is a Jewish response to Matthew's story, which Jews knew either in writing or from debates with Christians.

What about the name Panthera? It is a name well attested in the Roman army, the Latin form of the Greek *panther,* the word for an animal we call by the same name. Some think that in naming the man alleged to be Jesus' biological father the account gains historical credibility. However, the name looks suspiciously like an anagrammatic pun on the word *parthenos.* The "son of *Panthera*" could be a clever turn on the Christian claim that Jesus was the "son of a *parthenos.*"

So, about all that Celsus' work can tell us is that some second-century Jews had a story about Jesus' illegitimacy in answer to Christian claims based on Matthew's gospel. Whether any part of that story is based on anything from before the time when Matthew wrote is impossible to say.

JESUS IN JEWISH LITERATURE

Talmud

No references to Jesus appear in the earliest collection of rabbinic literature, the Mishnah, which was edited in the early third century. The Talmud, an encyclopedia of rabbinic teachings compiled over several centuries and edited into its final form sometime in the sixth or seventh century, contains several references to Jesus that pertain to our subject.

A few references to Jesus attributed to rabbis from the early second century call him "Ben Pantera" (Hebrew for "son of Panthera"). In one passage two rabbis argue over whether it is permissible to heal in the name of Jesus Ben Pantera.[4] Another passage attributes certain heretical teachings to him.[5] There must be some connection between this name and the story related by Celsus, but these rabbinic texts neither say nor imply that Jesus was illegitimate and make no reference at all to Jesus' origins. They seem to treat Pantera as a family name.

A few other references from this period apply another name to Jesus, "Ben Stada." The rabbis knew this was not his real name. It seems to have been the name of a Jew who had been put to death for promoting the worship of other gods. It was applied to Jesus as a kind of nickname because of his reputation among the rabbis for having taught Jews to worship false gods. Several passages say that Ben Stada had learned magic spells in Egypt and brought them back to Israel tatooed on his skin.[6]

The references to Ben Stada are relevant to our topic because a few of them—attributed to rabbis from the third, fourth, and fifth centuries—seem to identify Ben Stada with Ben Pantera. One such passage is clearly about Jesus because it says that Ben Stada/Ben Pantera was crucified on the day before Passover. Another passage records an argument over to whom these two names refer. One rabbi held that Stada is Mary's husband and Pantera is the name of her lover. Another rabbi theorized that Stada was Mary's nickname.[7] A rabbi from the third century is reported to have referred to Jesus as "the whore's son."[8]

Toledoth Yeshu

This work (the Hebrew title means "Life of Jesus") comes from the Middle Ages in various versions. It contains fanciful and defamatory stories about Jesus, an understandable reaction to the appalling persecution of European Jews carried out by Christians in his name. The stories incorporate all kinds of folklore, but may contain fossilized bits of much older tradition. This work is of interest here because its complete narrative of Jesus' birth incorporates some earlier rabbinic material. Here is a summary of relevant parts of the best attested version of the story.[9]

4. Jerusalem Talmud, Sabbath 14d
5. Tosefta, Hullin 2.24
6. For example, Jerusalem Talmud, Sabbath 12.4
7. Babylonian Talmud, Sabbath 104b
8. Pesiqta Rabbati 100B-101A
9. What follows is paraphrased from the summary in Schaberg, *Illegitimacy*, 175.

Joseph Pandera was a disreputable man of the tribe of Judah, who lived in Bethlehem. Near his house lived a widow and her beautiful virgin daughter named Miriam. Miriam was betrothed to Yohanan, a descendant of king David, a man who feared God and was learned in the Torah.

Toward the end of one Sabbath, Joseph Pandera, a handsome man who looked like a soldier, stared lustfully at Miriam. He knocked on her bedroom door and pretended that he was her betrothed husband, Yohanan. Even so, she was taken aback by this improper behavior and gave in to him only against her better judgment. When Yohanan visited her later, Miriam told him how astonished she was at him for having acted in a way so foreign to his character. It was in this way that they both discovered the crime of Joseph Pandera and Miriam's terrible mistake.

Yohanan went to his rabbi and told him about the tragic seduction. But since there were no witnesses Joseph Pandera could not be punished. When Yohanan learned that Miriam was pregnant, he left town and went to Babylonia.

Miriam gave birth to a son and named him Yehoshua, after her brother. This name was later shortened to Yeshu.

. . .

(Later in the story, Yeshu is an adult with a crowd of followers.) Those who defamed his birth he accused of seeking fame and power. Yeshu proclaimed, "I am the Messiah. Isaiah prophesied about me when he said, 'Look, a virgin will conceive, and give birth a son, and will name him Immanuel.'" He quoted other messianic passages and claimed, "My ancestor David prophesied about me: 'The Lord said to me, "You are my son, this day I have begotten you."'"

Like Celsus' story about Panthera, this account considers the virgin birth to be a story fabricated by Jesus himself. It's also interesting that this work goes out of its way to protect the moral reputation of Jesus' mother, portraying her as the innocent victim of a cruel hoax.

Conclusion

There are several references in the Talmud to Jesus under the names Ben Pantera and Ben Stada, but only a couple of them include the notion that he was illegitimate. This rabbinic testimony, intriguing though it may be, is too meager and too late to license any educated guesses about what Jews at the time of Matthew and Luke thought they knew about Jesus. The most that the medieval *Toledoth Yeshu* can tell us historically is that the rabbis *might* have known parts of its story about the birth of Jesus when they referred to him as Ben Pantera. Although we cannot rule out the possibility that there were pre-gospel Jewish accusations that Jesus was illegitimate, it seems more prudent to regard the rabbinic material as a polemical response to Christian claims about the virgin birth.

RESULTS

Let's recapitulate our results so far.

1. Mark's expression "son of Mary," although it worried Matthew and Luke enough to suppress it in their gospels, does not seem to insinuate that Jesus was illegitimate.
2. The malicious retort in John 8:41 does insinuate that Jesus was illegitimate, but does not imply any real knowledge about the circumstances of Jesus' birth.
3. The accusations reported in the Acts of Pilate that Jesus was "born of fornication" might be based on actual rumors going around in the second century.
4. Celsus' report that Jesus was the son of a Roman soldier reflects a Jewish story from the second century, but cannot be confirmed historically.
5. Oblique references to Jesus' illegitimacy in the rabbinic tradition and a medieval Jewish story about Jesus being a child of adultery probably originated as responses to Christian belief in the virgin birth and almost certainly do not reflect historical information.

So, was Jesus fathered by a man other than Joseph? Matthew seems to think so. But it's not until well into the second century that we pick up unambiguous evidence that anybody actually said so, and this evidence comes from opponents of Christianity. Those scattered accusations are best regarded as predictable rebuttals to Christian claims that Jesus was born of a virgin. It is highly doubtful that those who made such accusations knew, or even thought they knew, any facts about Jesus' origins.

Even if Jesus was illegitimate, that doesn't mean that his later detractors knew about it. Their accusation could well have been a gratuitous insult that just happened to be factually true. This possibility can be illustrated from the way we use insulting language. If someone who was born out of wedlock gets called a "bastard," it is probably true only by accident, just as a gay man can be called a "queer" by those who in fact know nothing about his sexual orientation. Words like "bastard" are random terms of abuse.[10]

The hypothesis that Jesus was conceived out of wedlock is unsupported

10. Someone unfamiliar with American culture could easily take our phrase "son of a bitch" to be a vicious insult against the addressee's mother. But it means nothing of the sort; it is frequently directed at inanimate objects.

by solid historical evidence. While we cannot rule it out completely, we need to be very skeptical of it. We can entertain it as a hypothesis, but cannot responsibly treat it as anything more than speculative. So, was Jesus fathered by a man other than Joseph? The simplest and most honest answer is, "Perhaps, but it's doubtful."

And yet there is Matthew's story, for which the most natural—and most Jewish—reading is that it presupposes that Jesus was conceived out of wedlock. Where did this presupposition come from? We don't know and, unless some new evidence comes to light, we never will. But there is one set of historical circumstances we need to investigate.

A PLAUSIBLE AND UGLY SCENARIO

In 4 BCE Sepphoris, a major city one hour's walk from Nazareth, took part in a rebellion against Roman rule. A Roman army was sent to punish Sepphoris. The Romans captured the city, burnt it to the ground, and sold its inhabitants into slavery. The villages surrounding Sepphoris were helpless before the Romans, who did with the villagers whatever they pleased. Everybody knew what happened when an invading army was making war on a civilian population. Women who had not fled or could not be safely hidden, especially the young ones, could expect to be raped. The babies born nine months later would be living reminders to the families and villagers of Israel's humiliation by its pagan enemies.

According to both Matthew and Luke, Jesus was born around the end of the reign of Herod the Great, who died in the same year Sepphoris was destroyed. This puts a Roman army on a punitive campaign in the Nazareth area during the range of years for the birth of Jesus.[11] Here our historical knowledge runs out. The most it can do is provide a framework for educated guesses about plausible scenarios. So although the following is plausible, it can only be speculation: *if* Mary was among the Jewish girls raped by the invading army, and *if* Jesus was born in 3 BCE, a Roman soldier might have been his biological father. Of course, we can't know whether this happened, nor even guess about its probability. All we can say is that it squares with what we know about Roman military history and the available evidence about the approximate year of Jesus' birth.

On the one hand, we cannot know whether Mary was raped nor whether Jesus was born nine months after Sepphoris was razed. On the other hand, historians cannot responsibly ignore that a Roman army bent on rape and pil-

11. The dating in Luke's story is vague enough to accommodate this scenario without difficulty. In Matthew's story Jesus is born a year or two *before* Herod dies. This does not rule out this scenario, however, unless one believes that Matthew's fictional infancy narrative happens to be precisely correct in its chronology. A mistake of a few years is well within a respectable margin of error for a narrative written nearly a century after the event.

lage was in just the right place at about the right time. We can do justice to both "hands" if we parlay this information, not for what it can tell us about Jesus, but rather for what it can tell us about how his contemporaries might have perceived him. Regardless of the actual facts of Jesus' birth, thirty years later people who knew or could guess his age and knew he was from Nazareth, might well put two and two together and wonder whether he was a child of Roman rape. It's a certainty that there were such children about the same age as Jesus in the villages near Sepphoris. Some of them probably grew up with him in Nazareth. When Jesus became a public figure, people who were offended by his teaching or behavior might dismiss him with contemptuous remarks like, "What do you expect from a man born like that?" Memories of the Roman brutalization of the population around Sepphoris would certainly be alive three decades later and so a rumor that Jesus was illegitimate would have an air of credibility.

Closing Thoughts

Before leaving this topic we need to face two issues which inevitably hover over discussions of this normally taboo subject and which can trouble those who have affection and reverence for the Christian tradition.

The first has to do with Mary. Some of the ancient sources we've examined defame her character. As a Catholic I am innately aware of the sensitivities that can be disturbed by these accusations. So I want to make it clear that from my perspective—one I hope I share with everyone in our culture—nothing in our modern discussion of the topic imputes moral blame to Mary. She was a young teenager when she gave birth to Jesus. The Infancy Gospel of James implies that Mary conceived soon after the onset of puberty and refers to her as a "child" during her pregnancy. The History of Joseph the Carpenter says that Mary was fourteen when she became pregnant. Neither of these is historical memory, but they show what ancient audiences accepted as the age for a woman to begin childbearing. But by *our* moral and legal standards, sex with a girl Mary's age is always an act of rape. If Jesus was illegitimate, his conception would have been the result of either physical violence or seduction. In either case Mary would have been a victim. If the perpetrator actually was a Roman soldier, her violation would have been painful and degrading in ways that I hope few of us can imagine.

The second issue has to do with theological implications. One famous scholar has worried that, "For many less sophisticated believers, illegitimacy would be an offense that would challenge the plausibility of the Christian mystery."[12] This may be so, but the same can be said for the scientific fact of evolution. A few centuries ago the same was true for the discovery that the

---

12. Brown, *Birth*, 530.

earth revolves around the sun. Many Christians past and present feared and rejected those truths because they seemed to undermine the truth of Christianity. Another prominent biblical scholar has a similar concern about the idea that Jesus was illegitimate, pointing out that it "causes shock in the pious and glee in the impious."[13] I don't doubt that this is a fair description of many people's initial reactions. (The idea deeply disturbed me when I first encountered it. Before I knew anything of the substance of the issue, I assumed, wrongly, that those who raised it were out to besmirch the Christian religion.) But in the world of the early Christians, the same was true about the idea of Jesus' crucifixion. We today are so habituated to the cross as a symbol of a great world religion that it takes a deliberate exercise of our imagination to accept that ancient people regarded this symbol with derision. To their way of thinking, anyone who had died such a horrible and shameful death must surely have been abandoned by God. Who could take seriously a religion that worships someone who was crucified? Paul was well aware how ridiculous this sounded to the people of his time, for he writes of the "stupidity"[14] of the whole notion of a crucified savior (1 Cor 1:23–25).

If the Son of God could leave this world as the innocent victim of horrifying violence, why is it unacceptable that he could come into this world through an act of violence against an innocent victim? If Christianity can believe that God could reverse the humiliation of Jesus' degrading death as a criminal by raising him from the dead, it can learn to believe that God could overturn the shame of Mary's degrading violation by making her the mother of the Messiah. It seems to me that not only is it theologically acceptable for Jesus to have been conceived in an act of Roman violence, but that such a beginning is symbolically appropriate for one who welcomed outcasts into God's kingdom and died a criminal's death under Roman rule.

I have to admit that because of that symbolic symmetry I find the notion of Jesus' illegitimacy theologically attractive. That is why I am perhaps overly skeptical about it historically: it's just "too perfect" theologically. What are the odds that historical events would exhibit a pattern that just so happens to confirm my beliefs about God?

13. Meier, *Marginal Jew*, vol. 1, p. 222.
14. The Greek word in 1 Cor 1:25 is *moron*, a word that lives on unchanged in English.

Son(s) of God in the Bible

SON OF GOD

AS A TITLE IN THE OLD TESTAMENT

The Old Testament uses the term "son of God" in four distinct ways.

1. *Angels* can be called sons of God (Gen 6:2; Job 1:6, 2:1, 38:7). In the Book of Job, one of the sons of God is called the "adversary" (Job 1:6, 21), in Hebrew *satan*, from which we get the name "Satan."

2. God calls *Israel* his son.

> Tell Pharoah that these are the words of Yahweh: "Israel is my firstborn son. I have told you to let my son go, so that he may worship me. You have refused to let him go, so I will kill your firstborn son." (Ex 4:22–23)

> When Israel was a boy I loved him,
> I called my son out of Egypt. (Hos 11:1)

3. The *Davidic king* is God's son.

In 2 Sam 7:11–16 the prophet Nathan relays to David God's promise to keep his family on the throne forever. Referring specifically to David's son Solomon, and by extension to all of the kings of David's lineage, God says,

> I will be his father and he shall be my son. (1 Sam 7:14; repeated in 1 Chr 22:10)

Psalm 2 was used to celebrate the coronation of a new king. In it the king sings,

> Of me God says, "I have enthroned my king on Zion, my holy
>   mountain."
> I will repeat Yahweh's decree:
> "You are my son," he said,
>   "today I have fathered you." (Ps 2:6–7)

In one section of Psalm 89 the psalmist reminds God of the covenant he made with David and his descendants. The psalm attributes to God these words about David:

> He will say to me, "'You are my father, my God,
>   my rock, my refuge."
> And I will name him my firstborn,
>   highest among the kings of the earth." (Ps 89:26–27)

4. A *righteous individual* can be called a son of God.

In Wis 2:10–20, evildoers conspire to murder a righteous man. Here is part of what they say.

> He says that the righteous die happy, and boasts that God is his father. Let's test the truth of his words, let's see what will happen to him in the end; for if the righteous man is God's son, God will stretch out a hand to him and save him from the clutches of his enemies. (Wis 2:16b–18)

Those who protect the fatherless become God's sons.

> Be a father to orphans
>   and like a husband to their mother;
> then the Most High will call you his son,
>   and his love for you will be greater than a mother's. (Sir 4:10)

This understanding of divine sonship is reflected in the words of Jesus:

> Love your enemies, and do good, and lend, expecting nothing in return. Your reward will be great, and you'll be sons of the Most High. (Luke 6:35)

The ways in which the Old Testament refers to different figures as sons of God shows the sense the term conveys: one who enjoys an unusually close relationship with God and who is expected to do God's will, that is, to obey God the way a son obeys his father. It is in this sense that the rabbis called some Jewish holy men and miracle workers sons of God. The term can apply to both angels and humans, and does not connote any sharing of divinity. In Judaism "son of God" was a title of special status, but had no metaphysical connotation. The notion that to be God's son means having a divine (or semi-divine) nature comes from the Greco-Roman world and is foreign to Judaism. It is also worth noting that "son of God" was never a designation for the messiah.

Divine Causality in Human Procreation

Much of what we today think of as natural processes was understood in the ancient world as the work of supernatural beings. Health and sickness or rainfall and drought, for example, were thought to result from the pleasure or displeasure of the gods. In projects requiring human effort, people knew that they had to do their part, but the final result was not up to them. The farmer had to till the soil and plant the crop, but only God could bring a good harvest. All ancient peoples, including the Israelites, looked at the world this way. When it came to human procreation, they obviously knew the role of sex, but they also assumed that successful pregnancies and safe deliveries were the work of God. Several passages in the Hebrew Bible speak of God causing conception and childbirth. Here are two examples.

- The very first child in human history was Cain. Eve gives God the credit for his birth.

   Adam had intercourse with his wife and she conceived and gave birth to Cain, saying, "I have made a man with the help of Yahweh." (Gen 4:1)

- The next passage is typical in that it simply assumes that God is the cause of human conception.

   Boaz took Ruth and she became his wife. He had intercourse with her, Yahweh made her conceive, and she gave birth to a son. (Ruth 4:13)

Several stories in the Bible credit God with overcoming human infertility, which in the ancient world was always considered to be a defect in the woman. Two of these stories describe God as "opening the womb" of the infertile woman.

When Yahweh saw that Leah was unloved, he opened her womb. . . and Leah conceived and gave birth to a son. (Gen 29:31–32)

Then God remembered Rachel. He heard her prayer and opened her womb. She conceived and gave birth to a son. (Gen 30:22–23)

Leah and Rachel were married to the same man, Jacob. Neither of the terse reports above mentions his involvement in the conception, but no one has ever imagined the Bible to imply that these sons of Leah and Rachel (Reuben and Joseph) were anything other than Jacob's biological children. The Old Testament never understands God's role in causing conception to exclude intercourse with a man.

Divine Fathering/Begetting

Closely connected to the notion of God having sons is the terminology of God "fathering" or "begetting." Our English vocabulary can get muddled here, so a brief explanation is in order. The verb "beget" has become archaic in our language. We know what the word means but do not use it in our own speech. Probably the only place we encounter the word nowadays is in the Bible. In modern English, when we describe a man's role in producing a child, we use the verb "to father." The relevant word in ancient Greek is the verb *gennan*, from which we get the English words "generate," generation," and "genitals." To avoid relying on archaic words in translating the Bible, in many New Testament passages we can render *gennan* with "to father." But in other passages there is a problem with translating it this way: in Greek *gennan* can have a masculine, feminine, or neuter subject, whereas in English only a man can father a child. So when the New Testament uses the verb with a subject like "spirit" or "water" the translation "to father" is inappropriate. (This is one of many cases in which the same Greek word calls for different English words in different contexts.) So it seems best to accept an inelegant compromise: render *gennan* with "to father" when the subject is masculine (the Greek word for "God" is masculine in gender), with the old fashioned "to beget" when the subject is neuter (as in "begotten" by the spirit, which in Greek is a neuter noun), and with "to give birth to" when the subject is feminine.[1]

CHRISTIANS AS FATHERED BY GOD

Some New Testament passages refer to baptism as a second birth.

> You have been born again, not of mortal parentage but of immortal, through the living and enduring word of God. (1 Pet 1:23; see also 1:3)

In the famous passage in which Jesus tells Nicodemus of the need for people to be "born again," baptism is referred to as "being begotten by water and spirit" (John 3:5).

The Gospel and First Letter of John use the terminology of divine fathering/begetting to refer to Christians.

> To those who believed in the light, it gave the right to become children of God. They were not born from sexual union, not from physical desire, and not from male willfulness; they were fathered by God. (John 1:12–13)

The language here is striking, for it explicitly denies that children of God have human parents. It is God alone who fathers them; their origin has nothing to do with human procreation.

> Everyone who does justice is fathered by God. (1 John 2:29)
> No one fathered by God commits sin because God's seed (*sperma*) remains in him. He cannot sin because he was fathered by God. (1 John 3:9)
> Love is from God, and everyone who loves was fathered by God. (1 John 4:7)
> Everyone who believes that Jesus is the Anointed One was fathered by God. (1 John 5:1)
> No one fathered by God sins; instead, the one fathered by God watches over him. (1 John 5:18)

---

1. There are separate Greek verbs (*sullambanein, kuein*) for a woman's act of conceiving.

The last example is especially interesting because it refers to Christians and to Christ in exactly the same way. The Gospel of John eloquently affirms that Jesus existed from all eternity as the Word of God. However, there is no evidence whatsoever that John believed in the virgin birth.[2] As far as John knew, the Word of God came into the world the way all of us do.

Two other occurrences of the concept of divine fathering in the New Testament show how widely early Christians could apply it.

1. In the Acts of the Apostles, in a speech attributed to Paul in Athens, Paul quotes and endorses an affirmation from Greek poetry: "We are all God's offspring (*genos*)" (Acts 17:28).

2. In the Letter to the Galatians, Paul develops an allegorical interpretation of the difference between Abraham's two sons: Ishmael, born to his slave Hagar, and Isaac, born to his aged wife Sarah. Ishmael, Paul asserts, "was fathered through flesh," while Isaac was fathered "through God's promise" (Gal 4:23). A few verses later, Paul contrasts the two sons: one was fathered "through flesh," the other "through spirit" (Gal 4:29). Paul can speak this way even though everyone knows that Abraham was the biological father of both boys. This by itself is a strong clue about how Jews and early Christians understood the language of divine begetting.

JESUS AS DIVINELY FATHERED/BEGOTTEN

Several passages in the New Testament refer to Jesus's conception.

Paul

Paul's sole reference to Jesus' birth states only that he "was born of a woman" (Gal 4:4). Although later in the same chapter Paul says that Isaac was "born through spirit" (Gal 4:29), he describes Jesus as one born like any other human being.

Paul's assumption that Jesus was conceived and born naturally is also evident when he refers to Jesus as

> God's son, who was descended from David through the flesh
> and was designated son of God in power through the spirit of
> holiness by resurrection from the dead. (Rom 1:3–4)

This statement tells us three things about Paul's understanding of Jesus.

1. Jesus had a biological father who was descended from David.

---

2. When the new disciple Philip tells Nathanael about Jesus, he says, "We have met the man spoken of by Moses in the Law and by the prophets: it is Jesus *son of Joseph* from Nazareth" (John 1:45). The Gospel of John has a number of passages in which people misunderstand who Jesus is or what he teaches, but in every case this gospel goes on to make it clear to the reader how this misunderstanding falls short of the truth. In 1:45, however, John gives no hint that Philip's description of Jesus as the "son of Joseph" is inadequate or mistaken.

2. Jesus' birth was "through the flesh," while his resurrection was "through the spirit." For Paul this means that God intervened in Jesus' resurrection, but not in his conception or birth.

3. Jesus was God's son by virtue of his resurrection, not of his birth.

Apparently Paul did not know about the virgin birth. Since he had spent two weeks talking to Peter and to James, the brother of Jesus (Gal 1:18–19), it seems that they did not know about it either. If they had, it is impossible to believe that they would not have mentioned such an important topic in two weeks of conversation. And certainly if Paul had heard about it from them he would have referred to it when he mentioned the birth of Jesus—a virgin birth is not the kind of information one forgets. Gal 4:4 is the earliest Christian reference to Jesus' birth, and Paul's silence about the virgin birth at this point strongly suggests that that belief did not yet exist.

1 John

As we discussed above, 1 John says that Jesus was "fathered by God" (1 John 5:18). But so are all those who do justice (1 John 2:29), love others (1

The "Only Begotten" Son

The Johannine writings say that Christians are fathered by God, but these texts also refer to Jesus as God's "only son." The Greek term is *monogenes*, literally, "only fathered," or "only begotten." The term occurs five times in the Gospel and First Letter of John. Here are two examples.

> This is how much God loved the world: he gave up an only son. (John 3:16)

> God sent his only son into the world so that we might live through him. (1 John 4:9)

The other three Johannine occurrences are in John 1:14, 18, and 3:18.

The only other use of this term in the New Testament is most interesting. It is found in Heb 11:17, which says that Abraham "was willing to sacrifice his only son." The author of Hebrews wrote the most sophisticated Greek in the New Testament and had a scholar's knowledge of the Old Testament. He must have known that Abraham had fathered two sons, Ishmael and Isaac. That this author can nevertheless refer to Isaac as Abraham's "only fathered" demonstrates that the term, which at first seems to be meant literally, was actually used as a rhetorical device for elevating one son to a level of importance above the other(s). And that is exactly how it is used by John: all Christians are "fathered by God" and yet Jesus was God's "only fathered."

John 4:7), or believe that Jesus is the Anointed (1 John 5:1). Moreover, the very same verse that refers to Jesus as "the one fathered by God" says that he watches over all the others who are fathered by God (1 John 5:18).

Psalm 2:7

In four places, the New Testament quotes God's words to the Davidic king in Ps 2:7 and applies them to Jesus: "You are my son, I have fathered you today" (Heb 1:5, 5:5; Acts 13:33; Luke 3:22; see Box 14.1). These quotations all carry the same connotation as the psalm verse itself: just as the king became God's son on the day of his coronation, so Jesus became God's son on a certain day. It's not clear which day the author of the Letter to the Hebrews has in mind, though the context suggests that it is the day when Jesus was seated

---

14.1   "Today I have fathered you."

Here are the four New Testament passages that quote Psalm 2:7.

When the son had accomplished purification from sins,
    he took his seat at the right hand of the Majesty on high,
as far superior to the angels
    as the name he has inherited is more excellent than theirs.
For to which of the angels did God ever say:
    "You are my son;
    today I have fathered you"? (Heb 1:3–5)

It was not Christ who glorified himself in becoming high priest, but rather the one who said to him:
    "You are my son;
    today I have fathered you." (Heb 5:5)

We ourselves are proclaiming this good news to you that what God promised to our ancestors he has fulfilled for us, their children, by raising up Jesus, as it is written in the second psalm:
    "You are my son;
    today I have fathered you." (Acts 13:32–33)

After Jesus had been baptized and while he was praying, the sky opened up, and the holy spirit came down on him in bodily form like a dove, and a voice came from the sky, "You are my son; today I have fathered you." (Luke 3:21–22)

at God's right hand, after his death on the cross (see Heb 1:4). In Acts, the day in question is the day of Jesus' resurrection. In Luke it is the day of his baptism.

Matthew 1:20

Matt 1:20 is the only New Testament passage that uses the terminology of divine begetting in a context that mentions Jesus' birth: the angel tells Joseph that Mary is pregnant "by a holy spirit."[3] In every other example from the Jewish and Christian scriptures (except for the Gospel of Luke), people who are described as sons of God or "fathered by God" or "begotten by the spirit" have two biological parents. That is one reason why I argue elsewhere in this book that Matthew probably did not intend to describe a virgin birth. That "probably" aside, the important point here is that in light of the way the Bible uses the terminology of divine begetting, we should not simply assume that Matthew believed in the virgin birth. Christians today see the virgin birth in Matthew's story because Christianity has always used Matthew's text as proof for that doctrine. But the interpretation of a passage need not correspond with its original intent; later readings do not certify earlier meanings.

WHEN DID JESUS BECOME GOD'S SON?

Putting the question this way might sound strange. In the traditional orthodox doctrine, the Son is the second person of the Trinity, co-eternal with the Father and the Holy Spirit. From that theological perspective, the idea of Jesus "becoming" God's son makes no sense because it implies a time when he was not the son of God. And yet in the New Testament, written long before the doctrine of the Trinity was formulated, there are passages which state that at a certain point in time God made Jesus his son, bestowing on him a special status he did not have the day before. This way of conceptualizing Jesus' sonship is known as Adoptionism, a term expressing the metaphor of God "adopting" Jesus as his son. Adoptionism was widespread among early Christians and remained a viable christological option for nearly three centuries before it was marginalized by the doctrinal decision of the great ecumenical councils and then suppressed by the authority of both the Catholic Church and the Roman Empire.

The question of when Jesus became God's son was answered differently at different times in early Christianity. If we arrange these answers in historical order, we can see distinct stages in the development of the belief that Jesus was the son of God. We can distinguish five such stages.

---

3. Luke attributes Jesus' conception to "a holy spirit" (Luke 1:35), but does not say that this spirit "begets" Jesus.

Stage 1: Before Mark

The earliest reference to Jesus becoming God's son is from Paul.

God's son who was descended from David through the flesh and designated son of God in power through the spirit of holiness by his resurrection from the dead. (Rom 1:3–4)

Paul clearly states that God "designated" Jesus to be his son by raising him
from death.

A passage in Acts also attests to this notion. It occurs in a speech attributed to Paul. After speaking of Jesus' death and resurrection (Acts 13:29–31),
Paul announces,

We have this good news for you: what God promised to the fathers, he
has fulfilled for us, their children, by raising Jesus, just as it is written in
the second psalm, "You are my son, today I have fathered you." (Acts
13:32–33)

The quotation of Psalm 2:7 helps us understand the logic at work here. In
Psalm 2 the heir to David's throne becomes God's son when he becomes king.
His coronation elevates him to a supreme status (king), which brings with it a
new relationship to God (son). Christians who applied this verse to Jesus must
have considered his resurrection to be analogous to a coronation: it elevated
him to a new exalted status, which entailed a new relationship to God.

A similar statement in Acts reflects this same concept, but without mentioning sonship.

Let the whole house of Israel know beyond any doubt that God has made
both Lord and Anointed this Jesus whom you crucified. (Acts 2:36)

Although Acts was written after Paul was dead, scholars have long recognized
that some of the theological affirmations in the speeches in Acts come from
the earliest years of Christian preaching.

Conclusion

The earliest understanding of how Jesus was God's son is that God made
him his son at the resurrection.

Stage 2: Mark

The next two stages in the development of the belief that Jesus was God's
son are evident in the synoptic gospels. The earliest gospel, Mark, shows Jesus
becoming the son of God at his baptism.

Jesus was baptized in the Jordan by John. And just as he got up out of the
water, he saw the skies torn open and the spirit coming down towards him

like a dove. There was also a voice from the skies: 'You are my special son—I fully approve of you." (Mark 1:9–11)

The way Mark uses symbolism here shows that Jesus' spiritual status changed at his baptism: the spirit descends on him and God tells him that he is "my special son."

Stage 3: Matthew and Luke

In the Gospels of Matthew and Luke Jesus is God's son from his conception. Luke explains that Jesus is God's son because God is directly responsible for his conception (Luke 1:35). Matthew makes no comparable claim. In his infancy narrative, Matthew focuses on Jesus as the son of Joseph and thus son of David. He does not say what makes Jesus the son of God and he never actually uses the term "son of God" in Matthew 1–2. Nevertheless, we can tell that Matthew considers Jesus to be the son of God from birth because the evangelist applies to the infant a prophecy about God's son (Matt 2:15).

Both Matthew and Luke incorporate Mark's scene of Jesus' baptism into their gospels (Matt 3:13–17; Luke 3:21–22). But by beginning their gospels with infancy narratives, Matthew and Luke create a story line within which the divine voice at the baptism confirms rather than confers Jesus' status as God's son. To reinforce this understanding, Matthew makes a small but significant change in the words Mark attributes to God. In Mark, God speaks *to* Jesus; in Matthew, God speaks *about* Jesus. Instead of Mark's "You are my special son—I fully approve of you," Matthew has, "This is my special son—I fully approve of him."[4] With this modification Matthew changes a scene in which Jesus becomes God's son to a scene in which God makes public what was true all along.

When we highlight the differences in the first three understandings of how Jesus came to be the son of God, and when we arrange them in the order in which they were written, we can see a retrograde movement of the point at which Jesus was believed to have become God's son:

- at his resurrection (Paul, early traditions in Acts, around 50)
- at his baptism (Mark, around 70)
- at his conception (Matthew and Luke, 85–100).

This realization helps us appreciate the context for the New Testament stories of Jesus' birth: they are Luke's and Matthew's way of expressing in narrative the belief that Jesus was the son of God from the very beginning of his life. That particular belief was the result of a process of development in christological thinking in which Jesus becomes God's son earlier and earlier in his life.

---

4. For the full passages, see Box 2.2, p. 25.

Stage 4: John

The Gospel of John extends this process to its logical extreme: Jesus was the son of God *before* his conception, indeed from all eternity. The famous first verse in this gospel expresses this belief by echoing the opening words of Genesis:

> In the beginning there was the divine Word.
> The divine Word was there with God,
> and it was what God was. (John 1:1)

That the Word is Jesus in a pre-human existence becomes clear in the equally famous declaration, "The Word became human and made itself at home among us" (John 1:14). John's gospel has no infancy narrative, no affirmation of the virgin birth, and no baptism scene.

Stage 5: After the New Testament

After the four canonical gospels were available in a collection, the Christian tradition blended John's belief in the Son's pre-existence, Matthew's and Luke's stories of the virgin birth,[5] and the developing doctrine of the Trinity. The result was a composite theological scenario: God the Son, pre-existent as the Word of God, came to earth in human form through the action of the Holy Spirit on the Virgin Mary. We find an example of how this scenario could influence the retelling of the biblical infancy story in a late second-century text.

> The Word changed his dwelling place and, coming late as a new light, he rose from the womb of the Virgin Mary. Coming down from heaven, he put on a mortal form. . . . The Word flew into her body. In time it was made flesh and came to life in her womb, was fashioned in mortal form, and became a boy by virgin birth. (Sibylline Oracles 8:456–458, 469–472)

Another interesting attempt to express this blend of beliefs in narrative form is found in the fourth-century History of Joseph the Carpenter. The author imagines Jesus consulting the other persons of the Trinity and choosing Mary to become his mother.

> I chose her. It was my decision, with the consent of my Father and the advice of the Holy Spirit. And I was made flesh of her, by a mystery beyond the grasp of created reason. (HistJos 5:1)

5. The Christian tradition assumed that Matthew was describing a virgin birth. See the cameo, "Can they all be wrong?" on p. 204.

The Virgin Birth in Context

Besides the tale of the virgin birth of Jesus, the ancient world knew other accounts of the extraordinary origins of extraordinary men. Each of these stories attributes the birth of a hero to direct supernatural intervention. There are two basic varieties of such accounts: Jewish stories about infertile women who miraculously conceive, and Greco-Roman tales of gods who father children with humans. The meaning the virgin birth of Jesus had for its original audiences emerged as they compared it to those other stories.

THE JEWISH CONTEXT

The Hebrew Bible tells of six barren women—the ancient world didn't know about male infertility—who conceive when God miraculously intervenes.

- Sarah, mother of Isaac (Gen 17:15–21; 21:1–3)
- Rebecca, mother of Jacob (Gen 25:21)
- Leah, mother of Reuben (Gen 29:31–32)
- Rachel, mother of Joseph (Gen 30:1–3, 22–24)
- the unnamed mother of Samson (Jud 13:2–25)
- Hannah, mother of Samuel (1 Sam 1:1–20)

The most developed and most important of these stories is the one about Sarah, who was both infertile and long past the age of childbearing. She was over ninety when she gave birth to Isaac (Gen 17:17). Like all the women in these stories, Sarah conceives a son after intercourse with her husband, but that in no way detracts from the divine miracle. In the Hebrew Bible God frequently acts through a human instrument and those events are no less the acts of God because of it. From a biblical perspective, Abraham's fathering of Isaac was just as much a miracle as Moses' parting of the Sea of Reeds. No matter what a prophet or a patriarch might do, a sea cannot be parted nor can an infertile woman conceive unless God intervenes.

The stories of the other five women all focus on God as the direct cause of their conceptions, though the narratives unfold that theme in different ways. God ends the infertility of Leah out of compassion for an unloved wife (Gen 29:30–32). God grants sons to Rebecca and Rachel in answer to their prayers (Gen 25:21, 30:22). In the story about the birth of Samson, an angel informs his mother that she will conceive (Judg 30:3). Hannah conceives Samuel after Yahweh "remembers" her heartfelt prayer for a son (1 Sam 1:10–11, 19–20).

How does the story of the virgin birth compare with these stories from the Hebrew Bible? Is Mary's conception more miraculous, that is, is it more clearly a sign of divine power? We need to consider this question from both ancient and modern perspectives, because our presuppositions are quite different from those that ancient readers brought to these stories. To us Mary's conception seems obviously more miraculous than those of Sarah and her counterparts—at least at first glance. Surely a conception that does not involve a male is a greater display of God's power than one that does. But if we think carefully about what these biblical conceptions entail, and if we bring in our modern knowledge about the biology of reproduction, it becomes more difficult to sustain that initial impression. For an aged woman like Sarah to conceive, God has to make up for the lack of an ovum; for a virgin to conceive, God has to make up for the lack of sperm. It seems arbitrary to regard one as more miraculous than the other.

From an ancient perspective the situation looked different because the available knowledge about reproduction was very limited. The ancient world did not know about human ova. It regarded pregnancy as the result of having male "seed" (Greek: *sperma*) grow within a woman, whose only role was to provide blood for the nourishment of the fetus and a place for it to grow. The failure to conceive was always attributed to a defect in the woman. She was "barren," the same term that applied to a field that failed to produce a crop. With these presuppositions, a virgin birth might well be thought to require an even more robust divine intervention than was needed for the pregnancies of Sarah or Hannah. To pursue the analogy, it is a greater miracle for crops to grow where no seeds have been planted than in a hitherto barren field. We can infer that is how Luke sees it, because he models Elizabeth after Sarah and Hannah and he wants his audience to perceive the miracle of Jesus' birth as surpassing the miracle of John's.

Another way of looking at this issue, however, was as relevant then as it is now. It has to do with the very concept of miracle. A miracle is more than an extraordinary event beyond human explanation. It is also, and essentially, a sign of divine providence and power.[1] Signs, by definition, have to be per-

1. For more on this definition see p. 255.

ceived. A miracle that no one knew about would be a contradiction in terms. One way to rank miracles, then, is to ask which one is more publicly and indubitably a sign of God's power. In our case of comparing Sarah and Mary, Sarah's age was a matter of public knowledge. When she gave birth, everyone recognized that an extraordinary event had occurred. People might have disagreed on how it happened (God, magic, some unknown natural process), but no one could doubt that a ninety-year old woman had swelled with child and then given birth. In Mary's case, the sign was not and could not be public because her status as a virgin was not a matter of public verification. The only person who knew for sure was Mary herself. Strictly speaking, a virginal conception would be, by definition, a private sign. The only way for anyone else to regard Mary's pregnancy as a miracle would be to *believe* that she was a virgin at the time. No belief is necessary in Sarah's case.

Let me pause for a clarification. Here I am not talking about believing in the actual fact of those births. One can easily think that the story about Sarah is fictitious or highly exaggerated. My point is that someone aware of Isaac's birth to an aged Sarah would need no faith to see that an extraordinary thing had happened. However, someone aware of Jesus' birth to a teenaged Mary would take it to be an extraordinary event only if faith added something to the picture. Teenagers have babies every day.

Imagine an argument between Lukan Christians and non-Christian Jews on this matter. The Christians maintain that Jesus' birth is a greater miracle than any other divinely engineered birth, greater than John's, Samuel's, or Isaac's. Only Jesus was born without a human father. The Jews, of course, are unconvinced. Everyone believes that God was directly involved in the births of Isaac and Samuel – the Christians would never doubt this because it says so in the Bible – but why should anyone believe that God was directly involved in the birth of Jesus?

That question leads to a crucial point. Christians who believe in the virgin birth do so because they trust the authority of the gospels or the church. Muslims believe that Jesus was born of a virgin because it says so in the Qur'an. Perhaps there are others as well who believe in the virgin birth; if so, I have no idea what authorities they rely on for this belief. What all these believers have in common is their *prior* belief that Jesus had an extraordinary and God-given status (e.g., Son of God, Messiah, prophet, illuminated teacher). Although it is astonishing what some people can believe, it nevertheless seems all but impossible that anyone would seriously believe Jesus to be an utterly ordinary human being who just happened to be born to a virgin. In other words, *the belief that Jesus was the son of God is logically prior to belief in the virgin birth*. People do not first believe in the virgin birth and then infer that because of this Jesus must be the son of God. As a miracle, the virgin birth is not only too private to adequately demonstrate divine power; it is hemmed in by circular reasoning as well, for it is a consequence of the very belief that is supposed to be a consequence of it.

THE PAGAN CONTEXT

In addition to biblical tales of miraculous births, the ancient world also knew pagan stories about gods who fathered children with human women. As we noted in Chapter 7, the purpose of all those stories was to account for the extraordinary achievements of the men who were born of these unions. From the hellenistic perspective such extraordinary accomplishments were beyond the abilities of mere humans. Since these men must therefore be partly divine, the ancient mind inferred that they had to be offspring of gods, and stories telling how this had come about were a common feature in biographies of great men. It is not surprising, therefore, that Matthew and Luke independently hit on the idea of adding infancy narratives to the framework for the life of Jesus they inherited from Mark. As we have seen, Luke clearly intends to say that Jesus had a divine father and a human mother. The choice to begin the account of Jesus' life and teachings with a story of his virgin birth is a

---

Emperors as Sons of God

Among the larger-than-life figures reputed to be sons of God, one group was of special interest to early Christians: the Roman emperors. They were acclaimed sons of God not so much because of what they had accomplished, but because of the power they embodied. The absolute power of the Roman Empire was proof enough to the ancient mind that the gods were behind it. Since the emperor was, in a very real sense, the incarnation of that power, it made sense that he must be the son of a god. The philosopher Celsus put it this way.

> The emperor is the man to whom all earthly power has been given. What you receive in life you receive from him. And that is what it means to be a god. (*True Doctrine* 10)

The first emperor of Rome, Julius Caesar, tried to enshrine that belief in stone, literally. After his military victories had brought Gaul (now called France) into the empire, Julius returned to Rome in triumph and built a grand new forum adjacent to the old one. There he built a temple to the goddess Venus Genetrix, Venus the Ancestress. Whose ancestress? Julius', of course. His family claimed to be descended from Venus through her son Aeneas, Rome's founding father. (Aeneas, son of Venus and the Trojan Anchises, was one of the few heroes with a divine mother and a human father, see the Appendix) It was Julius' adopted son Octavian who became Augustus Caesar, the emperor under whom Jesus was born. Octavian/Augustus was supposedly fathered by the god Apollo (see pp. 140–42). Four other first-century emperors—Tiberius, Nero, Titus, and Domitian—were officially called sons of God, though we have no stories about their miraculous conceptions. All of them had human fathers, other emperors who were themselves believed to be gods. Those men had become gods, that is, they had been "divinized" during their lives or after their deaths. The Latin language distinguished *divus* (a divinized man) from *deus* (a god). However, that distinction was lost in Greek, which translated both terms as *theos* (God or god).

The divinity of the emperors was advertised by inscriptions in highly visible public locations and on coins, all using the title "son of God" or some variation of it. People understood the imperial claims to divinity in different ways. Jews and Christians regarded them as idolatrous blasphemies. Others in the Greco-Roman world who were at home in polytheism had no theological objection to divine emperors. How did they take the claim that the emperors were the offspring of gods, including the stories about Venus being the ancestor of Julius and about Apollo fathering Augustus? We can only assume that some regarded the divine pedigree as factual while others regarded it as symbolic. Either way, the claim could not be dismissed. The emperor had to be divine, for how else could his power be explained? In Palestine there were temples to the goddess Roma and the god Augustus. Cities throughout the empire had similar temples and sponsored official rituals in which the emperors were worshiped. Christians living in this environment were thus surrounded by Roman assertions that the emperor was divine. For them there could be no doubt what was at stake in their belief that Jesus, a Jew put to death by Roman authority, was the one and only son of God.

(This cameo incorporates and expands on the seminal comments of John Dominic Crossan in "Infancy and Youth of the Messiah," pp. 72–73.)

good indication that Luke intended Jesus to compete with—and of course to outshine—other ancient teachers, rulers, and saviors. In fact, gentile audiences would have found it odd if Jesus' story did not begin with some account of his divine origin.

How did the story of Jesus' miraculous birth stack up against stories of other miraculous births? Early Christian apologists who debated with pagans drew attention to both the similarities and the differences between them. On the one hand, Christian writers made the point that pagans should find it easy to believe in the story of Jesus' birth because they accept similar stories about their own gods and heroes.

When we say that the Word, who is the First-begotten of God, was born for us without sexual union, Jesus Christ our teacher . . . we assert nothing new beyond what you already believe about those whom you call sons of Zeus. (Justin Martyr, *First Apology* 21)

If we say that the Word of God was begotten by God in an extraordinary manner, different from the ordinary method of conception, this is comparable to your claim that Hermes is the announcing Word of God . . . And even if we say that he was born to a virgin, this is comparable to what you say about Perseus. (Justin Martyr, *First Apology* 22)

On the other hand, Christian apologists drew distinctions between the story about Jesus and all the other ones. Such contrasts were intended to show that Jesus was different from and superior to his pagan competitors. Uniqueness was claimed for Jesus' story on two counts: it was asexual, and it really happened.

1. The pagan stories told of sexual encounters between gods and humans, whereas Jesus was conceived without divine intercourse.

> Some may misunderstand the prophecy about the virgin conceiving. Lest they bring against us the reproach that we bring against the poets who say that Zeus satisfied his lust with women, we will try to explain the prophecy clearly. "The virgin will conceive" means that the virgin will conceive without intercourse. (Justin Martyr, *First Apology* 33)

A prominent theme in both Jewish and Christian polemics against paganism was that the gods were described as being subject to human passions and as indulging their lusts, often with human partners. In fact, most pagan philosophers had long rejected these anthropomorphic tales. Four centuries before the birth of Jesus, Plato had denounced this kind of mythology because it gave bad example to the young and because it was a crude insult to the divine nature, which was pure spirit and therefore without bodily desires. Still, stories about gods who mated with humans were deeply ingrained in the hellenistic imagination. The second-century philosopher Plutarch informs us,

---

The Virgin Birth in Islam

The theological impulse to purge any hint of sexuality from the concept of God is unmistakably evident in the way Islam describes the virgin birth of Jesus. Several passages in the Qur'an adamantly insist that God cannot father a son. According to the Qur'an, God effortlessly brought about the virginal conception of Jesus, just as he had the creation of Adam. In both cases God simply gave the command, "Be."

> It is not befitting to God that he should father a son. Glory be to Him. When He determines a matter, He only says to it, "Be," and it is. (Qur'an 19:35)

> Mary said, "O my Lord, how will I have a son when no man has touched me?" He (the angel) said, "Such is the will of God. He creates whom He wills. When He decrees something, He only has to say, "Be," and it is. (Qur'an 3:47).

The fact of the intercourse of a male god with a mortal woman is conceded by all. (*Table Talk* 8.1)

Plutarch himself does not endorse this belief. His own position is rather complex and is remarkably similar to the later Christian treatment of this theologically sensitive topic. On the one hand, Plutarch shares the philosophical reluctance to attribute sexual passion to the gods.

That a god should take physical pleasure in a human body and its beauty: this, surely, is hard to believe. (*Life of Numa* 4.3)

On the other hand, he defends the possibility that gods might impregnate human women, with the understanding that the god's role would be purely spiritual and would involve no physical contact.

I do not consider it strange if the god does not approach a woman like a man does, but instead alters her mortal nature and by another kind of contact or touch, through other means, makes her pregnant with a more divine offspring. (*Table Talk* 8.1)

Matthew and Luke were both sensitive to the problem of how to recount the story of Jesus' conception without buying into the assumptions about divine-human procreation common in hellenistic culture. Matthew finesses the problem. When the angel informs Joseph about God's responsibility for Mary's pregnancy, Matthew takes refuge in the passive voice: "that which is begotten in her is of a holy spirit" (Matt 1:20). He thus avoids having to explain in what way the divine spirit is responsible for her pregnancy. (Remember that Matthew probably did not think that God was the *sole* cause of Mary's pregnancy.) Luke is more articulate on the matter and his solution shows some theological sophistication. He chooses biblical vocabulary that describes God's real, but non-physical, presence and power: "A holy spirit will hover over you and the power of the Most High will cast its shadow on you" (Luke 1:35, see p. 38).

2. The other distinction drawn by early Christian apologists between Jesus' birth and other miraculous births is a blunt one: our story is true and their stories are false.

Those other stories are really myths. People just invent tales like this about someone because they think he has greater wisdom and power than most other people. (Origen, *Against Celsus* 1.37)

To assert this point more forcefully, some Christians ascribed the pagan stories not to human imagination, but to Satan. The devil, knowing beforehand the details of the birth and life of the Son of God, inspired the pagan stories as deliberate imitations of the story of Christ, in order to lead people astray. This theory neatly explains the remarkable similarities between Christian and pagan stories; moreover, it brands the latter as not only false, but evil.

> ## 15.1   The Devil made them do it.
>
> You may rest assured that my knowledge of the scriptures and my faith in them have been well confirmed by the things that the Devil counterfeited in the fictions circulated among the Greeks, just as he accomplished them through the Egyptian magicians and the false prophets in the days of Elijah. For, when they say that Bacchus was born of Jupiter's union with Semele, and narrate that he was the discoverer of the vine, and that after he was torn to pieces and died, he arose again and ascended into heaven, and when they use wine in his mysteries, is it not evident that the Devil has imitated the prophecy of the patriarch Jacob, as recorded by Moses? And when it is asserted that Herakles, the son of Jupiter and Alkmene, was strong and jour-neyed across the whole earth, and that, after death, he, too, ascended into heaven, should I not conclude that the scriptural passage about Christ, "strong as a giant to run His course," was similarly imitated? And when the Devil presents Asclepius raising the dead to life and curing all diseases, isn't this also his way of imitating the prophecies about Christ?
> (Justin Martyr, *Dialogue with Trypho* 69)

THE MODERN CONTEXT

Unlike ancient readers, when we consider the story of Jesus' birth to a virgin we do not spontaneously make comparisons with the births of Plato or Pythagoras or Augustus. Those names are unfamiliar to most of us, except for students facing exams in Western Civilization and people interested in ancient history or philosophy. The stories about the miraculous births of such ancient heroes are all but extinct today, existing only as specialized academic knowledge among scholars. Being unfamiliar with those stories, most people don't notice how much they sound like the story about Jesus. The similarity does not ring in twenty-first century ears, as it did in those of the first. This is why some scholars have achieved a certain rhetorical success in arguing for a distinction between the Christian story and the pagan ones, defending the uniqueness of Jesus by dismissing the relevance of the other stories because none of them is about a virgin birth.[2] In the other stories, the mothers of the

---

2. Well, almost none, for there is one exception. As Justin Martyr was aware, the hero Perseus was born to a virgin. "In Greek mythology there is a story of how Perseus was born to Danae

heroes are married women who sleep with their husbands. Some of the stories even tell how the intervention of the god temporarily disrupted the couple's sex life.[3]

But what difference does this difference make? It's worth noting that this difference was not mentioned by the early Christian apologists. Then and now, the distinction that Mary was a virgin and the other women were not misses the point, which is that the conceptions did not involve a human male. Whether the mother had been sleeping with her husband on other occasions has nothing to do with it. The crucial question is not, "Did the child have a virgin mother?", but rather, "Did the child have a human father?". If Mary's virginity makes Jesus' birth more miraculous, as some modern Christians assert, must we say that Mary's conceiving Jesus without a human father would be less of a miracle if she had been, for example, a young widow instead of a betrothed virgin? Would Mary's conceiving Jesus without a human father be less miraculous if Jesus had not been her first child? Surely the passenger dignifies the vehicle, not the other way around.

In its original context, belief in the virgin birth was an affirmation of the supernatural identity of Jesus. In other words, *the affirmation of the virgin birth said something about Jesus, not Mary*. However, given the attitudes toward sexuality that prevailed in the hellenistic world into which Christianity expanded (see p. 262), this belief would inevitably focus more and more attention on Mary's virginity.

MARY, EVER VIRGIN

The increasing interest in Mary's sexual status is vividly illustrated in the Infancy Gospel of James. This imaginative second-century gospel is far less concerned with Jesus than with Mary; and what it likes best about this girl is her virginity. In this gospel Mary was a virgin not only at the time she conceived, but throughout her life. To establish this, the gospel develops three themes. First, it emphasizes that Mary was never Joseph's wife, nor even betrothed to him. He was her guardian and nothing more. Second, it explains away the New Testament references to Jesus' brothers: they were sons of Joseph by his past marriage, not children of Mary. Jesus grew up in their household, but he was not their brother. Third, Infancy James understands Mary's virginity in the most concrete manner possible: in this gospel her virginity not only means that she abstained from sex, it also means that she

while she was a virgin, when the one they call Zeus descended on her in the form of a shower of golden rain." (*Dialogue with Trypho* 67. See also the passing reference quoted above on p. 240). Although the legend of Perseus is the only pagan story about a virgin birth, it is not very useful as a comparison to the story of Jesus because Perseus was a hero from the mythic past and not a real historical figure.

3. See the stories about Alexander and Plato, pp. 138 and 145–46.

remained anatomically intact. Not only is Jesus' conception a miracle, but also his actual birth, for Mary delivered him without rupturing her hymen. This is dramatically demonstrated in what is surely the strangest episode in all the gospels: a midwife performs a gynecological inspection to verify Mary's virginal status after childbirth (InJas 19:18–20:2). That this scene strikes us as not only distasteful but as bizarre, shows how vastly different the early Christian world was from ours.[4]

Although we today might avert our imagination from the graphic details of that scene, we should not think that early Christians were shy about it. In the concrete value system of the ancient world, a woman's intact anatomy was her "certificate" of virginity, and in a world in which sexuality was fraught with moral danger, only virginity could guarantee a woman's virtue. Since early Christians knew next to nothing about the actual details of the life of Mary, they made her virginity the defining quality of her character. (Later tradition often referred to her simply as "the virgin.") As christology increasingly focused on Jesus' divinity, it became more important to imagine that his mother must have been morally perfect, in part because a son's moral character reflected on his parents and in part because Jesus had inherited his human nature solely from her, and that nature had to be sinless no matter how it interacted with his divinity.

It was in this theological context that the belief in Mary's lifelong virginity developed. The mainstream Christian tradition apparently could not imagine a sinless life that included sexual experience, not even sex within marriage. The fourth-century scholar Jerome went so far as to assert that *Joseph* was a lifelong celibate.

> Nowhere is it written that Joseph had another wife. He was the guardian of Mary, whom he was supposed to have to wife, rather than her husband. (*The Perpetual Virginity of Blessed Mary* 21).

The notion that Joseph was Mary's guardian and not her husband first appears in the Infancy Gospel of James, which clearly states that Joseph was a widower. So it is difficult to see how Jerome could deny knowing a written story about Joseph's marriage. That Joseph was formerly married is a crucial premise for Infancy James, since its author claims to be Joseph's son.

The assumption that a sinless life is a celibate life, at least for Jesus' family, persists even today in major segments of Christianity. The permanent virginity of Mary is dogma in the Catholic and Orthodox churches. Those who

---

4. At the women's college where I used to teach, I learned from experience to avoid any mention of this scene until after students had read it as their assignment. Formerly I had described this scene in the brief "what to look for as you read" introduction that I gave the day before we studied a text in class. Many students refused to believe that such a story could exist. Then, after they read it for themselves, few were willing to discuss it and all were relieved when we moved on to the next topic.

deny the doctrine of the virgin birth are regarded by many Christians not only to be rejecting the authority of the Bible and the church, but also to be impugning the virtue of Mary. A modern example of the Christian difficulty in reconciling holiness with sex comes from the reaction to the film *The Last Temptation of Christ*. This controversial movie offended many Christians for several reasons, but the scene found most disturbing depicted Jesus' dream that he is married and is making love with his wife. In the minds of many Christians, Jesus was too holy to be married.

Another reason why ancient Christians took such an interest in Mary's virginity was that they had come to construe it as a prerequisite for their own salvation. Within the framework of orthodox theology, human salvation depended on the atoning death of Jesus. Only a sinless savior could atone for humanity's sin. And Jesus could be sinless, it was assumed, only if he was born to a virgin. It was Augustine in the fifth century who articulated the theological rationale for this understanding. According to Augustine, the sin of Adam and Eve involved their "fall" into sexuality. This "original sin" is inherited by all and is transmitted to children because they are conceived in an act of sexual passion. Jesus could be free from original sin, therefore, only if he were conceived without sex:

> Jesus was begotten and conceived, then, without any indulgence of carnal lust, and therefore brought with him no original sin. (*Handbook* 41)

Augustine's reasoning involves three inferences:

- the efficacy of the atonement depends on Jesus' being sinless;
- Jesus' sinlessness depends on his birth to a sinless mother;
- his mother's sinlessness depends on her virginity.

In this way, Mary's virginity became crucial to the theology of atonement and was therefore considered a necessary part of God's plan for salvation. To this way of thinking, Jesus' death could not have atoned for sins if Mary had not been a virgin when she conceived him.

Augustine regarded all sexual behavior as sinful, even within marriage. While husbands and wives were expected to have sex—how else could there be children?—it nevertheless counted as a "venial" (as opposed to a "mortal," or deadly) sin. Married couples were thus doomed to sin—one reason why celibacy was considered spiritually superior to marriage. That is also why Mary had to be a lifelong virgin if she was to maintain the sinlessness proper to the Mother of God. Thomas Aquinas in the thirteenth century gives a clear example of this mindset.

> Because she conceived Christ without the defilement of sin, and without the stain of sexual intercourse, therefore did she bring Him forth without pain and without violation of her virginal integrity. (*Summa Theologica* Q. 35, art. 6, part 3)

Aquinas was sure that Mary had a painless delivery, not because the Bible says anything about this, but because it seemed to follow logically from her sinless conception of Jesus. Labor pain was considered to be woman's punishment for the sin of Eve (Gen 3:15), a punishment from which the sinless Mary was exempt. It was also theologically appropriate that Mary's "virginal integrity" be miraculously preserved, for why should the Mother of God be deprived, though no fault of her own, of the physical sign of her sinlessness?

CHRISTIAN REJECTION OF THE VIRGIN BIRTH

Aquinas' understanding of the virgin birth is historically far removed from that in the gospel(s), and belongs to a thought world fundamentally foreign to that of the gospel authors. But there is one conviction that Aquinas, and with him the great traditions of post-New Testament Christianity, have in common with the gospels. Or to be exact, this conviction is shared with the Gospel of Luke, since Mark and John and probably even Matthew disagree with Luke on this matter. This is the notion that Jesus had no human father because he was the son of God. As we have seen, this was originally a pagan notion. By enshrining it in his infancy narrative, Luke took a small but deci-

---

"Joseph fathered Jesus."

Another piece of evidence that sheds light on the Jewish-Christian rejection of the virgin birth comes from Syria and has to do with the genealogy of Jesus. The genealogy in Matthew's gospel uses the formula "A fathered B, B fathered C, etc.," starting with Abraham and ending with Joseph. When the genealogy gets to Jesus, Matthew breaks this pattern. Instead of saying, "Joseph fathered Jesus," Matt 1:16 reads,

> Joseph was the husband of Mary, from whom was born Jesus who is called the Anointed.

However, in an ancient Syriac translation of the gospels, Matt 1:16 was altered to read,

> Joseph, to whom Mary the virgin was betrothed, fathered Jesus who is called the Anointed.

The Christian scholars who produced this translation for Semitic Christians apparently believed that it was important to remove the ambiguity from the genealogy of Jesus and explicitly affirm the biological paternity of Joseph.

sive step in leading Christianity away from its Jewish roots. Nothing in Judaism would require Jesus to lack a human father in order to be God's son. But much in Judaism would require a holy man like Jesus *not* to have a mother impregnated extramaritally by an invisible mysterious power.

So it makes sense that to the best of our knowledge the only early Christians who rejected the virgin birth were the so-called Jewish Christians. Why did they do so? Living in Palestine and Syria and speaking Semitic languages (Aramaic and Syriac), they were less influenced by hellenistic theology than were Christians from gentile backgrounds, and to them making the Holy Spirit responsible for Mary's pregnancy was simply wrong, not only theologically, but even linguistically. That is because Jewish-Christians thought of the Holy Spirit as Jesus' *mother*. For example, the Jewish-Christian Gospel of the Hebrews had a distinctive version of the scene of Jesus' baptism in which Jesus reports,

> Just now my mother, the Holy Spirit, took me by the hair and brought me to Tabor, the great mountain. (Gospel of the Hebrews 4)

Jerome, who quoted this passage, explained it to his Latin-speaking audience.

> Now no one should be offended by this, because "spirit" in Hebrew is feminine in gender, while in our language it is masculine and in Greek it is neuter.[5] In divinity, however, there is no gender. (*Commentary on Isaiah* 11)

To those who spoke Semitic languages it made no sense that a female spirit and a human woman could together produce a child. A fascinating passage from a second-century Syrian writing uses this as an argument against those who believe in the virgin birth.

> Some say, "Mary conceived by the Holy Spirit." They are mistaken. They do not know what they are saying. How could a woman conceive by a woman? Mary is the young woman[6] whom no power defiled. . . The Lord would not have said "my Father who is in heaven" unless he had another father. He would have said simply "my Father." (Gospel of Philip 55)

The last sentence takes Jesus' habit of referring to God as "my father in heaven" to be proof that Jesus had two fathers, a spiritual one and a physical one. Having God for a heavenly father did not exclude Jesus from having Joseph for a biological father any more than Jesus having the Spirit for a

---

5. The relevant words are *ruach* in Hebrew, *spiritus* in Latin, and *pneuma* in Greek.

6. English translations of the Coptic Gospel of Philip all use "virgin" here. However, the Coptic text uses the Greek word *parthenos* in this passage and the usual sense of that term is "young woman." See pp. 189–90.

mother excluded Mary's giving him birth. The assertion that "Mary is the young woman whom no power defiled" invites elaboration. In a Jewish milieu no one could imagine that God would impregnate a woman apart from her act of intercourse with a man. Linguistically, Mary's pregnancy could not have been begun by the feminine Holy Spirit. Therefore, the only way to do without a human father for Jesus would be to hold some other god responsible for the pregnancy. Of course, for Christians such a charge would be blasphemous. Everyone knew about stories in which pagan gods had sex with humans, and Jews regarded those gods as demonic "powers." We see now what it meant to call Mary "the young woman whom no power defiled." In the minds of the Jewish-Christians, had Jesus been born to a virgin, it could mean only that there had been a physical union between a demon and Mary, a thought too shocking to consider. They would never call Mary a "virgin"—in our sense of the term.

It is fascinating indeed to see that some early Christians rejected the virgin birth in order to protect Mary's reputation for virtue and purity. Here the Jewish and hellenistic value systems come into sharp conflict, for Jews have never regarded sexuality as sinful. On the contrary, Judaism celebrates the holiness of marital sexuality, as, for example, in the tradition encouraging husbands and wives to sanctify the Sabbath by making love. All through the Hebrew Bible the plan of God moves forward with the births of boys destined to be patriarchs, prophets, and leaders of Israel, which means that God is working his will through the sexuality of their parents.

The Meaning of the Virgin Birth

Getting Started

Chapters 10-15 have led us through an array of linguistic, exegetical, historical, and cultural information and issues, all of them essential for an understanding of the virgin birth. Now that we have reviewed the evidence, we are in a position to make a judicious assessment of what it all means. As a warm up for this critical thinking about the virgin birth, I'd like to offer an observation, propose an experiment, and ask a question.

1. The observation is that people who believe in the virgin birth *want* it to be true. By contrast, there are many things that we believe even though we wish they weren't true. For example, we may reluctantly be forced to believe that our jokes are not funny, or that loved ones have betrayed us. But unlike those reluctantly accepted beliefs, the virgin birth is something that people believe only if they want to believe it. By the same token, people who don't want to believe it, don't. In the uneasy space between these two stances there are many—very many, I suspect—who want to believe this doctrine, but for various reasons, cannot. However, the opposite case is exceedingly difficult to imagine. Could there be anyone who, despite sincerely wanting not to believe this doctrine, nonetheless believes it to be true? It's hard to imagine how this could happen. The virgin birth is just not the kind of thing you can believe against your will.

2. Here's an experiment to back up that observation. In order to explore your own perspective on this issue, try this. Imagine that I were telling you, right here on this page, that the next chapter of this book laid out absolute proof of whether Jesus had a human biological father. This proof was going to be 100% convincing; everyone who has seen it, from militant atheists to the Pope himself, has agreed, either gladly or reluctantly, that this proof settles the

This chapter is built on the insights of John Dominic Crossan. The arguments on pp. 255–56 are taken from his "Infancy and Youth of the Messiah," pp. 74–76.

question once and for all. Now, catch yourself in the act of turning to that hypothetical chapter to find out whether the proof is proof for, or proof against, the historical truth of the virgin birth. Ask yourself: which outcome would you be hoping for? I'm assuming that no one reading this book would be neutral about this. So that question should be easy to answer. The more interesting, and more difficult, question is: *why would you care about the outcome ?*

3. This brings us to the last step in getting started. The "why" of our wishes in regard to the virgin birth points us to a question: what kind of miracle is the virgin birth? In the gospels this miracle is in a category all by itself. It does not compare with the other wonders, all of which occur for plain reasons. For example, take the miraculous healings in the gospels. They all address basic human needs. It's obvious why a compassionate God would empower people to heal others, or to deliver them from the grip of evil spirits. It's equally obvious that all of us would like to have such power or to receive its benefit. Or take the nature miracles in the gospels. These wonders also relate to fundamental human desires, such as the desire to control unruly and dangerous natural forces. Even the resurrection of Jesus speaks to our primal fears and hopes about death. But to what yearning does the virgin birth speak? It's difficult even to imagine an answer. Humans everywhere have to cope with disease, natural disasters, scarcity, and death. We respond to miraculous healings, nature miracles, and resurrection because they speak to the human condition; that is why they are almost instinctively apprehended as disclosures of the divine. The virgin birth, however, seems to float outside this constellation of meaning. Its relevance to human existence, and thus its religious significance, is not apparent to the modern mind.

This is an unusually clear reminder that the biblical books were written to speak to their own times and places and are under no obligation to make sense to us. If we want to understand the Bible we must do so on its terms, not ours. Often the challenge is to stop ourselves from reading our own meanings into the Bible. In a case like the virgin birth, however, there are no obvious relevant meanings for us to project. As we have seen, later generations did embroider the story with their own cultural interests. So it is essential for us to take what clues we can from the early sources and seek to understand what the first Christians made of this belief. Only then will we be in a responsible position to explore what is at stake in believing or not believing in the virgin birth today.

FACT AND MEANING

"Do you believe in the virgin birth?" is really two questions in one. It seems to be a question about Jesus' biological origin. This is so at one level, but only at the most literal level, which, as we will see, is of no religious importance in itself. The second, less obvious, but implied question is the one that really counts: "Do you believe that Jesus is the son of God, savior, messiah, etc.?" The first question is about a fact; the second is about a meaning. A fact without a meaning is, well, meaningless. Christians who assert the fact of the virgin birth do so because of what they think it means.

How tightly connected are these two questions? For many people, the two issues stand or fall together. It certainly makes sense to affirm both: "I believe that Jesus had no human father and that he was the Son of God." It makes equal sense to deny both: "I don't believe that Jesus is virgin born and neither do I believe that he was the Son of God." But does it make any sense to affirm one and deny the other? There are two possibilities here: 1) affirming the fact but denying its meaning, and 2) denying the fact but affirming the meaning. Let's consider both possibilities.

1. Can someone believe that Jesus had no human father, but deny that there was anything special about his spiritual identity? This is theoretically possible, but hardly seems worth the effort. Such a person would have no motivation to believe in the virgin birth in the first place (see p. 237). But even if someone who lacked any religious belief about Jesus nevertheless became convinced that Jesus was virgin-born, this odd conviction would amount to nothing more than a belief that Jesus' birth was a biological anomaly. Everyone else, including defenders of the traditional doctrine, would conclude that such a person had badly missed the point.

A real-life variation on this theme is the Muslim doctrine about Jesus. Christians are usually nonplussed to learn that Islam affirms the fact of Jesus' virgin birth while denying that Jesus was the Son of God. Islam teaches that Jesus was a prophet, indeed a special kind of prophet (in Arabic, a *rasulullah*, or "messenger of God") second in dignity only to Muhammad himself. However, in the Qur'an Jesus' virgin birth has nothing to do with his being a messenger of God. It is simply one of several miracles about his life. Islam holds Jesus and his virgin mother in very high esteem. Like other messengers of God, Jesus was a perfect human being, without sin. But he was a human being nonetheless. It is the gravest of sins in Islam to ascribe any degree of divinity to any human, including Jesus.

2. The truly interesting question is whether it makes any sense for someone to affirm the meaning of the virgin birth if he or she is unable to believe in it as a fact. Here is the point where Christian fundamentalists draw the line. While they can accept the reality that non-Christians deny the virgin birth, they do not tolerate Christians who cannot believe in the fact of it. According to fundamentalism, you are not a real Christian unless you affirm the literal truth of the virgin birth. From the fundamentalist perspective, unless you believe that Jesus was literally born of a virgin, you have no reason to believe that he is the savior or the Son of God.

Now this is not only a needlessly narrow way to frame the issue, it is plain wrong as a fact of history. The New Testament writings of Mark, John, and Paul show no hint whatsoever that these authors believed in the virgin birth; and yet each of them fully affirmed that Jesus is the savior and Son of God. (If someone responds that these authors really did believe in the virgin birth even though they didn't mention it, then he or she should be challenged to prove this claim from the Bible.)

Very few of us lose sleep worrying about whether fundamentalists consider us to be true Christians. And yet many of us accept their assumptions about how the virgin birth should be understood: that the only honest way to believe in the meaning of the virgin birth is to believe in it as a fact. Perhaps this assumption sounds to you like common sense. (If so, it shows how pervasive fundamentalist assumptions still are.) But that is a rather strange and stilted way to set the terms for religious faith, because that is not how Christians approach many other teachings of their religion. For example, all except fundamentalists can affirm the doctrine of creation, that God is the source of all that is, without feeling any need to take Genesis 1 as literal history. And even fundamentalists know that some biblical affirmations are metaphors; for example, that Jesus is the lamb of God. They affirm Jesus' "lambness" while understanding this metaphorically. It is really no different with the belief that Jesus is the son of God. Some Christians may claim that they believe this literally, but that's not actually what they mean unless they imagine that God has human DNA. They may believe that God miraculously created Jesus in Mary's womb, but that still amounts to a metaphorical way of thinking about Jesus as God's son. The only way to be the *literal* son of a father is to inherit his genes. Anything else is a non-literal use of the term.

A properly theological consideration of the stories of Jesus' birth has to be an engagement with their meaning. The question of whether the virgin birth was a biological fact is a separate issue, and by itself, one without theological significance. It is perfectly appropriate intellectually, and perfectly valid theologically, for Christians to take seriously the meaning of the virgin birth and at the same time to take it as a metaphor and not as a fact.

BELIEF IN THE VIRGIN BIRTH, BACK THEN

As we noted above, to engage the meaning of the virgin birth we need to start by discerning the meaning it had for the Christians who first affirmed it. Only then can we explore what is at stake in affirming or denying that meaning today. As we also saw above, the early Christian presentation of the virgin birth took shape at the intersection of two cultures, each with its own set of miraculous birth stories. Since meaning always comes from context, the virgin birth had two distinct but related meanings, depending on which set of miraculous birth stories a given audience took to be the context for understanding Jesus'. There are two sets, and therefore two possible contexts.

1. One set of context stories is the miraculous births reported in the Hebrew Bible: the births of Isaac, Jacob, Reuben, Joseph, Samson, and Samuel. What did the virgin birth of Jesus mean for Christians who understood it in the context of those stories? That depends largely on what these men have in common. They are a diverse group. Isaac and Jacob were patriarchs, Joseph a sage, Samson a military hero, Samuel a prophet.[1] About all they have in common is that they were men in whose lives the plan of God moved forward. Yet they were no more crucial to God's will for Israel, nor were their lives any more guided by God, than others who were born without direct divine intervention. For example, it is not clear that a miraculous birth adds something to the religious significance of Isaac or Samuel that is missing from the lives of Joshua or Elijah. God's direct intervention in bringing Isaac or Samuel into the world to carry out his will seems no more special than the ways in which God chose such heroes of Israel's faith as Abraham, Moses, David, or Jeremiah, all of whom were dramatically summoned to their missions through visions or prophets.

Therefore, to consider the meaning of the virgin birth of Jesus against the background of the miraculous births in the Hebrew Bible gives it no specific significance beyond the general sense that Jesus, like those born miraculously before him, had a special role in furthering the purpose of God. It's a safe bet that early Christians held Jesus' birth to be a greater miracle than those other births and took this as divine confirmation that Jesus was not simply like those Old Testament heroes, but greater than all of them. However, a debate over whether it was more miraculous for the teenage virgin Mary or the ninety year old Sarah to conceive is one that can go either way (see p. 237).

2. The other miraculous birth stories against which the virgin birth of Jesus acquired its meaning for early Christians are the ones about the Greek and Roman sons of God. All but forgotten today, these stories influenced the early Christian understanding of Jesus more than did those about Isaac and company, for three reasons. First, as part of hellenistic culture they were known by more Christians than were stories from the Hebrew Bible. Second, the Israelite heroes were from the distant past, whereas most Greco-Roman sons of God were much more recent or even contemporary figures. Third, the Greco-Roman heroes were more immediately comparable to Jesus in that they allegedly lacked

---

1. Reuben is a very minor character in the Bible. His only significant deed is saving the life of his brother Joseph. His other brothers wanted to kill Joseph, but Reuben convinced them to throw him down a well rather than murder him outright. Reuben planned to come back later and rescue Joseph, but before he could do so, the brothers sold Joseph to slave traders (Gen 37:20-28). Ironically, that is how Joseph got to Egypt, where years later he was able to save his family from starvation. Reuben was thus unknowingly an instrument of providence.

human fathers. The meaning of this was obvious to the hellenistic mind: someone who was fathered by a god was, by definition, a son of God. That is also the logic of Luke's story. Even though Luke preempts the literal hellenistic inclination to assume that God physically fathered Jesus, he shares the hellenistic logic that Jesus was the son of God because, like Adam (see Luke 3:38), he had no human father.

By far the most important difference between the two sets of stories—the miraculous birth stories in the Hebrew Bible, and the Greco-Roman ones—is that the early Christians believed the former but not the latter. Christians might have argued that Jesus was greater than Isaac or Samuel, but they did not doubt that those men had been born by God's direct intervention. But when it came to the Greco-Roman stories, Christians were unwilling to argue that Jesus was a greater son of God than Plato or Augustus. Rather, Christians asserted that in comparison to men like those, Jesus was the *only* son of God. In their minds, Alexander and Pythagoras were not fathered by gods at all.

Many Christians disbelieved the Greco-Roman stories about gods who fathered human sons for the same reason that those Christians—along with Jews—disbelieved all the stories about the pagan gods: those gods simply did not exist. We need to be careful here, however, because many other Christians believed that those beings did exist, though not at the same level of existence as the Christian God. In any case, when Christians denied miraculous birth stories involving pagan deities, it was a rejection only of their literal truth. We know that some pagans also declined to take such stories literally, but nevertheless regarded them as important expressions of symbolic truths. Here, at the level of the meaning of the stories, is a crucial place where early Christians dissented from some of the most basic values of their surrounding culture. Above all, Christians disbelieved these stories *because Christians rejected their meaning.*

What we need to keep in mind in assessing these stories is that even though they tell of someone's birth, they are really statements about that person's whole life. In the ancient world, an extraordinary birth got its significance from the context of a "godly" life: Alexander's accomplishments were so extraordinary that people decided after the fact that there had to be something supernatural about him. The meaning of a story about a miraculous birth is thus retrospective. Early Christians understood this full well. The second-century Christian scholar Origen explains,

> These stories are really myths. People just invent tales like this about someone because they think he has greater wisdom and power than most other people. So they say that his body was originally composed from superior and more divine seed, thinking this to be an appropriate beginning for those who surpass ordinary human nature. (*Against Celsus* 1.37)

In order to verify for yourself that a miraculous birth has meaning only in retrospect, try the following thought experiment. Imagine that you have a cousin, Jennifer, who works in a convenience store, loves her husband and children, and spends most of her free time watching television. Her life is completely normal and utterly average. Now imagine that one of your relatives tells you that Jennifer was born to a virgin. Wanting to warn your aunt, Jennifer's mother, about this weird family gossip, you tactfully tell her about this rumor. To your total amazement your aunt confirms it: yes, she did indeed become pregnant while still a virgin several months before her wedding. Your aunt is quite rational and you know her to be scrupulously honest. Completely baffled, you bring up the topic with her husband. Your uncle tells you that he loves Jennifer like his own daughter, but that he is not her biological father and, because he believes his wife, he is convinced that no one else is either.

What would you make of all that? The natural suspicion would be that such a story is a pathetic attempt to cover up pre-marital sex. But everything you know about your aunt makes it impossible for you to believe that she is either lying or deluded. So imagine yourself being willing to believe this improbable story. What on earth could Jennifer's virgin birth mean? That strange event would just sit there as an extremely bizarre fact, utterly unexplainable, but otherwise without significance. Jennifer would still be the same old Jennifer to you.

This thought experiment should bring us to think critically about the very concept of "miracle." Here is one place where definitions really matter, so let's be precise. Let's reserve the term "miracle" for theological use. (A frog with three eyes would not be a miracle; it would be an accident.) Theologically, a miracle is not merely an unexplainable event. It is a surprising, unexpected event that is a sign of God's power and presence. We consider something to be a miracle not merely because its explanation eludes us, but also because we see it as an act of God. If someone possessed amazing and unexplainable powers, but used them only for selfish or evil purposes, or to amuse friends by performing weird stunts, we might be very impressed, but would not view those events as miracles.

For early Christians the virgin birth of Jesus was believable *only* because it was *Jesus'* birth. In his life they recognized the presence of God. The reason why non-Christians didn't believe in the virgin birth of Jesus was not that they were skeptical about the possibility that children could be born without human fathers. Everybody accepted that possibility: some literally and some metaphorically (see the text by Iamblichus on pp. 150–51). Non-Christians didn't believe in the virgin birth of Jesus because they didn't see what could be divine about him. Celsus, a Roman intellectual who despised Christianity and wrote an energetic refutation of it, leaves no doubt about this. From his perspective, the story about the virgin birth of Jesus was nonsense precisely because a low achiever like Jesus could not have had a divine father. In Celsus' estimation, Jesus had done nothing heroic. He had used magic to trick people into believing teachings that did not make the world a better place. Celsus was not surprised that most of Jesus' followers were ignorant illiterates.

> I doubt very much that any really intelligent man believes these doctrines of the Christians, for to believe them would require one to ignore the sort of unintelligent and uneducated people who are persuaded by them. (*The True Doctrine* 4)

BELIEF IN THE VIRGIN BIRTH TODAY

So, do you believe in the virgin birth? If that is a question about a biological fact, then the question is not a live option for many Christians today. Some cannot believe that anyone, even Jesus, could be born that way. Others may be open to the theoretical possibility of such a miracle, but can find no objective evidence that Jesus was born without a human father. And many Christians simply cannot make themselves believe something merely because the Church or the Bible says so. On the other hand there are numerous Christians who do believe in the virgin birth solely on the authority of the Church or the Bible. But many of these have apparently given little or no thought to what this belief is all about. And even those whose belief in this doctrine is reflective and sincere are dealing with it in a context so different from that of the early Christians that this belief cannot affect their lives the way it affected the lives of those first believers. No Christian today, not even someone who believes in the virgin birth literally, has to grapple with the issue as the Gospel of Luke poses it: Jesus or Augustus? Luke's audience had to make a choice whether Jesus or Caesar was the Son of God. That was a decision about God, not about biology. No contemporary Christian, not even one who stoutly affirms that Jesus is the Son of God, has lost any sleep wondering whether Augustus was divine. Today, 99.9% of Christians wouldn't even understand the question.

Then and now, the question about the virgin birth comes down to whether you believe in its meaning: do you see in Jesus' life the presence and power of God? And this question is rooted in a more basic one: How do you imagine God? Can you see God in the imperial might and majesty of Rome incarnated in the person of the emperor? Or can you see God in, for instance, the vision of justice and compassion for the powerless incarnated in the historical Jesus? I say "for instance" because there is more to Jesus than that, and thus more to the question about God. So fill that in for yourself. What do you see in Jesus? Is what you see there a manifestation of God?

But beware. Unless you keep those questions within the boundaries of a strictly intellectual exercise, they will push you into a confrontation with your own values. This can be risky, because values have to do with how we live. Seeing God in the historical Jesus entails a willingness to live within Jesus' vision of the kingdom of God. This is what is ultimately at stake in the question about the virgin birth and divine sonship of Jesus. If you say that you see the presence and power of God in the life and teachings of Jesus, then this stance of yours should mean that you are willing, for example, to seek the kingdom of God among the marginalized nobodies of our society. If you aren't, then it's just talk, no matter how high-minded.

Christians who insist that the Bible (or the traditional creeds) must be taken literally or not at all are committed to a quite different perspective on the meaning of Christian faith. Those who defend this diminished sense of orthodoxy think that the reason it takes a lot of faith to be Christian is that one has to believe strange things like a literal virgin birth and a physical resurrection. But to many others, the far more profound challenge is to trust that Jesus was right in his vision of a God who sides with the victims of empire, not with its beneficiaries. And trusting that Jesus was right means living as if he was.

IS JESUS THE ONLY SON OF GOD?

The theological approach to the virgin birth discussed above proposes a way to take it seriously without taking it literally. This way is to refocus the question, away from "What happened to Mary?" and toward "What do you make of Jesus?" When we translate that question into theological terms, it becomes "What do you imagine God to be like?", which in turn boils down to "How are you willing to live?" This way of framing the issue shows how one can take the virgin birth seriously, and believe in it with integrity, no matter what one thinks about Jesus' biological origins.

I'm well aware that many Christians will be impatient with all this. There are those who will still insist that the meaning of the virgin birth cannot be separated from its literal truth. Indeed, for them the truth of its meaning *depends* on its truth as a fact. When the issue is flattened out like that, the only way to affirm that Jesus was God's son is to also believe that he had no human father. But as we saw above, the notion that Jesus could not be the Son of God if he had a human father is a hellenistic (i.e., pagan) assumption, not a Jewish (i.e., biblical) one. In its most consistent form, this approach assumes that unless you can believe that Jesus was literally born of a virgin you can have no reason at all to see divinity in him. I don't know how many defenders of the doctrine are willing to be that consistent. Christians who object when other Christians take the virgin birth metaphorically are surely not troubled by the possibility that those whom they criticize might find God in Jesus.[2] Rather, their objection commonly reflects the fact that the metaphorical reading does not exclude the possibility of seeing God in others besides Jesus. That is why some insist on the literal fact of the virgin birth: if it is biologically true, that implies more than that Jesus was the son of God; it means that he was—and is—the *only* son of God. As we have seen, the "only son" terminology comes from the First Letter and Gospel of John, where it is an awkward (and illogical) way of putting Jesus in a category all by himself, above Christians who are also "fathered by God" (see p. 228). But that is not the reason why modern biblical and doctrinal literalists embrace that term with such fervor. They use it to deny the validity of every religion or system of belief other than their own by implying a rhetorical equivalence: "Jesus is the only Son of God" = "Jesus is the only savior" = "Christianity is the only true religion" = "We are right and everyone else is wrong." From this perspective, Christianity cannot be a true religion unless it is the *only* true religion.

But more and more Christians are coming to repudiate the idea that religious truth is a zero sum game, as if in order for us to be right everyone who believes differently must be wrong. They feel no need to think that if Jesus is God's son no one else can be. They find that way of thinking not only unnecessary, but untenable. And it is untenable not because of some fuzzy thinking in which everyone's opinion is equally valid, but because the notion of sincere Buddhists, Muslims, Jews, etc., being excluded from God's salvation cannot be squared with what many of us know from our own experience of other religions and of those who live them. But an even more important reason for rejecting the "only Jesus" dogma is that a God who would refuse salvation to such people cannot be reconciled with the God revealed in the life and teachings of Jesus.

2. Perhaps some object because they think that facts are somehow truer than symbols. If so, they are mistaken. Facts by themselves are mute; symbols speak to us where we live and breathe. People who are willing to die for their country do not put their lives on the line for the fact that a certain piece of geography exists, but rather for what their country symbolizes. When a young man swears that he is willing to fight to defend the Constitution, no one thinks he is referring to the paper and ink with which it's written. What commands loyalty is the meaning of the Constitution, what it stands for and the way of life it charters. Do those who say, "I pledge allegiance to the flag," imagine they are referring to a piece of colored fabric?

The Infancy Gospel of James

Title

The "Infancy Gospel of James" is the modern name for this text that has different titles in its various ancient and medieval manuscripts. The oldest extant manuscript bears the title "Birth of Mary, Revelation of James." Both that title and the modern one are only partial descriptions of the contents of this book.

Contents

The narrative begins with the annunciation and birth of Mary, mother of Jesus, and ends a short time after the birth of Jesus, with the murder of Zechariah, father of John the Baptizer. Jesus is born about two-thirds through the narrative. The first half of this gospel tells of the annunciation and conception of Mary; her birth, infancy, and extraordinary childhood; and God's selection of Joseph, here cast as an aged widower with adult sons, to be Mary's guardian (not her husband). The second half of this gospel (the selection presented below) generally follows an outline that combines scenes from Matthew and Luke. It tells of the annunciation of Jesus' birth to Mary; her visit with Elizabeth; Joseph's dilemma over Mary's unexplained pregnancy; a public inquiry into Mary's condition which exonerates both her and Joseph; the journey to Bethlehem and Joseph's search for a midwife; Jesus' birth in a cave; a physical certification of Mary's post-partum virginity with two confirmatory miracles; the visit of the Magi; Herod's massacre of the infants; Mary's hiding of Jesus (there is no escape to Egypt in this gospel); a miraculous hiding of John; and the murder of Zechariah.

This chapter draws heavily on *The Infancy Gospels of James and Thomas* by Ronald Hock. The comments on the following passages incorporate Hock's material: 11:2, 12:2, 13:6, 15:17, 16:3, 20:1, 20:6, 21:1, 22:4, 24:9. Used with permission.

The Infancy Gospels

Consider the annunciation to Mary in Luke's gospel. Luke introduces her simply as a girl from Nazareth betrothed to man named Joseph (Luke 1:27). Then the angel Gabriel tells her that she will be the mother of the Son of God. That slim narrative scaffolding is sufficient for Luke's purposes, but later generations of Christians who treasured this story and revered Mary because of it were understandably curious. Out of all the girls in Israel, why was Mary chosen to be the mother of the Lord? What kind of extraordinarily pious life must she have led to deserve this honor? What kind of people were her parents? Was the hand of God evident in her birth, as it was in the birth of her son?

Or consider the annunciation to Joseph in Matt 1:18–23. That laconic scene bristles with unanswered questions. How did Joseph and Mary meet? How did he discover that she was pregnant? What words passed between them on that occasion? What kind of person was this man whom God chose to raise and protect his son?

Inquiring minds wanted to know. And Christian storytellers stepped up to satisfy this natural curiosity about the Savior's earthly origins. Since the canonical gospels were silent on these matters, the only constraints on the Christian imagination were the conventions of ancient biographies, which did not demand that stories be factual, but only that they be appropriate reflections of someone's true nature. In a culture in which stories were virtually the only form of entertainment, tales about Mary and Joseph and the child Jesus proliferated. Such stories were acceptable as long as they edified and entertained. By the late second century the Infancy Gospel of James was offering pious and satisfying answers to all the questions mentioned above.

There were, of course, other questions and areas of curiosity about Jesus' early years and the storytelling we see preserved in the infancy gospels rose to meet them. Just who were those people referred to in the New Testament as the brothers and sisters of Jesus? (See Infancy James and the History of Joseph the Carpenter.) The only story in the Bible about the young Jesus recounts his visit to the temple at age twelve; what kinds of things was the divine child doing before that? (See the Infancy Gospel of Thomas.) What happened when the family fled to Egypt and during the time they lived there as refugees? (See the Arabic Infancy Gospel and the Gospel of Pseudo-Matthew.) How did Joseph relate to his divine son; and, since the New Testament gospels seem to imply that Joseph died while Jesus was young, what was his death like? (See the History of Joseph the Carpenter.)

The primary purpose of the infancy gospels was to fill out the story of the early life of Jesus. Some of the material in these gospels also glorifies Mary. (See Infancy James and the Arabic Gospel.) Some of the stories press theological points. (Pseudo-Matthew, for example, reports that Jesus' early life fulfilled more prophecies than are listed in Matthew.) Some stories are told to support a certain theological perspective. (See the excerpts from the Vision of Isaiah and the Latin Infancy Gospel, both of which promote Docetism.) A few stories were designed to give Jesus and his mother a competitive edge over popular deities of the ancient world. (See the Arabic Gospel 20–21.) Still, most of the material in the infancy gospel tradition does not seem to be strongly motivated by apologetic or theological agendas.

Even if these gospels were not written to score points in theological controversies, they nevertheless are permeated by specific religious beliefs, most universally the divinity of Jesus. In several of the infancy gospels Jesus' divinity completely eclipses his human nature. A number of stories show him working miracles before he can walk. However, other stories betray a concern to keep Jesus human. The Infancy Gospel of Thomas is a fascinating exercise in giving concrete expression to the belief that Jesus was both human and divine. How would a youngster who had both the power of God and the childish emotions of a five-year-old interact with his playmates? How would an eight-year-old who had the fullness of divine knowledge behave in school when forced to learn his ABCs? The stories in Infancy Thomas are entertaining to be sure, and their religious content is, from our perspective, somewhat unsophisticated; but they are also vivid examples of the storyteller's craft tackling a theological problem.

The stories about the young Jesus are almost all miracle stories of one kind or another. Infancy Thomas tells of Jesus between age five and twelve, and every story in it pictures him wielding miraculous power – sometimes to devastating effect – or showing off his supernatural knowledge. Later gospels go a step further by recounting miracles worked by Jesus when he was a baby, sometimes directly (as in Pseudo-Matthew), sometimes through the mediation of his mother (the Arabic Gospel). It was probably inevitable that, as the centuries went by, the miracles got more and more fantastic. For example, in the fifth-century Arabic Gospel, playmates who ditch Jesus turn into goats. And in the eighth-century Gospel of Pseudo-Matthew, Jesus tames dragons, pets wild lions, and makes a palm tree bow down to his mother.

Relationship to Matthew and Luke

The Infancy Gospel of James relates to the stories in the canonical gospels in several ways. Sometimes it condenses them and sometimes it elaborates them. Sometimes Infancy James follows the canonical story closely and sometimes alters it considerably. Infancy James also contains a fair amount of material not based on Matthew or Luke. Whether the author was familiar with the non-biblical stories from earlier Christian storytelling or whether he wrote them himself is impossible to determine.

What is clear from a close analysis of the narrative is that the author assumed his readers were familiar with the characters in Matthew and Luke. This indicates that he intended his gospel to supplement, not replace, the canonical infancy narratives. This is important because it means that the author expected Christians to accept both his narrative and the canonical originals, even though his gospel sometimes differs dramatically from them. In this the author succeeded admirably, judging from the influence this gospel had on later Christian doctrine about Mary and from the numerous examples over many centuries of Christian art depicting scenes from this gospel.

Influences

Besides relying on the early chapters of Matthew and Luke for narrative material, the author also borrows many phrases from throughout Matthew, Luke, John, Acts, and even 1 Peter. In addition, he makes extensive use of the Septuagint—which seems to be his sole source for information about Judaism—in bits of dialogue and narrative descriptions. In several passages the author enhances the portrayals of his characters by explicitly comparing them to Old Testament figures.

The author was also familiar with Greco-Roman literature, especially with the Greek romances, which were popular narratives about lovers overcoming obstacles that separate them and enduring ordeals for the sake of their mutual love. Our author borrows phrases, plot devices, and conventions of behavior from these ancient romances. The most pronounced point of contact with these writings is the emphasis on the value of sexual purity, a virtue much admired in the Greco-Roman world. Their celebration of the idealized fidelity and chastity of their characters comports with the unifying theme of the Infancy Gospel of James: Mary's extraordinary purity. Especially in the first half of this gospel, Mary's purity is so elaborately portrayed that the primary message of this gospel seems to be that Mary was chosen to be the mother of the son of God because of her unique and exemplary purity.

Authorship and Date

The author claims to be James (25:1), who in the New Testament is one of the brothers of Jesus.[1] The author further claims that he wrote this work just after the death of Herod (4 BCE). If this were true, this gospel would come from Jesus' own family, from an eyewitness to many of the events in the story, and would have been written while Jesus was still in diapers. Both of the author's claims are false. Literary analysis has demonstrated that the author used the gospels of Matthew and Luke, which were written between 85–100 CE, and the James known as the "brother of the Lord" died in 62 CE.

The author is thus pseudonymous. As for when this gospel was written, as with so many ancient writings, we do not know. Our only secure evidence is that it was known by Clement of Alexandria, who died before 212 CE. A late second-century date is a good guess. The gospel was written in Greek. Our earliest complete manuscript comes from the early fourth century.

THE INFANCY GOSPEL OF JAMES 11–25

At this point in the narrative, Mary is a young teenager living in the home of Joseph, an older widower with grown children, who was chosen by lot to be her guardian.

---

1. See, however, the comment on 25:1, p. 272.

Mary has been chosen by lot to spin thread for an ornate veil in the temple. Joseph, a carpenter, has been away from home for a long time building houses.

11 And she took her water jar and went out to fill it with water. ²Suddenly there was a voice saying to her, "Greetings, favored one! The Lord be with you. Blessed are you among women." ³Mary began looking around, both right and left, to see where the voice was coming from. ⁴She became terrified and went home. After putting the water jar down and taking up the purple thread, she sat down on her chair and began to spin the thread.

⁵Suddenly a heavenly messenger stood in front of her and said, "Don't be afraid, Mary. You see, you've found favor in the sight of the Master of all. You will conceive by his word."

⁶But as she listened, Mary was puzzled and said, "Am I going to conceive by the Lord, the living God, the way every woman does who gives birth?"

⁷And the messenger of the Lord replied, "No, Mary. The power of God will cast its shadow on you. And so the child to be born will be called holy, son of the Most High. ⁸You will name him Jesus because he will save his people from their sins."

⁹And Mary said, "In the presence of the Lord, here I am, his slave. I pray that everything you've told me comes true."

12 And she finished spinning the purple and the scarlet thread and took her work up to the high priest. ²The high priest accepted it and blessed her and said, "Mary, the Lord God has extolled your name and so you will be blessed by all the generations of the earth."

³Mary rejoiced and left to visit her relative Elizabeth. ⁴She knocked at the door. Elizabeth heard her, tossed aside the scarlet thread, ran to the door, and opened it for her. ⁵And she blessed her and said, "Who am I that the mother of my Lord should visit me? Look, the baby inside me has jumped for joy and blessed you."

⁶But Mary forgot the mysteries which the heavenly messenger Gabriel had spoken, and she looked up to the sky and said, "Who am I, Lord, that every generation on earth should congratulate me?"

⁷She spent three months with Elizabeth. ⁸Day by day Mary's womb kept swelling. She became frightened and returned home, where she hid from the people of Israel. ⁹She was just sixteen years old when these mysterious things happened to her.

13 She was in her sixth month when one day Joseph came home from his building projects, entered his house, and saw that she was pregnant. ²He struck himself in the face, threw himself to the ground on sackcloth, and began to cry bitterly: "How can I show my face to the Lord God? ³What prayer can I say for her since I took her in as a virgin from the temple of the Lord God and didn't protect her? ⁴Who has set this trap for me? Who has done this evil thing in my house? Who has lured this virgin away from me and violated her? ⁵I'm reliving the story of Adam, aren't I? Adam was off by himself praying when the serpent came and found Eve. He deceived and corrupted her. Now the same thing has happened to me."

⁶So Joseph got up from the sackcloth and summoned Mary and said to her, "God has taken special care of you–how could you have done this? ⁷Have you forgotten the Lord your God? You were raised in the Holy of Holies and fed by a heavenly messenger. Why have you brought shame on yourself?"

⁸But she began to cry bitter tears: "I'm innocent. I'm still a virgin."

⁹So Joseph said to her, "Then where did the child you're carrying come from?"

¹⁰She replied, "As the Lord my God lives, I don't know."

14 Now Joseph became very frightened. He no longer spoke with her as he pondered what he was going to do with her. ²He said to himself, "If I try to cover up her sin, I'll end up going against the Law of the Lord. ³But if I disclose her condition to the people of Israel, I'm afraid that her pregnancy might be heaven-sent and I'll end up handing over innocent blood to a death sentence. ⁴So what should I do with her? I guess I'll divorce her quietly."

⁵But that night a messenger of the Lord suddenly appeared to him in a dream and said: "Don't be afraid of this child, because a holy spirit is responsible for her pregnancy. ⁶She will give birth to a son and you will name him Jesus because he will save his people from their sins." ⁷Joseph got up from his sleep and praised the God of Israel, who had done him this favor. ⁸And so he began to protect the child.

15 Then Annas the scholar came to him and said to him, "Joseph, why haven't you attended our assembly?"

²And he replied, "I was worn out from my trip and I rested my first day home."

³Then Annas turned and saw that Mary was pregnant.

⁴He left in a hurry to see the high priest and said to him, "You remember Joseph, don't you–the man you yourself vouched for? Well, he has committed a serious offense."

⁵The high priest asked, "In what way?"

⁶"Joseph has violated the virgin he received from the temple of the Lord," he replied. "He has stolen her wedding and hasn't disclosed this to the people of Israel."

⁷The high priest asked him, "Has Joseph really done this?"

⁸Annas replied, "Send temple assistants and you'll find the girl pregnant."

⁹And so the temple assistants went and found her just as Annas had reported. So they brought her, along with Joseph, to the court.

¹⁰ "Mary, why have you done this?" the high priest asked her. "Why have you humiliated yourself? ¹¹Have you forgotten the Lord your God? You were raised in the Holy of the Holies and were fed by heavenly messengers. ¹²You heard their hymns and danced for them; you of all people–why have you done this?"

¹³And she wept bitterly: "As the Lord God lives, I stand innocent before him. I'm still a virgin."

¹⁴The high priest said, "Joseph, why have you done this?"

¹⁵And Joseph said, "As the Lord lives, I am innocent. I had nothing to do with this."

¹⁶And the high priest said, "Don't perjure yourself; tell the truth. You've stolen her wedding and haven't disclosed this to the people of Israel. ¹⁷And you haven't humbled yourself under God's mighty hand, so that your offspring might be blessed."

¹⁸But Joseph was silent.

16 Then the high priest said, "Return the girl you received from the temple of the Lord."

²And Joseph, bursting into tears. . .

³The high priest said, "I'm going to give you the Lord's drink test. It will disclose your sin clearly to both of you."

⁴The high priest took the water and made Joseph drink it and sent him into the wilderness, but he returned unharmed. ⁵And he made the child drink it, too, and sent her into the wilderness. She also came back unharmed. ⁶And everybody was surprised because their sin had not been revealed. ⁷And so the high priest said, "If the Lord God has not exposed your sin, then neither do I condemn you." So he let them go. ⁸Joseph took Mary and returned home, celebrating and praising the God of Israel.

17 Now an order came down from Augustus the Emperor that everybody in Bethlehem of Judea be counted in a census.

²And Joseph wondered, "I'll register my sons, but what am I going to do with this child? How will I register her? ³As my wife? I'm ashamed to do that. As my daughter? The people of Israel know she's not my daughter. ⁴This day belongs to the Lord; he will do whatever he decides."

⁵So he saddled his donkey and had her get on it. His son led it and Samuel brought up the rear. ⁶As they neared the three mile marker, Joseph turned around and saw that she was gloomy. ⁷He said to himself, "Perhaps the baby she is carrying is causing her discomfort." ⁸Joseph turned around again and saw her laughing and said to her, "Mary, what's going on with you? One minute I see you laughing and the next minute you're gloomy."

⁹She replied, "Joseph, it's because I imagine two peoples in front of me, one weeping and mourning and the other rejoicing and celebrating."

¹⁰Halfway through the trip Mary said to him, "Joseph, help me down from the donkey—the child inside me is ready to be born."

¹¹And he helped her down and said to her, "Where will I take you to give you some privacy, since this place is out in the open?"

18 He found a cave nearby and took her inside. He stationed his sons to guard her ²and went to look for a Hebrew midwife in the countryside around Bethlehem.

³"Now I, Joseph, was walking along and yet not going anywhere. ⁴I looked up at the dome of the sky and saw it standing still, and then at the clouds and saw them stopped in amazement, and at the birds of the sky suspended in midair. ⁵As I looked down on the ground, I saw a bowl lying there and workers reclining around it with their hands in the bowl; ⁶some were chewing and yet did not chew; some were picking up something to eat and yet did not pick it up; and some were putting food in their mouths and yet did not do so. ⁷Instead, they were all looking upward.

⁸"I saw sheep being herded along and yet the sheep stood still; ⁹the shepherd was lifting his hand to strike them, and yet his hand remained raised. ¹⁰And I observed the current of the river and saw goats with their mouths in the water and yet they were not drinking. ¹¹Then all of a sudden everything and everybody went on with what they had been doing.

19 "Then I saw a woman coming down from the hill country. She asked, 'Where are you going, sir?'

²I replied, 'I'm looking for a Hebrew midwife.'

³She inquired, 'Are you an Israelite?'

⁴I told her that I was.

⁵'And who's the one having a baby in the cave?' she asked.

⁶'My betrothed,' I replied.

⁷She asked me, 'You mean she isn't your wife?'

⁸I told her, 'She is Mary, who was raised in the temple of the Lord; I obtained her by lot as my wife. ⁹But she's not really my wife; she's pregnant by a holy spirit.'"

¹⁰"Really?" the midwife said.

¹¹"Come and see," Joseph responded.

¹²So the midwife went with him. ¹³As they stood in front of the cave, a dark cloud overshadowed it. ¹⁴The midwife said, "I've really been privileged, because today my eyes have seen a mystery: salvation has come to Israel."

¹⁵Suddenly the cloud withdrew from the cave and a light appeared inside it that was so intense their eyes could not bear to look. ¹⁶And a little later that light receded until an infant became visible. He came and took the breast of his mother Mary.

¹⁷Then the midwife shouted: "What a great day this is for me! I've seen this new miracle!"

¹⁸And the midwife left the cave and met Salome and said to her, "Salome, Salome, let me tell you about a new marvel: a virgin has given birth, something we all know is impossible!"

¹⁹And Salome replied, "As the Lord my God lives, unless I insert my finger and examine her, I will never believe that a virgin has given birth."

20 The midwife entered and said, "Mary, position yourself for an examination. You are facing a serious test."

²And so Mary, when she heard these instructions, positioned herself, and Salome inserted her finger into Mary. ³And then Salome cried aloud and said,

"I'll be damned because of my transgression and my disbelief; I have put the living God on trial. ⁴Look! My hand is disappearing! It's being consumed by flames!"

⁵Then Salome fell on her knees in the presence of the Master, with these words: "God of my ancestors, remember me because I am a descendant of Abraham, Isaac, and Jacob. ⁶Do not make an example out of me for the people of Israel, but give me a place among the poor again. ⁷You yourself know, Master, that I've been healing people in your name and have been receiving my payment from you."

⁸And suddenly a messenger of the Lord appeared and said, "Salome, Salome, the Master of all has heard your prayer. ⁹Hold out your hand to the child and pick him up, and then you'll have salvation and joy."

¹⁰Salome approached the child and picked him up and said, "I'll worship him because he's been born to be king of Israel." ¹¹And Salome was instantly healed and left the cave acquitted.

¹²Then a voice said abruptly, "Salome, Salome, don't report the mysteries you've seen here until the child goes to Jerusalem."

21 Joseph was about ready to depart for Judea when a great uproar broke out in Bethlehem in Judea. ²It all started when magi came inquiring, "Where is the one born to be king of the Judeans? We have observed his star at its rising and have come to pay him homage."

³When the news reached Herod, he was visibly shaken and sent his assistants to the magi. ⁴He also sent for the high priests and questioned them in his palace: "What has been written about the Anointed? Where is he supposed to be born?"

⁵They said to him, "In Bethlehem, Judea, that's what the scriptures say." ⁶And he dismissed them.

⁷Then he questioned the magi: "What sign have you seen regarding the one who has been born king?"

⁸The magi said, "We saw a star in the sky that was so brilliant that it dimmed the other stars to the point where they were no longer visible. That is how we know that a king was born for Israel. We have come to pay him homage."

⁹Herod instructed them: "Go and begin your search, and if you find him, report back to me, so I can also go and pay him homage."

¹⁰The magi departed. And there it was: the star they had seen in the East showed them the way until they arrived at the cave; then the star stopped directly above the head of the child. ¹¹After the magi saw him with his mother Mary, they took gifts out of their pouches: gold, frankincense, and myrrh.

¹²Since they had been advised by the heavenly messenger not to go into Judea, they returned to their country by another route.

22 When Herod realized he had been duped by the magi, he flew into a rage ²and dispatched his executioners with instructions to kill all the infants two years old and younger.

³When Mary heard that the infants were being killed, she was frightened ⁴and took her child, wrapped him in strips of cloth, and put him in a feeding trough used by cattle.

⁵As for Elizabeth, when she heard that they were looking for John, she took him and went up into the hill country. ⁶She kept searching for a place to hide him, but there was none to be had. ⁷Then she groaned and said out loud, "Mountain of God, please take in a mother with her child." You see, Elizabeth was unable to go on climbing. ⁸But suddenly the mountain was split open and let them in. This mountain allowed the light to shine through to her, ⁹since a messenger of the Lord was with them for protection.

23 Herod, though, kept looking for John ²and sent his agents to Zechariah, who was serving at the altar. They asked him, "Where have you hidden your son?"

³But he answered them, "I am a minister of God, attending to his temple. How should I know where my son is?"

⁴So the agents left and reported all this to Herod, who got angry and said, "Is his son going to rule over Israel?"

⁵He sent his agents back with this message: "Tell me the truth. Where is your son? Don't you know that your life is in my hands?"

⁶The agents went and reported this message to him.

⁷Zechariah answered, "I am a martyr for God. Take my life. ⁸The Master, though, will receive my spirit because you are shedding innocent blood at the entrance to the Lord's temple."

⁹And so at daybreak Zechariah was murdered, but the people of Israel did not know that.

24 At the hour of formal greetings the priests departed, but Zechariah did not meet and bless them as was customary. ²And so the priests waited around for Zechariah, to greet him in prayer and to praise the Most High God.

³But when he did not show up, they all became fearful. ⁴One of them, however, summoned up his courage, entered the sanctuary, and saw dried blood next to the altar of the Lord. ⁵And a voice said, "Zechariah has been murdered! His blood will not be cleaned up until his avenger appears."

⁶When he heard this utterance he was afraid and went out and reported to the priests what he had seen and heard. ⁷And they summoned up their courage, entered, and saw what had happened. ⁸The panels of the temple cried out and the priests ripped their robes from top to bottom. ⁹They didn't find Zechariah's body, but they did find his blood, which had turned to stone. ¹⁰They were afraid and went out and reported to the people that Zechariah had been murdered. ¹¹When all the tribes of the people heard this, they began to mourn; and they beat their breasts for three days and three nights.

¹²After three days, however, the priests deliberated about whom they should appoint to Zechariah's post. ¹³The lot fell to Simeon. ¹⁴This man, you

see, is the one who was informed by the holy spirit that he would not see death until he had seen the Anointed in the flesh.

25 Now I, James, am the one who wrote this account at the time when an uproar broke out in Jerusalem at the death of Herod. ²I withdrew to the desert until the uproar in Jerusalem died down. ³There I praised the Lord God, who gave me the wisdom to write this account.

⁴Grace will be with all those who fear the Lord. Amen.

Birth of Mary

Revelation of James

Peace to the writer and the reader.

———— ❧ ————

11:2 *Greetings, favored one! The Lord be with you.* This part of the supernatural message is taken from Gabriel's greeting in Luke 1:28, but the next part, *Blessed are you among women*, comes from Elizabeth's greeting in Luke 1:42.

11:5–7 is an abbreviated paraphrase of Luke 1:30–35.

11:6 *the way every woman does who gives birth.* Mary believes the angel's announcement that God will bless her conception. However, her question assumes that conceiving "by the word" of the Lord need not entail a miracle. The angel's answer in the next verse allows the author to clarify that Mary will conceive and still remain a virgin.

In some manuscripts 11:6 reads, "If I am going to conceive by the Lord, the living God, will I also give birth the way every woman does?" In that version of the question Mary understands that she will conceive miraculously and goes on to ask whether she will have a natural delivery.

11:8 comes word for word from Matt 1:21, where it is addressed to Joseph.

11:9 closely follows Luke 1:38.

12:2 The high priest's words recall those of Luke 1:46, 48, though with some striking changes, such as their being said to Mary, not by her, and their reversing the subject and object, so that it is Mary, not the Lord, who is exalted.

12:3 This is the first mention of Elizabeth in this gospel, even though Zechariah has been prominently featured. The author assumes that readers are familiar with Elizabeth from the Gospel of Luke. This is one of many indications that Infancy James was intended to supplement, not replace, the canonical infancy narratives. It also shows that the author expects readers to accept his narrative *and* the canonical originals, from which it differs dramatically.

12:3–7 is loosely based on Luke 1:39–56.

12:6 That Mary could forget what the angel had told her is implausible in the extreme. However, it does explain her question, *Who am I?*

12:8 In Luke 1:24, it is Elizabeth who remains secluded from public view during her pregnancy.

12:9 *sixteen years old.* The ancient manuscripts differ considerably here about Mary's age. Most read "sixteen," but others put her anywhere from twelve to seventeen. Twelve fits best with the story line of Infancy James. The gospel earlier reported that Mary was twelve (8:3) when she left her home in the temple to live in Joseph's house and the narrative does not give the impression that much time went by before she conceived.

13:5 That *Adam was off by himself praying when the serpent came and found Eve* is an imaginative embellishment of Gen 3:1–7.

13:6 *how could you have done this?* This is the very question that God put to Eve in Gen 3:13.

13:8 *I'm still a virgin* is what Mary says to Gabriel at the annunciation in Luke 1:34.

13:10 Mary's response is intelligible only in light of 12:6: that she forgot what the angel had told her.

14:3 The *death sentence* is confusing. Deut 22:23–24 prescribes capital punishment for a betrothed woman who has consensual sex with another man, because that amounts to adultery. But in this gospel Mary is not betrothed. If a non-betrothed woman had consensual sex, she could be punished only if she later married a different man and her husband charged her with not being a virgin at the time of their marriage (Deut 22:13–21).

14:4 That Joseph should *divorce her quietly* makes no sense here because they are neither betrothed nor married. The author is clearly dependent on Matt 1:19.

14:5 The command here, *Don't be afraid of this child*, differs significantly from the parallel account in Matt 1:20 ("Do not be afraid to take Mary as your wife") . The difference is deliberate, reflecting the very different relationship between Joseph and Mary in this gospel. Referring to Mary as a child (*paida*) accentuates the disparity in their ages.

14:6 is copied from Matt 1:21.

15 In Matthew, Joseph covers up the cause of Mary's pregnancy by completing their marriage. People have no reason to think that he is not Jesus' biological father. In the present gospel, Joseph and Mary do not marry, so there is no way to prevent public suspicion.

15:6 *He has stolen her wedding* means that he has married her in secret. This seems to imply that Joseph could have lived with Mary as her husband, as long as he publicized his intention to do so. This is puzzling.

15:11 This was narrated earlier in the gospel, at 8:2.

15:17 The wording of *humbled yourself under God's mighty hand* comes from 1 Pet 5:6.

16:2 There is probably a gap in the original text here, for no verb accompanies the participle *bursting*. How much has dropped out is difficult to tell, but perhaps nothing more than "said nothing" is missing.

16:3 The *Lord's drink test* seems to be based on the ritual test for wives suspected of adultery in Num 5:11–31. The ritual here is rather different, especially in its application to the man.

16:7 *Neither do I condemn you* echoes the words of Jesus to the adulteress in John 8:11.

17 From this point the gospel begins to follows the outline of Luke 2:1–20, occasionally inserting material from Matt 2:1–12, 16.

17:1 The census applies only to Bethlehem, whereas in Luke 2:1 it was for the whole world.

17:2 Earlier in this gospel Joseph had stated, "I already have sons and I'm an old man" (9:8).

17:5 The identity of *Samuel* is unknown. Joseph and Mary obviously do not live in Bethlehem, but this gospel neither tells where they live nor mentions Nazareth. The author probably assumes that readers know from Luke's gospel that they live in Nazareth.

17:9 This enigmatic remark may be based on Luke 2:34, where Simeon says that Jesus will grow up to be the cause of "the fall and rise of many in Israel."

17:11 Contrary to the Gospel of Luke, here Jesus is not born in Bethlehem itself.

18:1 Jesus is born in a *cave* outside Bethlehem. Luke sets the birth in a travellers' shelter in the town (Luke 2:7). In Matthew, Mary and Joseph live in Bethlehem (Matt 2:11) and it is assumed that Jesus, like all babies, was born at home.

18:3–11 Joseph's vision, which begins with his claim to be *walking along and yet not going anywhere*, describes an experience in which everything—the winds, birds, workers, herds, herders, and himself—are momentarily frozen in whatever activity they were engaged in. This moment would seem to be the time when, back at the cave, Jesus was born.

19:6 That Joseph calls Mary his *betrothed* reflects Luke 2:5, but contradicts the present gospel, which elsewhere emphasizes that Joseph is merely Mary's guardian.

19:13 Perhaps the *dark cloud* is meant to recall the cloud that enveloped Mount Sinai when Moses received the covenant from God (Ex 19:16–18).

19:15 The intense light hides the actual birth and bathes the scene in a miraculous glow. Perhaps this also symbolizes the arrival of "the light of the world" (John 8:12). The Latin Infancy Gospel (see pp. 288-89) elaborately develops the theme of light at the nativity. For example, "when the light was born it increased and outshone the light of the sun with its dazzling brightness" (Latin Gospel 73:4).

19:18 *Salome* is a new character in this gospel. *A virgin has given birth.* Matthew and Luke claim that Mary conceived as a virgin, but this gospel makes the unprecedented claim that she remained a virgin—in the sense of being anatomically intact—after childbirth. How the midwife knows this is not explained.

19:19 *Unless I insert my finger* recalls the language and story of doubting Thomas, who demanded to probe the wounds of the risen Jesus before believing in the miracle of his resurrection (John 20:24–25).

20:1 *serious test:* Just as the high priest tested Mary to verify that she was a virgin (see 15:10–13; 16:3–5), so now Salome must examine her to confirm that she remains a virgin after giving birth.

20:6 *Give me a place among the poor:* The manuscripts vary widely at this point. Some have "Restore me to my parents," while others have "restore my hand" or "restore my full health."

20:11 That Salome leaves *acquitted* recalls the wording of Luke 18:14, in the parable in which the toll collector leaves the temple acquitted after acknowledging his sinfulness.

21:1 Since the author knows that Bethlehem is in Judea, the phrase *depart for Judea* seems to be a mistaken reference to Jerusalem. The author probably means that Joseph planned to take Mary and Jesus to the temple in Jerusalem, as in Luke 2:22–24. The author again writes *Judea* in 21:12 when he obviously means "Jerusalem."

21:2–12 The visit of the magi follows very closely the scene in Matt 2:1–12.

21:10 This star is more fantastic than the one in Matthew's story: here it moves into the cave and rests over Jesus' head.

22:1–2 is based on Matt 2:16.

22:4 *wrapped him in strips of cloth and put him in a feeding trough*. These details recall Luke 2:7, but here they are Mary's way of hiding Jesus from Herod's soldiers. Presumably the baby was covered with some hay. This gospel has no story about Jesus and his parents fleeing to Egypt to escape Herod's wrath (Matt 2:13–15).

22:5–9 Only Luke tells of the birth of John the Baptizer and only Matthew tells of Herod's slaughter of the infants. When those two gospels are blended together, a narrative problem arises that does not exist when each gospel is read on its own: since John is only six months older than Jesus (Luke 1:36), how did he escape the massacre of baby boys? Infancy James solves this problem: John and his mother are miraculously hidden by a mountain (22:8) and protected by an angel (22:9).

23:2 Zechariah's presence at the altar, where he will be killed, shows that the author has identified this Zechariah, the father of John, with another Zechariah, mentioned in Matt 23:35, who reportedly was murdered. When readers of Infancy James encounter Matt 23:35 in its own context, they will understand Jesus to be referring to John's father, not to some prophet from the Old Testament.

24:1–2 This report assumes that Zechariah was the high priest, whereas in Luke 1:5 he is an ordinary priest.

24:5 The identity of Zechariah's avenger, and how the priest's murder was avenged, remains a mystery.

24:9 Presumably the killers had disposed of Zechariah's body.

24:13–14 This gospel identifies the new high priest with *Simeon*, the holy man who prophecies over the baby Jesus in the temple in Luke 2:25–26.

25:1 *James* is presumably the same man known in the New Testament as the brother of Jesus (Mark 6:3, Matt 13:55, Gal 1:19). However, in this gospel James is not Jesus' brother. He is an adult son of Joseph and thus not related to Jesus at all since Joseph is not married to Jesus' mother. It is impossible for anyone, much less James himself, to have written this gospel when Herod died in 4 BCE. See p. 262.

The Infancy Gospel of Thomas

Title

This gospel used to be known as "The Gospel of Thomas the Israelite" or simply "The Gospel of Thomas." It was renamed in the mid-twentieth century in order to distinguish it from the Gospel of Thomas discovered at Nag Hammadi in Egypt, a gospel composed entirely of sayings of Jesus. The ancient title of the present gospel was probably "The Boyhood Deeds of Our Lord Jesus Christ," an apt description of its contents.

Contents

The only story in the canonical gospels about Jesus as a boy is the scene of his visit to the temple in Jerusalem at age twelve (Luke 2:41–52). Christians were understandably curious about Jesus' early years, and the Infancy Gospel of Thomas is an attempt to fill this twelve-year gap in Jesus' biography. The gospel is a collection of self-contained stories highlighting Jesus' miraculous powers. There are fifteen separate stories in all, many of them quite brief. They are very loosely connected: a few stories contain references to earlier ones (e.g., 14:2) and four reports of Jesus' age—he is five at 2:1, six at 11:1, eight at 12:4, and twelve at 19:1—are the only indications of narrative structure.

The stories in the first part of the gospel tell of Jesus at play and at school. The most prominent theme here is Jesus' lethal temper: two of his playmates are struck dead after Jesus curses them (3, 4). In school he humiliates his teachers by showing that he knows far more than they (6–8, 14). The rest of the gospel features Jesus using his powers to help out with household chores (11), farm work (12), and his father's carpentry (13), and to aid the suffering: he heals two

This chapter draws heavily on *The Infancy Gospels of James and Thomas* by Ronald Hock. The comments on the following passages incorporate Hock's material: 3:2, 6:23, 8:3, 9:5, 11:3, 15:1–7, 16:1, 19:1–12, 19:8–10. Used with permission.

severe injuries (10, 16) and raises three people from death (9, 17, 18). The gospel ends with a slightly modified version of Jesus' visit to the temple (19).

That last story is the only one in the gospel taken from the New Testament. A few other passages echo expressions or wording in the canonical texts. For example, in 6:6 Jesus describes himself in the distinctive language of John's gospel (John 4:34, 5:24). 6:16 uses the metaphor of a "clashing symbol" from 1 Cor 13:1. And the report in 11:4 that Mary "kept to herself the mysteries that she had seen him do" is modeled on Luke 2:51.

Biographical Function

The stories in this gospel meet the expectations that ancient audiences brought to the childhood stories of famous men. Such stories in ancient biographies were designed to be previews of the adult hero's character. They featured signs that the boy was divinely favored, portrayed him as a child prodigy,[1] and foreshadowed the man's future greatness in the way the boy played and did his chores. Accordingly, the Infancy Gospel of Thomas portrays Jesus as surpassing his teachers in knowledge (e.g., 6:18, 7:10, 15:6), dwells on the divine origin of his wisdom (7:4–5, 19:10), and amply displays his miraculous abilities. People in the narrative recognize that "the spirit of God dwells in this child" (10:4) and conclude that he must be either God or an angel (7:11, 17:4). Towards the end of the gospel a crowd acclaims his supernatural origin and anticipates his salvific mission: "This child's from heaven—he must be, because he has saved many souls from death, and he can go on saving all his life" (18:3).

Christology

This gospel expresses its christology most directly in statements Jesus makes about himself. Even as a five-year old he knows that he is the incarnate Son of God sent to earth for human salvation.

> I am the Lord of these people. (6:5)
> When the world was created, I existed along with the One who sent me to you. (6:10b)
> I've come from above to rescue those below and call them to higher things. (8:2)

Interspersed with these affirmations of high christology are stories in which Jesus is portrayed as a vengeful, impulsive, and arrogant child.

- Two of Jesus' playmates die after he curses them. The grieving parents threaten Joseph: "Teach your boy to bless and not curse, or else you can't live with us in the village. He's killing our children!" (4:4)

1. See Box 3.4, pp. 69–70.

- Later in the story there is this chilling report: "From then on no one dared to anger him for fear of being cursed and maimed for life" (8:4).
- When Jesus' teacher falls into a coma after Jesus curses him, Joseph warns Mary, "Don't let him go outside, because those who annoy him end up dead" (14:5).

Many modern readers are offended by stories of Jesus slaying playmates who incur his childish wrath. Others regard these stories as humorous. The gospel itself hints that early Christians were somewhat uncomfortable with these stories since it points out that "all those who had fallen under [Jesus'] curse were instantly saved" (8:3) and that the teacher whom Jesus had cursed was later restored to consciousness (15:7). Both of those reports fit awkwardly into the overall narrative (see the Comments) and so are almost certainly later additions to the gospel. They hint that the early Christians who retold these stories were uneasy with them, though not so uneasy as to leave them untold. What seems incongruous to us is that these stories exist alongside stories of Jesus healing the injured and raising the dead. We do not know whether early Christians felt any tension between these two types of stories. Both of them depict Jesus wielding supernatural power and so are imaginative expressions of the Christian belief in Jesus' divinity.

The stories in the Infancy Gospel of Thomas may be theologically unsophisticated, but they show that some early Christians were thinking through the implications of their belief that Jesus was both human and divine. It's one thing to think of the eloquent and restrained adult Jesus as God in human form, but what about his childhood? How would God act if he had the interests and emotions of a five-year old? The apparently unseemly stories of Jesus humiliating his teachers, blinding his neighbors, and lethally cursing his playmates display a certain level of theological honesty: a boy-God would be both charming and very dangerous. It's worth noting that Infancy Thomas arranges its stories so that as Jesus grows older he loses his temper less and increasingly uses his power to help and to heal. Perhaps this reflects a plan by the author to portray a divine brat growing into his godliness.

Author, Attestation, Date

Nothing is known of the author. Only some of the manuscripts attribute the gospel to Thomas and one attributes it to James. The original text was probably anonymous. Copies of the gospel exist in various ancient versions in Greek, Syriac, Latin, and Slavonic. The earliest extant manuscript is in Syriac from the sixth century. The gospel was originally written in Greek, probably in the mid-second century, since at least one of its stories was known to Christian writers in the late second century.

THE INFANCY GOSPEL OF THOMAS

1 I, Thomas the Israelite, am reporting to you, all my non-Jewish brothers and sisters, to tell you about the extraordinary childhood of our Lord Jesus Christ—what he did after his birth in my part of the world. This is how it all started.

2 When this boy, Jesus, was five years old, he was playing at the ford of a rushing stream. [2]He was collecting the flowing water into ponds and with a single command he made the water instantly pure. [3]He then made soft clay and shaped it into twelve sparrows. He did this on the sabbath, and a lot of other boys were playing with him.

[4]But when a Jew saw what Jesus was doing while playing on the sabbath, he immediately went off and told Joseph, Jesus' father: "See here, your boy is at the ford and has violated the sabbath by taking mud and making twelve birds with it."

[5]So Joseph went there, and as soon as he spotted him he shouted, "Why are you doing what's not permitted on the sabbath?"

[6]But Jesus simply clapped his hands and shouted to the sparrows: "Go on, fly away, and remember me, you who are now alive!" And the sparrows took off and flew away noisily.

[7]The Jews watched with amazement, then left the scene to report to their leaders what they had seen Jesus doing.

3 The son of Annas the scholar was standing there with Jesus. He took a willow branch and drained the water Jesus had collected. [2]Jesus saw what had happened and got angry and said to him, "Damn you, you ungodly ignoramus! What harm were the ponds of water doing you? From now on you, too, will dry up like a tree, and you'll never produce leaves or roots or bear fruit."

[3]In an instant the boy had completely withered away. Then Jesus departed and left for the house of Joseph. [4]The parents of the boy who had withered away picked him up and were carrying him out, in grief because he was so young. And they came to Joseph and accused him: "It's your fault—your boy did all this."

4 Later on he was going through the village when a boy ran by and bumped him on the shoulder. Jesus got angry and said to him, "Your journey is over." [2]And all of a sudden he fell down and died.

[3]Some people saw what had happened and said, "Where has this boy come from? Everything he says happens instantly!"

[4]The parents of the dead boy came to Joseph and blamed him, saying, "Teach your boy to bless and not curse, or else you can't live with us in the village. He's killing our children!"

5 So Joseph summoned his child and scolded him in private, "Why are you doing all this? These people hate and harass us because they are suffering." [2]Jesus said, "I know that the words I spoke are not my own. Still, I'll keep quiet

for your sake. But those people must take their punishment." At that very moment his accusers were struck blind.

³Those who saw this were very frightened and didn't know what to do. All they could say was, "Every word he says, whether good or bad, turns into a fact—a miracle, even!" ⁴When Joseph saw that Jesus had done such a thing, he got angry and grabbed his ear and pulled very hard. ⁵The boy became infuriated with him and replied, "It's one thing for you to seek and not find; it's quite another for you to act this unwisely. ⁶Don't you know that I don't really belong to you? Don't get me angry."

6 A teacher by the name of Zacchaeus was listening to everything Jesus was saying to Joseph, and was astonished. He said to himself, "He is just a child, and he's saying this!" ²And so he summoned Joseph and said to him, "You have a bright child, and he has a good mind. Hand him over to me so he can learn his letters. I'll teach him everything he needs to know so he won't be out of control."

³Joseph replied, "No one can control this child except God alone. Don't consider him to be a small cross, brother."

⁴When Jesus heard Joseph saying this he laughed and said to Zacchaeus, "Believe me, teacher, what my father told you is true. ⁵I am the Lord of these people and I'm present with you and have been born among you and am with you. ⁶I know where you've come from and how long you'll live. I swear to you, teacher, I existed when you were born. If you wish to be a perfect teacher, listen to me and I'll teach you a wisdom that no one else knows except for me and the One who sent me to you. ⁷It's you who happen to be my student. I know how old you are and how long you have to live. ⁸When you see the cross that my father mentioned, then you'll believe that everything I've told you is true."

⁹The Jews who were standing by and heard Jesus marveled and said, "How strange and paradoxical! This child is barely five years old and yet he says such things. In fact, we've never heard anyone say the kinds of things this child does."

¹⁰Jesus said to them in reply, "Are you really so amazed? Rather, consider what I've said to you. The truth is that I also know when you were born, and your parents, and I announce this paradox to you: when the world was created, I existed along with the One who sent me to you."

¹¹The Jews, once they heard the child speaking like this, got angry but were unable to say anything back. ¹²But the child skipped forward and said to them, "I've made fun of you because I know that your tiny minds marvel at trifles."

¹³When, therefore, they thought that they were being comforted by the child's exhortation, the teacher said to Joseph, "Bring him to the classroom and I'll teach him the alphabet."

¹⁴Joseph took him by the hand and led him to the classroom. ¹⁵The teacher wrote the alphabet for him and began the instruction by repeating the letter alpha over and over again. But the child clammed up and did not answer him for a long time. ¹⁶No wonder, then, that the teacher got angry and struck him on the head. The child took the blow calmly and replied to him, "I'm teaching

you instead of being taught by you: I already know the letters you're teaching me, and your condemnation is great. To you these letters are like a bronze pitcher or a clashing cymbal, which can't produce glory or wisdom because it's all just noise. [17]No one can understand the extent of my wisdom." [18]When he got over being angry he rapidly recited the letters from alpha to omega.

[19]Then he looked at the teacher and told him, "Since you don't know the real nature of the letter alpha, how are you going to teach the letter beta? [20]You phony, if you know, teach me first the letter alpha and then I'll trust you with the letter beta." [21]He began to quiz the teacher about the first letter, but he was unable to say anything.

[22]Then while many were listening, he said to Zacchaeus, "Listen, teacher, and observe the arrangement of the first letter: [23]How it has two straight lines or strokes proceeding to a point in the middle, gathered together, elevated, dancing, three-cornered, two-cornered, not antagonistic, of the same family, providing the alpha has lines of equal measure."

7 After Zacchaeus the teacher had heard the child expressing such intricate allegories regarding the first letter, he gave up trying to defend his teaching. [2]He spoke to those who were present: "Poor me, I'm completely at a loss, wretch that I am. I've heaped shame on myself because I took on this child. [3]I beg you, brother Joseph, take him away. I can't bear his harsh stare or his lucid speech. [4]This child is no ordinary mortal; he can even tame fire! Perhaps he was born before the creation of the world. [5]What sort of womb bore him, what sort of mother nourished him? I don't know. [6]Poor me, friend, I've lost my mind. [7]I've deceived myself, I'm totally miserable. I struggled to get a student, and it turns out I have a teacher. [8]Friends, think of the shame: I'm an old man, but I've been defeated by a mere child. [9]Now I can only despair and die because of this boy; I can't look him in the face. [10]When they say that I've been defeated by a small child, what can I say back? And what can I report about the lines of the first letter which he told me about? I just don't know, friends. For I don't know its beginning or its end. [11]So I have to ask you, brother Joseph, to take him back to your house. What great thing he is—God or angel or whatever else I might call him—I don't know."

8 While the Jews were advising Zacchaeus, the child laughed loudly and said, "Now let the infertile bear fruit and the blind see and the deaf hear in the understanding of their heart: [2]I've come from above to rescue those below and call them to higher things, just as the one who sent me to you commanded me."

[3]When the child stopped speaking, all those who had fallen under the curse were instantly saved. [4]And from then on no one dared to anger him for fear of being cursed and maimed for life.

9 A few days later Jesus was playing on the roof of a house when one of the children playing with him fell off the roof and died. When the other children saw what had happened, they ran away and left Jesus all by himself.

²The parents of the dead child came and accused Jesus: "You troublemaker you, you're the one who threw him down."

³Jesus responded, "I didn't throw him down; he threw himself down. He just wasn't being careful; he jumped down from the roof and died."

⁴Then Jesus himself jumped down from the roof and stood over the body of the child and shouted in a loud voice: "Zeno!"—that was his name—"Get up and tell me: Did I push you down?"

⁵He got up immediately and said, "No, Lord, you didn't push me down; you raised me up."

⁶Those who saw this were astonished. The child's parents worshiped Jesus and praised God for the miracle that had happened.

10 A few days later a young man in the neighborhood was splitting wood when his axe slipped and cut off the bottom of his foot. He was dying from the loss of blood.

²The crowd rushed there in an uproar, and the boy Jesus ran up, too. He forced his way through the crowd and grabbed hold of the young man's wounded foot. It was instantly healed.

³He said to the young man, "Get up now, split your wood, and remember me."

⁴The crowd saw what had happened and worshiped the child, saying, "Truly the spirit of God dwells in this child."

11 When he was six years old, his mother sent him to draw water and bring it back to the house. ²But he lost his grip on the pitcher in the jostling of the crowd, and it fell and broke. ³So Jesus spread out the cloak he was wearing and filled it with water and carried it back to his mother.

⁴His mother, once she saw the miracle that had occurred, kissed him; but she kept to herself the mysteries that she had seen him do.

12 Again, during the sowing season, the child went out with his father to sow their field with grain. While his father was sowing, the child Jesus sowed one measure of grain. ²When he had harvested and threshed it, it yielded one hundred measures. ³Then he summoned all the poor in the village to the threshing floor and gave them grain. Joseph carried back what was left of the grain. ⁴Jesus was eight years old when he did this miracle.

13 Now Jesus' father was a carpenter, making plows and yokes at that time. He took an order from a rich man to make a bed for him. ²When one board of what is called the crossbeam turned out shorter than the other, and Joseph didn't know what to do, the child Jesus said to his father Joseph, "Put the two boards down and line them up at one end."

³Joseph did as the child told him. Jesus stood at the other end, grabbed hold of the shorter board, and, by stretching it, made it the same length as the other.

⁴His father Joseph looked on and marveled, and he hugged and kissed the child, saying, "How lucky I am that God has given me this child."

14 When Joseph saw how earnest the child was, and how intelligent he was for his age, he again resolved that it was high time for Jesus to learn to read. So he took him and handed him over to another teacher. ²The teacher said to Joseph, "First I'll teach him Greek, then Hebrew." This teacher, of course, knew of the child's previous experience at school and was afraid of him. Still, he wrote out the alphabet and instructed him for quite a while, though Jesus was unresponsive.

³Then Jesus spoke: "If you're really a teacher, and if you know the letters well, tell me the meaning of the letter alpha, and I'll tell you the meaning of beta."

⁴The teacher became exasperated and hit him on the head. Jesus got angry and cursed him, and the teacher immediately passed out and fell facedown on the ground.

⁵The child returned to Joseph's house. But Joseph was upset and instructed his mother: "Don't let him go outside, because those who annoy him end up dead."

15 Some time later another teacher, a close friend of Joseph, said to him, "Send the child to my schoolroom. Perhaps with some flattery I can teach him his letters."

² Joseph replied, "If you can muster the courage, brother, take him with you." And so he took him along with much fear and trepidation, but the child was happy to go.

³ Jesus strode confidently into the schoolroom and found a book lying on the desk. He picked up the book but did not read the letters in it. Rather, he opened his mouth and spoke by the power of the holy spirit and taught the Law to those standing there.

⁴A large crowd gathered and stood listening to him, and they marveled at the maturity of his teaching and his readiness of speech—a mere child able to say such things.

⁵When Joseph heard about this he feared the worst and ran to the schoolroom, imagining that this teacher was having trouble with Jesus.

⁶But the teacher said to Joseph, "Brother, please know that I accepted this child as a student, but already he's full of grace and wisdom. So I'm asking you, brother, to take him back home."

⁷When the child heard this, he immediately smiled at him and said, "Because you have spoken and testified rightly, that other teacher who was struck down will be healed." And right away he was. Joseph took his child and went home.

16 Joseph sent his son James to bundle up some wood and carry it back to the house, and the child Jesus followed. While James was gathering the firewood, a viper bit his hand. ²And as he lay sprawled out on the ground, dying, Jesus came and blew on the bite. Immediately the pain stopped, the animal burst open, and James got better on the spot.

17 After this incident a baby in Joseph's neighborhood became sick and died, and his mother grieved terribly. Jesus heard the loud wailing and the uproar that was going on and quickly ran there.

²When he found the child dead, he touched her chest and said, "I say to you, infant, don't die; live, and be with your mother."

³And immediately the infant looked up and laughed. Jesus then said to the woman, "Take your child, offer her your breast, and remember me."

⁴The crowd of onlookers marveled at this: "Truly this child was God or a heavenly messenger of God—whatever he says instantly happens." But Jesus left and went on playing with the other children.

18 A year later, while a building was under construction, a man fell from the top of it and died. There was quite a commotion, so Jesus got up and walked over. ²When he saw the man lying dead, he took his hand and said, "I say to you, sir, get up and go back to work." And he immediately got up and worshiped him.

³The crowd saw this and marveled: "This child's from heaven—he must be, because he has saved many souls from death, and he can go on saving all his life."

19 When he was twelve years old his parents went to Jerusalem, as usual, for the Passover festival, along with their fellow travelers. ²After Passover they began the journey home. But while on their way, the child Jesus went back up to Jerusalem. His parents, of course, assumed that he was in the traveling party. ³After they had traveled one day, they began to look for him among their relatives. When they did not find him, they were worried and returned again to the city to search for him.

⁴After three days they found him in the temple area, sitting among the teachers, listening to the Law and asking them questions. ⁵All eyes were on him, and everyone was astounded that he, a mere child, could interrogate the elders and teachers of the people and explain the main points of the law and the parables of the prophets.

⁶His mother Mary came up and said to him, "Child, why have you done this to us? Don't you see that we've been worried sick looking for you."

⁷ "Why are you looking for me?" Jesus said to them. "Don't you know that it's my destiny to be in my father's house?"

⁸Then the scholars and the Pharisees said, "Are you the mother of this child?"
⁹She said, "I am."

¹⁰And they said to her, "You more than any woman are to be congratulated, for God has blessed the fruit of your womb! For we've never seen nor heard such glory and such virtue and wisdom."

¹¹Jesus got up and went with his mother, and was obedient to his parents. His mother took careful note of all that had happened. ¹²And Jesus continued to excel in learning and gain respect.

¹³To him be glory for ever and ever. Amen.

————— ⌒⌒⌒ —————

1 The gospel is attributed to *Thomas the Israelite*. In John's gospel the apostle Thomas is known as Didymus, which means "twin" (e.g., John 11:16). This apostle is presumably the same man as the Didymus Judas Thomas who figures in the Gospel of Thomas and the Judas Thomas, the twin of Jesus, who is the hero of the *Acts of Thomas*.

2:3, 6 This miracle is also attested in the Qur'an: "Jesus will say, 'I bring you a sign from your Lord. From clay I will make for you a likeness of a bird. I shall breathe into it and, by God's leave, it shall become a living bird'" (3:49; also 5:113).

3:1 *Annas the scholar* also appears in the Infancy Gospel of James (InJas 15). In the canonical gospels, Annas is a high priest (see Luke 3:2; John 18:13, 24; Acts 4:6).

3:2 *dry up like a tree.* This metaphor may derive from the story of Jesus cursing the fig tree (Mark 11:12–14).

5:2 *I know that the words I spoke are not my own.* The original wording of this sentence is uncertain. It is further confusing that Jesus accepts Joseph's rebuke but then punishes his accusers, though they have done nothing wrong.

6:5–8, 10 The five-year old Jesus is fully aware of his divine nature and eternal existence. The language here has a Johannine flavor, especially the phrase *the One who sent me* (vv. 6, 10), which is used frequently in John (e.g., 4:34, 5:24).

6:15 *alpha.* This gospel portrays Jesus learning the Greek alphabet as though Greek were his native language. See also 14:2, which presupposes a bilingual environment.

6:16 Such corporal punishment was standard in ancient education.

6:18 *Alpha* and *omega* are the names of the first and last letters of the Greek alphabet. Other ancient versions of this gospel use the names of the letters of the language in which they are written.

6:19–23 The reference to the *real nature of the letter alpha* and the cryptic statement in vv. 22–23 reflect the ancient belief that the shapes of letters had esoteric meanings.

6:23 *How it has two straight lines.* These are the only words in this difficult sentence that make sense. The rest of the translation is guesswork. Unfortunately, this strange disjointed sentence was garbled in the copying process. Some of the words are not even listed in Greek dictionaries. No wonder Zacchaeus despairs of taking Jesus on as a student.

7:4 The remark that Jesus *can even tame fire* may allude to a lost episode.

7:11 *God or angel.* The Greek language never capitalizes *theos*, the word for "God," and the grammar of this sentence leaves it unclear whether *theos* means "a god" or "God." The capitalized *God* in the translation reflects a guess about the ancient author's intended meaning.

8:1 It is unclear to whom this refers.

8:2 This christological statement is reminiscent of the distinctive language of the Gospel of John.

8:3 It is not clear who *those who had fallen under the curse* are. It seems to refer to those whom Jesus has killed and maimed: the boy who emptied the ponds

Jesus had made (3:3), the boy who bumped him (4:2), and those who were blinded (5:2). However, if that is what the phrase means, it makes for an awkward story line since the two boys seem to have been dead for quite some time. 8:4 further complicates the logic of the scene and makes little sense following 8:3. In light of its poor fit in the narrative flow, 8:3 seems to have been added to the sequence of episodes in order to alleviate some Christian discomfort with the notion that Jesus would use his powers for such violent and disproportionate revenge.

9:4 That Jesus *jumped down from the roof* without injury might be another demonstration of his miraculous powers.

9:5 *Lord.* Here is the only place in this gospel in which Jesus is addressed by any title.

9:6 That the parents *worshiped Jesus* and *praised God* reinforces the gospel's high christology.

11:1–4 Jesus' mother is a minor character in this gospel. She is unnamed and appears only three times: here, 14:5, and chapter 19.

11:2 Jesus' superhuman abilities apparently do not prevent him from having accidents.

11:3 It is not clear whether the pitcher was full of water when it broke, so that Jesus gathered up the spilled water in his garment, or whether the pitcher was empty, so that Jesus poured well water into his cloak.

11:4 *she kept to herself the mysteries which she had seen him do.* The language here reflects Luke 2:19, "Mary took all this in and reflected on it," and Luke 2:51, "His mother took careful note of all these things."

12:2 *one hundred measures.* The yield is perhaps inspired by the parable of the sower (Mark 4:8, Matt 13:8, Luke 8:8).

14:1–4 This story is somewhat loose in its narrative logic. Although the teacher knows about Jesus' previous school experience, he starts by trying to teach him the Greek alphabet, something the boy has already proven he knows (6:18). Also, if the teacher *was afraid of him* (14:2), why does he provoke him with physical abuse (14:4)?

15:1–7 Yet a third teacher attempts to teach Jesus his letters. This time, however, the teacher defers to Jesus' superiority and no one gets hurt.

15:7 The narrator seems unconcerned about how long the teacher in 14:4 had lain unconscious: see the vague *some time later* in 15:1.

16:1 *his son James.* James is listed among the brothers of Jesus in Mark 6:5 and Matt 13:55. Paul identifies him as "the Lord's brother" (Gal 1:19). It is not apparent whether this gospel assumes that James and Jesus are full brothers or whether it takes James to be an adult son of Joseph by from an earlier marriage, as in the Infancy Gospel of James.

17:3 The detail about feeding the resuscitated baby resembles Jesus' similar command to give Jairus' revived daughter something to eat (Mark 5:43, Luke 8:15).

17:4 *was God.* The unusual use of *was* may be a deliberate echo of the opening words of John's gospel: "In the beginning was the Word, and the Word was with God, and the Word was God." See also the comment on 7:11.

19:1–12 This is the only story in this gospel that is taken from another gospel (Luke 2:42–51). The narrative follows Luke's account closely, with a few modifications.

19:5 This verse elaborates on the Lukan original in order to spotlight the boy's extraordinary wisdom. Note especially the emphatic description of Jesus as *a mere child*.

19:8–10 These verses have no parallel in Luke, although v.10a draws on what Elizabeth says to Mary in Luke 1:42. These verses replace the report in Luke 2:50 that Jesus' parents "did not understand what he was talking about." Instead of that negative comment, this gospel addresses an admiring beatitude to Mary.

TWO DOCETIC BIRTH STORIES

DOCETISM

Docetism is the name of a belief that arose in early Christian history and has persisted ever since. Since the New Testament presents Jesus both as human and divine, early Christian thinkers experimented with a variety of formulations of faith in their attempts to clarify and reconcile those two aspects of the scriptural portrait. One of these formulations was Adoptionism, the belief that the man Jesus was promoted to divine status when God "adopted" him as his son (see p. 230). Docetism takes a diametrically different position: Jesus is the Son of God from all eternity, fully and solely divine. He was not truly human, but only appeared to be so. (The term "Docetism" comes from the Greek *dokein*, "to seem.") The docetic Jesus is God posing as a human being.

The formal doctrines of the great councils of bishops in the fourth, fifth, and sixth centuries explicitly condemned Docetism and held that Jesus was both fully divine and fully human. No mainstream church officially endorses Docetism, yet it still functions today as a kind of common-sense christology for large numbers of Christians, laity and clergy alike. Though seldom spelled out in public, there can be little doubt that Docetism is an implicit belief of many Christians who worship the divine Christ.

Docetism was as widespread in early Christianity as it is today. Docetists who told stories about the birth and infancy of Jesus could easily use them to emphasize his fully divine status. Presented below are two brief excerpts–from much longer writings–that narrate Jesus' "birth," though the idea of Jesus actually being born is problematic for Docetism. From a docetic perspective, it was unnecessary and unseemly for the mother of God to undergo the pain of childbirth. In the two stories below there is no physical birth at all: the divine infant miraculously appears from Mary's body without any transitional event.

THE VISION OF ISAIAH

This work is not a gospel, but is important to us because it contains a unique narrative of the birth of Jesus. The Vision of Isaiah was originally an independent work, strongly influenced by Gnosticism, that was incorporated into a longer text known as the Ascension of Isaiah. The Vision of Isaiah, which now comprises chapters 6–11 of the Ascension of Isaiah, tells what the prophet Isaiah sees when he leaves his body and is escorted to the seventh heaven by an angel. There Isaiah sees the reward awaiting the righteous and learns of Christ's future descent to earth. To get to the physical world, Christ must descend through the different heavens. Along the way he disguises himself by taking on the appearance of the hostile angels who live in each heaven. He arrives to earth disguised as a human infant. No one except Mary and Joseph know his real identity. This is a key concept for the gnostic theology of the Vision. The present physical world is controlled by evil spiritual adversaries who hold humans in subjugation by keeping them ignorant of their true spiritual natures. The heavenly revealer sneaks into this world disguised as a human in order to set humankind free. He brings the revelation that enables humans to know the truth about themselves and thereby attain salvation.

Our excerpt from the Vision of Isaiah (Ascension of Isaiah 11) tells the story of the birth of Jesus from this gnostic perspective, using the basic details from Matthew and Luke for its narrative framework. The story is marked by two distinctive emphases: the secrecy surrounding Jesus' "birth" and heavenly origin, and the miraculous appearance of the infant without physical childbirth, after only two months of pregnancy. Both elements are expressions of Docetism.

The narrative in the Vision of Isaiah is a perfect example of how the story of Jesus' birth was creatively shaped by Christian storytellers to make it serve particular theological agendas.

The Vision of Isaiah was written in Greek in the early second century. This section of it (Ascension of Isaiah 11) exists only in an Ethiopic translation.

THE VISION OF ISAIAH
Ascension of Isaiah 11

The angel who talked with me and conducted me said, "Pay attention, Isaiah, son of Amoz. . . ²And I saw a woman named Mary, a descendant of David the prophet. She was a virgin, and was betrothed to a man called Joseph, a carpenter, who also was of the seed and family of the righteous David, of Bethlehem in Judah. ³And he came into his portion. And when she was betrothed, she was found to be pregnant, and Joseph, the carpenter, wanted to divorce her. ⁴But the angel of the Spirit appeared in this world, and after that Joseph did not divorce her, but kept her, without telling anyone about the situation. [5]He did not approach Mary, but kept her as a holy virgin, even though she was pregnant. [6]And she did not move in with him for two months.

[7]When those two months were over, and Joseph was in his house with his wife Mary, [8]it so happened, while they were both alone, that Mary all at once looked and was amazed to see a small child. [9]When her amazement wore off, she found that her womb was as it had been before she was pregnant. [10]When her husband Joseph said to her, "What was it that amazed you?", his eyes were opened and he saw the child and praised God, that the Lord had come to his portion. [11]And a voice came to them: "Don't tell anyone about this vision."

[12]But rumors about the child caused a stir in Bethlehem. [13]Some said, "The virgin Mary has given birth before she was married two months." [14]Many others said, "She has not given birth. The midwife has not been to her house and we have heard no cries of pain." And they were all in the dark concerning him. They all knew about him, but no one knew where he had come from.

[15]And they took him and moved to Nazareth in Galilee. [16]I saw and declare in the presence of the other prophets standing here that this was hidden from all the heavens and all the princes and every god of this world. [17]And I saw that in Nazareth he nursed at the breast, like babies usually do, so that he would not be recognized.

———— ❧ ————

2 Mary is *a descendant of David*. Matthew gives no information about Mary's genealogy. Luke says that she was a relative of Elizabeth, who was of the priestly house of Aaron.

4–5 We are not told what the angel said to Joseph, but since he learns from the vision that Mary was still a virgin, the narrative presupposes the scenario in Matt 1:18–23.

13 This seems to reflect a report that Jesus was born very early in the marriage. The author could therefore be responding to insinuations that Jesus was illegitimate.

14 That Jesus came into this world without his mother experiencing pain or needing a midwife is also attested in the Odes of Solomon, Christian hymns from the early second-century.

> The Holy Spirit spread his wings over the womb of the Virgin, and she conceived, and gave birth to a child, and became a Virgin Mother with much mercy. She grew great with child and painlessly brought forth a son. And so that nothing might be done unnecessarily, she did not ask for a midwife to help her. (Odes of Solomon 19)

15 As in Matthew, the family moves to Nazareth, but without a layover in Egypt. The Vision of Isaiah gives no reason for the move, though the context, and the theme of secrecy in the story, implies that the parents wanted to move away from Bethlehem, where the boy had become an object of curiosity and rumor.

16 This verse seems to be directed against the stories in Matthew 2. *Hidden from all the heavens* rules out the story of the star and the magi; *hidden from all the princes* rules out the story about Herod. Jesus' birth is also hidden from *every god of this world*, that is, from the evil spiritual powers who tyrannize humanity until the coming of the savior.

There is an echo of this theme of the secret arrival of the savior in the letters of Ignatius of Antioch.

> The virginity of Mary and her childbirth, and likewise also the death of the Lord: these were hidden from the ruler of this world. These are three mysteries to be shouted out; they were worked in the silence of God. (Letter to the Ephesians 19:1)

17 The infant does not nurse because he needs nourishment, but only to maintain his disguise as an ordinary human baby. This is another docetic element in the Vision.

THE LATIN INFANCY GOSPEL

This untitled gospel was written sometime in the Middle Ages. Most of it is based on the Infancy Gospel of James and the Gospel of Pseudo-Matthew. The brief excerpt included here, however, tells a story found nowhere else. The birth of Jesus is depicted in shimmering and blazing light. This tableau is based on a brief description in Infancy James (see InJas 19:15–16), but expands on it with vivid imagination. Perhaps this scene is a literal attempt to narrate the arrival of "the light of the world" (John 8:12). We do not know how far back this scene goes in the history of Christian storytelling. Nothing in it would seem out of place in the early Christian centuries.

This gospel, and this scene especially, presents the nativity story from a docetic perspective. Here Jesus is born from an overwhelming light (73:4; 74:1) that "took the shape of a baby" (74:2). Clearly this is no human child: he is weightless, needs no diapering, and does not cry (74:3–4).

The Latin Infancy Gospel is attested in two manuscripts from the thirteenth and fourteenth centuries.

THE LATIN INFANCY GOSPEL 73–74

73 As the time got close the power of God showed itself openly. ²The girl stood staring at the sky and became like a grapevine. For now the goal of all that is good was coming near. When the light had emerged, Mary saw the one to whom she had given birth, and she worshiped him. ³The child himself shone brightly, like the sun. He was beautiful and wonderful to look at because he alone appeared as peace, spreading peace everywhere. At the time when he was born many invisible beings proclaimed "Amen" with one voice.

⁴And when the light was born it increased and outshone the light of the sun with its dazzling brightness. The cave was filled with a bright light, along with the sweetest fragrance. ⁵The light was born just as dew falls from heaven to earth. Its aroma is more fragrant than any perfume.

74 I stood there paralyzed with amazement and overcome with awe. I was staring at the intense brightness of the light that had been born. ²After a while the light slowly receded and took the shape of a baby, and then immediately became an infant like other newborn babies. ³I summoned the courage to reach over and touch him. Awestruck, I picked him up and was terrified because, unlike other newborns, he was weightless. I examined him and saw that there was nothing foul about him. ⁴His whole body was shimmering like the dew of the Most High God. He was light to carry and magnificent to see. I was amazed because he did not cry as newborns usually do. ⁵While I held him and looked into his face, he smiled at me with the sweetest smile, and opened his eyes and gazed at me. And all at once a bright light shot from his eyes like a brilliant flash of lightning.

———————— ❧ ————————

73:2 *grapevine.* This baffling sentence may be the result of a copyist's mistake. The Latin word for "grapevine," *vinea,* could well be an inadvertent transcription of *nivea* ("snow white"). This would change the meaning to "she became snow white," which is still puzzling, but fits in with all the bright light in the story. Perhaps *nivea* is itself the result of a confusion in translation from a Greek source: "like snow" (*hos chion*) is very close to "like a pillar" (*hos kion*), which would make sense if meant as a description of the girl standing motionless.

73:3 *many invisible beings proclaimed "Amen" with one voice.* This might be inspired by a vivid scene in the Book of Revelation:

> Then I heard every creature in heaven and on earth and under the earth and in the sea, everything in the universe, cry out:
>
> > "To the one seated on the throne and to the Lamb
> > be blessing and honor and glory and might,
> > forever and ever."
>
> The four living creatures answered , "Amen." (Rev 5:13–14)

74:1 *I.* The narrator is a midwife named Zachel whom Joseph found and brought back to the cave where Mary had given birth. This matches the story in Infancy James 18–20, except there the midwife is unnamed.

74:3 *nothing foul.* A euphemism for the absence of excrement, reflecting the docetic belief that a fully human nature was beneath the dignity of the Son of God.

THE HISTORY of JOSEPH THE CARPENTER

Contents

This book is a life of Joseph, told in the first person by Jesus to his disciples. The opening scene explains that the apostles wrote this story down and left it in "the library in Jerusalem." The narrative begins by summarizing Joseph's life before he met Mary. He was a priest and a carpenter with a wife, four sons (Judas, Justus, James, and Simon) and two daughters (Assia and Lydia). His wife died when she was eighty-nine years old.

Our selection from the History of Joseph includes chapters 3–9, 11, and a snippet from chapter 17. These tell about Joseph coming to be the guardian of Mary (3–4); her miraculous pregnancy (5); the angel's revelation to Joseph (6); Jesus' birth in Bethlehem (7); Herod's search for the infant and the escape to Egypt (8); the family's return to Nazareth (9); Jesus' perfect childhood (11); and a reminiscence of a miracle Jesus performed when he was a child (17). The rest of the book is an extended narrative of Joseph's death when he was 111 years old. He dies in the presence of Mary and Jesus, with whom he speaks at length on his deathbed, addressing him as "my savior," "the deliverer of my soul," and "my God."

Sources

The narrative in our selection from the History depends primarily on story lines from Matthew and Infancy James, into which Luke's episode of the journey to Bethlehem is incorporated. In addition, the author may have known, or at least been aware of, stories about Jesus' naughty behavior as a boy, such as the stories in the Infancy Gospel of Thomas. Chapter 11 looks like a repudiation of such tales, which would be theologically unacceptable in a work which portrays Jesus as the second person of the Trinity and tells of his consulting with the Father and Holy Spirit on the choice of his future mother.

Distinctive Features

The History of Joseph has a number of original elements: Mary as step-mother to James, the young son of Joseph (4); the pre-existent Son of God choosing who will be his mother (5); Satan as the ally of Herod (8); a description of Jesus' model behavior as a child (11); and an otherwise unattested childhood miracle (17).

Origin

About all that can be said of the origin of this work is that it comes from Egypt, probably in the fourth century. It was originally written in Coptic, but survives only in an Arabic translation.

THE HISTORY OF JOSEPH THE CARPENTER

3 When righteous Joseph lost his wife, my blessed, holy, and pure mother Mary was already twelve years old. ²Her parents had dedicated her to the temple when she was three years old, and she had stayed in the temple of the Lord for nine years. ³Then when the priests saw that the holy and God-fearing virgin was growing up, they said to one another, "We should find a righteous and reverent man to whom Mary can be entrusted until she is married. ⁴If she stays in the temple, she will go through what women experience. We would sin if we let that happen and God would be angry with us."

4 So they put out the word at once and assembled twelve old men from the tribe of Judah. They wrote down the names of the twelve tribes of Israel. And the lot fell on the reverent old man, righteous Joseph. ²Then the priests said to my blessed mother, "Go with Joseph, and live with him until you get married." Righteous Joseph welcomed my mother and brought her into his home.

³And Mary found James the Less in his father's home, broken-hearted and sad because he had lost his mother. She raised him and that is why Mary was called the mother of James. ⁴Joseph left her at home and went off to the shop where he plied his trade as a carpenter. The holy virgin lived in his home for two years until she was exactly fourteen years old.

5 I chose her; it was my decision, with the consent of my Father and the advice of the Holy Spirit. And I was made flesh of her, by a mystery beyond the grasp of created reason. ²Three months into her pregnancy righteous Joseph returned from his workplace. When he discovered that my virgin mother was pregnant, he was very perplexed, and thought of sending her away secretly. ³He was so afraid and upset, and had so much anguish in his heart, that he could not eat or drink that day.

6 Around noon the prince of angels, holy Gabriel, appeared to him in a dream with instructions from my Father. He said to him, "Joseph, son of David, don't be afraid to marry Mary, for she is pregnant by the Holy Spirit. ²She will give birth to a son whose name will be Jesus. He is the one who shall rule all the nations with an iron rod." After he said this, the angel left him.

³Joseph got up from his sleep and did as the angel of the Lord had told him. And Mary lived with him.

7 Some time later Augustus Caesar, the king, issued a decree for a census of the whole inhabited world, with each man to be counted in his own city. ²So the old man, righteous Joseph, got up and went to Bethlehem. He took the virgin Mary with him, because it was almost time for her delivery. ³Joseph signed the census list, because Joseph, the son of David and spouse of Mary, belonged to the tribe of Judah. ⁴And my mother Mary gave birth to me in Bethlehem, in a cave near the tomb of Rachel, the wife of the patriarch Jacob and the mother of Joseph and Benjamin.

8 Now Satan went and told this to Herod the Great, father of Archelaus. This was the same Herod who had my friend and relative John beheaded. ²Herod searched diligently for me because he assumed that my kingdom was going to be an earthly one. ³But Joseph, that reverent old man, was warned of this in a dream. He got up and took my mother Mary, while I lay in her arms. ⁴Salome also accompanied them on the journey.

⁵So he left home and settled in Egypt. He stayed there for a whole year, until Herod's hatred faded away.

9 Now Herod died the worst kind of death, atoning for shedding the blood of the innocent children he maliciously slaughtered. ²Once that ungodly tyrant Herod was dead, they came back to the land of Israel, and lived in Nazareth, a city in Galilee. ³Joseph went back to his carpentry and earned his living by working with his hands; ⁴for, as the law of Moses commands, he never tried to live off someone else's labor. . .

11 Justus and Simeon, Joseph's oldest sons, were married and had families of their own. Both of his daughters were also married and lived in their own homes. ²Judas and James the Less still lived with my virgin mother in Joseph's home. I lived with them, just as if I were one of his sons.

³In my whole life I did nothing wrong. I called Mary my mother and Joseph my father, and I obeyed them in everything. ⁴I never argued with them, as others whom earth produces usually do but did as I was told. I never once made them angry, or said anything against them. ⁵On the contrary, I loved them with deep affection, like the apple of my eye. . .

17 [*spoken by Joseph on his deathbed*] "My Lord, I also remember the day when the boy died of snakebite. His relatives said that you had killed him and they wanted to hand you over to Herod. But you raised him from the dead and gave him back to them."

——— ∾∾∽ ———

3:2–4 This story is taken from Infancy James 7–8.

3:4 The *sin* is one against ritual purity. The Law considered a woman ritually unclean during her period (see Lev 15:19–24). Mary would thus "pollute" the temple when she began to menstruate.

4:1 Selection by *lot* was believed to indicate God's choice (see Acts 1:15–26, where the lot is used to pick a replacement for Judas). The details of how Joseph was selected are sketchy. In Infancy James 8–9, all the widowers in Israel assemble and God's choice of Joseph is signaled when "a dove came out of his staff and perched on his shoulder" (InJas 9:6). Later in the History of Joseph the Carpenter we are told that Joseph was ninety years old when he became Mary's guardian.

4:3 *James the Less.* All four lists of the twelve apostles in the canonical gospels include two men named James. The first one is mentioned with his brother John; they are the sons of Zebedee. The second James is the son of Alphaeus. Church tradition distinguished James son of Zebedee from James son of Alphaeus, calling the first one James the Great and second one James the Less. The unflattering title is based on Mark 15:40, which refers to "James *ho mikros*," which means either "the small one" or "the younger one."

4:3 *mother of James.* This seems to be an attempt to explain Mark 15:40, which lists "Mary of Magdala, and Mary the mother of James the Less." The author assumes that the Mary in that verse is also the mother of James and that the James in that verse is the one who was Jesus' brother (Mark 6:3; Gal 1:19). Both assumptions are erroneous. According to the canonical gospels, Jesus had two disciples named James (e.g., Mark 3:17, 18), neither of whom was his brother. The obvious intent of this imaginative explanation of how Mary became known as the mother of James is to reconcile the biblical information that Jesus had a brother named James with the Christian belief (not attested in the New Testament) that Jesus was Mary's only child.

5:1 This reflects the doctrine of the Trinity and the belief that the Son of God existed prior to his incarnation in the person of Jesus. That belief precludes the notion that Jesus *became* God's son at his resurrection (as in Rom 1:4) or baptism (as in Mark 1:11) or even at his conception (as in Luke 1:32). The metaphysical status of Jesus' nature as the Son of God was a matter of fierce dispute among Christians in the fourth century when this narrative was written.

5:2 That Joseph *thought of sending her away secretly* is taken from Matt 1:19.

6:1 *Gabriel.* The angel who appears to Joseph in a dream is unnamed in Matt 1:20. Gabriel is the name of the angel who appears to Mary in Luke 1:26. We see here one example of the standard Christian practice of combining details from different gospels into a composite story: in this case the angel's name comes from Luke, the angel's words from Matt 1:20–21.

6:2 *rule the nations with an iron rod.* An expression from Rev 12:5 and 19:15, probably based on Ps 2:9: "You will break the nations with an iron rod and dash them into pieces like a potter's vessel."

7:1–2 The story of the census and the trip to Bethlehem comes from Luke.

7:3 *spouse of Mary.* In Luke's gospel Mary and Joseph are betrothed and not yet fully married when they journey to Bethlehem. Our author makes this "mistake" because, in combining the narratives of Matthew and Luke, he has Joseph comply with the angelic command to take Mary as his wife (a detail found only in Matthew) before the couple goes to Bethlehem (an episode found only in Luke).

7:4 *in a cave.* Here the narrator follows the story in Infancy James (18:1) instead of the story in Luke, which has Jesus born in a stable (Luke 2:7).

near the tomb of Rachel. This detail is inspired by the prophecy quoted in Matt 2:18.

8:1 *Satan.* In Matthew, Herod hopes to learn the whereabouts of the newborn Jesus from the magi (Matt 2:7–8). In the History of Joseph there are no magi. Instead, Herod learns about Jesus from Satan himself.

Herod, father of Archelaus. This information comes from Matt 2:22.

the same Herod. Actually it was Herod Antipas, son of Herod the Great, who murdered John.

8:2 *He assumed that my kingdom was going to be an earthly one* echoes John 18:36: "My kingdom is not an earthly one."

8:3–5 is based on Matt 2:13–15.

8:4 *Salome* appears without introduction and does nothing in the story. In the Infancy Gospel of James, Salome is the midwife who verifies that Mary is an anatomically intact virgin after giving birth to Jesus (Infancy James 19–20). The History of Joseph, however, does not mention a midwife. In Infancy James, a mysterious man named Samuel accompanies Mary and Joseph on the trip to Bethlehem (InJas 17:5). Perhaps the Salome here is a garbled reference to that Samuel. Another possibility is the Salome in Mark 15:40, one of the women who looked after Jesus' needs and accompanied him to Jerusalem.

9:1 Herod the Great died in 4 BCE after a long illness. However, *the worst kind of death* makes more sense as a reference to the death in 44 CE of Herod Agrippa, ruler of Palestine and grandson of Herod the Great. According to Acts 13:21–23 this Herod was struck down by an angel when a crowd acclaimed him a god; "he was eaten by worms and died."

Shedding the blood of the innocent children refers to Herod the Great's massacre of baby boys in Matt 2:16.

11:2 *Judas and James the Less.* Mark 6:3 mentions three brothers of Jesus: James, Judas, and Simon. It also mentions Jesus' sisters but gives no names.

11:3 *In my whole life I did nothing wrong.* This is a very different picture of Jesus' childhood behavior than the one in the Infancy Gospel of Thomas and seems intended as a rejection of it.

17 This story is unattested elsewhere, although it seems to combine elements of Infancy Thomas 9 and 16. The reference to *Herod* contradicts the report that he had died before Jesus' family returned from Egypt (HistJos 9:1–2). Our fourth-century author seems not to realize that there are three Herods in the New Testament: Herod the Great at the time of Jesus' birth; his son, Herod Antipas, ruler of Galilee when Jesus was an adult; and the first Herod's grandson, Herod Agrippa, mentioned in Acts of the Apostles. Our author mistakenly thinks that the first two Herods are the same man in 8:1; in 9:1 he seems to confuse Herod the Great with his grandson.

Th Arabic Infancy Gospel

This infancy gospel calls itself the "Book of Joseph the High Priest." It is largely a derivative work, but includes a fair amount of material found nowhere else. It tells the story of Jesus from his birth to his twelfth year.

Contents

The gospel can be divided into four parts.

The first part (chapters 1–9) is relatively brief. It recounts Jesus' birth, the visit of the magi, and the family's flight from Bethlehem toward Egypt. The narrative follows Luke, Matthew, and Infancy James, with some original material.

The second part (chapters 10–25) is composed almost entirely of miracle stories set during the journey to and sojourn in Egypt. The young Jesus' time in Egypt is passed over in silence by the canonical gospels. The Infancy Gospel of James excludes the journey to Egypt[1] and Infancy Thomas begins its story when Jesus is five years old, ostensibly after the family has returned from Egypt. Jesus' Egyptian experience thus remained a topic of curiosity and it was only a matter of time until Christian storytellers filled in this gap in the life of the baby Jesus. As far as we know, the material in this section of the Arabic Infancy Gospel is original to it.

The third part (chapters 26–49), about half the text of the gospel, tells mostly of various miracles worked by the child Jesus in his hometown, after the family gets back from Egypt. Though several of the stories in this section are unique to this gospel, most are based on Infancy Thomas.

The last part (chapters 50–55) contains a highly embellished version of

---

[1]In Infancy James, Jesus eludes Herod's soldiers when Mary hides him in the feeding trough (InJas 22:3).

Jesus' visit to the temple at age twelve. The gospel concludes with a doxology, preceded by a report that Jesus lived in obscurity until he was thirty.

Distinctive Features

The primary purpose of the Arabic Infancy Gospel is to celebrate the wonders worked by Jesus as an infant and a boy, but this gospel is designed also to exalt his mother Mary. Throughout the narrative she is referred to as "the Lady Mary." Many of the miracle stories, especially those in the Egyptian section of the gospel, honor Mary as much as they glorify Jesus. These miracles are orchestrated by Mary: they are worked, under her supervision, through physical contact with the infant Jesus or with his clothes or bathwater.

The stories about the miracles of the boy Jesus tone down, but do not eliminate altogether, the malevolent quality of some of the stories in Infancy Thomas. In the Arabic Infancy Gospel, Jesus injures or kills only two people (a boy who deliberately knocks him down and a teacher who whips him), a significantly lower casualty count than in Infancy Thomas. In two episodes, Jesus goes on to repair the damage done by his naughty behavior, when he sees the distress it causes others (see chapters 37 and 40).

Another distinctive feature of the Arabic Infancy Gospel is its casting of several minor characters from Jesus' adult life in scenes from his childhood. One episode spotlights the two thieves who will be crucified along with him (see chapter 23). In addition, Jesus heals three boys who in later life will be his disciples: Bartholomew, Judas (see chapter 35), and Simon the Canaanite.[2]

Origin and Attestation

The Arabic Infancy Gospel was originally composed in Syriac, probably in the fifth or sixth century. It exists only in Arabic translation, hence its name. However, because few scholars of early Christianity can read ancient Arabic, this gospel is known to Western scholars primarily by way of a Latin translation prepared in 1697. That Latin translation is the basis for the few English versions of this gospel, including the one below.

The Selections

The chapters presented here make up about one-third of the total text of the gospel. They are:

- An opening report (1) and an original story about the magi (7–8).
- Five stories about the trip to Egypt, all unique to this gospel (17, 19, 20–21, 23, 24).
- Five stories about Jesus' boyhood not found in Infancy Thomas (27, 35, 37, 40, 41).

[2]This person is the other Simon besides Simon Peter. He is called "the Canaanite" in Mark 3:18 and Matt 10:4 and "the Zealot" in Luke 6:15.

• An elaborate version of Jesus' adventure in the temple (50–53) and the explanation for the "hidden years" prior to his baptism (54).

THE ARABIC INFANCY GOSPEL

1 [2]When Jesus was lying in his cradle, he said to his mother Mary, "I am Jesus, the Son of God, the Logos, to whom you have given birth, just as the angel Gabriel announced to you. My Father has sent me for the salvation of the world."

The Magi

7 When the Lord Jesus was born in Bethlehem of Judea, in the time of King Herod, magi arrived from the East in Jerusalem, just as Zeradusht had predicted. [2]They carried with them gifts of gold, frankincense, and myrrh. And they worshiped him and offered him their gifts. [3]The Lady Mary, having very little of her own, took one of the strips of cloth she had wrapped around the baby and gave it to the magi, who accepted it from her with the greatest honor. [4]At that very hour, an angel appeared to them in the form of the star that had guided them on their journey. [5]And they left, following the lead of the star's light, until they arrived in their own country.

8 Their kings and leaders met with them and asked what they had seen and done, what routes they had taken, and what they had brought back with them. [2]The magi showed them the strip of wrapping cloth that the Lady Mary had given them. [3]They then celebrated a festival, and, according to their custom, lit a fire and worshiped it, and threw that wrapping cloth into it; and the fire took hold of it and engulfed it. [4]And when the fire had gone out, the wrapping cloth was exactly as it had been before, as if the fire had never touched it. [5]Then they began to kiss it, and place it on their heads and their eyes, saying, "This certainly is the truth beyond doubt. Surely it is a great thing that the fire was could not burn or destroy it." [6]Then they took it, and with the greatest honor, stored it among their treasures.

Stories from the Journey to Egypt

17 A woman took scented water to give the Lord Jesus a bath. [2]After she had bathed him, she took the bathwater and poured some of it on a girl whose body was white with leprosy, and washed her with it. Immediately the girl was cleansed of her leprosy. [3]The people of the town said, "There can be no doubt that Joseph and Mary and that boy are gods, not humans." [4]And when they were getting ready to leave, the girl who had suffered from leprosy approached them and asked them to take her with them.

19 They arrived at another city and wanted to spend the night there. [2]So they turned off the road and came to the house of a man who was newly married, but, because he was under the influence of witchcraft, was unable to

Isis and Mary

The Transformations of Lucius is a very famous story from the ancient world. This novel, the first in Western literature, was nicknamed *The Golden Ass*. Lucius, the main character, is a vain young man who dabbles in witchcraft in the pursuit of amorous adventures. He wants to turn himself into an owl so that he can fly at night into the bedroom of the beautiful woman with whom he is infatuated. But his plans go terribly wrong when he accidentally applies the wrong potion and turns himself into an ass. Trapped in this animal's body, Lucius endures an amazing series of misfortunes and degradations: some of them humorous, some violent, and some pornographic. Eventually he is restored to his human form by the great Egyptian goddess, Mother Isis. Lucius devotes the rest of his life to spreading the gospel of this beneficent deity.

The novel's author, Apuleius, was a priest of Isis and wrote his novel as an allegory praising Isis for her power to save her followers from their lower natures and bring them to eternal life. Known as the Queen of Heaven, Isis was much beloved throughout the ancient world and was the most revered deity in Egypt. She was commonly portrayed in art with her infant son, the god Horus, on her lap or at her breast. The long tradition in Christian art of the Madonna with child descends directly from the iconography of Isis.

The story in the Arabic Gospel 20–21 shows the holy Mary, in Egypt, with Jesus on her lap, performing the very same miracle as the one made famous by Apuleuis. The message of the miracle story would have been crystal clear to ancient audiences: Mary and Jesus were every bit as powerful as the most powerful deity from Egypt.

---

enjoy his wife. ³When they had spent the night with him, the spell on him was broken. ⁴The next morning when they were getting ready for their journey, the bridegroom would not let them go, and prepared a great banquet for them.

20 So they set out the next day. As they approached another city, they saw three women weeping as they were leaving a cemetery. ²When the Lady Mary saw them, she told the girl who accompanied her, "Ask them what's the matter, or what disaster has happened to them."

³They didn't answer the girl's questions, but instead asked her, "Where do you come from and where are you going? The day is already over and night is almost here."

⁴"We are travellers," said the girl, "and we're looking for an inn for the night."

⁵They said, "Come with us, and spend the night at our house." ⁶So they followed them and were brought into a new house with lovely decorations and furniture. ⁷Now it was winter. The girl went into the women's bedroom and again found them again weeping and lamenting. ⁸Next to them was a mule covered with cloth of gold. The women put sesame in front of him; and they were kissing him and giving him food.

⁹The girl asked, "My ladies, what's going on with this mule?"

¹⁰With tears in their eyes, they said, "This mule here used to be our brother, born of the same mother as ourselves. When our father died, he left us great wealth, but only one brother. ¹¹We did our best to get him married, and were arranging his wedding. But some women, out of mutual jealousy, secretly cast a spell on him. ¹²One night, just before dawn, while the door of our house was shut, we discovered that our brother had been turned into a mule, as you see him now. ¹³And we are sorrowful, as you can see, having no father to comfort us. There is not a wise man, or magician, or enchanter in the world that we haven't sent for; but nothing has done us any good. ¹⁴And whenever our hearts are overwhelmed with grief, we get up and go away with our mother here, and weep at our father's grave, and come back again."

21 When the girl heard all this, she said, "Be brave and don't weep, for the cure for your misfortune is near; in fact, it's right next to you, in the middle of your own house. ²I used to be a leper; but when I saw that woman with her baby, whose name is Jesus, I sprinkled my body with the water in which his mother had washed him, and I was cured. ³I know he can cure your affliction too. So get up and go to my mistress Mary. Bring her into your house, tell her your secret, and plead with her to take pity on you."

⁴After the women had listened to the girl, they hurried to the Lady Mary and brought her into their bedroom and sat down in front of her, weeping. ⁵"Lady Mary, our mistress, have pity on your servants; for no one older than us, and no head of the family, is left—neither father nor brother—to live with us. ⁶This mule that you see used to be our brother; women have made him this way with witchcraft. So we beg you to have pity on us."

⁷Then, grieving at their situation, the Lady Mary picked up the Lord Jesus and put him on the mule's back. ⁸She wept along with the women and said to Jesus Christ, "My son, heal this mule by your mighty power, and make him a man endowed with reason as he was before."

⁹And when the Lady Mary spoke these words, he was transformed, and the mule became a young man, free from every defect. ¹⁰Then he and his mother and his sisters worshiped the Lady Mary, and lifted the boy above their heads, and began to kiss him, saying, ¹¹"Blessed is she who bore you, O Jesus, savior of the world; and blessed are the eyes that enjoy the happiness of seeing you."

23 They left that place and came to a desert. Joseph and the Lady Mary heard that it was infested by robbers and so they decided to cross that area at night. ²But on their way through, they saw two robbers lying in wait, and a large gang of robbers, their partners, sleeping there with them. ³Now those two robbers, into whose hands they had fallen, were Titus and Dumachus. ⁴Titus said to Dumachus, "I'm asking you: let these people go so our partners don't see them."

⁵But Dumachus refused. So Titus said again, "Take forty of my drach-

mas; they're yours for the keeping." At the same time he handed him the belt from around his waist, hoping he wouldn't open his mouth and speak out.

[6]And the Lady Mary saw that the robber had done them a favor and said to him, "The Lord God will uphold you with his right hand and will grant you forgiveness of your sins."

[7]And the Lord Jesus said to his mother, "Thirty years from now, mother, the Jews will crucify me in Jerusalem, and those two robbers will be hung on the cross along with me, Titus on my right and Dumachus on my left; [8]and when that day is over, Titus will go before me into paradise."

[9]And she said, "God spare you that, my son."

[10]And they went from there toward a city of idols; but as they got close to it, it was changed into sand dunes.

24 From there they turned off the road to that sycamore tree which is now called Matarea, [2]and the Lord Jesus made a spring bubble up in Matarea, in which the Lady Mary washed his shirt. [3]And from the sweat of the Lord Jesus which she wrang out, balsam was produced in that region.

Stories from Jesus' Childhood

27 When they went into the city of Bethlehem, they saw there many serious diseases afflicting the eyes of the children, who were dying as a result. [2]And a woman was there with a sick son, who was very close to death. [3]She brought him to the Lady Mary, who saw him as she was bathing Jesus Christ. The woman said to her, "My Lady Mary, look at my son of mine, who is suffering from a terrible disease."

[4]The Lady Mary listened to her and said, "Take a little my son's bathwater and sprinkle it on him."

[5]So she took a little of the water, as the Lady Mary had told her, and sprinkled it on her son. [6]And after this his illness abated; and when he had slept a little, he woke up safe and sound. [7]His mother rejoiced at this and took him back to the Lady Mary. And she said to her, "Give thanks to God, because he has healed your son."

35 Another woman was living in the same place; she had a son named Judas who was tormented by Satan. [2]Whenever Satan seized him, he used to bite anyone who came near him; and if no one was around he would bite his own hands and arms. [3]When the mother of this poor creature heard about the reputation of the Lady Mary and her son Jesus, she got up and brought her son Judas to the Lady Mary. [4]Meanwhile, James and Joses had taken the child, the Lord Jesus, with them to play with the other children. They and the Lord Jesus had left the house and sat down when Judas, possessed by the devil, came up and sat down on Jesus' right. [5]Just then he was attacked by Satan, as he often was, and tried to bite the Lord Jesus. [6]He was unable to bite him, so he punched Jesus on his right side and made him cry. [7]And immediately Satan came out of that boy, running away like a mad dog. [8]This boy who hit Jesus, and out from whom Satan fled in the shape of a dog, was Judas Iscariot, who betrayed him to the Jews; [9]and that same side on which Judas hit him, the Jews pierced with a spear.

37 One day, when the Lord Jesus was running around playing with some boys, he passed the shop of a dyer named Salem. In his shop were many pieces of cloth he was going to dye. [2]The Lord Jesus went into his shop, picked up all the pieces of cloth, and threw them into a tub full of indigo. [3]When Salem came and saw his cloth ruined, he started to shout in a loud voice at Jesus. [4]"How could you do this to me, son of Mary? You have destroyed my reputation in this town; everyone has ordered the color of their choice, but you have come in here and ruined all of them."

[5]The Lord Jesus answered, "I will change the color of any piece of cloth that you want changed." [6]And he immediately began to take the pieces of cloth out of the tub, each of them colored the way the dyer wanted, until he had taken all of them out. [7]When the Jews saw this amazing miracle, they praised God.

40 One day the Lord Jesus went outside and saw the boys who had gathered to play. He followed them, but the boys hid from him. [2]When the Lord Jesus came to the door of a certain house, he saw some women standing there and asked them where the boys had gone. [3]They answered that no one was there. He then asked, "Who are they over there in the furnace?"

[4]They replied that they were three-year-old goats. And the Lord Jesus shouted, "You goats there, come over here to your shepherd." [5]Then the boys, who had been changed into goats, came out and started to prance around him.

[6]When the women saw this, they were deeply shocked and trembling with fear, and they immediately pleaded with the Lord Jesus: "Lord Jesus, son of Mary, you are truly the good shepherd of Israel. [7]Have mercy on your servants who stand before you and have never doubted you; for you have come, O Lord, to heal, and not to destroy."

[8]And when the Lord Jesus answered that the children of Israel were like the Ethiopians among the peoples, the women said, "Lord, you know everything, and nothing is hidden from you. [9]Now we are begging you in your mercy to restore these boys, your servants, to their previous condition."

[10]So the Lord Jesus said, "Come on, boys, let's go play." [11]And immediately, while these women were standing there, the goats were changed into boys.

41 Now in the month of Adar, Jesus was acting like a king and assembled the boys. They spread their clothes on the ground and he sat down on them. [2]Then they put a crown made of flowers on his head, and stood next to him, on the right and on the left, like royal servants, as if he were a king. [3]And the boys grabbed whoever passed by there and dragged them in front of him and told them, "Come here and worship the king; then you can go on your way."

Jesus' Stay in the Temple

50 When he was twelve years old, they took him to Jerusalem for the festival. [2]When the festival was over, they went home, but the Lord Jesus stayed behind in the temple among the teachers and elders and scholars of Israel. [3]He was asking them questions in various fields of knowledge and in turn was answering them. [4]For example, he asked, "Whose son is the Anointed One?"

"The son of David," they answered him.

[5]To this he replied, "Is he in the spirit calling him his lord when he says, 'The Lord said to my lord, "Sit at my right, until I make your enemies grovel at your feet?"'"

[6]The head of the teachers asked him, "Have you read the scriptures?"

"Both the scriptures," said the Lord Jesus, "and the things contained in the scriptures." [7]And he explained the scriptures, and the Law, and the ordinances, and the statutes, and the mysteries that are contained in the books of the prophets—things beyond the understanding of any created being.

[8]That teacher therefore said, "I have not acquired such knowledge; until now I have not even heard of such things. [9]Tell me, who do you think this boy will turn out to be?"

51 A philosopher who happened to be there, a skillful astronomer, asked the Lord Jesus whether he had studied astronomy. [2]And the Lord Jesus answered him, and explained the number of the spheres, and of the heavenly bodies, their natures and operations; their opposition; their aspect, triangular, square, and hexagonal; [3]their course, direct and retrograde; the twenty-fourths, and sixtieths of twenty-fourths; and other things beyond human reason.

52 There was also among those philosophers an expert in natural science, and he asked the Lord Jesus whether he had studied medicine. [2]And he, in reply, explained to him physics, metaphysics, hyperphysics, and hypophysics; [3]the functions and humors of the body, and their effects; also the number of members and bones, of veins, arteries, and nerves; also the effects of heat and dryness, of cold and moisture, and what these cause; [4]the perceptions and powers of the soul, and how it influences the body; the faculties of speech, anger, and desire, and how they operate; finally, their conjunction and disjunction, and other things beyond the reach of any created intellect. [5]Then that philosopher stood up and worshiped the Lord Jesus, and said, "O Lord, from this time on I will be your disciple and servant."

53 While they were speaking to each other about these and other things, the Lady Mary arrived, after three days of searching for him with Joseph. [2]So when she saw him sitting among the teachers asking and answering questions, she said to him, "My son, how could you do this to us? Your father and I have been worried sick searching for you."

³But he said, "Why are you searching for me? Don't you know that I have work to do in my father's house?"

⁴But they did not understand what he said. Then those teachers asked Mary whether he was her son. ⁵When she nodded that he was, they said, "Blessed are you, O Mary, for having raised such a son."

⁶Jesus returned with them to Nazareth and obeyed them in everything. ⁷His mother kept all these words of His in her heart. ⁸And the Lord Jesus grew in size, and in wisdom, and in favor in the eyes of God and the people.

The Hidden Years

54 And from that day he began to hide his miracles and mysteries and secrets. ²He paid attention to the Law, until he was thirty years old, when his Father publicly acknowledged Him at the Jordan by this voice sent down from heaven: ³"This is my special son; I fully approve of him," the Holy Spirit being present in the form of a white dove.

———— ⌘ ————

1:2 *Logos* is Greek for "word." The newborn Jesus thus introduces himself in the terms of John 1:1: "In the beginning was the Word, and the Word was in God's presence, and the Word was God."

7:1 *Zeradusht* is a garbled form of the name Zarathustra, the Persian prophet known in the West as Zoroaster. The Arabic Gospel correctly understands the magi to be Zoroastrian priests.

just as Zeradusht had predicted: This reflects the tradition that Zoroaster prophesied that, in the final period of cosmic history, a mighty redeemer would be sent to earth, and that Zoroaster's followers would see the star announcing his arrival.

7:3 The mention of *the strips of cloth* is another indication that the infancy gospel tradition blended Luke and Matthew into one hybrid story: the magi appear only in Matthew, the strips of cloth only in Luke.

8:3 In Zoroastrianism, *fire* is the symbol of God's presence. Zoroastrian temples have a sacred flame, which is tended by priests and treated with great reverence. Worshippers can bring offerings, which are given to God by being burned in the holy fire. The Arabic Gospel thus portrays the magi treating the cloth with respect, as something fit to be offered to God in a sacred ceremony.

19 This is the only story in all the gospel tradition in which Jesus' power is used to cure male impotence.

27 *Bethlehem:* In chapter 26, after the family gets back from Egypt, an angel instructs Joseph to move to Nazareth, a detail based on Matt 2:21–23. There is no apparent reason why the story in chapter 27 is set in Bethlehem instead of in Nazareth. This is not the result of a copyist's error, because Bethlehem is mentioned again in chapters 32 and 33. Perhaps this geographical mismatch is evidence that the material in the next section of this gospel was taken from an earlier collection of stories about the infant Jesus during the time *before* the family fled

from Bethlehem to Egypt. In any case, the end of the Arabic Gospel presupposes that the family lived in Nazareth, for that is where Jesus returns with his parents after his adventure in the temple (53:6).

40:3 *in the furnace*: Perhaps an unused potter's kiln is meant. Or perhaps this is a mistake in the Latin translation of this gospel: *fornax* ("furnace") could be a misspelling of *fornix* ("archway").

40:8 *the children of Israel were like the Ethiopians among the people*: This is adapted from the prophet Amos.

> "Are you not like the Ethiopians to me,
>> O people of Israel?" says Yahweh.
> "Did I not bring up Israel from the land of Egypt,
>> and the Philistines from Caphtor,
>> and the Syrians from Kir?" (Amos 9:7)

The point for Amos, and this gospel, is that the people of Israel are no more precious to God than any other people.

41 This story is similar to one told about the young Cyrus, future emperor of Persia (see p. 69). Perhaps the story here was deliberately modeled after that earlier one.

50:4–5 In the synoptic gospels, this exchange is part of a hostile encounter between the adult Jesus and the Pharisees (Mark 12:35–37; Matt 22:41–46; Luke 20:41–44).

50:9 This question mimics what the relatives and neighbors of Zechariah and Elizabeth say about baby John at his circumcision (Luke 1:66).

51:3 *twenty-fourths and sixtieths of twenty-fourths*: Jesus explains the positions and motions of the heavenly bodies at each hour (a twenty-fourth of a day) and each minute (a sixtieth of an hour).

52:2 *physics, metaphysics, hyperphysics, and hypophysics*: Metaphysics is the branch of philosophy dealing with ultimate realities, things "beyond" (*meta*) the physical. *Hyperphysics* and *hypophysics* are not actual fields of philosophy; these terms are artificial words—in Greek *hyper* means "above" and *hypo* means "below." The message is that Jesus understood every conceivable field of knowledge, even ones that do not yet exist.

52:3 *humors of the body*: In ancient and medieval physiology, the overall functioning of the body was determined by the mix of the four "humors," or essential bodily fluids: blood, phlegm, yellow bile, and black bile. Whichever humor predominated in an individual's constitution determined his or her temperament: sanguine, phlegmatic, choleric, or melancholic.

53:6 Although the stories in chapters 27–49 are set in Bethlehem, the narrative here presupposes, along with Luke and Matthew, that the family lived in Nazareth. See the comment on chapter 27.

54 This report bridges the gap in the gospel tradition between Jesus at age twelve and at age thirty. It also explains why this gap in the story of Jesus' life exists: Jesus intentionally lived in obscurity until his baptism.

The Gospel of
Pseudo-Matthew

This work bears the title "The Birth of the Blessed Mary and the Infancy of the Savior." Most of it is based on Infancy James and Infancy Thomas, which it freely revises, expanding most of the stories, changing details in the narrative, and omitting some material altogether.

Contents

Chapters 1–17 retell the Infancy Gospel of James. Pseudo-Matthew deletes all the material in Infancy James about Zechariah and John the Baptizer. It embellishes a number of the episodes in its source and makes a few alterations in the plot. For example, Joseph agrees to be Mary's guardian only temporarily, until he decides which of his sons she should marry. In the meanwhile, five other young women from the temple accompany Mary to live with her in Joseph's house. The most developed revision of Infancy James is that this new gospel elevates Mary's saintliness far beyond her portrayal in that earlier one. Pseudo-Matthew lavishly describes the girl's exemplary piety, profound religious learning, and scrupulous observance of the Law. It adds hagiographical touches, such as the reports that angels obeyed her and that sick people were healed when they touched her. Pseudo-Matthew also surpasses Infancy James in emphasizing Mary's virginity. When the high priest wants her to marry his son, she declines and declares her intention to live in permanent celibacy; the gospel points out that Mary was the first person ever to choose this way of life. Later in the story, Pseudo-Matthew dramatically underscores Mary's post-partum virginity when one of the midwives who examines her after her delivery exclaims, "A virgin has conceived, a virgin has given birth, and a virgin she remains."

Chapters 18–25 are made up of material unique to this gospel: miracle stories from the family's journey to Egypt. Like the Arabic Infancy Gospel,

Pseudo-Matthew thus exploits the only narrative gap in the canonical story left unfilled by either Infancy James or Infancy Thomas. The episodes in 18–25 might be based on a source unknown to us, but are more likely the original compositions of the author of this gospel, judging from the fact that four of the five miracles in this section are said to have happened in fulfillment of scripture (see below).

Chapters 26–41 basically retell the Infancy Gospel of Thomas. Pseudo-Matthew omits three of that earlier gospel's miracle stories and the episode about Jesus' visit to the temple at age twelve. As with the material from Infancy James, the stories from Infancy Thomas are here told at greater length and with added details, some of them intended to make Jesus look less malicious. Chapters 35, 36, and 40 contain new stories about the young Jesus.

Chapter 42 closes the narrative with a depiction of Jesus presiding over the household meals of his extended family. The final lines of the gospel tell how his relatives revered him and report that a divine light would shine on him whenever he slept.

Fulfillment of Prophecy

A distinctive feature of this infancy gospel is its theme of prophecy fulfillment. In several episodes the narrator breaks into the story to inform us that a certain event fulfilled a passage from scripture, which he then quotes. With this device the pseudonymous author imitates Matthew's gospel and subtly reinforces the claim that the present gospel was written by Matthew himself. In all, the text quotes six prophecies that were fulfilled.

- An ox and a donkey worship the newborn Jesus (PsMatt 14), which fulfills two prophecies: "The ox knows its owner, and the donkey its master's feeding trough" (Isa 1:3), and "Between two animals you are made known" (Hab 3:2).
- Dragons worship Jesus (PsMatt 18), which fulfills "Praise the Lord from the earth, you dragons" (Ps 148:7).
- Lions, leopards, and wolves peacefully mingle with the family's livestock (PsMatt 19), which fulfills "Wolves will graze with lambs; the lion and the ox will eat hay together" (Isa 65:25).
- Jesus miraculously speeds along the family's journey to Egypt, enabling them to cover a month-long route in one day (PsMatt 22); and, when Jesus enters an Egyptian temple, its idols fall to the ground (PsMatt 23). These two events fulfill the prophecy, "Look, the Lord will enter Egypt on a swift cloud, and all the artifacts of the Egyptians will be removed from before his face" (Isa 19:1).
- When Jesus was brought to school, he took over from the teacher of the

Law and spoke in the spirit, "as if a stream of water were gushing from a living spring" (PsMatt 39). This fulfilled "The river of God is full of water; you have provided grain for them, for thus is its preparation" (Ps 65:9).

The last episode is based on one from the Infancy Gospel of Thomas. The others are reported only in Pseudo-Matthew.

Cover Letters

The second line of the gospel's text, immediately following the title, claims that the work was "written in Hebrew by the blessed evangelist Matthew and translated into Latin by the blessed presbyter Jerome."

The text then contains two cover letters. The first is from two bishops to Jerome, the fourth-century scholar who translated the Bible into Latin. The bishops express their concern over infancy gospels that "contain many things contrary to our faith." They complain that infancy gospels are effective vehicles by which heretics can spread their odious influence. "Heretics, in order to teach bad doctrines, have mingled their own lies with the excellent birth of Christ, so as to hide the bitterness of death within the sweetness of life." The bishops have heard that Jerome has in his possession an infancy gospel written in Hebrew by Matthew himself and they urge Jerome to translate it and thereby provide an orthodox infancy gospel which can drive out the heretical ones.

The second letter is Jerome's reply to the bishops. He explains that Matthew did not intend this Hebrew infancy gospel to be widely distributed. However, a heretic, a Manichean named Leucius, has published a misleading translation of this work, which led to its condemnation by a council of bishops. Jerome hopes that his translation will set the record straight and "expose the deception of heresy." He declares that he has no intention of adding this "little book" to the canonical scriptures; his only aim is to "translate a writing of an apostle and evangelist."

The letters are forgeries written by the author to reassure suspicious authorities by establishing an orthodox pedigree for this pious gospel. Whether because of these letters, or because of the inherent appeal of its stories, Pseudo-Matthew found a wide audience in the Middle Ages and inspired much medieval art. It was through this gospel that many of the infancy legends found their way into popular lore.

Date and Attestation

Pseudo-Matthew was used as the basis for some tenth-century poetry on the nativity of Mary. Beyond that, there is no evidence indicating when this gospel was written. Sometime in the eighth or ninth century is a good guess. The gospel was composed in Latin; nothing in its language hints that it was translated from Hebrew, as its spurious cover letters claim. There are over 130 manuscripts of this text, all of them in Latin. The earliest extant copy is from the eleventh century.

The Selections

The selections from Pseudo-Matthew featured here amount to about one fifth of the total text and include all the stories about Jesus unique to this gospel.

- Two brief excerpts from chapter 13 and chapter 14 are vignettes from the birth scene.
- Chapters 18–25 narrate the infant's miracles during the trip to Egypt.
- Chapter 29 retells an episode from Infancy Thomas, with some interesting revisions.
- Chapters 35, 36, and 40 are miracle stories from Jesus' childhood not found in Infancy Thomas, nor anywhere else.
- Chapter 42 is the final scene in the gospel.

THE GOSPEL OF PSEUDO-MATTHEW

Excerpts from the Birth Story

13 [12]When Mary entered the cave, it began to shine as brightly as if it were noon. The divine light remained in the cave day and night as long as Mary was there.

And there she gave birth to a son. [13]As soon as he was born he stood on his feet and angels surrounded him and worshiped him, saying, "Glory to God in the highest, and on earth peace to those of good will.". . .

[32]A huge star, larger than any star that has ever existed since the beginning of the world, shined gloriously over the cave from evening until morning. [33]The prophets who were in Jerusalem said that this star pointed out the birth of Christ, who was going to restore the promise, not only to Israel, but to all peoples.

14 On the third day after the birth of the Lord, Mary left the cave and entered a stable. She put the boy in a feeding trough and an ox and a donkey knelt down and worshiped him. [2]This fulfilled what was spoken through Isaiah the prophet:

> The ox knows its owner
> and the donkey its master's feeding trough.

[3]These same animals, the donkey and the ox, having him present between them, worshiped him continuously. [4]This fulfilled what was spoken through Habakkuk the prophet:

> Between two animals you are made known.

The Journey to Egypt

18 Mary arrived at a certain cave and wanted to take a rest in it. She dismounted her donkey and sat down with the child Jesus on her lap. There were three boys traveling with Joseph, and a girl with Mary. ²All of a sudden a bunch of dragons came out the cave. The children saw them and screamed in terror. ³Then Jesus climbed down from his mother's lap and stood in front of the dragons. They worshiped Jesus and then backed away. ⁴This fulfilled what was spoken through the prophet David:

> Praise the Lord from the earth, you dragons.

⁵Then the baby Jesus walked in front of them and commanded them not to hurt anyone. Mary and Joseph were very afraid that the dragons would injure the child. ⁶So Jesus said to them, "Don't be afraid, and don't think of me as a baby. I am and always have been perfect and all the wild animals must be tame around me."

19 Lions and leopards likewise worshiped him and accompanied them in the desert. ²Wherever Mary and Joseph went, these animals walked in front of them, showing them the way and expressing their loyal devotion, reverently bowing their huge heads. They showed their submission with their cringing tails. ³When Mary saw the lions and the leopards and other kinds of wild animals surrounding them, she was very frightened at first. ⁴But the infant Jesus looked into her face with a smile and said, "Don't be afraid, mother; they didn't come here to harm you; they are eager to obey us." These words took away all the fear from her heart.

⁵The lions kept walking with them and with the oxen and the donkeys and the pack animals who carried their supplies. Even though they stayed close to them, they did no harm to any of them. ⁶The family had brought sheep and rams with them from Judea, and they walked among wolves without fear; neither of them harmed the other. ⁷This fulfilled what was spoken through the prophet:

> Wolves will graze with lambs;
> the lion and the ox will eat hay together.

⁸There were two oxen pulling a wagon in which they carried their supplies, and the lions guided them on their journey.

20 On the third day of their journey Mary became exhausted by the oppressive heat of the desert sun. She saw a palm tree and said to Joseph, "Let me rest a little in the shade of that tree." ²So Joseph hurried up and led her to the palm and helped her get down from her animal.

³While Mary was sitting there, she looked at the palm tree's foliage and noticed that it was full of fruit. She said to Joseph, "I wish we could get some fruit from this palm."

⁴Joseph said to her, "I'm surprised you said that. You can see how tall this palm tree is. How can you even think about eating its fruit? ⁵I'm more

concerned about the lack of water here; our water bags are empty and there's nothing with which we and our animals can quench our thirst."

⁶Then the baby Jesus, who was smiling and sitting on his virgin mother's lap, said to the palm, "You tree there, bend down and refresh my mother with your fruit." ⁷At these words the palm immediately lowered its top down to Mary's feet; and they picked fruit from it, which they ate for their refreshment.

⁸After they had picked all its fruit, it remained bent down and waited for him who had commanded it to bend down to give the order to get up. ⁹Then Jesus said, "Raise yourself, you palm tree; be strong, and join those trees of mine in my father's paradise; open up the stream of water hidden in the ground beneath your roots, and let the waters flow, so we can quench our thirst." ¹⁰The palm raised itself, and immediately a spring of water began pouring through its roots, water that was exceptionally clear and cool and sweet. ¹¹When they saw the spring of water, they rejoiced greatly, and they and their livestock and pack animals all drank as much as they wanted and gave thanks to God.

21 The next day, as they were leaving that place to continue their journey, Jesus turned to the palm and said, "You palm tree, I give you the honor of having one of your branches carried by my angels and planted in my father's paradise. ²I am bestowing this blessing on you, so that it will be said to everyone who wins any contest, 'You have won the palm of victory.'"

³While he was saying this, an angel of the Lord suddenly appeared, standing above the palm tree. He took one of its branches and flew to heaven with it in his hand. ⁴When they saw this, they fell facedown, as if they were dead. Jesus said to them, "Why are your hearts gripped with fear? ⁵Don't you see that this palm tree, which I have had carried to paradise, will be there for all the saints in that place of delight, just as it was here for us in this place of desolation?"

22 While they were travelling, Joseph said to Jesus, "Lord, this oppressive heat is roasting us. If it pleases you, let's take the route by the sea, so we can rest in the towns along the coast."

²Jesus said to him, "Don't be afraid, Joseph. I will shorten your trip: you will travel in one day what would normally take you thirty." ³And even as they were speaking, they looked ahead and began to see the mountains and cities of Egypt.

⁴Rejoicing and exulting, they crossed into the region of Hermopolis and entered an Egyptian city called Sotinen. ⁵Since they knew no one there from whom they could ask for hospitality, they went to a temple which was called the "Capitol of Egypt." ⁶Now in this temple there were three hundred and fifty-five idols; each one had its own day for receiving divine honor in sacriligeous rituals.

23 And it happened that when Mary entered the temple with the baby, all the idols fell to the ground; all of them were lying facedown, shattered and smashed to pieces. In this way they plainly showed that they were nothing. ²This fulfilled what the prophet predicted:

> Look, the Lord will enter Egypt on a swift cloud,
> and all the artifacts of the Egyptians will be removed from
> before his face.

24 When Affrodosius, the governor of that city, was informed of this, he went to the temple with his whole army. ²When the priests of the temple saw Affrodosius entering the temple with his army, they assumed he was going to take revenge on those who had caused the gods to fall down. ³But when he entered and saw all the idols lying facedown, he went up to Mary, who was carrying the Lord in her arms. ⁴He worshiped him, and said to his whole army and all his friends, "If he were not the Lord of our gods, our gods would not have fallen on their faces before him; nor would they be lying prostrate in His presence. They are silently professing that he is their Lord. ⁵So unless we do what we have seen our gods doing, we all might be in danger of incurring his anger and of being destroyed, just as it happened to Pharaoh, king of the Egyptians. ⁶He was drowned in the sea with his whole army because he did not believe in such mighty powers." ⁷Then all the people of that city believed in the Lord God through Jesus Christ.

25 A short time later an angel said to Joseph, "Go back to the land of Judah, for those who were seeking the boy's life are dead."

Episodes from Jesus' Childhood

29 All of a sudden a boy, an evildoer, ran up and bumped into Jesus' shoulder, trying to tease him or hurt him. And Jesus said to him, "You won't make it back safe and sound from where you're going." And immediately the boy fell down and died.

²The parents of the dead boy saw what happened and shouted, "Where does this child come from? It's obvious that every word he says comes true; it's often carried out before he even speaks." ³The parents of the dead boy came to Joseph and told him, "Take that Jesus away from here. We cannot have him living with us in this town; or at least teach him to bless, not curse."

⁴Joseph came up to Jesus and scolded him. "Why do you do things like this? A lot of people are in grief and have turned against you. ⁵They hate us because of you and we have to put up with their recriminations."

⁶And Jesus answered Joseph, "No son can be wise unless his father teaches him what there is to know at this time; and a father's curse can hurt only an evildoer."

⁷Then they gathered against Jesus and accused him to Joseph. When Joseph saw this, he was terrified, fearing the violence and uproar of the people of Israel. ⁸Then Jesus grabbed the dead boy by the ear and lifted him off the ground in front of them. They saw Jesus speaking to him like a father to his son. ⁹The boy's spirit returned to him, and he came back to life. And all of them were amazed.

35 There is a road that goes from Jericho to the Jordan river, to the place where the children of Israel crossed, which is also where they say the ark of the covenant rested.

²When Jesus was eight years old he left Jericho and headed for the Jordan. ³Next to the road, near the bank of the Jordan, there was a cave where a lioness was nursing her cubs; it was not safe for anyone to walk past it. ⁴Jesus, on his way from Jericho, knowing that that cave was where the lioness had given birth to her cubs, went into it in front of everyone. ⁵When the lions saw Jesus, they ran to meet him and worshiped him. Jesus sat down in the cave and the lion's cubs ran around at his feet, nuzzling him and playing with him. ⁶The older lions stood at a distance with their heads bowed and worshiped him, showing their affection for him with their tails.

⁷Then the people who did not see him because they were standing a long way off said, "He would not voluntarily have offered himself up to the lions unless he or his parents had committed serious sins."

⁸The people were thinking along these lines and were overcome by sorrow when, all of a sudden, in full view of the people, Jesus came out of the cave with the lions parading in front of him and the cubs playing with each other at his feet. ⁹Jesus' parents stood a long way off and watched with their heads bowed. The people also stood at a distance because of the lions; no one dared approach them. ¹⁰Then Jesus began speaking to the people. "The wild animals are so much better than you are: they recognize their Lord and give him glory, while you humans, who have been made in the image and likeness of God, do not know him! ¹¹Wild animals know me and are tame; humans see me but do not acknowledge me."

36 After all this, Jesus crossed the Jordan with the lions as everyone watched. ²And the water of the Jordan was parted, on the right and on the left. ³Then, in front of everyone, he said to the lions, "Go in peace and harm no one; but don't let anyone hurt you either, until you get back to the place from which you've come." ⁴They told him good-bye, not only with their gestures but with their voices as well, and went home. ⁵Then Jesus went home to his mother.

40 After all this, Joseph moved from there with Mary and Jesus to Capernaum by the seashore, because of the malice of his enemies.

²When Jesus was living in Capernaum, there was a very rich man named Joseph in the city. He had wasted from his disease and died, and was lying dead on his couch. ³When Jesus heard the people in the city mourning, and weeping, and lamenting for the dead man, he said to Joseph, "Why don't you show some generosity to this man, seeing that he has the same name as you?"

⁴And Joseph answered, "What makes you think I have the power to do anything for him?"

⁵Jesus said to him, "Take the kerchief on your head, and go put it on the dead man's face, and say to him, 'Christ save you.' ⁶The dead man will be healed immediately and will get up from his couch."

[7]When Joseph heard this, he left in obedience to Jesus' command; he ran and entered the dead man's house, and put the kerchief he was wearing on his head on the face of the man on the couch, and said, "Jesus save you." [8]The dead man immediately got up from his bed and asked who Jesus was.

The Conclusion of the Gospel

42 Joseph came to a feast with his two daughters and his sons, James, Joseph, Judah, and Simeon. [2]Jesus met them with his mother Mary, along with her sister Mary, daughter of Cleophas, whom the Lord God had given to her father Cleophas and her mother Anna, because they had offered Mary the mother of Jesus to the Lord. [3]Her sister had been given the same name, Mary, for the consolation of her parents. [4]And when they all had gathered, Jesus sanctified and blessed them. [5]He was the first to start eating and drinking; for none of them dared to eat or drink, or to break bread, or even to sit down at the table, until he had first sanctified them. [6]If he happened not to be there, they used to wait for him. And when he didn't want to come for dinner, neither Joseph nor Mary, nor his brothers, the sons of Joseph, came.

[7]His brothers kept his life as a lamp before their eyes; they watched him closely and revered him. [8]And whenever Jesus slept, whether during the day or at night, the brightness of God shined on him, to whom be all praise and glory for ever and ever. Amen, amen.

13:12 Jesus is born in a *cave*, as in Infancy James 18–19. The *divine light* in the cave is based on InJas 19:15–16.

13:13 *Glory to God* . . . This is what angels sing for the shepherds in Luke 2:14.

14:1 *left the cave and entered a stable*: The Infancy Gospel of James, the source for most of the material in the first part of Pseudo-Matthew, has no feeding trough in the cave where Jesus was born. Pseudo-Matthew, however, needs a feeding trough (a detail from Luke 2:5) to set the scene for a fulfillment of prophecy and so moves Mary from the cave to a place where a feeding trough is available.

14:2 The quotation is from Isa 1:3.

14:4 The quotation is from the Septuagint version of Hab 3:2, which is markedly different from the Hebrew original.

18:4 The quotation is from Ps 148:7 LXX. The English word "dragon" comes from the Latin *draco*, a transliteration of the Greek *drakon*. The Hebrew text of this verse from the Psalms refers to sea monsters.

19:7 The quotation comes from Isa 65:25.

23:1 This scene is modeled on 1 Sam 5:1–4, in which the statue of the Philistine god Dagon falls on its face and breaks into pieces when the Philistines bring the ark of the covenant, which they had captured from the Israelites, into Dagon's temple.

23:2 The quotation is from Isa 19:1.

29:1 This story is a revision of Infancy Thomas 4–5. In that story the boy seems to run into Jesus accidentally (InThom 4:1); here the boy does it on purpose and with evil intent.

29:3 InThom 5:2 reports that the people who complain about Jesus are struck blind. Nothing dire happens to them here.

29:4 According to InThom 5:4, Joseph deals with Jesus by physically punishing him; here Joseph uses words instead of violence.

29:6 InThom 5:5–6 portrays Jesus answering Joseph defiantly and with a thinly-veiled threat; here Jesus replies with filial respect.

29:8–9 In Infancy Thomas 4–5, the slain boy is left dead; here Jesus resurrects him.

35:1 See Josh 3:14–17.

36:2 This description is based on Josh 3:16 and 2 Kgs 2:8.

40:1 The family's move to *Capernaum* explains what the canonical gospels do not: how it was that Jesus came to live in that town. Mark 2:1 tells that Jesus had a house in Capernaum. Matt 9:1 refers to Capernaum (though not by name) as "his own town."

40:7–8 Miracles worked though contact with handkerchiefs are also reported in Acts 19:11–12.

42:2 *her sister, Mary, daughter of Cleophas*: This is an interpretation of the confusing description in John 19:25 of the women who stood by the cross of Jesus: "Jesus' mother, his mother's sister, Mary of Clopas, and Mary of Magdala." John is probably referring to four different women and leaving Jesus' aunt unnamed. Pseudo-Matthew understands "Mary of Clopas" in John 19:25 to be the *daughter* of Cleophas—Clopas and Cleophas are variants of the same name—and the the same woman as "his mother's sister." PsMatt 42:2 then explains why there were two sisters with the same name: the second daughter was a kind of replacement for the first. In the Infancy Gospel of James, Mary's parents offered her to God by taking her to live in the temple when she turned three years old (Infancy James 7). It is puzzling that Pseudo-Matthew construes Mary to be Cleophas' daughter, whereas Infancy James identifies Mary's father as Joachim.

Appendix

THE BIRTHS OF AENEAS AND JESUS

Aeneas, son of Anchises and a prince of Troy who survived the Trojan war, was a cultural hero well known from Italy to Asia Minor. A number of cities and regions claimed him as their founder, asserting thereby their connections with the illustrious Trojans. Julius Caesar, the first emperor of Rome, claimed Aeneas as his ancestor, which gave his clan not only a heroic lineage, but a divine one as well, for Aeneas' mother was the goddess Aphrodite (whom the Romans called Venus). Aeneas first appears in literature as a minor character in the *Iliad*, Homer's epic poem about the fall of Troy. Aeneas is best known in Western culture as the hero of the *Aeneid*, Vergil's magnificent epic about the origins of Rome and the bane of generations of high school Latin students.

The story of Aeneas' birth—or, more precisely, of his conception—is found in the *Hymn to Aphrodite*, a poem from the seventh century BCE ascribed to Homer. It tells of Aphrodite's seduction of Anchises and her prediction of the future greatness of their son-to-be. There are a number of verbal and narrative similarities between the Hymn and the annunciation scenes in Luke's gospel that merit our attention.

THE HYMN TO APHRODITE

Aphrodite had the ability to smite gods and goddesses with overpowering desires
for mortal men and women. Not even Zeus could resist her spells. To give her a taste of

After this book was written, but before it was printed, I had the good fortune of attending a lecture by Dennis MacDonald, in which he introduced some fascinating parallels between Luke's infancy narrative and the Homeric *Hymn to Aphrodite*. Professor MacDonald was kind enough to send me his unpublished work on this topic and graciously gave permission for me to make use of it in this appendix. What follows relies heavily on MacDonald's findings. The translation of the excerpts from the Hymn is based on Charles Boer's *The Homeric Hymns* (Dallas: Spring Publications, 1970), pp. 72–80.

her own medicine, Zeus puts into Aphrodite's heart an urgent yearning for a mortal man, Anchises. As soon as she sees him, "she loved him and a terrifying desire seized her heart." She then sets out to seduce him.

[81]Aphrodite, the daughter of Zeus, stood in front of Anchises in the form and size of a young girl, lest he recognize her and be terrified. Anchises saw her and marvelled at her, amazed at [85]her appearance and expensive clothes. . . . Love gripped Anchises, and he spoke to her: [91]"Great lady, you must be one of the blessed ones: Artemis or Leto or the golden Aphrodite or noble Themis or bright-eyed Athena. . . . [100]I'll build an altar to you, on some high spot visible from all around. I'll offer lavish sacrifices to you in every season. . . .

[107]Aphrodite, daughter of Zeus, replied: "Anchises, the most splendid man who lives on the earth, [110]I'm not a goddess at all. Why do you take me for one of the immortals? I'm a mere mortal, and the mother who bore me was just a woman. My father's famous name is Otreus – perhaps you've heard of him – he rules over all of Phrygia."

Aphrodite explains that Hermes, the divine messenger, had whisked her away from her home and brought her to Anchises.

[126]"Hermes told me that I would be called a wedded wife of Anchises, and that I would bear you splendid babies. . . [133] Take me, a girl inexperienced in love-making, and introduce me to your father and your good mother and your brothers. . ."

The goddess filled his heart with a sweet longing. Love seized Anchises, and he spoke these words: [145]"If you really are a mortal, and the mother who bore you really was a woman, and if Otreus is in fact your father's name, as you say, and if you really do come here through the will of the immortal guide, Hermes, then you will be called my wife forever. No one, neither god nor mortal, will stop me right here and now [150]from making love to you . . . who look so much like a goddess."

[155] Then he took her hand. Aphrodite, smiling, turned her head and, with her lovely eyes lowered, walked toward his bed. . . . He took off her beautiful clothes and removed her girdle [165]and put them on a silver chair, he, Anchises! And then, by destiny and the will of the gods, he lay with her, a mortal, with an immortal goddess. And he didn't even know it.

Aphrodite casts Anchises into a deep sleep, while she dresses and resumes her divine appearance. She then awakens him.

[177] "Get up, son of Dardanus! Why do you sleep so deeply? Tell me: do I look the same to you now as when you first saw me?" [180]He did what she said and woke up at once. But when he saw her neck and the lovely eyes of Aphrodite, he was terrified and averted his eyes. He covered his own beautiful face with a cloak, and begged her in these words: [185]"When I first saw you, goddess, I knew right away you were divine. But you weren't honest

with me. Now at your knees I beg you, in the name of Zeus, don't let me live the rest of my life impotent. Have pity on me. [190]For a man who sleeps with an immortal goddess is virile no longer."

Aphrodite, daughter of Zeus, responded to him, "Anchises, most glorious of mortal men, cheer up and do not fear greatly in your heart. You have nothing terrible to fear from me, [195]nor from the other blessed ones, because you are loved by the gods. You will have a dear son, who will rule among the Trojans, and his children's children after him, descendants forever. His name will be Aeneas,[1] because of the terrible anguish I feel for letting myself fall into bed with a mortal man. . ."

[277] "I will return in five years and bring you your son. And when you see the child for the first time you'll be delighted. He'll be especially godlike. Take him with you to windy Troy. And if any mortal man ever asks you who was the mother of this sweet boy, remember to give this story: 'They say he's the child of a flower-like nymph, [285]one of those who live on this mountain covered with woods.' But if you let it out and foolishly brag that you made love with the crowned Aphrodite, Zeus will be furious and strike you with a smoking thunderbolt. Guard this secret [290]and never mention my name: avoid the wrath of the gods."

When she had said this, she flew into the windy sky.

PARALLELS TO LUKE

There are three scenes in Luke 1–2 in which angels announce a miraculous birth: the annunciation of John to Zechariah, the annunciation of Jesus to Mary, and the proclamation of Jesus to the shepherds. The number and

Hymn to Aphrodite 79–81, 181–82, 191–98	Luke 1:11–13
Anchises was alone in the hills, playing his lyre.	*Zechariah was alone in the sanctuary of the Temple offering incense.*
Aphrodite, the daughter of Zeus, stood in front of him	A messenger of the Lord appeared to him standing to the right of the altar.
When he saw Aphrodite's neck and lovely eyes, he was terrified and averted his eyes	When he saw him, he was terrified and overcome by fear.
Aphrodite responded to him, "Anchises,	The messenger said to him, "Zechariah,
cheer up; do not fear greatly in your heart. . .	do not fear
for you are loved by the gods.	for your prayer has been heard.
[Anchises earlier had prayed that the goddess give him offspring.]	*[His prayer was for a child.]*

1. Aeneas' name is here connected to the Greek word *ainos*, which means "awful."

You will have a dear son
His name will be Aeneas."
*[Zeus later punished Anchises for reveal-
ing that he had slept with a goddess.]*

Your wife will bear you a son
and you will name him John."
*[The angel punished Zechariah for doubt-
ing the promise.]*

Hymn to Aphrodite 81, 181–82, 191–98, 291

Aphrodite
stood in front of him . . . .

When he saw Aphrodite's neck
and lovely eyes, he was terrified
and averted his eyes . . . .
Then Aphrodite responded to him,
"Anchises, cheer up; do not fear
for you are loved by the gods.

You will have a dear son
His name will be Aeneas.
who will rule among the Trojans,
and his children's children after him,
descendants forever. . ."

When she had said this,
she flew into the windy sky.

Luke 1:26, 28–35, and 38

The messenger Gabriel was sent from
God to a town in Galilee . . . . When
he had come into her room, he said,
"Greetings, favored one! The Lord
be with you."
At these words
she was terrified and wondered what
this greeting could mean.
And the messenger said to her,
"Mary, do not fear,
for you have found favor with God.
You will conceive in your
womb and give birth a son
and will name him Jesus.
and he will rule over the house of
Jacob
forever, and his dominion will have
no end."
And the messenger left her.

Hymn to Aphrodite 54–55, 78–79, 81, 181–82, 191–96, 291

Anchises was grazing his cattle
among the steep slopes of Mount
Ida. . . . All the other herdsmen were
following their cattle . . .
Aphrodite, daughter of Zeus,
stood in front of him . . . .
When he saw Aphrodite's neck
and lovely eyes, he was terrified . . . .
Then Aphrodite responded to him,
"Anchises, cheer up; do not fear

Luke 2:8-15

Now in the same area there were
shepherds living outdoors keeping
watch over their flock at night.

And a messenger of the Lord
stood in front of them, and the glory
of the Lord shined around them,
and they were terrified.
And the messenger said to them,
"Do not fear,

for you are loved by the gods.

You will have a dear son
who will rule among the Trojans . . ."
When she had said this,
she flew into the windy sky.

for I bring you good news of a great
joy
Today your Savior is born,
who is the Anointed, the Lord."
And the messengers went up from
them into the sky.

quality of the parallels between these scenes and the Hymn to Aphrodite suggest that Luke was consciously imitating the Hymn.

In the ancient world everyone who learned to read and write Greek did so by practicing with Homer, so it's a safe assumption that Luke knew the famous Homeric Hymns. Educated members of Luke's audience who would recognize the echoes of the Hymn would see that Luke was making the connections between the stories of Jesus and Aeneas in order to portray Jesus as superior to Rome's ancestral hero. From a Christian perspective, the most important difference between the two figures is that Aeneas is the son of a goddess, one of many deities, whereas Jesus is the son of the one and only Most High God. Several other points of contrast reinforce Jesus' superiority to Aeneas.

- Aphrodite lies to Anchises; Gabriel is truthful with Mary.
- Anchises is not aware of what he is really doing; Mary gives her informed consent.
- Aeneas is conceived in a sexual encounter between a deity and a human; there is no physical contact between God and Mary.
- Aphrodite deeply regrets what she has done; Mary rejoices over what has happened to her.
- Aeneas' birth is announced once, Jesus's twice, the second time by an army of angels.
- Aeneas and his dynasty will rule over Troy forever; Jesus will be the savior of the whole world.

For Further Reading

Brown, Raymond. *The Birth of the Messiah*. Garden City, NY: Doubleday, 1977.
An indispensable reference for all serious study of the infancy narratives.
Though written for scholars, this nearly 600-page commentary can be of
immense value to the resolute non-specialist. Brown presents an over-
flowing wealth of information and interacts responsibly with all the sec-
ondary literature. His historical judgments are critical but very guarded.
Brown's treatment of the virgin birth goes about as far as possible for a
book that carries the Imprimatur (the official certification from the
Catholic Church that a book contains no doctrinal errors). *Birth of the
Messiah* was republished in 1993, with an extensive supplement evaluating scholarly work on the topic that had appeared since 1977.

Freed, Edwin D. *The Stories of Jesus' Birth: A Critical Introduction*. Sheffield:
Sheffield Academic Press, 2001.
A useful guide for general readers to the study of the infancy narratives.
For Freed, the infancy narratives are not historical, but rather "beautiful
and edifying legends, myths, and poetry." Freed treats the full text of the
narratives and all the important topics, but this book is not a commentary. The author asks more questions than he answers, and urges readers
to decide for themselves.

Hock, Ronald F. *The Infancy Gospels of James and Thomas*. The Scholars Bible.
Santa Rosa: Polebridge Press, 1995.
The best and most important book on these two gospels. It contains a
new critical Greek text of each gospel, with critical apparatus, Scholars
Version translation, detailed comments, substantial introductions, and
scholarly bibliographies. Hock is especially attentive to the hellenistic lit-
erary conventions at work in these gospels.
Also available from Polebridge Press is "Away With the Manger," a

four-hour video in which Hock expertly discusses these infancy gospels for a general audience. This video is an excellent resource for college, seminary, or adult education classes.

Sawicki, Marianne. "Son of God's Slavewoman." In *Seeing the Lord: Resurrection and Early Christian Practices*. Minneapolis: Augsburg Fortress, 1994. Pp. 95–118.

In this fascinating and learned investigation into the annunciation story, Sawicki draws on the Septuagint, the targums, and the Infancy Gospel of James to argue that Luke's story of the annunciation preserves the memory of a Jewish legal debate over Jesus' legitimacy.

Schaberg, Jane. *The Illegitimacy of Jesus*. New York: Harper & Row, 1987.

On the basis of a detailed analysis of Matthew 1 and Luke 1, Schaberg argues that behind both Matthew and Luke is a tradition that Jesus was illegitimately conceived. Schaberg's work is a model of rigorous scholarship, as well as an insightful and sensitive treatment of a controversial subject.

Spong, John Shelby. *Born of a Woman*. San Francisco: Harper San Francisco, 1992.

A lively and reverent discussion of the infancy narratives by a popular author who is also a bishop. Spong understands the virgin birth as a myth and assesses its negative effects on Christian attitudes towards sex. This book is a fine example of how to take the Bible seriously without taking it literally.

Van Aarde, Andries. *Fatherless in Galilee: Jesus as Child of God*. Harrisburg, Trinity Press International, 2001.

Arguing that Jesus grew up without a father, van Aarde investigates the social and religious consequences of Jesus' marginal status. This book explores the way Jesus' own experience of being fatherless inspired his calling God father, his critique of patriarchal values, and his compassion for outcasts and the vulnerable.

About the Translations

Translations of the Hebrew Bible in this book are variously from the New Revised Standard Version, the New English Bible, and the New American Bible. all of which I have modified in a number of places. Translations of the Septuagint are my own.

The translation of the New Testament gospels used in this book is the Scholars Version, which I have occasionally modified. The full Scholars Version translation of the four biblical gospels, plus sixteen other early Christians gospels, including the Infancy Gospels of James and Thomas, is available in *The Complete Gospels*, edited by Robert J. Miller.

Chapter 6. In preparing the translations from Pseudo-Philo and Josephus, I consulted the works of Harrington and Thackeray, respectively. The extract from the Book of Memory comes, with minor revisions, from the article by John Dominic Crossan.

Chapter 7. In preparing the translation from Pausanius, I consulted Jones' translation. The translations of Plutarch and Diogenes Laertius are revisions of the ones by Robert Funk. In translating the extract from Dio Cassius, I consulted the work of Earnest Cary. For my translation of Suetonius, I consulted Cartlidge and Dungan, J. C. Rolfe, and Robert Graves. In preparing the translation from Philostratus, I revised the translation of Funk and consulted an early edition of Cartlidge and Dungan's anthology. I consulted Cartlidge and Dungan in translating the selections from Diodorus of Sicily and Iamblichus. For the latter, I also consulted Thomas Taylor's translation.

Chapter 17 and 18. The translations of the Infancy Gospels of James and Thomas are based on Hock's translation for the Scholars Version, which I have modified in many places.

Chapter 19. The translation from the Ascension of Isaiah is a revision of the one by Flemming and Duensing. In translating the excerpt from the Latin Gospel, I consulted the version by Cullmann.

Chapter 20. The translation of the History of Joseph the Carpenter is a revision of the one in *The Ante-Nicene Fathers*.

Chapter 21. The translation of the Arabic Infancy Gospel is a revision of the one in *The Ante-Nicene Fathers* and the excerpts by Cartlidge and Dungan.

Chapter 22. In preparing the translation of the Gospel of Pseudo-Matthew, I consulted the one in *The Ante-Nicene Fathers* and the selections by Cartlidge and Dungan.

Translations
Consulted

Cartlidge, David and Dungan, David, trans. *Documents for the Study of the Gospels*. Revised and enlarged edition. Minneapolis: Fortress Press, 1994. Pp. 132–36.

Cary, Earnest, trans. *History of Rome,* by Dio Cassius. Vol. 4. Loeb Classical Library. Cambridge: Harvard University Press, 1969. Pp. 409–11.

Crossan, John Dominic. "From Moses to Jesus: Parallel Themes." *Bible Review* 2.2 (1986) Pp. 22, 26.

Cullmann, Oscar, trans. "Extract from the Latin Infancy Gospel in the Arundel Manuscript." In *New Testament Apocrypha*. Ed. Wilhelm Schneemelcher. Vol. 1. Philadelphia: Westminster, 1959. Pp. 413–14.

Flemming, J. and Duensing, H, trans. "The Ascension of Isaiah." In *New Testament Apocrypha*. Ed. Wilhelm Schneemelcher. Vol. 2. Philadelphia: Westminster, 1964. P. 657.

Funk, Robert W., trans. *The Acts of Jesus*. San Francisco: HarperSanFrancisco, 1998. Pp. 502–3, 505, 507.

Graves, Robert, trans. *The Twelve Caesars,* by Suetonius. Baltimore: Penguin Books, 1957. Pp. 100–102.

Harrington, D. J., trans. "Pseudo-Philo." In *The Old Testament Pseudepigrapha*. Ed. James H. Charlesworth. Vol 2. Garden City, NY: Doubleday & Company, 1985. Pp. 315–16.

Hock, Ronald F., trans. *The Infancy Gospels of James and Thomas*. The Scholars Bible. Santa Rosa: Polebridge Press, 1995. (Also available in *The Complete Gospels*, pp. 369–96.)

Jones, W. H. S., trans. *Description of Greece,* by Pausanius. Vol. 2. Loeb Classical Library. Cambridge: Harvard University Press, 1971. Pp. 65–69.

Miller, Robert J., trans. and ed. *The Complete Gospels*. Santa Rosa: Polebridge Press, 1994.

Robert, Alexander and Donaldson, James, eds. *The Ante-Nicene Fathers*. Vol. 8. Grand Rapids: Eerdmans, no date.
"Gospel of Pseudo-Matthew," pp. 368–83;
"History of Joseph the Carpenter," pp. 388–94;
"The Arabic Gospel of the Infancy of the Saviour," pp. 405–15.

Rolfe, John C., trans. *The Twelve Caesars,* by Suetonius. Vol 1. Loeb Classical Library. Cambridge: Harvard University Press, 1951. Pp. 263–71.

Taylor, Thomas, trans. *The Life of Pythagoras,* by Iamblichus. In *The Pythagorean Sourcebook and Library*. Compiled by Kenneth Sylvan Guthrie. Grand Rapids: Phanes Press, 1987. Pp. 58–59.

Thackeray, H. St. J., trans. *Josephus*. Vol. 4. Loeb Classical Library. Cambridge: Harvard University Press, 1957. Pp. 252–61.

Works Consulted

Boslooper, Thomas. *The Virgin Birth*. Philadelphia: Westminster Press, 1962.

Borg, Marcus and Wright, N. T. "The Birth of Jesus." In *The Meaning of Jesus: Two Visions*. San Francisco: Harper San Francisco, 1998. Pp. 171–86.

Brown, Raymond. *The Birth of the Messiah*. Garden City, NY: Doubleday, 1977.

Cary, M., et al. (eds). *The Oxford Classical Dictionary*. Oxford: At the Clarendon Press, 1949

Cartlidge, David & Dungan, David. "Birth and Youth." In *Documents for the Study of the Gospels*. Revised and enlarged edition. Minneapolis: Fortress Press, 1994. Pp. 129–36.

Crossan, John Dominic. "From Moses to Jesus: Parallel Themes." *Bible Review* 2.2 (1986): 18–27.

— "The Ethical Reason." In *The Birth of Christianity*. San Francisco: Harper San Francisco, 1998. Pp. 26–29.

— "The Infancy and Youth of the Messiah." *In The Search for Jesus*. Ed. Hershel Shanks. Washington: Biblical Archaeology Society, 1994. Pp. 59–81.

Davies, W. D. and Allison, Dale C. *The Gospel According to St. Matthew*. Vol 1: *Chapters 1–7*. International Critical Commentary. Edinburgh: T & T Clark, 1988.

Delling, G. *"parthenos."* In *Theological Dictionary of the New Testament*. Ed. G. Kittel and G. Friedrich. Vol 5. Grand Rapids: Eerdmans, 1968. Pp. 827–37.

Evans, C. F. *Saint Luke*. Philadelphia: Trinity Press International, 1990.

Fitzmyer, Joseph. *The Gospel According to Luke I–IX*. Anchor Bible 28. Garden City, NY: Doubleday, 1981.

Flemming, J. and Duensing, H. "The Ascension of Isaiah." In *New Testament Apocrypha*. Ed. Wilhelm Schneemelcher. Vol. 2. Philadelphia: Westminster Press, 1964. Pp. 642–63.

Freed, Edwin D. *The Stories of Jesus' Birth: A Critical Introduction*. Sheffield: Sheffield Academic Press, 2001.

Funk, Robert W. "Birth and Infancy Stories." In *The Acts of Jesus*. San Francisco: Harper San Francisco, 1998. Pp. 497–526.

Harrington, D. J. "Pseudo-Philo." In *The Old Testament Pseudepigrapha*. Ed. James H. Charlesworth. Vol 2. Garden City, NY: Doubleday, 1985. Pp. 297–303, 315–16.

Hendrickx, Herman. *The Infancy Narratives*. London: Geoffrey Chapman, 1984.

Hock, Ronald F. *The Infancy Gospels of James and Thomas*. The Scholars Bible. Santa Rosa: Polebridge Press, 1995.

Johnson, Marshall D. "Genealogies of Jesus." *Forum* 2,1 New Series (1999): 41–55.

Luz, Ulrich. *Matthew 1–7: A Commentary*. Minneapolis: Augsburg Press, 1989.

McGaughy, Lane. "Infancy Narratives and Hellenistic Lives." *Forum* 2,1 New Series (1999): 25–39.

Meier, John P. "In the Beginning . . . The Origins of Jesus of Nazareth." In *A Marginal Jew: Rethinking the Historical Jesus*. Vol. 1 New York: Doubleday, 1991. Pp. 205–52.

Miller, Robert J. "Historical Method and the Historical Jesus." In *The Jesus Seminar and its Critics*. Santa Rosa: Polebridge Press, 1999. Pp. 27–45.

— "Back to Basics: A Primer on Historical Method." *The Fourth R* 11.6 (November–December 1998): 11, 14–17, 20.

Obbink, H. W. "On the Legends of Moses in the Haggadah." In *Studia Biblica et Semitica T. C. Vriezen Dedicata*. Ed. W. C. van Unnik and A. S. van der Woude. Wageningen: Veenman, 1966. Pp. 252–64.

Schaberg, Jane. "A Cancelled Father." *Forum* 2,1 New Series (1999): 57–76.

— *The Illegitimacy of Jesus*. New York: Harper & Row, 1987.

Talbert, Charles. "The Concept of Immortals and Mediterranean Antiquity." *Journal of Biblical Literature* 94 (1975): 419–36.

Index of Quotations

Entries in bold are extended passages followed by comments.

Index of Topics